"Thomas Watson deserves far more attention than he has received in the past. Thankfully, Yarran Johnston has provided us a fresh and practical way into this Puritan and his work. Drawing particularly on Augustine, Bernard, and Calvin to historically anchor Watson's approach, Johnston helps us understand how this minister distinctly understood and encouraged true godliness. In this, Watson is well worth our attention."

Dr. Kelly M. Kapic

Professor of Theological Studies,

Covenant College, Georgia, United States

"A huge hole has been filled! Finally we have an extensive and careful work on the significant Puritan, Thomas Watson. Yarran Johnston has done a superb job unpacking Thomas Watson's understanding of godliness and doing so in his historical context and the broader Christian tradition. What we discover is a rich and profound theology of Christian living that will be of great benefit for both pastors and people in our contemporary context. Johnston's work will help anyone who wants a stable Christian walk in an unstable world."

Dr. Martin Foord

Lecturer in Systematic Theology,

Evangelical Theological College Asia, Singapore

"Thomas Watson represents the very best of Puritanism. He is affectionately regarded for his lucid expositions of key theological themes, with an almost unmatched ability for his turn of phrase. As Yarran Johnston shows in this book, Watson's picture of godliness represents a sort of "body of divinity." What we get in this volume is not only an in depth look at Watson's theology but also a historical look at the Puritan movement. Not all works of historical theology can warm the soul, but this one certainly does."

Dr. Mark Jones

Senior Minister,

Faith Presbyterian Church (PCA), Vancouver, Canada

I0806555

"A concern for Godliness stood at the heart of the English Puritan movement. Yet, strangely, few scholars have analyzed what godliness meant in this context. Yarran Johnston helps to fill this gap in the literature by expanding our understanding of godliness through the eyes of Thomas Watson, who was one of its ablest and thorough defenders during mid to late seventeenth century. His study is sensitive to the times in which Watson lived and gives readers a window into a key characteristic of Puritanism through an analysis of Watson's extensive writings."

Dr. Ryan M. McGraw

Academic Dean and Morton H. Smith Professor

of Systematic Theology,

Greenville Presbyterian Theological Seminary, United States

"Yarran Johnston's sympathetic although not uncritical account of the life and teaching of one of the best known Puritans, Thomas Watson, is well informed and fills a significant gap in scholarly literature. He sets Watson's numerous writings, of which A Body of Divinity is the best-known, in their context and analyses his theologically grounded affectional piety most helpfully. The very clarity of Johnson's exposition makes this also a dangerous book since it challenges a reader's own piety. Take up and read!"

Rev. Dr. Rowland S. Ward

Research Lecturer,

Presbyterian Theological College, Melbourne, Australia

Studies in Reformed Thought
Monograph Series

Volume 1

Enamoured with Piety

Godliness As The Pervading Theme In The Thought And Ministry Of Thomas Watson (C. 1620-1686)

Yarran Johnston

Series Editor: Rowland S. Ward

Enamoured with Piety

Studies in Reformed Thought

ISSN: 2652-7677

Tulip Publishing,

PO Box 3150, Lansvale,

NSW, Australia 2166

For information, head to:

www.tulippublishing.com.au

PAPERBACK ISBN: 978-0-6487250-6-0

HARDBACK ISBN: 978-0-6487250-7-7

DIGITAL ISBN: 978-0-6487250-9-1

Book and Cover design by Tulip Publishing

Front Cover Illustration: An etching of Crosby Hall at Bishopsgate in London England, where Thomas Watson was to minister between 1672-1680.

Charts on pages 20-21 by Basileia Creative.

10 9 8 7 6 5 4 3 2 1

NATIONAL LIBRARY OF AUSTRALIA

A catalogue record for this book is available from the National Library of Australia

Series Preface

Over the last 30 or so years we have seen a renewal of scholarship on the Reformation period and a major shift away from the lop-sided scholarship that had developed from the mid 19th century. While John Calvin (1509-64) was always a highly significant figure in the articulation of the Reformed faith in the 16th century, he was neither the first in order of time or the standard to which all deferred. The contribution of others is becoming increasingly recognised. Scholarship on the Westminster Assembly (1643-53) has greatly advanced and the significance of the Assembly for theology, worship, and church government is newly appreciated. The essential continuity between the earlier and later periods is also recognised. Treating the use of scholastic tools as indicating a fundamental rationalism and the claim of a rationalistic deduction from a central principle, such as predestination, are now widely seen for the mistakes that they are. The Puritans have come back into focus and the picture is more attractive than the common caricatures. Always concerned lest the church slip into doctrinal error or mere formalism, the Puritan emphasis on warm-hearted piety is something today's church needs to hear. Likewise, the ongoing theological developments that have occured since the 17th century within Reformed Christendom have opened up specific arguments and debates, many bringing clarity where such clarity and correction was needed.

The *Studies in Reformed Thought Monograph Series* will cover, Lord-willing, many such topics, shining light on the different debates and theological intersections that have played out within the hallowed halls of church history. The series particularly will have the laudable aim of promoting Australian contributions to Reformed scholarship and making them available at a reasonable price point for students, pastors and scholars world-wide. The intent is not to further a mere antiquarian interest but to uncover the past in a way which is faithful to the sources and speaks with relevance for the present day.

Dr. Rowland S. Ward, Series Editor

To Helen,

A godly wife, devoted mother and great encouragement to many.

CONTENTS

Part 4: Practical Divinity: Watson's Catalyst for Godliness

Part 5: "Divine Consolation:" Sustaining godliness through trials

Part 6: Conclusion

Excurses

Acknowledgements

My sincere thanks to Brett Lee-Price, Rev Dr Rowland Ward and the team at Tulip Publishing for their interest and investment in the publication of this project. I acknowledge with gratitude the Rev Drs Richard Gibson and Andrew Prince at Brisbane School of Theology, for their willingness to supervise my research and for the hours they spent reading over drafts and providing helpful suggestions and corrections to this work in the earlier stages of its life. The assistance of librarians is indispensable to any research work and I have been particularly assisted in the acquisition of much needed resources by Helen Johnston and Elizabeth Greentree at the Brisbane School of Theology and Annette McGrath, at the Queensland Theological College. I am grateful to the Rev Dr Keith Condie for providing advice in the early stages of research and suggested useful literature, which helped me deepen my understanding of Puritanism and work out how to highlight Watson's distinctive contribution. Thanks is also due to Profs Tom Schwanda, Kelly Kapic, Tim Cooper, Ryan McGraw, Dr. Mark Jones, and the Rev Dr Martin Foord who have each taken the time to read draft manuscripts of this work and provide the insightful feedback and constructive criticism that has helped the book develop and mature.

The period of life spent working on this project has been a season of incredible hardships and joys and my wife Helen has been my companion in every trial and celebration. I thank her from the bottom of my heart for enabling me to undertake and complete this work in the midst of everything else that has occurred in our lives these past five years. My children Kirrily and Hilkiah have provided much joy and respite from academic work as we embarked on adventures that took me far away from the darkened corners of a library. My mother, Sandra Johnston, deserves special thanks for helping to care for the children, enabling me to research and write at times that would have otherwise been impossible. Regrettably I could never offer appropriate thanks to every individual friend who provided their support and encouragement, in this small space. But I do wish to make special mention of Steve Nation, Mike Thompson, Mikael Rantala, Daniel Carkeet and Allan Adams, all of whom have helped me to weather storms and press on with writing. The final and greatest thanks must go to my great God and Saviour for His sustaining grace. May He be glorified as you, the reader, consider the meaning of godliness in the pages that follow.

Abbreviations

Watson[†]

Anatomy	*God's Anatomy Upon a Man's Heart (1649)*
APA	*A Plea for Alms (1658)*
APG	*A Plea for the Godly (1672)*
APL	*A Pastor's Love (1662)*
Autarkeia	*Autarkeia, or The Art of Divine Contentment (1653)*
Beatitudes	*The Beatitudes (2nd ed. 1671)*[*]
BPD	*A Body of Practical Divinity (1692)*[**]
Charter	*The Christian's Charter (1652)*
CM	*A Christian on the Mount (1657)*
DC	*A Divine Cordial (1663)*
DSD	*Duty of Self-Denial (1675)*
Eucharist	*Holy Eucharist/Fiery Serpents/Spiritual Vine (1668)*
GMP	*The Godly Man's Picture (1666)*[**]
HTS	*Heaven Taken by Storm (1669)*
JG	*Jerusalem's Glory (1661)*
Mischief	*The Mischief of Sinne (1671)*[*]
Paramythion	*Paramythion. A Word of Comfort to the Church of God (1662)*
Repentance	*The Doctrine of Repentance (1668)*[*]
RTI	*Religion Our True Interest (1681)*
Seven Sermons	*Seven sermons on several select subjects (1689)*
SSD	*The Saint's Spiritual Delight (1657)*
UMC	*The Upright Man's Character and Crown (1657)*

† Quotations from Watson's works (and other primary sources) replicate the original text (including italics, punctuation, capitalisation etc) of the edition referenced, apart from minor edits to modernise obsolete spelling, for the sake of enhanced readability.

* Where alternative editions of these works include minor texts referred to, full publication details are given.

** Where modern reprints of these titles are referred to instead of the original, full publication details are given.

Other abbreviations

CCP	*J. Coffey and P. Lim, The Cambridge Companion to Puritanism*
CR	*A. G. Matthews, Calamy Revised.*
CSPD	*Calendar of State Papers Domestic (Charles II, 1660-1685).*
DNB	*Dictionary of National Biography 1885-1900.*
HDSE	*R. H. Fritze and W. B. Robison eds. Historical Dictionary of Stuart England 1603-1689.*
ODNB	*The Oxford Dictionary of National Biography*
PRRD	*R. A. Muller, Post-Reformation Reformed Dogmatics. Vols. I-IV.*
SLC	*The Solemn League and Covenant*
TCP	*Text Creation Partnership (Oxford University)*
WCF	*The Westminster Confession of Faith*
WLC	*The Westminster Larger Catechism*
WSC	*The Westminster Shorter Catechism*

PART 1

Godliness, Thomas Watson and English Puritanism

Introduction

In 1990, J. I. Packer noted that, despite there being a long interest in Puritan history, ecclesiology and politics, "only recently have Puritan theology and spirituality (that is, to use their own word, godliness) begun to receive serious scholarly attention."[1] Subsequent years have continued to see the spirituality of English Puritanism (and its New World derivative in North America) receive a more thorough treatment.[2] "Godliness" was a key term in the vocabulary of this historical religious movement. However, its meaning is often assumed and undeveloped in academic studies of Puritanism.[3]

Thomas Watson (c. 1620-1686) devoted much of his ministry to elucidating what godliness meant to Late English Puritans. He produced detailed treatises on this subject, which are unsurpassed in depth and accessibility by any of his more well-known contemporaries. By virtue of the republication of these works, Watson has become a representative spokesperson for the Puritan movement concerning this integral element of their spirituality. Yet he has received disproportionately little attention from scholars of Puritanism. There has been a welcome, recent interest in the mystical and meditative elements of his approach to spirituality. Likewise, there are numerous, passing references to Watson in major studies of Puritan spirituality. However, for a man who has been described as "the most readable of the Puritans" and the "pithiest of

1. He continues: "Only recently has it been noted that a devotional quickening occurred throughout the divided Western church during the century after the Reformation and that Puritanism was a foremost expression (the foremost expression, I would contend) of this stirring." J. I. Packer, *A Quest for Godliness: The Puritan Vision of the Christian Life* (Wheaton: Crossway, 1990): 12.
2. See the survey of literature below for some of the notable works covering this subject.
3. A notable example would be Patrick Collinson's introductory essay "The Godly: Aspects of Popular Protestantism" in his *Godly People: Essays on English Protestantism and Puritanism* (London: Hambledon Press, 1983): 1-17. While Collinson provides a detailed account of what those he identifies as "the godly" *did*, he does not elucidate what they would have understood "godliness" to be in its essence.

Presbyterians," there remains a lack of substantial studies dedicated to his thought and piety.[4]

Godliness as a spiritual posture, characterised chiefly by an appropriate, affectional response toward God, is the pervading theme of Watson's entire thought and ministry. His spiritual theology and practice exemplify English Puritan devotion in its mature form. This is demonstrated by both his positive commitments to piety and his negative reactions to perceived ungodliness. Watson presents his piety in harmony with contemporary Puritan consensus. But he takes pains to demonstrate that it is derived from the testimony of Scripture and the doctrinal basis of the Westminster standards. On the other hand, a consistent juxtaposition exists in his works between godliness and impiety. This includes Watson's polemics against aberrant forms of religious devotion and his pastoral concern to encourage godliness in the midst of the harsh religious conformity enforced in the Restoration period.

Key works on godliness

Several of Watson's works are of particular importance to this study of his understanding of godliness.[5] *The Godly Man's Picture* was produced at the mid-point of his pastoral ministry. It provides an extensive treatment of what Watson considered to be the key characteristics of godliness. This work remains in print and is the most accessible Puritan work for today's Christian readers wishing to gain an introductory understanding of the movement's concept

4. The 20th century re-publishers of *A Body of Divinity* had this to say about its author: "Watson conveys his thorough, doctrinal and experimental knowledge of the truth in such an original, concise, pithy, pungent, racy, rich and illustrative style that he is rightly regarded as the most readable of the Puritans." Watson, *A Body of Divinity* (Edinburgh: Banner of Truth, 1965): back cover. See also Alan Sell, "The Doctrinal and Ecumenical Significance of the Great Ejectment" in *The Great Ejectment of 1662: Its Antecedents, Aftermath and Ecumenical Significance*, ed. Alan Sell (Eugene: Wipf & Stock, 2012): 224.
5. Watson, *The Godly Man's Picture* (1666) (Oxford: Text Creation Partnership [TCP], 2004). http://purl.ox.ac.uk/ota/A65296. Other works of comparable topical concern from the period include Richard Baxter, *Saint or Brute* (1662) (Oxford: TCP, 2006): http://purl.ox.ac.uk/ota/A27016; Richard Alleine, *Vindiciæ pietatis* (1660) (Oxford: TCP, 2009): http://purl.ox.ac.uk/ota/A74976; Vincent Alsop, *Decus & tutamen* (1696) (Oxford: TCP, 2010): http://purl.ox.ac.uk/ota/A25204. Each of these works elaborate on the nature of godliness and how to live in accordance with it, but these works are less well known than *Godly Man's Picture* and lack the anatomical extensiveness of Watson's approach to the topic.

of godliness.[6] Yet its wealth as a resource for scholarship remains untapped. Watson penned another treatise dedicated to godliness in his final years, with *Religion our True Interest* becoming the final book published within his lifetime. In this capstone work Watson does not merely revisit godliness as a favourite theme. He provides his readers with an extended reflection upon the kind of piety required in the dark circumstances that the Puritans found themselves in during this period of English history. The posthumous work, *A Body of Practical Divinity* can be regarded as his "*magnum opus*."[7] This work demonstrates how his confessional, systematic theology and affectional piety were integrated.

Puritanism

A study of this nature cannot afford to succumb to the notorious academic "quagmire" that is the task of defining *Puritanism*.[8] The immensity of scholarly debate surrounding this issue cannot be adequately treated here. But neither can the subject be completely evaded. Watson's significance as a representative of *Puritan* piety cannot be appreciated apart from a working definition of these key terms.

Brian H. Cosby's attempt, after a diligent survey of the historiography of Puritanism, serves as an appropriate reference point for the use of these terms in this study.

> A 'Puritan' was one who, politically, reacted against the *via media* of the Elizabethan Settlement in favour of a more thorough reformation in England; who, socially, promoted evangelism, catechism, and spiritual nourishment through the preaching and teaching of the Bible; who, theologically, held the views of

6. Whilst perhaps not falling within the parameters of traditionally accepted methodology, in the digital age an author's enduring popularity and relevance is undoubtedly measurable, to some extent, by how highly they rank in listings on internet search engines and online bookstores. Searches for a combination of "Puritan" and "godliness" on leading search engine Google and booksellers Amazon.com reveal that Watson's works tend to be the top primary sources to appear. This approach, despite its unconventionality, lends weight to the suggestion that he is the leading Puritan voice on this important emphasis in the early 21st century.
7. Barry Till, "Watson, Thomas," *ODNB* (Oxford: Oxford University Press, 2004): ¶5. https://doi.org/10.1093/ref:odnb/28867 Accessed 6/10/15; Joel Beeke and Randall Pederson, *Meet the Puritans* (Grand Rapids: Reformation Heritage Books, 2006): 608.
8. Randall J. Pederson, *Unity in Diversity: English Puritans and the Puritan Reformation, 1603-1689* (Leiden: Brill, 2014): 310.

> Luther's doctrine of faith (*sola fide*), Calvin's doctrine of grace (*sola gratia*), and the Reformers' doctrine of Scripture (*sola scriptura*); and who, devotionally, strove for personal holiness, a practical faith, communion with God, and the glory of God in all things.[9]

This general definition captures the essence of Puritanism as a mid-sixteenth to late seventeenth century, English religious movement. English Puritanism can be described ecclesiologically as "deutero-Protestantism;"[10] theologically as Reformed;[11] and devotionally as "pietist[ic]."[12] Thus, for the purposes of this study, Watson is referred to as a Puritan to denote his identification with a historical movement which derived much of its heritage from the Reformed tradition and strove to complete the work of Reformation from within the English Church, before eventually being driven out of it.[13]

There is no consensus among Puritan scholars about how to divide the movement into historical phases. However, it is commonplace to identify such phases with the reigns of particular monarchs or royal

9. Brian H. Cosby, "Towards a Definition of 'Puritan' and 'Puritanism': A Study in Puritan Historiography," *Churchman* 122:4 (2008): 307. For other, helpful and recent attempts to survey and define Puritanism, see John Coffey and Paul Lim, "Introduction" in *The Cambridge Companion to Puritanism*, eds. John Coffey and Paul Lim (Cambridge: Cambridge University Press, 2008): 1-6; Pederson, *Unity in Diversity*, 28-30, 32-33.
10. I.e. seeking to reform the faith, worship and structure of the English Church from within until—like Luther and other Protestant reformers—they eventually found themselves expelled from the Church. See Leland Ryken, *Worldly Saints: The Puritans as they Really Were* (Grand Rapids: Zondervan, 1986): 7; Beeke and Pederson, *Meet the Puritans*, 3-4. Historian of English Presbyterianism, Polly Ha, has suggested that while Puritan attempts at "completing reformation of the Church of England" could be understood as a kind of "Second Reformation," some of the early Congregationalists may have understood their quest as a "Third Reformation"—continuing reform where the Presbyterians would have stopped short. Ha, *English Presbyterianism, 1590-1640* (Stanford: Stanford University Press, 2011): 7, 203.
11. I.e. Protestant with a dominant Calvinist/Genevan flavour.
12. I.e. characterised by daily, heartfelt, spiritual exercises; a commitment to constant, holy living; and a concern for sincere correlation between the individual's public/private or internal/external religious devotion. See Joel Beeke and Mark Jones, *Puritan Theology: Doctrine for Life* (Grand Rapids: Reformation Heritage Books, 2012): 847-850.
13. It is outside the scope of this study to evaluate the extent to which it is helpful to refer to the religion of the New England colonists (beyond the first generation of pilgrims) as Puritanism. Suffice it to say that there are a range of common elements between the theology and spirituality of the two movements separated by the Atlantic Ocean. However, the ecclesiological project, historical circumstances and geopolitical realities of devout New Englanders were substantially different to their English counterparts. See Charles Pastoor and Galen Johnson, *Historical Dictionary of the Puritans* (Lanham: Scarecrow Press, 2007): 5.

houses e.g. "Elizabethan" or "Early Stuart" Puritanism.[14] This study will refer to three distinct phases of the Puritan movement, each consisting of roughly four decades and directly tied to monarchial reigns and pivotal events in British history. Early Puritanism (c. 1560-1603) is synonymous with "Elizabethan Puritanism" and covers the period of early angst and controversy within the established Protestant Church over matters such as liturgy, vestments and ecclesiology. Middle Puritanism (1603-1649) has also been termed "Early Stuart Puritanism."[15] It began with high hopes for progressive reform under James I/VI, deteriorated into the repressive climate of the Laudian arch-episcopate under Charles I and culminated in the English Civil Wars and the only regicide in English history. Late Puritanism (1649-1689) includes the decade of Puritan ascendancy (1649-1659) and its political decline into religious nonconformity (1660-1689).[16]

Watson's Late English Puritan milieu

It is to this last generation of English Puritans that Watson belongs and their collective piety that he represents. The late English Puritans inherited their devotional ethos from the preceding century of their devout English forebears, including the likes of William Perkins, William Ames and Richard Sibbes.[17] Puritans

14. E.g. Patrick Collinson, *The Elizabethan Puritan Movement* (Oxford: Clarendon, 1990); Tom Webster, "Early Stuart Puritanism," in *CCP*.
15. Webster, "Early Stuart Puritanism," 48; P. R. Schaefer refers to the "middle period" of English Puritanism between 1590-1640. Schaefer, *Spiritual Brotherhood: Cambridge Puritans and the Nature of Christian Piety* (Grand Rapids: Reformation Heritage Books, 2013): 85. Kindle Edition.
16. See Dewey Wallace, *Spirituality of the Later English Puritans: An Anthology* (Macon: Mercer University Press, 1987). These phases can be employed for the purpose of exploring the context of particular figures' upbringing and ministry. For instance, Thomas Watson was born into the environment of Middle Puritanism, but became active in ministry during the Late Puritan phase. When speaking of English Puritans, it is inadvisable to extend the term beyond those who were born after the Middle Puritan phase or whose ministry occurred after the Late Puritan period (e.g. renowned Bible commentator Matthew Henry is often called a Puritan, but would be better designated an English nonconformist).
17. See Tom Schwanda, "'Sweetnesse in Communion with God:' The Contemplative Mystical Piety of Thomas Watson," *Journal for the History of Reformed Pietism* 1:1 (January 2015): 57; Norbert Haukenfrer, "Bellows of Affection: The Meditative Spirituality of Thomas Watson" (MCS thesis, Vancouver: Regent College, 1998): 13; Richard Lovelace, "The Anatomy of Puritan Piety: English Puritan Devotional Literature, 1600-1640" in *Christian Spirituality: Post-Reformation and Modern*, eds. Louis Dupre and Don Saliers (New York: Crossroad, 1989), 3:299; William S. Barker,

from each historical phase shared the conviction that they could distil the Church's devotional practice to a point of utmost biblical fidelity. This naturally led to severe conflict with religious groups that Puritans perceived to be unfaithful to the biblical vision for Christian piety. Late English Puritans were confronted with the resurgence of Arminian, Anglo-Catholicism in Restoration England. The threat of a national return to Catholicism remained present, while theological error proliferated due to religious policies of toleration. This religious context led Watson to articulate his piety in contradistinction to other contemporary varieties he felt had diverged from biblical fidelity.

Late English Puritanism also had a theological context that distinguishes it from the two preceding phases of Puritan history. This period was marked by widespread confessionalism, as the Reformed branches of English Christianity sought to codify their respective tenets of faith.[18] The great formative exercise in Reformed dogma undertaken by the Westminster Assembly (1643-1648) occurred during the closing years of the Middle Puritan period. Watson's age and inexperience precluded him from participating in the Assembly. But his *Body of Divinity* (1692) became the most widely-distributed, early exposition of the *Westminster Shorter Catechism* (WSC), surpassing comparable works in substance and extensiveness. This establishes Watson as the most important practical English divine to produce a detailed programme of piety as the natural outcome of the doctrinal system transmitted by the WSC.

Finally, the climate facing Puritans, following the Restoration of the monarchy, required a robust pastoral vision for confirming one's fellow travellers in godliness when difficulties arose. Watson's works show that he had given serious consideration to the question of what it meant to exhibit godliness in harsh social conditions. His personal history tells the story of someone who often experienced persecution and marginalisation despite having considerable prominence and a number of privileged friends. The tenor of his writings on godliness reflects this *milieu* and highlights the concerns of nonconformist pastors in the reign of Charles II.

"A Body of Divinity by Thomas Watson" in *The Devoted Life: An Invitation to the Puritan Classics*, eds. Kelly M. Kapic and Randall C. Gleason (Downers Grove: IVP, 2004), 205.

18. Richard A. Muller, *Post-Reformation Reformed Dogmatics* (Grand Rapids: Baker, 2003): 1:31.

The structure of this study

The next chapter in this section surveys the existing literature on Watson and the most pertinent studies on Puritan spirituality. This will assist in establishing the relative neglect of Watson and the specific topic of godliness in Puritan studies. Chapter 2 provides a biographical overview of Watson's life to give historical context for the development of his piety. Key events that shaped Watson's outlook and ministry are highlighted. The biography also situates his major works on godliness in relation to these historical elements. Because this study attempts to provide the most comprehensive account of Watson's affectional piety to date, it provides a natural opportunity to expand upon existing biographical material.

The second section, consisting of chapters 3-6, approaches Watson's notion of godliness through the lens of spiritual theology. I examine his interaction with biblical data and his exposition of the nature of godliness in *Godly Man's Picture* and *Religion our True Interest*. Watson presents a picture of godliness that is chiefly affectional. That is to say, it consists mainly in the appropriate response of the heart towards God as He is revealed in Scripture. But the extensiveness of his treatment of the subject allows us to see the whole range of dimensions that are present in his understanding of piety. After establishing what godliness means for Watson, I proceed to consider his proposed means for cultivating it in the life of the Christian. Previous scholarship has rightly noted the meditative and mystical aspects of Watson's piety. However, this study will demonstrate that meditation itself—while vital for Watson—was but one of several, indispensable means of growth in his schema of practical piety. The final chapter in this section outlines several important aims or outcomes of godliness that Watson set forth as incentives for those pursuing it. For Watson, godliness has a unique capacity for glorifying God, while benefiting both the godly individual and their neighbours.

The third section explores Watson's doctrine of godliness as historical theology. Chapter 7 establishes the common themes that make Watson's approach to godliness representative of the late English Puritan movement. This is achieved by drawing on the secondary literature on Puritan spirituality and the writings of key Puritans, including Richard Baxter, John Owen and Stephen Charnock. This is followed by a consideration of Watson's indebtedness to the piety of his earlier Puritan predecessors from the late sixteenth and early-mid seventeenth century. Chapter 8 explores the reactive element of Watson's piety. Watson expressed his commitment to godliness in deliberate contradistinction to the doctrine and practice of Roman and Anglo-Catholicism. He adopted the same stance towards various sects and religions that were erroneous from a Puritan perspective. This leads to a polemical edge in many of his devotional writings which precludes the possibility of genuine piety where devotion is based on faulty doctrine.

The chapters in the fourth section explore the relationship between Watson's emphatic commitment to piety and his systematic theology. Watson's best-known work, *Body of Divinity*, serves as his most thorough attempt to deal with the major doctrines of the Christian faith. Watson greatly expands upon the WSC's statements and draws out a wide range of pietistic and practical applications for each significant doctrine treated.[19] In so doing, Watson was improving upon the merely doctrinal formulations of the WSC and creating a "practical divinity" that moved Christians beyond confessional subscription to responsive, godly piety. The entirety of his catechetical endeavour served to advance his vision of godliness.

The fifth section investigates how Watson sought to promote godliness among a religious community that found itself subject to marginalisation and persecution in Restoration England. The trajectory of Watson's ministry forged his identity as a member of and pastor to a godly, afflicted minority within a perverse generation. For much of his ministry, Watson executed his pastoral charge in a climate where manifesting Puritan or Presbyterian convictions could invite serious consequences. The consolatory literature he produced was not thematically separate from his emphasis on godliness. Rather, these works were pastoral exhortations to his fellow-travellers to persevere in piety under severely unfavourable conditions.

The final section concludes the study with an overview of the main aspects of Watson's affectional piety discussed in earlier chapters. It also highlights possible areas for further research related to Thomas Watson, godliness and Puritan spirituality.

---

19. See also Barker, "A Body of Divinity," 204.

Chapter 1
A Scholarly "Quest for Godliness"? Watson's Place in Puritan Studies

The considerable academic interest in the piety of English Puritanism would initially seem to suggest that scholars have embarked on something of a "quest for godliness" (to borrow from Packer)—seeking to understand that which lay at the heart of Puritan devotion. Yet, as noted in the introduction, the watchword of *godliness* itself has often received a cursory treatment in the relevant literature. It is this neglect of godliness that calls for an extensive study of the theme in one of its most articulate proponents. Studying Watson's abiding fixation with the importance of godliness will contribute to the existing literature by enhancing our appreciation of the object of this quest. Situating the insights of the limited amount of literature on certain aspects of Watson's thought and devotion within the broader context of his commitment to godliness will also assist us in understanding the motivations of this notable Puritan figure.

The mystical element of Watson's spirituality

Watson has received the most attention from those who have identified contemplative traits in his spirituality. Norbert Haukenfrer's thesis, "Bellows of Affection: The Meditative Spirituality of Thomas Watson," was the earliest and most substantial study of this element of Watson's piety. However, it remains unpublished after twenty years and as a masters-level work it lacks the depth of a doctoral or postdoctoral study. Nevertheless, it cannot be ignored due to the lack of a more extensive study. Haukenfrer describes Watson's piety as a "meditative spirituality of the heart" and establishes the link between his emphases on godliness and meditation.[1] As suggested by the title, *Bellows of Affection* highlights the role of meditation in

1. Haukenfrer, "Bellows of Affection", vii.

"flam[ing] the affections of the heart."[2] Jennifer Neimeyer does not indicate any awareness of Haukenfrer's work in her article, "Thomas Watson: The Necessity of Meditation," but picks up on many of the same themes.[3] Her main claim is that, "Watson viewed meditation as most foundational to personal piety."[4] She considers Watson's treatise on Meditation to have exalted this discipline above all other spiritual duties—establishing it as the most important aspect of true piety. Haukenfrer and Neimeyer have both rightly identified meditation as a crucial component of Watson's piety. Yet, as I will discuss in Chapter 5, focusing on this element exclusively runs the risk of reducing his devotional outlook to one narrow aspect.

Tom Schwanda, a scholar of the history of Christian spirituality, has made two recent and welcome contributions to our understanding of Watson's piety.[5] Schwanda builds upon earlier works, acknowledging the aforementioned studies and situating Watson within the development of Christian spirituality. He goes beyond the merely meditative aspect in characterising Watson's piety as "contemplative-mystical." From this perspective, he explores the extent to which the pre-Reformation devotional practices of medieval monasticism influenced his approach to spirituality. "Sweetnesse of Communion" has a particular focus on the influence of Bernard of Clairvaux upon Watson's attitudes towards the practice of contemplation and his mystical interpretation of the biblical Canticles. Schwanda's discussion of the role of the Lord's Supper, prayer and meditation in Watson's contemplative-mystical piety explores Watson's emphasis on how the Spirit works through such practices. It also notes how godly affection must be joined to these spiritual disciplines for them to be genuine. Importantly, Schwanda notes that for Watson and other Puritans, any spiritual experience through the ordinances came as a result of God's grace, rather than the process itself. He also states that there was no discernible shift in Watson's emphasis on contemplative-mystical themes between his early writings and those after the Great Ejection.

In "The Saints' Spiritual delight and desire to be with Christ" —the most recent publication relating to Watson's spirituality—

2. Haukenfrer, "Bellows of Affection," 114.
3. Jennifer Neimeyer, "Thomas Watson: The Necessity of Meditation," *Puritan Reformed Journal* 2:1 (2010): 166-181.
4. Neimeyer, "Thomas Watson," 167
5. Schwanda, "Sweetnesse," 45-68; Schwanda, "The Saints' Desire and Delight to be with Christ" in *Puritanism and Emotion in the Early Modern World*, eds. Alec Ryrie and Tom Schwanda (Basingstoke: Palgrave Macmillan, 2016).

Schwanda builds on his earlier study of Watson's "contemplative, mystical piety." He draws out the aspect of the Christian's longing to be with Christ and attain the beatific vision.[6] Schwanda again demonstrates connections between Watson's approach to piety and that of Bernard of Clairvaux and other Catholic mystical, devotional writers.[7] The relationship between spiritual duties in the present life and the fulfilment of spiritual desire in the age to come is explored in detail. Schwanda shows that Watson emphasised the cultivation of a proper emotional response to God in this life through the appropriate duties.[8] At the same time, he anticipated the fullness of divine delight when the believer beholds his glory for eternity. Because this fullness is unattainable in the present life, Schwanda shows how Watson emphasised catching a "glimpse" of God in the ordinances in the meantime—thus giving definite form to the importance of spiritual duties.[9]

Other resources pertaining to Watson's thought, practice and significance

Watson's piety and theology have been examined in a more general manner by authors such as William S. Barker, Christopher Jenkins, Chris Lee and Jack Hughes. Barker provides the best published overview of Watson's general theological framework in an introductory essay to *A Body of Divinity.* He explores the connection between Watson's theology and that of the Westminster Assembly, whose WSC forms the skeleton for his *Body of Divinity.* He establishes that Watson is representative of "standard seventeenth-century Calvinism," while highlighting the topics that he placed more emphasis upon than the WSC he used as his basis.[10] Barker demonstrates a keen appreciation of Watson's context—aptly listing both his theological influences and the adversaries to which he reacted. This essay conveys the dimension of Watson's "practical divinity" and closes by suggesting that it is the theological undergirding of practical devotion, along with an emphasis on meditation and other spiritual duties that predominantly characterise Watson's work.[11]

6. Schwanda, "Saints' Desire," 80-87.
7. Schwanda, "Saints' Desire," 72-74.
8. Schwanda, "Saints' Desire," 76-78.
9. Schwanda, "Saints' Desire," 87-88.
10. Barker, "A Body of Divinity," 206.
11. Barker, "A Body of Divinity," 208-209.

Although implicit in some of the discussions of Watson's practical bent, Barker does not mention godliness as a central theme for Watson and in *Body of Divinity.*

The works of Jenkins and Lee are aimed at a more popular audience. While they lack scholarly depth and theological breadth, they provide a number of insights into Watson's piety overlooked by others. Jenkins provides a useful overview of the characteristics of godliness in his study of *Godly Man's Picture* and holds Watson forward as a positive exemplar of Puritan piety.[12] The constraints of the conference paper format mean that Jenkins has only scratched the surface of the significance of *Godly Man's Picture*—not only for understanding Watson's piety, but as a remarkable anatomy of Puritan godliness.

Lee's article also traces themes without providing in-depth analysis, but ranges beyond a single work in an attempt to summarise Watson's overall outlook.[13] Lee lacks a dedicated section on godliness—his brief remarks on holiness being the closest he gets. But his observations about Watson's view of suffering, affliction, persecution and encouragement are noteworthy and more substantial than what is found in other works. "At a time when Protestants in general and Non-Conformists in particular were being persecuted, Watson was a good shepherd that settled the sheep. Watson did not shy away from the problem of pain that seemed to affect the godly more than the sinful."[14]

Hughes produced the only doctoral thesis to focus on Watson.[15] However, its scope is limited to Watson's mastery of homiletic imagery and thus offers little direct material on his piety. Watson's evocative power of communication is a key component of his enduring readability through the centuries, contributing, in turn, to his emergence as a Puritan spokesperson on godliness. Yet his illustrative techniques fall outside of the scope of this study, except where they are employed to convey a sense of his affectional piety.[16]

---

12. Christopher Jenkins, "Thomas Watson and how to live a Godly Life" in *The Power of God in the Life of Man* (London: Westminster Conference, 2005): 27.
13. Lee, "Thomas Watson as Pastor and Scholar," *Founders Journal* 88 (Spring 2012): 3-22.
14. Lee, "Thomas Watson," 9.
15. Published as Jack Hughes, *Expository Preaching with Word Pictures* (Fearn: Christian Focus, 2001).
16. For other published studies that make a contribution to our understanding of Watson, but fall outside the purview of this study's focus on his central emphasis, see John D. Wilsey, "English Puritan views on Assurance: John Owen and Thomas Watson"

Several of the works mentioned above contain biographical sketches of Watson's life. Other notable accounts of his life, which are drawn upon in the biographical section below, include older sketches by Edmund Calamy III, Walter Wilson, Charles Spurgeon and E. I. Carlyle, along with more recent contributions by Barry Till, Dewey Wallace and Joel Beeke.[17]

Notable works on Puritan piety, theology and history

Our study of Watson's piety is a subset of the wider scholarly interest in Puritan spirituality. Neither the extent to which Watson is representative of Late English Puritan devotion nor the distinctiveness of his contribution can be ascertained without the assistance of the existing literature in this field. It is necessary, therefore, to chart some of the key works which stand behind this study.

1980s

While there had been a number of notable works on Puritan spirituality prior to the 1980s—including the contributions of Gordon Wakefield and Irvonwy Morgan—this decade saw a blossoming of interest in Puritan spirituality. Charles Hambrick-Stowe approaches Puritanism as a devotional movement, which—notwithstanding its distinctiveness—shared some key commonalities with Catholic devotion.[18] He identifies a clash between the priority of external, "liturgical forms" of worship and vital, inward "heart religion" as the impetus for Puritan spirituality.[19] At the end of the decade, Richard Lovelace remained concerned that "no work has appeared which adequately grasps Puritan piety both in its distinctiveness and in its relation to medieval piety and to the developing stream of Christian experience after the seventeenth century."[20] While

https://www.academia.edu/11430265/ Accessed 30/09/15; Mark Kim, "Michael Horton's Covenant Theology as a Defense of Reformation Theology in the Context of Current Discussions" (ThD Thesis, Toronto: Wycliffe, 2013).

17. See bibliography for a complete list of these sources.
18. Hambrick-Stowe, *The Practice of Piety: Puritan Devotional Disciplines in Seventeenth-Century New England* (Chapel Hill: University of North Carolina Press, 1986). Hambrick-Stowe focuses on New England, but his insights are pertinent to the English Puritanism of the same period.
19. Hambrick-Stowe, *Practice of Piety*, 43.
20. Lovelace, "Anatomy of Puritan Piety," 295.

addressing this lacuna, the strength of Lovelace's contribution is his grasp of theologically-fuelled heart affections towards God as the substance of godliness. He summarises affective Puritan spirituality as "an experience which is neither intellectual nor emotional nor volitional, but which takes place in a ground of the personality underlying all these faculties."[21]

Dewey Wallace also identifies connections between the spirituality of the Puritans and their English and Continental Reformation predecessors. This situates English Puritanism as part of a wider revival of piety across Christian traditions during this period. Wallace argues, convincingly, that Later English Puritan spirituality focused on the "cultivation of the religious life," following their severe political marginalisation in post-Restoration England.[22] Godliness offered a vital, uncontroversial point of unity for a species of irenic nonconformists fatigued by the intra-Puritan theological conflicts of the Interregnum years. In terms of substance, Wallace proposes that:

> [t]he Puritan spirituality of the latter seventeenth century was less a new departure than it was the refinement, intensification, and sometimes narrowing of earlier themes of Puritan piety. One of these themes was that true religion must be an inner, spiritual experience.[23]

An emphasis on regeneration was one area where this intensification occurred, "Puritans after 1660 had no new doctrines to offer, though perhaps they intensified the new birth as an individual experience."[24] Wallace also identifies the importance of meditation and "heavenly mindedness" in Puritan spirituality—a theme which has been explored by numerous scholars since. The role of the Holy Spirit and significance of sincere affections in this phase of Puritan piety are also highlighted. Wallace proceeds to cast light on the reactive aspect of Puritan devotion—especially in response to the Arminianism that was rampant in the Restored English Church. The case is made well that persecution at the hands of ecclesiastical foes shaped Puritan theology and piety as much as their enemies' objectionable doctrines. "Puritan writers, especially after 1660 with the failure of Puritan hopes, devoted considerable attention to the afflictions of the godly."[25]

21. Lovelace, "Anatomy of Puritan Piety," 320.
22. Wallace, *Spirituality*, xiv.
23. Wallace, *Spirituality*, xv.
24. Wallace, *Spirituality*, xv.
25. Wallace, *Spirituality*, xxiv.

Wallace's contribution also outlines the late Puritan programme of piety, which included: "reading, attendance at sermons, conferring with the spiritually mature, partaking of the sacrament of the Lord's Supper, prayer and meditation" and the production of "affectionate divinity" manuals (devotional works wherein systematic theology is applied to produce a range of affective responses and godly actions).[26]

1990s

The 1990s saw the further publication of significant examinations of Puritan piety. J. I. Packer's *A Quest for Godliness* is a survey of Puritanism as a devotional movement, written from a sympathetic, evangelical perspective with a view to retrieve helpful emphases and practices for the benefit of contemporary Christianity. While Packer gives a detailed account of Puritan theology, spirituality, worship and ministry throughout this work, perhaps his greatest contribution is the following overview of the movement's distinctive characteristics:

> Puritanism was at heart a spiritual movement, passionately concerned with God and godliness ... Into its making went Tyndale's reforming Biblicism; John Bradford's piety of the heart and conscience; John Knox's zeal for God's honour in national churches; the passion for evangelical pastoral competence that is seen in John Hooper, Edward Dering and Richard Greenham; the view of Holy Scripture as the 'regulative principle' of church worship and order that fired Thomas Cartwright; the anti-Roman, anti-Arminian, anti-Socinian, anti-Antinomian Calvinism that John Owen and the Westminster standards set forth; the comprehensive ethical interest that reached its apogee in Richard Baxter's monumental *Christian Directory*; and the purpose of popularising and making practical the teachings of the Bible that gripped Perkins and Bunyan, with many more. Puritanism was essentially a movement for church reform, pastoral renewal and evangelism, and spiritual revival; and in addition—indeed, as a direct expression of its zeal for God's honour—it was a world-view,a total Christian philosophy, in intellectual terms a Protestantised and updated medievalism, and in terms of spirituality a reformed monasticism outside the cloister and away from monkish vows.[27]

After an extensive overview of the issues surrounding the academic definition of Puritanism, Christopher Durston and Jacqueline Eales defer to William Haller's earlier observation that it was "a spiritual

26. Wallace, *Spirituality*, xxv.
27. Packer, *Quest for Godliness*, 28.

outlook, way of life, and mode of expression."[28] As an outlook it included: an emphasis on predestination;[29] an appreciation of the "enormous gulf" between sinful humans and their holy Creator;[30] the significance of spiritual conversion; the struggle for assurance of salvation;[31] an accordant "need for constant self-examination and vigilance against sin and temptation, and a deep sense of personal unworthiness;"[32] a desire to purify the worship of the church in conformity with the Scriptures;[33] bibliocentrism;[34] anti-Romanism; and a vision for moral, societal reform. Its mode of expression included communal solidarity in a distinctive lifestyle of piety, not limited to strict sabbatarianism and a regimen of religious duties.[35]

2000-present

Inquiry into Puritan piety has continued into the 21st century. *The Cambridge Companion to Puritanism* succeeds in setting out the present landscape of Puritan studies, by drawing together several of the leading authorities on Puritanism. The contributions of Patrick Collinson, Spurr, Hambrick-Stowe and Wallace are of particular assistance in coming to appreciate the historical background and devotional context of English Puritanism.[36] A clear juxtaposition exists between certain scholarly approaches to Puritan spirituality in the last fifteen years. In the works of David Como and Theodore Bozeman, English Puritanism is presented as an overly rigid, "disciplinarian" religious movement, which sought to combat the widespread laxity its adherents perceived in their society and yet itself provoked the theological and ethical reactions that would come to be known as "antinomianism."[37] Bozeman offers a range

28. C. Durston and J. Eales, "Puritan Ethos" in *The Culture of English Puritanism 1560-1700*, eds. C. Durston and J. Eales (London: Palgrave MacMillan, 1996).
29. Durston and Eales, 7-8.
30. Durston and Eales, 9.
31. Durston and Eales, 11.
32. Durston and Eales, 12.
33. Durston and Eales, 17-20.
34. Durston and Eales, 16-17.
35. Durston and Eales, 20-27.
36. P. Collinson, "Antipuritanism" in *CCP*, 19-32; J. Spurr, "Later Stuart Puritanism" in CCP, 89-107; C. Hambrick-Stowe, "Practical Divinity and Spirituality" in *CCP*, 191-205; D. Wallace, "Puritan polemical divinity and doctrinal controversy" in *CCP*, 206-222.
37. David Como, *Blown by the Spirit: Puritanism and the Emergence of an Antinomian Underground in pre-Civil-War England* (Stanford: Stanford University Press, 2004); Como, "Radical Puritanism" in *CCP*, 241-258; Theodore Bozeman, *The Precisianist*

of critiques of Puritan spirituality which require some discussion at key points in this study of Watson's piety. Chief among them are his suggestions that: 1) Despite being vehemently anti-Catholic, Puritans borrowed heavily from the Roman framework of piety; 2) There is a fundamental tension at the heart of Puritan spirituality between its commitment to "Solifidianism" and its stress upon the rigorous execution of religious duties; 3) Puritan pastors struggled to admit or realise that their pious strictures were largely unattainable and were likely to cause more spiritual anguish than delight across the board.[38]

A very different approach has been taken by the circle of authors associated with Reformation Heritage Books, who commend the positive elements of Puritan piety to today's Christian reader, while maintaining academic integrity in their treatment of these subjects. Representatives of this approach include Joel Beeke and Mark Jones' *A Puritan Theology: Doctrine for Life*, which includes an insightful chapter on the Puritans' "Pilgrim Mentality," expounding what it means for them to be "biblically based, pietistic, churchly, warfaring, methodical, and two-worldly."[39] Individual exemplars of Puritan piety are also showcased in the *Profiles in Reformed Spirituality* series which provide introductory sketches to several key figures and excerpts from their devotional writings.[40] While this is an excellent series, the lack of a work featuring Watson is a glaring omission.

In tracing the heritage of Jonathan Edwards' piety, Brad Walton provides valuable analysis of the English Puritan understanding of spiritual affections.[41] Watson and Edwards drew from the same stream of earlier Puritan influences in formulating their piety. Since Watson often fails to signal which Puritan predecessors he is indebted to, Walton's study is useful for comparative purposes.

Raymond Brown's *Spirituality in Adversity* is the premiere study on Puritan piety in the context of suffering during the Post-Restoration period.[42] Brown discusses how the nonconformists active

---

Strain: Disciplinary Religion and Antinomian Backlash in Puritanism to 1638 (Chapel Hill: University of North Carolina Press, 2004).

38. Bozeman, *Precisianist Strain*, 4, 12-13, 74-83, 178-180.
39. Beeke and Jones, 858.
40. For a full list of titles in this series, see Dustin W. Benge, "Sweetly Set on God" *The Piety of David Brainerd* (Grand Rapids: Reformation Heritage, 2016): v.
41. Brad Walton, *Jonathan Edwards: Religious Affections and the Puritan Analysis of True Piety, Spiritual Sensation and Heart Religion* (Lewiston: Edwin Mellen, 2002).
42. Raymond Brown, *Spirituality in Adversity: English Nonconformity in a Period of Repression, 1660-1689* (Milton Keynes: Paternoster, 2012).

in this period understood their suffering theologically and what means they advocated for promoting piety in the face of adversity. This provides much of the necessary context for evaluating both Watson's typicality and distinctiveness in relation to the afflictions endured by fellow members of the Late English Puritan movement.

Finally, one of the most important studies in recent years to consider the role of religious devotion in the history of seventeenth century England is Alec Ryrie's Being Protestant in Reformation Britain.[43] While the period of Ryrie's focus does not extend beyond Middle Puritanism into Watson's ministry, his survey of how pious affections and spiritual duties shaped the daily concerns of British Protestants in the preceding century is invaluable for our understanding of the pedigree of Late Puritan spirituality.

The relationship of this study to existing literature

This work seeks to build upon the small, existing body of secondary literature concerned with Thomas Watson, while also highlighting his relevance to broader studies of English Puritan spirituality. The meditative element of Watson's piety identified by Schwanda, Neimeyer and Haukenfrer will be affirmed. However, this aspect will be contextualised as one component of Watson's broader commitment to affectional godliness. Schwanda has come further than the previous studies by covering the principles and practices that characterise Watson's devotion with considerable breadth. However, there is an opportunity to develop many of his insights into a fuller assessment of Watson's piety. This study will also relativise the importance of meditation in Watson's programme for cultivating godliness, by demonstrating that it was part of a more fully-orbed approach to religious devotion than Neimeyer and Haukenfrer's earlier studies might suggest. The following chapters will also expand upon the elementary treatments of Watson's theology and spirituality found in Barker, Jenkins and Lee. The relationship between the theology of the Westminster Assembly and Watson's piety—noted by Barker—is explored more substantially in Chapters 9 and 10. A more comprehensive treatment of the themes present in *Godly Man's Picture* is presented in Chapter 4. The roles of self-denial and suffering in Watson's piety—as identified by

43. Alec Ryrie, *Being Protestant in Reformation Britain* (Oxford: Oxford University Press, 2013).

Lee—require more attention and are treated in Chapters 5 and 12 respectively.

With respect to the general secondary literature on Puritan spirituality, this study of Watson provides an opportunity to illustrate and qualify Wallace's assessment of later English Puritan spirituality. Watson epitomises many of the characteristics delineated by Wallace. These include his concentrated focus on personal piety, practical divinity, the use of key means in cultivating godly affections, and the sustenance of godliness amongst marginalised nonconformists. By focusing on one notable late English Puritan who does not feature in Wallace's study, this book presents Watson as a case study in the spirituality of the period. This allows for a deepened understanding of the above aspects, while asking how Watson might challenge previous understandings of Puritan piety in its mature phase. Chapters 11-12 provide a broader context for the relationship between godliness and consolation in Watson's ministry, by drawing upon Brown's survey of nonconformist responses to adversity. While *Spirituality in Adversity* identifies many of the responses that characterise his approach to affliction, Watson's lifelong trajectory of hardship and marginalisation gives him a distinctive voice on the question of how adversity affects piety.

Thomas Watson's
Life & Ministry

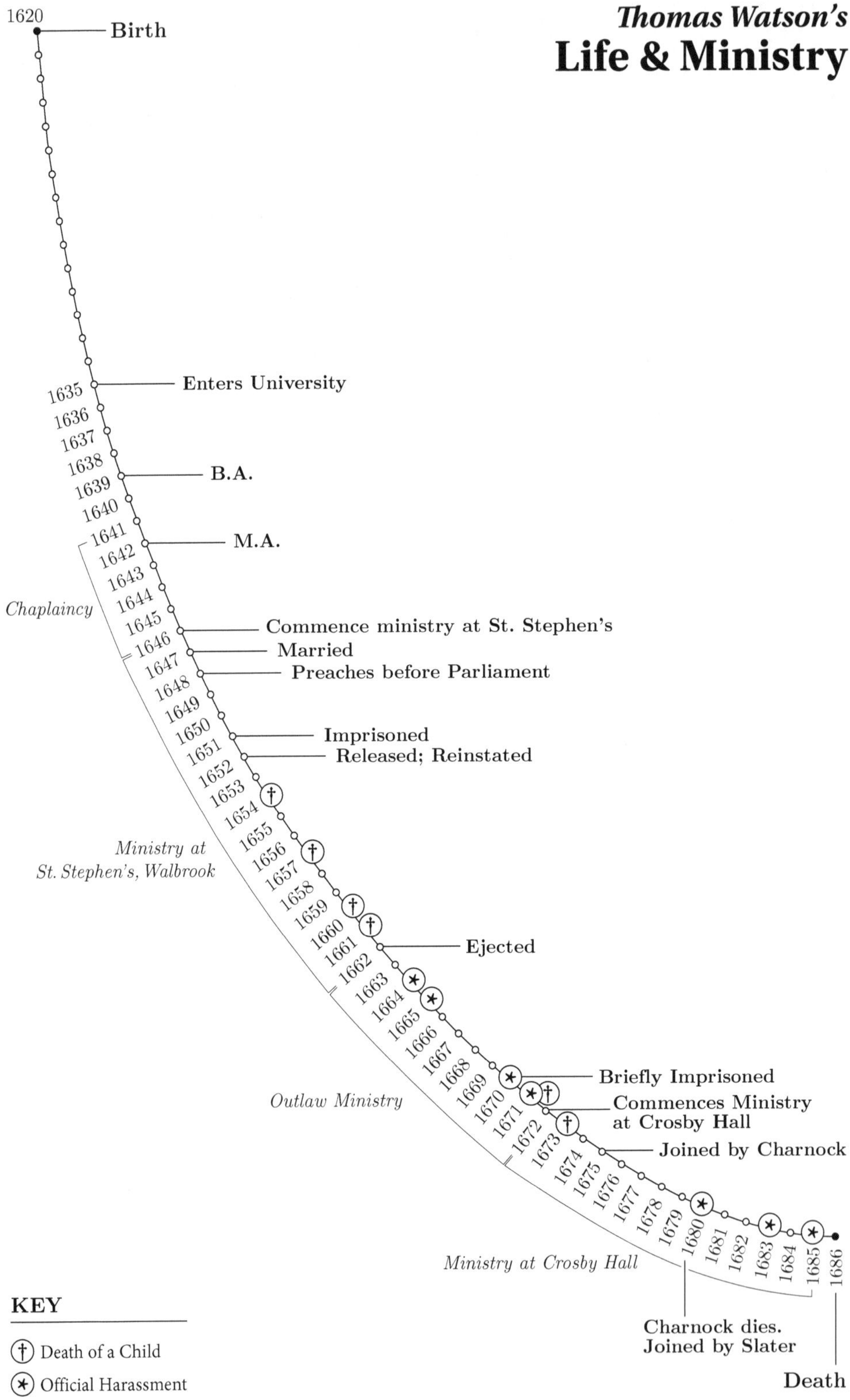

Contemporaneous Events

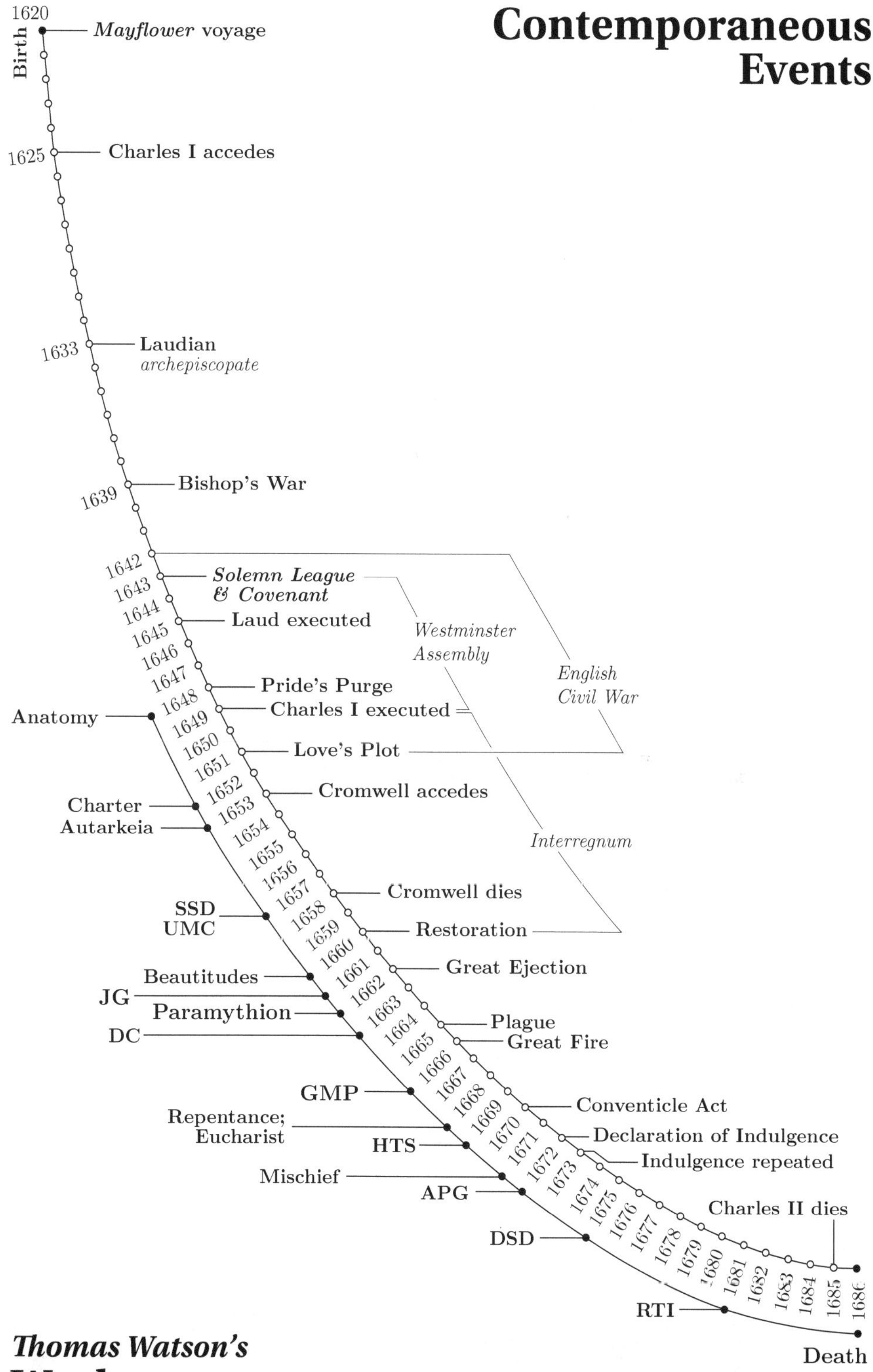

Thomas Watson's
Works
Refer to List of Abbreviations

Chapter 2
An "Exemplary Life and Conversation:"*
Thomas Watson (c. 1620-1686)

Early Life and Ministry (pre-1646)

*"The School of Saints:"*** *Education at Emmanuel College, Cambridge (1635-1642)*

Watson first appears in records as an Arts student at Cambridge on 4 July, 1635.[1] His enrolment papers indicate he originated from Yorkshire and 1620 has been the most commonly estimated date for his birth.[2] Watson entered Emmanuel College, an institution established for the purpose of training preachers and ministers and with a reputation for a strong Puritan theological heritage.[3] The choice of Emmanuel suggests prior exposure to the Puritan ethos and perhaps an intention to pursue theological training for clerical ministry.[4] Watson was recognised as a hard-working student.[5] After completing the B.A. in 1639, he continued studying at Cambridge until he graduated with a Master of Arts in 1642.[6]

Watson's studies occurred during a tumultuous time in British history. A hybrid of theological anti-Calvinism and high church ceremonialism, associated with William Laud (Archbishop of

---

* Title taken from publisher's introduction to 1689 edition of Seven Sermons.

** Title taken from Charles Spurgeon, "Brief Memoir of Thomas Watson" in *Thomas Watson, A Body of Divinity* (Edinburgh: Banner of Truth, 1965): vii.

1. Till, "Watson," 1.
2. Till, "Watson," 1; Beeke and Pederson, 605.
3. Charles Spurgeon, "Brief Memoir of Thomas Watson," vii-viii.
4. See R. McDermott, "Introduction" in Thomas Watson, *Jerusalem's Glory* (Fearn: Christian Focus, 2002): 12. Although it must be acknowledged that Emmanuel was not a uniform production line of Presbyterian or even Puritan ministers as S. Bryn Roberts points out in *Puritanism and the Pursuit of Happiness: The Ministry and Theology of Ralph Venning* (Woodbridge: Boydell Press, 2015): 36-37.
5. Spurgeon, "Watson," viii.
6. Spurgeon, "Watson," viii.

Canterbury from 1633) had been increasingly disrupting the English Church's existing "Calvinist mainstream" for some years.[8] Laud was known for his strict enforcement of religious uniformity and intolerance towards dissenters. This is illustrated by the misstep that brought about his downfall. In 1640, parliament held Laud responsible for the "Bishop's wars" between England and Scotland—conflicts instigated, in part, by his attempts to compel the Scottish Kirk to use a prescribed liturgy.[9] He was imprisoned until his execution in 1645.

As Watson was completing his Master of Arts degree, the religiously-charged English Civil War began. The country was plunged into turmoil for the next decade. The causes of the war are too complex to delve into here. But animosity towards the oppressive religious policies of the Laudian party was one factor that fuelled the momentum leading to the outbreak of the conflict. Together with the vast majority of faculty and students at Emmanuel College, Watson signed his name to Parliament's *Protestation Oath* in early 1642. This bound him to uphold Reformed Protestantism and demonstrate loyalty towards the King in the face of a perceived Catholic threat.[9] This was the tense climate in which he graduated and entered ministry.

The following year, Watson would sign another pledge, which had an even greater impact on his outlook in subsequent years of ministry. In 1643, the English Parliamentarians were eager to secure a military alliance with the Scots against Royalist forces in the First English Civil War. A key plank in the arrangement which eventuated was a shared commitment to a fresh religious settlement in England through the *Solemn League and Covenant* (SLC). The reformed religion would be preserved and promoted, and church government reformed so that a resumption of the previous Prelacy was excluded and a Presbyterianism akin to that which existed in Scotland would result—at least in the Scots' interpretation.[10] The

7. John Spurr, *English Puritanism* (London: MacMillan, 1998): 11-12; H. G. Alexander, *Religion in England 1558-1662,* London History Studies No. 4 (London: University of London Press, 1968): 148-151; Robert Letham, *The Westminster Assembly* (Philipsburg: P&R, 2001): 20-21.
8. Martyn Bennett, *Historical Dictionary of the British and Irish Civil Wars 1637-1660* (London: Rowman & Littlefield, 2016): 48.
9. Parliamentary Archives (United Kingdom), *Emanuel College—The whole number therein as ... taking the Protestation* (1642). http://digitalarchive.parliament.uk/HL/PO/JO/10/1/78/61 Accessed 06/12/17.
10. See Rowland S. Ward, "Introduction," *The Westminster Assembly's Grand Debate*, ed. Chris Coldwell (Dallas: Naphtali Press, 2014): xvi-xxi.

SLC made it clear that its signatories would seek their religious reforms while making every effort to "preserve and defend the King's Majesty, person and authority."[11] Watson was a true believer in the SLC and its objectives. His political actions in the following years can be understood as attempts to act consistently with his undertakings in this covenant.

"My Much Honoured Lady:"[*] Chaplaincy to Mary Vere (1642-46)

During the same period following his graduation, Watson became chaplain to the Puritan patroness Lady Mary Vere, Baroness of Tilbury.[12] The two shared similar theological convictions. Vere was known to be strongly Calvinistic in theology and associated with the Continental Reformed churches—having spent time in the Netherlands where her late husband's career as a military campaigner and governor had been concentrated.[13] She was a well-connected noblewoman, with her daughter Anne marrying Sir Thomas Fairfax (commander-in-chief of Parliamentary forces in the English Civil War) and was held in high esteem by Parliament.[14] Watson enjoyed a lifelong friendship with Vere and her family. This is attested by her leaving him £30 in her will.[15] Watson also dedicated *The Beatitudes* to the Earl and Countess of Clare, Vere's son-in-law and daughter, in 1660 and Holy Eucharist to Dorothy Wolstenholme, another of her daughters, in 1668.[16]

Lady Vere appears to have spent most of this period at a residence in Clapton, Hackney—about four miles out of the centre

11. *Solemn League and Covenant* (1643) Art. III https://en.wikisource.org/wiki/Solemn_League_and_Covenant Accessed 21/02/18.

* Title taken from Watson's dedicatory epistle to Lady Vere in the 1654 edition of *The Christian's Charter*.

12. Schwanda, "Sweetnesse," 34-63.

13. Till, "Watson," 1; Jacqueline Eales, "Vere, Mary," *ODNB* (Oxford: Oxford University Press, 2008): 1. https://doi.org/10.1093/ref:odnb/40534 Accessed 6/10/15; Barker, "A Body of Divinity," 200.

14. During the period Watson was living in her household, Vere "was briefly entrusted by parliament with the care of two of [Charles I's] children," (namely Princess Elizabeth and Henry, later Duke of Gloucester), while the war raged on in England. Eales "Vere," 4.

15. For Lady Vere's will and testament, see National Archives, PROB 11/338/214 (1672). http://www.oxford-shakespeare.com/Probate/PROB_11-338_ff_167-8.pdf Accessed 20/04/2018..

16. See also *Beatitudes* (1660) and *Holy Eucharist* (1668) (Oxford: TCP, 2004).

of London. However, her family's estates centred around Hedingham Castle in Essex where she died in 1670.[17] It is plausible that Watson's first pastorate came about through Lady Vere's connection with Sir Robert Harley (1579-1656), a prominent Puritan parliamentarian.[18] Harley was High Steward of Hereford and Deputy Lieutenant of Herefordshire, where Watson ministered briefly.[19] He was known for appointing Puritan ministers to local pulpits where he held influence.[20] Also plausible is that Watson met his wife Abigail (daughter of Puritan minister John Beadle, from Barnston, Essex) during his period in Vere's service, due to her family's connection with the area.[21] The pair married in 1647, around the same time he was beginning a new chapter of ministry in London.

"The Godly Preacher:" Forty Years of Pastoral Ministry (1646-1686)*

*"My dearly beloved:"** St. Stephen's Church, Walbrook*

Watson began pastoring St. Stephen's Church in 1646-1647, as the first Civil War ended. St. Stephen's was a parish church within the City of London, only a few miles away from the Vere residence in Hackney. It has been described as being "among the most important and influential parochial communities in Puritan London" and notable for the wealth and power of its membership.[22] Watson now had a pulpit ministry at the heart of English society. The rectorship of St. Stephen's had been something of a politicised office in the years prior to Watson's appointment to it. This was not surprising, due

17. Thomas Seccombe, "Vere, Horace," *ODNB* (1904): 238. https://en.wikisource.org/wiki/Vere,_Horace_(DNB00) Accessed 22/03/17.
18. Vere had played a key part in advocating for a marriage between Harley and her niece Brilliana Conway (1598-1643). J. Eales, "Anne and Thomas Fairfax, and the Vere Connection," in *England's Fortress: New Perspectives on Thomas, 3rd Lord Fairfax*, eds. Andrew Hopper and Philip Major, (London: Routledge, 2014): 159.
19. A. G. Matthews, *Calamy Revised* (London: Clarendon, 1988): 513.
20. John P. Ferris, "Harley, Sir Robert (1579-1656)" in *The History of Parliament: the House of Commons 1604-1629*, eds. Andrew Thrush and John P. Ferris (Cambridge: Cambridge University Press, 2010): 16. http://www.historyofparliamentonline.org/volume/1604-1629/member/harley-sir-robert-1579-1656 Accessed 06/12/17.
21. Haukenfrer, "Bellows of Affection," 42.

* Title taken from publisher's introduction to Watson's *Seven Sermons*, vii.

** Title taken from *APL*, 1.

22. Tai Liu, *Puritan London: A Study of Religion and Society in the City Parishes* (Newark: University of Delaware Press, 1986): 24, 61.

to the combination of the Church of England's established nature, the central location of the parish and the presence of local vested interests. The prominent London livery company, the Worshipful Company of Grocers had long exercised its influence whenever the senior clerical office in this church needed to be filled.[23] Watson's immediate predecessor Humphrey Chambers (later a Westminster divine) had been chosen as rector with popular backing from parishioners in 1644.[24] This followed the disaffection and division which had characterised the consecutive tenures of the three rectors who preceded him.[25] Watson was selected by the Grocers, rather than the congregation, but appears to have gained a broad support base that he maintained throughout his time at St. Stephen's.[26]

Watson was clearly a committed Presbyterian by the time he became rector. He was chosen as a replacement delegate to attend the Third Classis of the London Presbytery as a minister, as early as January 1647.[27] He would be involved in the Presbyterian governance of the churches under this classis until the Restoration in 1660.[28] Watson was not a member of the Westminster Assembly, probably by virtue of his youth and inexperience.[29] He did, however, subscribe

23. For a detailed account of the Grocers' involvement in determining the senior minister at St. Stephen's, Walbrook, see Joseph P. Ward, *Metropolitan Communities: Trade Guilds, Identity and Change in Early Modern London* (Stanford: Stanford University Press, 1997): 101-110.
24. J. P. Ward, *Metropolitan Communities*, 107-109.
25. J. P. Ward, *Metropolitan Communities*, 107-109; John Benjamin Heath, *Some account of the Worshipful Company of Grocers of the City of London* (London: W. Marchant, 1829): 99-101. Heath notes that earlier (i.e. 1635), even King Charles himself had written to the Company of Grocers to exercise his own wishes as to who would become the next rector of St. Stephen's.
26. It has been suggested that Watson became a lecturer (a junior position within the parish, which involved delivering regular sermons) at the church in 1646 and assumed the rectorship in 1655 or 1656. Beeke and Pederson, *Meet the Puritans*, 605. This is doubtful because it is predicated upon Watson succeeding Ralph Robinson as rector, when there is little evidence that Robinson ever held that office at St. Stephen's (he was however the minister of St. Mary Woolnoth, the neighbouring parish to St. Stephen's, Walbrook from 1643-55 and another leading London Presbyterian, see E. C. Vernon, "Robinson, Ralph," *ODNB* https://doi.org/10.1093/ref:odnb/23864 Accessed 06/10/15). Watson's appointment at St. Stephen's can, in fact, be tied to a clear historical event, i.e. the vacancy left by Humphrey Chambers in 1647. See J. P. Ward, *Metropolitan Communities*, 109.
27. Harry B. Wilson, *A History of the Parish of St. Laurence Pountney, London* (London: Rivington, 1831): 92.
28. Wilson, *History of St. Laurence*, 93.
29. Cf. Beeke and Jones, *Puritan Theology*, 59. The erroneous description of Watson as a "Westminster divine" has been questioned by at least one review of this work. See Kevin Bidwell, "A Puritan Theology (Review)" *Evangelical Times* (July 2013) https://www.evangelical-times.org/book/13010/a-puritan-theology/ Accessed 13/03/18.

his name to the *Westminster Confession's* "Epistle to the Christian Reader," as an endorsing minister in an edition dated 1658.[30]

Inter malleum et incudem:[*] *Watson's activities during the Civil Wars (1648-1651)*

In Watson's first year of ministry at St. Stephen's, one of the church's elders, John Warner, served as Lord Mayor of London in 1647.[31] This further demonstrates the significance of this congregation in the political life of England's capital. It is not surprising then that Watson would soon find himself embroiled in England's political turmoil as the second and third chapters of the English Civil War continued to affect the stability of the nation. The English Civil Wars are popularly conceived of as a mortal struggle between Puritan Roundheads and establishmentarian Cavaliers. Such a dichotomy fails to grasp the complex place of most Presbyterians in the struggle. They had led the parliamentary challenge against the king and his forces in the First Civil War. Yet most Presbyterians desired the reform of religion without the overthrow of the king. In January 1649, following the Second Civil War, Watson joined many of his coreligionists in signing *A Serious and Faithful Representation of the Judgment of the Ministers of the Gospel within the Province of London.* This document addressed the leaders of the military on the matter of preserving the life of the king and the functions and powers of parliament.[32] However, the Independents, with their strength concentrated in the New Model Army, took an uncompromising position concerning how to deal with the king. They consolidated their power by side-lining the Presbyterians and anyone who might attempt to negotiate with the deposed monarch.[33] At the close of 1648, "Pride's Purge" occurred—effectively a *coup d'état* by Independent parliamentarians and the military to wrest control of the House from Presbyterians, which led to the establishment of the

30. See "To the Christian Reader," in *The confession of faith together with the larger and lesser catechismes* (London: J. Rothwel, 1858).

* Title taken from *Anatomy*, 52. Trans. "Between a hammer and an anvil."

31. Wilson, *History of St. Laurence*, 93.

32. D. Neal, *History of the Puritans or Protestant Non-Conformists* (New York: Harper & Bros. 1843): 92.

33. David Plant, "Pride's Purge, 1648," *British Civil Wars Project* (2008) http://bcw-project.org/church-and-state/second-civil-war/prides-purge Accessed 20/04/18; Plant, "Army Remonstrance," BCWP (2008) http://bcw-project.org/church-and-state/second-civil-war/army-remonstrance Accessed 20/04/18.

'Rump Parliament."[34]

Three weeks after Pride's Purge, on 27 December, Watson appeared before Parliament to preach at an end-of-year, day of fasting.[35] He preached the message that was to become his earliest published work, *God's Anatomy upon Man's Heart.*[36] Watson's address demonstrates a mixture of typical pastoral concern for the souls of his hearers and a personal concern about the state of the nation. This appears in his introductory remarks, "And certainly, that may be one reason why there is so much State-affliction, because there is so little Soul-affliction. Our condition is low, but our hearts are high."[37] As several scholars have noted, Watson preached a bold, even defiant, sermon that dealt with characteristic Puritan themes like sincerity of heart and the danger of hypocrisy.[38] But the application targeted the behaviour of specific parliamentarians, with Trevor-Roper suggesting, "there could be no doubt [to the hearers] of whom he was thinking."[39] Watson's specific targeting of covenant-breaking went to the core of his political contentions with the dominant Independents.[40] At this crucial moment in English history, for the hour or so that he spoke to this chamber filled with Independent-aligned politicians, Thomas Watson was momentarily

34. Bennett, *Historical Dictionary*, 238.
35. Hugh Trevor-Roper suggests that Watson's nominating MP, John Rolle had likely been forced out of Parliament by Pride's Purge, but that the nomination was honoured rather than being revoked. Trevor-Roper, *The Crisis of the Seventeenth Century: Religion, the Reformation and Social Change* (Indianapolis: Liberty Fund, 1999): 308; However, it appears that Rolle died the month before Watson's sermon, suggesting that perhaps Watson's participation in the fast was a courtesy to the deceased. William A. Shaw, "Rolle, John," *DNB* 1885-1900 Vol. 49 (London: Smith, Elder & Co., 1897): https://en.wikisource.org/wiki/Rolle,_John_(1598-1648)_(DNB00) Accessed 02/05/18.
36. Trevor-Roper, *Crisis*, 309.
37. Anatomy, 2.
38. Trevor-Roper, *Crisis*, 308; Wilson, *Pulpit in Parliament*, 155.
39. Trevor-Roper, *Crisis*, 308.
40. "[L]et us look upon our solemne League and Covenant, I tremble when I read it; we covenanted not only against Prelacy, but Popery; not only Hierarchy, but Heresie; not only Sinne, but Schisme; and have we not gone against the letter of it? how is the Covenant slighted, as an *Almanack out of date*? Those that did once lift up their hand to it, do now lift up their heele against it ... Covenant violation is an high affronting sinne, and an affront will make God draw his sword; to set our hand and seale to the Covenant, and then to teare off the Seal, if the Covenant will not hold us, God hath Chaines that will." *Anatomy*, 26-27. Both sides in the disputation between Presbyterians and Independents saw the other as guilty of neglecting or even nullifying the covenant. See Edward Vallance, *Revolutionary England and the National Covenant: State Oaths, Protestantism and the Political Nation 1553-1682* (Suffolk: Boydell Press, 2005): 159-160.

the chief representative of English Presbyterianism as he aired their grievances with the *junta.*

Charles I was executed several weeks later on charges of treason, despite Watson and other Presbyterians protesting to Cromwell that this action was too extreme. Watson again joined a number of London Presbyterian ministers in expressing alarm over the regicide and seeking to distance themselves from any allegations of complicity. He signed his name to *A Vindication of the Ministers of the Gospel in and about London, from the unjust aspersions cast upon their former actings for the Parliament, as if they had promoted the bringing of the King to capital punishment.* This was published shortly after the king's death in January 1649.[41] *God's Anatomy* was published at the same time.[42]

Watson's commitment to the SLC did not end with the death of the king and the ascendancy of the Independents. His monarchist (as opposed to “Royalist”)[43] and Presbyterian convictions led him to take serious and risky action. He joined with some fellow, influential Presbyterians in what would become known as Love's Plot, a concerted effort to re-establish the Stuart monarchy under Charles' son (who became Charles II). The fact that Watson and his co-conspirators had been communicating with exiled members of the royal family and their Scottish allies, was discovered by the authorities in May 1651. Many of them were arrested and jailed in the Tower of London. Christopher Love was singled out as the “ringleader” of the plot and executed in August to send an unmistakeable message to would-be collaborators with the heir to the throne.[50] Watson's “humble petition” to Parliament was considered on 15th October, along with similar pleas from his fellow plotters. All were pardoned of treason and released shortly afterwards, after five months imprisonment.[45]

41. See Cornelius Burges, *A Vindication of the Ministers of the Gospel in and about London* (London: AM, 1648): https://catalog.hathitrust.org/Record/102258099 Accessed 25/06/18. Dewey D. Wallace Jr. “Thomas Watson” in *Puritans and Puritanism in Europe and America*, eds. Francis J. Bremer and Tom Webster (Santa Barbara: ABC Clio, 2006): 266.
42. Trevor-Roper, *Crisis*, 309.
43. I propose that while royalist describes those who supported the King politically and the established church religiously, another term is needed to represent Watson and the other Presbyterians, who supported Charles I and II as monarch, while expressing Puritan concerns about their religious policies. Monarchist has been adopted for this purpose.
44. Haukenfrer, “Bellows of Affection,” 31; David Underdown, *Royalist Conspiracy* (New Haven: Yale, 1960): 49.
45. “15 October 1651,” in *Journal of the House of Commons*: Volume 7, 1651-1660

*"Great fame and popularity as preacher"** *Ministry during the Interregnum* (1652-1660)

After regaining his liberty, Watson resumed his pastoral duties at St. Stephen's for the next decade. Historian, Tai Liu, suggests he enjoyed "the undiminished support of his parishioners" throughout the period.[46] The substantial £30 increase in his stipend in 1658 from £120 to £150 is cited as evidence.[47] In truth, Watson had been offered several other pastoral posts that would have had higher pay attached to them during this period, but was reluctant to leave St. Stephen's, as he felt that God had made his ministry there fruitful over the years.[48] According to vestry records, the increase of his "maintenance" was in response to the many hardships Watson had faced and recognised his sacrificial decision to remain in the parish.[49] Spurgeon similarly suggests Watson was popular with his parishioners and that his ministry was blessed: "The church was constantly filled, for the fame and popularity of the preacher were deservedly great. Going in and out among his flock, fired with holy zeal for their eternal welfare, his years rolled on pleasantly enough amid the growing respect of all who knew him."[50] But Spurgeon's summary overlooks the sombre detail of the deaths of four of Watson's children between his reinstatement and ejection from ministry at St. Stephen's.[51] During this period, Watson produced an important work on affectional piety and its relationship to devotional disciplines. *The Saint's Spiritual Delight* (1657) and its adjoined treatises, represent his most detailed presentation of the role of meditation in cultivating godliness. The lack of persecution (relative to other periods of his ministry) and need for solace in the face of familial deaths were factors which may have made this season conducive to a focus on the contemplative dimension of his piety.[52]

(London: His Majesty's Stationery Office, 1802), 27-29. *British History Online*, http://www.british-history.ac.uk/commons-jrnl/vol7/pp27-29. Accessed February 16, 2018.

* Title taken from E. I. Carlyle, "Watson, Thomas," *DNB* 1885-1900 Vol. 60 (London: Smith, Elder & Co., 1899): https://en.wikisource.org/wiki/Watson,_Thomas_(d.1686)_(DNB00) Accessed 02/05/18.

46. Liu, *Puritan London*, 61.
47. Liu, *Puritan London*, 61.
48. White, *History of Walbrook*, 371.
49. White, *History of Walbrook*, 371.
50. Spurgeon, "Watson," viii.
51. Haukenfrer, "Bellows of Affection," 43-44.
52. For a discussion of how opportunities for meditation and reflection amongst English Puritans were impacted by later developments see Brown, *Spirituality in Adversity*, 204-205.

Watson's significance as a preacher during this period is further demonstrated by his addresses to the Lord Mayor and Aldermen of the City of London on three separate occasions from 1656-8.[53] *The One Thing Necessary* (1656) provides an early example of Watson's emphasis on fear and love as indispensable, affectional elements of piety.[54] *The Upright Man's Character and Crown* (1657) presents godliness in sharp contrast to opportunistic hypocrisy—in a manner reminiscent of *God's Anatomy.*[55] Watson also took this opportunity to counsel the civic leaders about the peace they could enjoy in their conscience and in the face of death, if they possessed godliness.[56] Another significant theme introduced in this sermon and further emphasised in the subsequent *A Plea for Almes* (1658) was the relationship between godliness and generosity or mercy.[57] In 1659 he delivered a sermon on the subject of Judgement Day, as part of the morning exercises at St. Giles in the Fields (a Presbyterian sermon series designed to present a comprehensive account of Reformed orthodox doctrine in the face of the perceived danger posed by Socinianism and other heterodox movements).[58] Watson used this platform to remind the saints of the great separation at the end of history between the godly and the wicked and condemned several groups he saw as deniers of the doctrine of divine judgement.[59]

Watson's stature also led to active involvement in Presbyterian ecclesiastical activities throughout this period.[60] One of the Long Parliament's final actions, before its dissolution in 1660, was the appointment of Watson and 30 other prominent Presbyterians as commissioners for the approbation of ministers throughout England and Wales.[61] Watson was esteemed enough by his fellow

53. Haukenfrer, "Bellows of Affection," 20.
54. See Watson, *The One Thing Necessary* (1656) (Oxford: TCP, 2005). http://purl.ox.ac.uk/ota/A65304.
55. *UMC*, 14-15.
56. *UMC*, 49-50
57. *APA*, 3. This theme also appears prominently in Watson's *Beatitudes*.
58. Paul Lim, *Mystery Unveiled: The Crisis of the Trinity in Early Modern England* (Oxford: Oxford University Press, 2012): 13.
59. He names "Epicures and Atheists," "Lucianists and Platonists" and "Photinians." Watson, "The Day of Judgement Asserted" in *The Morning Exercise Methodized* ed. Thomas Case (London: R. W., 1676): 448-450.
60. See also Haukenfrer, "Bellows of Affection," 19-20. Watson was "an assessor of London Provincial Assembly 2 Feb. 1651-2: scribe of 3rd Classis 1652." *CR*, 513.
61. "March, 1659/60: An Act for Approbation and Admission of Ministers of the Gospel to Benefices and Publick Lectures," *Acts and Ordinances of the Interregnum, 1642-1660* (London: Royal Stationary Office, 1911): 1459-1462. *British History Online* http://www.british-history.ac.uk/no-series/acts-ordinances-interregnum/pp1459-1462

Presbyterians that they would entrust him with the duty of screening new candidates for ministry. In practical terms, his appointment meant nothing—as the return of episcopacy in the Restoration prevented him from exercising this office. But it does demonstrate the influence he might have exerted had the Presbyterians managed to remain ascendant under Charles II.

"The Bond of the Covenant:" The Restoration and the Great Ejection (1660-1662)*

The Restoration of the Stuart Monarchy occurred on 29 May 1660. Watson's first work in this new period was published barely a month after the king's return. *The Beatitudes* (1660), is both Watson's largest sustained exposition of a biblical passage and his major work on practical religion in the New Testament.[62] It introduced Watson's readers to many of the most substantial aspects of his affectional piety. The way of godliness is presented as the means to eternal felicity, along with present enjoyment of God.[63] The character and fate of the godly is sharply contrasted with that of the wicked, with Watson offering comfort to the sincere Christian at the hour of death and beyond.[64] The importance of positive duties for cultivating godliness is further emphasised. The idea of negative means for growth, such as "godly sorrow," repentance, self-denial and persecution, is also introduced and features prominently across the work.[65] As I will demonstrate below, this work reveals Watson's dire assessment of England's spiritual state at the time.

Perhaps he already had a sense of what was to come. Despite his consistent in-principle support of the Stuart monarchy, its Restoration was not a positive development for Watson and many of his Presbyterian peers. As H. G. Alexander puts it, 'Some [Presbyterians] were still foolish enough to think that Charles might agree to the imposition of a Presbyterian system since he had himself taken the Covenant when he went to Scotland in 1650.'[66]

Accessed 25/06/18.

* Title taken from *BPD*, 1:93.

62. *Beatitudes* is approximately three times the size of later expositions of Matthew 11:12 (*Heaven Taken by Storm*) and Malachi 3:16-18 (*Religion our True Interest*).

63 *Beatitudes*, 30, 33.

64. *Beatitudes*, 37-38.

65. E.g. *Beatitudes*, 84, 394-457. We will discuss these themes and others in Chapter 5.

66. Alexander, *Religion in England*, 219.

But as he goes on to explain, the political landscape of Restoration England meant that Presbyterians would scarcely achieve any of their aims through negotiations with the new king.[67] Attempts to use parliamentary procedures to reinstate the SLC as a binding force on the nation failed.[68] By May 1661, parliament was in fact ordering that the SLC be publicly incinerated.[69] Spurr blames the Presbyterians' "disunited and inept showing at the [second Savoy] conference" in 1661 for their ultimate failure to achieve what they had hoped for.[70] He goes on to note that the outcome of that conference, in terms of religious settlement, was far more problematic for nonconformists than the impositions of Laud in the period before the civil wars.[71]

Those who supported the Covenant and could not conform to renewed uniformity being established in the national church would soon face a difficult ultimatum. The Corporation Act (1661) began the process of enforcing conformity throughout the country, by establishing mandatory religious requirements for certain positions within society.[72] In May 1662, Parliament passed a new Act of Uniformity. It required strict adherence to the revised Prayer Book from all ministers by 24 August or removal from their positions within the church.[73] Renunciation of the SLC was another requirement of the Act, which someone like Watson could never bring himself to do.[74] As many as two thousand dissenting ministers were expelled from the ministry of Church of England that year in the Great Ejection. Gary S. De Krey notes that "[t]he diocese of London was the most heavily purged in the country."[75] Watson was one of sixty-four London ministers to suffer this fate.

The loss of his living and consignment to outlaw status would have caused Watson considerable hardship. But during the trying period of 1661-1663, Watson's writings convey his earnest concern for God's people.[76] *Jerusalem's Glory* (1661) reveals a deep concern

67. Alexander, *Religion in England*, 219.
68. Vallance, *Revolutionary England*, 181.
69. Vallance, *Revolutionary England*, 181.
70. Spurr, *English Puritanism*, 129.
71. Spurr, *English Puritanism*, 129.
72. William Gibson, *Religion and the Enlightenment 1600-1800: Conflict and the Rise of Civic Humanism in Taunton* (Oxford: Peter Lang, 2007): 118.
73. Calvin Lane, *The Laudians and the Elizabethan Church: History, Conformity and Religious Identity in Post-Reformation England* (London: Routledge, 2013): 138.
74. See Spurr, *English Puritanism*, 130; Spurr, "From Puritanism to Dissent," 237; Lane, *The Laudians*, 138.
75. Gary S. De Krey, *London and the Restoration, 1659–1683* (Cambridge: Cambridge University Press, 2005): 87.
76. McDermott, "Introduction," *Jerusalem's Glory*, 19-20.

for the state of the church in England and how sincere Christians should respond to the situation. *Paramythion* (1662) along with the final sermons he preached at Walbrook before being ejected, demonstrate his pastoral love and determination to bring comfort to the faithful in the wake of persecution.[77] *A Divine Cordial* (1663) provides a timely exposition of Romans 8:28 for those Christians trying to make sense of their lives in the midst of the political and religious disturbances of the previous years.[78]

The Godly Duckling: Watson's Outlaw Ministry (1662-72)

The next decade saw Watson continue his ministry, as a covert Presbyterian preacher, holding meetings for nonconformist believers "in barns, homes, and woods."[79] He faced harassment over his religious activities numerous times throughout the remainder of his life. The civil authorities were alerted to his unauthorised preaching at least twice in 1664-5 and Watson was jailed briefly in 1670 due to the perceived incendiary nature of one of his sermons.[80] Records also show that several of Watson's meeting houses were brought to the attention of authorities and confiscated or vandalised during the early 1670s.[81] Watson came to be identified with a group of Presbyterians informally referred to as Ducklings. The moniker came about because prior to the 1672 Indulgence these ministers decided that it was preferable to exercise their ministry outside the established church.[82] They were thus prepared to "take the plunge in

77. Compare Haukenfrer, "Bellows of Affection," 40-41. In 1663, the recently appointed government censor, Roger L'Estrange suggested that passages from *Paramythion* were seditious statements intended to support the regicides John Barkstead and Miles Corbet, who were executed around the time of its publication. This is a highly dubious claim, given Watson's consistent opposition to Charles I's execution—even if his disenchantment with the restored monarchy is taken into account. L'Estrange, *Considerations and Proposals In Order to the Regulation of the Press* (1663), 16. http://purl.ox.ac.uk/ota/A47832; Haukenfrer, "Bellows of Affection," 36.
78. McDermott, "Introduction," *Jerusalem's Glory*, 16, 19-20; Lee, "Thomas Watson," 5, 17.
79. Beeke and Pederson, *Puritans*, 606.
80. *CR*, 513; Wallace, "Watson," 266. "Jittery London magistrates briefly imprisoned Thomas Watson and Thomas Vincent on charges of treason for preaching on Hebrews 12:4 'Ye have not yet resisted unto blood, striving against sin.'" Richard L. Greaves, *Enemies under His Feet: Radicals and Non-conformists in Britain 1664-1677* (Stanford: Stanford University Press, 1990): 156.
81. Greaves, *Enemies*, 160, 203; W. T. Whitely, "The Great Raid of 1670 on certain London churches under the new Conventicle Act," *Baptist Quarterly* 9:4 (1938): 249.
82. Spurr, *English Puritanism*, 138.

breaking the law and setting up conventicles."[83] Joseph Williamson, who coined the term, numbered Watson among half a dozen "leaders of the vulgars and men of great interest," suggesting he viewed him as a major figure within the Duckling faction.[84] Ducklings were distinguished from the Dons. These were ministers who opted to abide by the Five Mile Act's demand for "Nonconformist ministers to take an oath not to seek changes in the church or state or not to live within five miles of any place where they had formerly ministered."[85] It has been suggested that Watson subsequently took the oath in 1666, in order to live in London after the Act came into effect.[86] But there is reason to question whether this actually happened.[87]

London residents faced two great calamities in the 1660s—the Great Plague of 1665 and the Great Fire of London in 1666. The Plague claimed upwards of 70,000 lives.[88] The Fire "consumed two thirds of the parish churches"[89] and "13,200 houses."[90] Watson interpreted both events as God's "afflictive providences" designed to produce contrition amongst the English. He said of the fire, "God hath set our houses on fire, that we may run to him by Repentance."[91]

---

83. C. G. Bolam and Jeremy Goring, "The Cataclysm" in *The English Presbyterians: From Elizabethan Puritanism to modern Unitarianism*, eds. C. G. Bolam and Jeremy Goring (London: Allen & Unwin, 1968): 87.
84. CSPD, Vol. 12 (1671-1672): 28. See also F. H. Blackburne Daniell's prefatory remarks to this volume, xviii; Greaves, *Enemies*, 218; De Krey, *London and the Restoration*, 120.
85. Richard Greaves, "Presbyterians, Religious," in *HDSE*, 420.
86. Whitely, "The Great Raid," 259; Wallace, "Watson," 266.
87. The claim appears to have first been made in CR. But it is probably based on a misunderstanding of Richard Baxter's comment, "Mr. Calamy, Watson, Gouge, and many others, had taken the Oath this Week, but for this unhappy Accident." *Reliquiæ Baxterianæ or, Mr. Richard Baxters narrative of the most memorable passages of his life and times* (1696) (Oxford: TCP, 2003): 3:14. http://purl.ox.ac.uk/ota/A27006. The context suggests that in February 1665 Watson and others had been inclined to take the oath, but changed their minds when it became apparent that such an undertaking could be interpreted as a violation of the *Solemn League and Covenant.* This interpretation of Baxter is supported by the fact that Gouge appears to have never taken the oath. See Alexander Gordon, "Gouge, Thomas," *Dictionary of National Biography* (1885-1900) Vol. 22. https://en.wikisource.org/wiki/Gouge,_Thomas_(1609-1681)_(DNB00) Accessed 25/06/18. It is further suggested by Watson's classification as a Duckling in the 1670s and his being fined in 1681 under the Five Mile Act (which would have been inapplicable had he taken the oath).
88. Stephen Porter, *The Great Plague* (Stroud: Amberly, 2009): 57; The death toll was high as 110 000, representing "one quarter or more of the permanent resident population." Mark Heumann, "London, Plague of," in *HDSE*, 309.
89. De Krey, *London and the Restoration*, 90.
90. Mark Heumann, "London, Great Fire of," *HDSE*, 308.
91 *Repentance*, 165-166.

He even went as far as to suggest that the fact the great fire began on a Sunday ought to be interpreted as a divine punishment on England for "Sabbath profanation."[92] Yet given Watson's exposition of Romans 8:28 a few years earlier, his perspective on divine providence would have identified God's blessing upon the godly in these dark times. Ejected Puritan ministers found opportunities to preach in churches abandoned by their ministers during the plague, while the devastation of the fire facilitated a burgeoning of nonconformist meeting spaces to replace burned down churches.[93]

Watson wrote his most significant work on godliness as deaths from the bubonic plague were subsiding. *Godly Man's Picture* was published a few weeks after Charles II returned to London—six months before the city would be scarred by the Fire. The extent to which the recent epidemic impacted the composition of this work is uncertain. Watson does employ disease-imagery to illustrate certain points in *Godly Man's Picture*, including several references to "the plague".[94] One suspects that the high death toll would have increased interest amongst the reading public in a work purporting to describe "a Man that shall go to Heaven." Likewise, the new opportunities for nonconformist ministry in London may have generated greater potential readership for a book advancing the Puritan ideal of godliness than what would have existed a year earlier. There is little historical record of Watson's activities in London in the years immediately following the fire. He does not appear to have suffered from persecution or harassment during these years and produced several publications, including *The Doctrine of Repentance* (1668), *The Holy Eucharist* (1668) and *Heaven Taken by Storm* (1669). In 1669, he participated in a preaching conference at Hackney alongside other leading nonconformists such as John Owen and Thomas Brooks.[95]

A survey of Watson's powerful friends and foes during this period further establishes his significance in the religious and political life of the nation—particularly that of the capital. The

92. *BPD*, 2:348.
93. Porter, Great Plague, 121; Spurgeon, "Watson," x; Beeke and Pederson, *Puritans*, 606. See also Haukenfrer, "Bellows of Affection," 40-41.
94. E.g. *GMP*, 122, 193, 204-205, 284.
95. Dewey Wallace, "Pinner's Hall," in *Puritans and Puritanism in Europe and North America*, eds. Francis Bremer and Tom Webster (Santa Barbara: ABC Clio, 2006): 478. Francis J. Bremer, *Congregational Communion: Clerical Friendship in the Anglo-American Puritan Community 1610-1692* (Boston: Northeastern University Press, 1994): 213.

Puritan noblewoman Mary Rich, Countess of Warwick, was an admirer and possible patroness.[96] A connection with the influential Whig politician (and later Duke of Devonshire), William Cavendish (1640-1707), also seems likely, as Watson succeeded in renting a congregational meeting space from his family in 1669.[97] Watson's imprisonment in the Tower of London and bare escape from execution in 1651, may have made him more cautious in subsequent years. However, he remained active in some of the political developments in Restoration London. His connection to the Puritan-friendly Lord Mayor of the City of London, Sir William Turner, is revealed by the dedication of his *Heaven Taken by Storm.* De Krey relates how many of London's influential dissenters threw their weight behind Turner in the hopes of seeing his term as civic head extended beyond the normal one year term.[98] They were confident that Turner would have ensured that the religious and political environment of the city remained more favourable to nonconformists.[99] When this failed to come to fruition, resistance to the Conventicle Act continued. Attempts by the enforcers of religious conformity to shut down meetings or apprehend nonconformist ministers were met by open, mass defiance.[100] Watson found himself at the centre of this struggle, when the new Lord Mayor Samuel Starling sent the constabulary to arrest him while preaching in 1670. Starling acted upon reports that Watson would incite the congregation to violent resistance in his sermon.[101] Watson's auditors physically blocked the City officials from approaching him. A significant controversy arose between the Lord Mayor and Watson's allies, the local Whig politicians John

96. The Countess visited Watson in his wife's hometown of Barnston and attended his preaching on more than one occasion. *CR*, 513. Charlotte Fell Smith, her biographer, suggests that Watson was among the ministers Rich "patronised," though this may simply refer to her attendance of his sermons rather than implying financial support. *Mary Rich, Countess of Warwick* (London: Longmans, Green & Co., 1901): 213. An interesting connection however is the fact that Watson's father-in-law John Beadle was previously chaplain to the Countess's father-in-law Robert Rich, 2nd Earl of Warwick. See John Craig, "Beadle, John," *Puritans and Puritanism*, 22.
97. Whitely, "The Great Raid," 249; See also Greaves, *Enemies*, 203. This property was reportedly "seized for Anglican use [in] 1671." *CR*, 513.
98. De Krey, *London and the Restoration*, 108-9.
99. De Krey, *London and the Restoration*, 108-9.
100. De Krey, *London and the Restoration*, 112.
101. Apparently he had been preaching on the subject of "holy violence," which was the central idea in his work Heaven Taken by Storm, published the year before. See Justin Champion, "Heaven Taken by Storm: Christopher Hill, Andrew Marvell and the Dissenting Tradition," Christopher Hill Memorial Lecture (London, 2019). https://www.versobooks.com/blogs/4311-heaven-taken-by-storm-christopher-hill-andrew-marvell-and-the-dissenting-tradition Accessed 11/09/19.

Jekyll and James Hayes, over the incident.[102] After being arrested for their defence of Watson, Jekyll and Hayes took legal action against Starling, which ultimately came to naught when Parliament voted, several months later, to resolve the matter in favour of the Lord Mayor.[103] While this was not a short term victory for the nonconformist activists, De Krey has presented this as one of several, significant acts of resistance to establishmentarian assaults on their religious freedoms, which gradually weakened the efficacy of their persecutors' attempts at suppression.[104]

Watson's connection to these figures and events not only highlights his significance as a London Presbyterian minister. It suggests that he was part of the dissenting political movement that sought to establish lasting religious freedoms in the capital and mitigate some of the harsh, excessive restrictions enacted by the Restoration government.[105] There is further evidence for this in the fact that Watson contributed a substantial amount of money (£450) to what has come to be known as the 1670 Dissenting Subscription. This was an enormous loan made by prominent religious dissenters to Charles II (who had been seeking to borrow funds from the London corporations to little avail) as a gesture of goodwill.[106] They hoped their generosity would dispose Charles towards more favourable religious policies.[107] Watson and four fellow ministers obtained a private audience with the king, on 9 November 1671.[108] Charles assured them that he was personally against the suppression of their religious liberty and would seek to ameliorate

102. Jekyll was a significant parishioner at Watson's St. Stephen's congregation and a co-conspirator in the Love plot, who remained a staunch ally. See De Krey, *London and the Restoration*, 110; Elizabeth Clarke, "Elizabeth Jekyll" in *The Encyclopedia of English Renaissance Literature*., eds. Garrett Sullivan and Alan Stewart (Chichester: Wiley & Blackwell, 2012): 1:541. Clarke has called the ensuing dispute "one of the most controversial Nonconformist trials in the Restoration." Politics and Religion, 182. Henry Mares refers to it as the "cause celebre" of opponents to the Conventicles Act. "Criminal Informations of the Attorneys-General in the King's Bench from Egerton to North" in *Law and Legal Process: Substantive Law and Procedure in English Law History*, eds. Matthew Dyson and David Ibbetson (Cambridge: Cambridge University Press, 2013): 173.
103. De Krey, *London and the Restoration*, 112.
104. Gary S. De Krey, "The First Restoration Crisis: Conscience and Coercion in London, 1667-73," *Albion* 25:4 (1993): 577.
105. De Krey suggests Watson was among "an elite group of Reformed Protestants and sectarians who were actively committed to the achievement of liberty for conscience." *London and the Restoration*, 125.
106. De Krey, *London and the Restoration*, 125.
107. De Krey, *London and the Restoration*, 125-134.
108. Baxter, *Reliquiæ Baxterianæ*, 3:87.

the circumstances for dissenters.[109] The king made his short-lived Declaration of Indulgence a few months later.

During this period, several of Watson's opponents also targeted him over his published works. John Birkenhead lampooned his style and several of his sayings in *Cabala* (1663).[110] Significantly, Birkenhead named Watson as one of the principal Presbyterian figures that his stereotypical nonconformist minister "Lewis" sought to emulate.[111] Simon Patrick, Bishop of Ely, attacked Watson's *Doctrine of Repentance* in print in 1668, mocking his literary style as "childishness."[112] Patrick's targeting of Watson is notable, as Keeble has described this tract as part of "a concerted press campaign to kill any initiative toward alleviating the proscription of dissent."[113] These attacks reinforce the sense that Watson was a notorious, leading nonconformist in the eyes of Restoration London's religious establishment.

"Holy Antiperistasis:" Nonconformist Ministry in the later reign of Charles II (1672-86)*

In 1672, when the Declaration of Indulgence came into effect, Watson began to hold meetings in his home. He was soon given the use of Crosby Hall, a 15th century mansion at Bishopsgate, London, by its owners the Langham family.[114] Sir John Langham, an influential London nonconformist of Presbyterian convictions died in 1671 and passed the estate on to his son Stephen Langham, who allowed the property to be utilised for public worship.[115] According to Charles

109. Baxter, *Reliquiæ Baxterianæ*, 3:87; Matthew Henry, *The Life of Mr. Philip Henry* (London: J. S. Hughes, 1825): 128. Watson was among the London, nonconformist ministers being monitored by the State Department during this period, with five references to him by Joseph Williamson in the *State Papers* of November 1671. See *CSPD* (Jan-Nov 1671), 11:556, 560, 561, 568; Greaves, *Enemies*, 218.
110. Birkenhead, *Cabala, or, An impartial account of the non-conformists private designs, actings and ways* (1663) (Oxford: TCP, 2009): 6, 14, 23, 28, 35-36. http://purl.ox.ac.uk/ota/A28205
111. Birkenhead, *Cabala*, 36. Noted in Kinda Skea, "The Ecclesiastical Identities of Puritan and Nonconformist Clergy, 1640-1672" (PhD Thesis, Leicester: University of Leicester, 2015): 24-25.
112. See Simon Patrick, *A Friendly Debate between a Conformist and a Non-conformist* (London, 1668): 20-24. https://archive.org/details/frienbe00patr Accessed 21/06/18.
113. N. H. Keeble, *The Restoration: England in the 1660s* (Oxford: Blackwell, 2002): 124.
* Title taken from *RTI*, 6.
114. Spurgeon, "Watson," x; Till, "Watson," 2; *CR*, 513. His licence was granted on 18 April, 1672. *CSPD*, Vol. 12 (1671-1672): 341.
115. Charles W. F. Goss, *Crosby Hall: A Chapter in the History of London* (London:

Goss, "Watson succeeded in bringing together a very nourishing congregation" and was "admired by a large circle of friends."[116] The Declaration of Indulgence only remained in effect for twelve months. The meetings at Crosby Hall were once again illegal. It is difficult to gauge the extent to which Watson and the congregation suffered from legal harassment for the remainder of the decade. All of the histories suggest that the congregation at Crosby Hall remained stable thereafter. However, there are several records of Watson preaching in other London locations during this period while under the surveillance of the authorities.[117] Richard Baxter also wrote, around this time, that Watson was one of those ministers "who by Preaching more openly than the rest, and to greater Numbers, are under more Men's displeasure and censure."[118] Watson continued to be referred to in printed religious controversies in this period. In 1674, a London rector, William Sherlock, viciously criticised what he perceived as Watson's grotesque misinterpretation of Scriptural imagery in several of his sermons.[119] Watson's reputation was defended in several counterblasts to this work, in the months following.[120] Watson was also named in William Penn's *A Just Rebuke* (1674) in retaliation for his endorsement of Peter Faldo's *Quakerism no Christianity* (1674).[130]

Crowther & Goodman, 1908): 104.

116. Goss, *Crosby Hall*, 105-6.

117. E.g. "Chequer Yard, Dowgate Hill, in 1676" (and again in 1680). *CR*, 513; Walter Besant, *London in the Time of the Stuarts* (London: A&C Black, 1903): 156. There is also a record of Watson preaching at the headquarters of the Worshipful Company of Grocers 3 June 1678. *CSPD* Vol 20. (Mar-Dec, 1678): 203. This was unlikely to have been a regular meeting place, but rather an indicator that Watson continued to enjoy a close association with the company that held a powerful grip on his previous parish of St. Stephen's.

118. Baxter, *Reliquiæ Baxterianæ*, 3:95.

119. William Sherlock, *A Discourse Concerning the Knowledge of Jesus Christ* (1674) (Oxford: TCP, 2005). http://purl.ox.ac.uk/ota/A59816. Sherlock attacks the following of Watson's works. "Christ's Loveliness," 67, 70, 114; *Charter*. 68; "Spiritual Vine," 68; *Eucharist.*, 121. See E. Clarke, *Politics, Religion and the Song of Songs in Seventeenth Century England* (Basingstoke: Palgrave Macmillan, 2011): 178-183.

120. See Samuel Rolls, *Prodromus* (1674): 12-14. Google Books edition. https://books.google.com.au/books?id=cH5nAAAAcAAJ; Henry Hickman, *Speculum Sherlockianum* (London: Thomas Parkhurst, 1674): 22-25. Google Books edition. https://books.google.com.au/books?id=9NekFwfGjz4C; Robert Ferguson, *The Interest of Reason in Religion* (1675) (Oxford: TCP, 2005): xiii, xiv, 382-384. http://purl.ox.ac.uk/ota/A41173; Edward Polhill, *An Answer to the Discourse of William Sherlock* (London: Foster, 1675): 90-95, 128-133. Google Books edition. https://books.google.com.au/books?id=ETR9QYJcPtUC Accessed 21/06/18. Clarke, *Politics, Religion and the Song of Songs*, 184, 186, 231-232.

121. William Penn, *A Just Rebuke to One and Twenty Learned and Reverend Divines Being*

In 1675, Stephen Charnock became Watson's co-pastor at Crosby Hall. Charnock was a fine Late English Puritan theologian, renowned for his *Existence and Attributes of God.* Charnock died in 1680 and was replaced by Samuel Slater, who appears to have co-pastored with Watson and carried on as a minister at Crosby Hall for several years after the latter's death.[122] Unresolved issues surrounding the nation's religious policy led to Watson becoming one of many nonconformists to suffer intensified persecution during the early-mid 1680s.[123] In line with Baxter's remarks a few years earlier, Watson seems to have been specifically targeted due to his influence and the size of his meetings. Historical records indicate that his conventicle meeting at Chequers Yard in 1680 attracted around 300 attendees.[124] He was charged three times under the Conventicle Acts in 1681, 1683 and again in 1685 (the year before his death).[125]

Significantly, his only major work published during this period was his exposition of Malachi 3:16-18, *Religion Our True Interest* (1681). This was a second treatise on godliness following the earlier *Godly Man's Picture*, but with a more particular focus on the fear of God. As I will discuss further in Chapter 11, this treatise is significant for understanding Watson's piety in its historical context, as it represents his attempt to promote godliness in "the dregs of

---

an Answer to an Abusive Epistle Against the People Call'd Quakers (1674) (Oxford: TCP, 2007). http://purl.ox.ac.uk/ota/A54003

122. Goss, *Crosby Hall*, 106; Walter Wilson, *The History and Antiquities of Dissenting Churches and Meeting Houses* (London W. Button & Son, 1808): 331, 339.

123. Gary Brady describes the so-called "Tory revenge" which began in 1681, "the most severe persecution of the period" experienced by "Dissenters" at the hands of the establishment. *The Great Ejection* (Darlington: EP, 2012): 90-91. Sandra Hynes agrees, noting "the period between 1681 and 1686 was particularly harsh for Dissenters." "Mapping Friendship and Dissent" in *Varieties of Seventeenth and Early Eighteenth-Century English Radicalism in Context*, eds. Ariel Hessayon and David Finnegan (London: Routledge, 2016): 209.

124. Besant, *London in the Time of the Stuarts*, 156. Historical Manuscripts Commission, *The Manuscripts of the Duke of Leeds* (London: HMSO, 1888): 16.

125. Wallace, "Watson," 266; Richard Greaves, *Glimpses of Glory: John Bunyan and English Dissent* (Stanford: Stanford University Press, 2002): 529fn; Till, "Watson," 2. The 1681 charge was for "not repairing to church" (i.e. attending the state parish church) and violating the Five Mile Act. *CSPD* Vol. 22 (Sept 1680- Dec 1681), 592. Watson was liable for £440. James Ferguson has linked the charges against Watson and a group of notable nonconformists to the treason proceedings against the Earl of Shaftesbury, by virtue of his chaplain, Robert Ferguson, being among them. Ferguson, *Robert Ferguson, "The Plotter"* (Edinburgh: David Douglas, 1887): 58. If accurate, this would again place Watson's sufferings in the midst of the power struggle between England's Whig and Tory factions during this period.

time."[126] Watson published two smaller works that are pertinent to his emphasis on godliness, during his Crosby Hall ministry. *A Plea for the Godly* (1672) expounds Proverbs 12:26, "The Righteous is more excellent than his Neighbour." It is similar to *Godly Man's Picture*, in that it delineates the qualities of the godly. However, it is a much shorter piece than its predecessor and Watson uses the language of "righteousness" far more than godliness in his treatment of the subject.[136] *The Duty of Self-Denial* (1675) explores an aspect of devotion that was crucial to Watson's understanding of piety. I will discuss its significance further in Chapter 5. Watson's decreased output in this period cannot be readily explained. It is possible that he concentrated on pulpit ministry during the Crosby Hall years and that his posthumous *Body of Divinity* was the fruit of his catechetical labours during the 1670s.

"He being dead yet speaketh:" Death, Legacy and Summary*

*"The Day-break of Eternal Brightness:"** Watson's Death (1686)*

As Watson's health faded in 1686, he left London for Essex, his wife's home county, where he would die on 28 July.[128] While pious details surrounding the death of a religious figure should raise suspicions of hagiography, every account of Watson's death suggests that he died whilst in private prayer in his home, aged in his mid-late sixties.[129] He was buried in his father-in-law's grave at Barnston, Essex. His contemporary Henry Newcome reports, in his diary entry of December 3, 1692, "Mr. Watson, I have heard, died poor, when most thought he had been very rich, but he had some children that

126. *RTI*, 6.
127. E.g. *APG*, 1-4.
* Title taken from Scripture reference in *BPD*, 1:i.
** Title taken from *BPD*, 1:225.
128. *CR*, 513.
129. Watson's death in his prayer closet would be an appropriate finish to a life and ministry marked by prayerful devotion. It is consistent with the recurrent account in his biographies of his impressing Bishop John Richardson with his ability to pray extemporaneously and Mary Rich's account of her chaplain John Woodrooffe being healed by God after Watson prayed for him. Rich, *Memoir of Lady Warwick* (London: Religious Tract Society, 1847): 130-131.

exhausted him to nothing."[130]

Several funeral sermons delivered by Watson are extant, but the details of his own funeral are not. In *lieu* of formal eulogies, we have the tribute of his publisher shortly after his death: "his Name is so savoury among all those, that either heard him Preach, read his Writings, or were acquainted with his Exemplary Life and Conversation (he having with that great Apostle taken sufficient care, that while he Preached to others he might not be a cast away himself)."[142] In his endorsement of the original edition of *A Body of Divinity*, William Lorimer briefly commented that Watson was regarded as "a grave, serious, modest, good Man."[132] A later admirer noted "He was so well known in [London] for his piety and usefulness ... [and] carried a general respect from all sober persons along with him to his grave."[133]

"His works preserved his fame long after his death:"[*] Watson's Enduring Legacy

Watson's works have continued to be read in the subsequent centuries after his death, down to the present day.[134] While the majority of his influence has been felt in the Anglosphere, his works were also read by Calvinists and Lutherans throughout Europe. The century after his death saw multiple texts translated into languages as diverse as German, Dutch, Danish and Welsh.[135] More recently, select works

130. Henry Newcome, *Autobiography* (Manchester: Charles Simms, 1852): 276. Richard Baxter seems to have been aware of Watson's financial hardships several years earlier, as he arranged to have him sent £2 around the Christmas of 1683, as part of a "distribution to poore Ministers." N. H. Keeble and Geoffrey F. Nuttall, *Calendar of the Correspondence of Richard Baxter* Vol. II 1660-1696 (Oxford: Clarendon, 1991): 257-258. The probate of his will occurred on 24 August 1686 and his estate including "leasehold in London" and "Personalty c. £400." *CR*, 513.

131. "The Publisher to the Reader," Watson, *Seven Sermons* (1689). The publisher's identity is undisclosed, but Watson's usual distributor, Thomas Parkhurst (c.1632–1711), is the most likely candidate.

132. Lorimer, "To the Reader," *BPD*.I-III. (1692): i.

133. This quote can be traced back to Calamy's *Nonconformist Memorial*, though it is not certain whether it was present in Calamy's original (which would put it closer to Watson's death) or added by his successor Samuel Parker in a 1775 revision.

* Title taken from Carlyle, "Watson," *DNB* https://en.wikisource.org/wiki/Watson,_Thomas_(d.1686)_(DNB00)

134. For example, *Autarkeia* was circulating in its nineteenth edition in 1719, while *Body of Divinity* was in its seventh edition in 1782.

135. Schwanda, "Sweetnesse," 37-38; Gina Dahl, *Book Collections of Clerics in Norway, 1650-1750* (Leiden: Brill, 2010): 90, 171. According to Dahl, Watson was one of the

have been published in Spanish, Hungarian, Polish, Russian, Korean and Chinese.[136] His enduring influence amongst English speaking Christians can be illustrated via an example from each century subsequent to his lifetime. In 1719, his *The Christian Soldier or Heaven Taken by Storm* was "instrumental in the conversion of Col. James Gardiner."[137] Gardiner was a renowned officer in the 1745 war against the Jacobites and the subject of a popular biography by the minister Philip Doddridge.[138] Charles Spurgeon, the leading English Baptist of the 19th century, was well acquainted with Watson's writings. He quotes Watson close to a hundred times in his influential commentary on the Psalms, *The Treasury of David.* He offered the following endorsement:

> Watson was one of the most concise, racy, illustrative and suggestive of those eminent divines who made the Puritan age the Augustan period of evangelical literature. There is a happy union of sound doctrine, heart-searching experience and practical wisdom throughout all of his works.[139]

Spurgeon goes on to suggest that *Body of Divinity* was something of a standard text for the theological formation of many Christians in Britain. "For many a year, this volume continued to train the common people in theology, and it may still be found very commonly in the cottages of the Scottish peasantry."[140] The republishers of *Body of Divinity*, Banner of Truth Trust, noted in 1965 that it was the first ever text they released as a publishing house. In the 1986

most popular English Puritans amongst Norwegian clergy in the period covered in her book. 249. His works were also present in the library of Swedish bishop Haquin Spegel (Archbishop of Uppsala and Primate of Sweden 1711-1714). Nicholas Hope, *German and Scandinavian Protestantism 1700-1918* (Oxford: Clarendon, 1995): 126. The broadest collections appear to be in German [See Hans Schneider, *A Catalogue of British Devotional and Religious Books in German Translation, from the Reformation to 1700* (Berlin: de Gruyter, 1996): 413-417] and Dutch [Johannes Fabricius, *Al de Theologische en Practicale Werken van de Godvruchtige en zeer Geleerde Heer Thomas Watson* (Utrecht: Kemmer, 1665)]. For Welsh see, *Yr happusrwydd o nesau at Dduw; wedi ei egluro mewn pregeth, ar Salm lxxiii.28* (Cardiff, 1790).

136. Schwanda, "Sweetnesse," 37-38. Works translated into Spanish include: *BPD.I-III* (Tradato de Teologia; Los Diez Mandamientos; El Padre Nuestro); *The Lord's Supper* (La Cena del Señor); *The Saint's Spiritual Delight* (El Deleite Espiritual del Creyente) and *Christ's Loveliness* (La hermosura de Cristo). Various other translations of *BPD* include: 系统神学 (Chinese); Praktyczne wymiary pobożności (Polish); 신학의체계 (Korean); Основы практического богословия (Russian).
137. Schwanda, "Sweetnesse," 37.
138. Schwanda, "Sweetnesse," 37; Spurgeon, "Watson," xi.
139. Spurgeon, "Watson," vii.
140. Spurgeon, "Watson," xi.

reprint they continued to describe it as "one of [our] best sellers and consistently the most useful and influential of our publications."[141] The Trust's endorsement of Watson in their 1992 republication of *Godly Man's Picture* (which has continued to be reprinted into the 21st century) serves as a suitable addendum to the eulogies above.

> Few preachers in the Puritan era (or any other period of church history) match Thomas Watson for his ability to combine rich spirituality, nourishing doctrine and sane wisdom with fascinating illustration and a pleasant style ... Watson is always the essence of sanity and reliability.[142]

Summary

Like all previous biographies, this sketch of Watson's life remains incomplete—due to a lack of historical sources specifically relating to the events of his life. This difficulty is compounded by his own habit of relative silence regarding his personal life. However, it is clear that Watson was a well-regarded pastor and preacher in London and played a significant role in the Presbyterian and Puritan movements during the years of the Civil War, Interregnum and Restoration period. His personal sufferings ranged from losing several of his children to experiencing loss and imprisonment as the results of persecution for his religious and political convictions. This contributed to his theology and piety being necessarily practical and durable under pressure. His convictions regarding God and godliness cannot be explained simply as reactions to the religious climate and political turmoil of Watson's England. Yet they certainly cannot be understood without grasping the impact of these factors on his life and thought. Similarly, Watson's perspective that the godly were frequently on the wrong side of worldly trends and human politics stood behind the stances and actions taken throughout his turbulent life. This perspective would have been reinforced rather than formed by his experiences in the Civil War years and beyond.

141. Watson, *A Body of Divinity* (Edinburgh: Banner of Truth, 1965): cover insert.
142. Watson, *The Godly Man's Picture* (Edinburgh: Banner of Truth, 1992): back cover.

Summary of PART 1

We have identified a lacuna in substantial scholarship regarding the thought and ministry of Thomas Watson. This is made more stark by his considerable contribution to seventeenth-century devotional literature concerning godliness—a well-known emphasis of English Puritan spirituality. This chapter has sought to lay the foundation for the rest of this study of how this key motif pervades his theology, devotion and praxis. Having provided a detailed introduction to what is presently known of Watson's life and demonstrating where this study of his piety will sit in relation to existing scholarship on Puritan spirituality, the following chapter will aim to establish the core subject matter of the book, by a thorough investigation and analysis of the nature of godliness in Watson's thought.

PART 2

"The Grand Errand of Godliness"

Watson's Spiritual Theology

Watson's chief contribution to our understanding of Puritan piety is his detailed presentation of godliness from the perspective of his religious community. *Godly Man's Picture* is a dedicated treatise on this subject, functioning as a devotional, spiritual theology of godliness and delineating its nature for Watson's readers. *Religion our True Interest*, approaches the subject from a different angle—focusing on the aspect of reverent fear. This work boldly asserts Watson's vision of piety in what he viewed as "evil" and "corrupt times."[1] The following chapters present Watson's schema of godliness, beginning with its nature as a spiritual phenomenon and proceeding to the practical means of cultivating it and the teleological goals of such piety. I contend that while godliness encompasses several aspects of Christian spirituality for Watson, at its core this phenomenon was the affective response of a regenerate heart that had encountered the revealed glory of God. Watson's programme for the Christian life was therefore centred upon the stimulation of godly affections as the key means of obtaining the objectives of the faith.

1. *RTI*, 13.

Chapter 3
"Opening the Nature of Godliness:"*
Definition of key terms

Godliness and *Godly*

One of the aims of this study is to provide clarity concerning what Watson—and by extension other Puritans—meant by the term *godliness*. The space of three centuries between our context and theirs and the nebulous or conflated usage of godliness in evangelical Christianity today means that a shared understanding of this word should not be assumed. Yet, as already stated, it has often been insufficiently expounded by the literature and therefore requires some explication here.

Watson's preliminary definition of godliness

In the introduction to *Godly Man's Picture*, Watson makes some preliminary, definitional statements about godliness, before undertaking his larger task of exploring its characteristics in much greater detail. He first asserts that "Godliness consists in an exact harmony, between holy Principles and Practises."[1] For Watson, in order to be godly, the way one lives (i.e. their "practices") must consistently reflect what one professes to believe (i.e. their "principles"). In the second chapter of the work, "Opening the Nature of Godliness," the initial proposition is expanded by a more substantial definition,

> Godliness is the sacred impression, and workmanship of God in a man, whereby of carnal he is made spiritual. When Godliness is wrought in a person, he doth not

* Title taken from *GMP*, 5.

1. *GMP*, ii.

> receive a new soul, but he hath *another spirit,* Numb. 14. 24. The *faculties* are not new, but the *qualities;* the Strings are the same, but the Tune is mended.[2]

From these two introductory remarks and the seven "maxims" posited thereafter, Watson makes it clear that godliness has two essential prerequisites: 1) theological truth to which the subject responds and 2) a divine regenerative work on the subject's heart.

Watson's accent on these aspects is demonstrated clearly in his seven maxims. His first maxim declares that "Godliness is a *Real* thing ... it hath Truth for its foundation" and comes from God Himself.[3] True godliness can only come about in response to the reception of true revelation of God, from God. He continues by describing godliness as "intrinsical," "supernatural" and "extensive." Taken together, these three maxims speak of a spiritual transformation of the heart, by an act of God Himself. This transformation permeates the entire being, radically realigning the understanding, will and affections.[4] The next maxim makes Watson's emphasis on godliness as affectional piety very clear. "Godliness is an *intense* thing; it doth not lie in a dead formality and indifferency, but is vigorous and flaming ... He is godly whose devotion is inflamed, and his heart boils over in holy affections."[5] The affectional aspect of godliness is the nexus between "holy principles and practices" that makes their correspondence possible. The regenerate Christian's "vigorous and flaming" response to the revealed truths of God not only characterises them as godly, but enables them to live in God's ways. The alternative—an emotional and spiritual state of "indifferency" (as Watson puts it)—was perceived as an ever-present danger by a range of approaches to piety in Britain during this period, according to Alec Ryrie.[6]

Terms such as "piety," "fear of God" and "religion" are inseparably linked to godliness in Watson's writings.[7] Each of these terms is used interchangeably with godliness in the opening section of *Godly Man's Picture*. Watson wants his readers to be "enamoured with piety" as they

---

2. *GMP*, 5
3. *GMP*, 5-6.
4. *GMP*, 6-7.
5. *GMP*, 7.
6. Ryrie, *Being Protestant*, 20-22, 70.
7. S. Yuille notes the synonymity of several of these terms in *Puritan Spirituality: The Fear of God in the Affective Theology of George Swinnock* (Milton Keynes: Paternoster, 2007): 14.

see the sublimity of godliness.[8] Godliness is religion in true form, as opposed to false forms of religion built on "feverish conceit," "fancy" or external morality.[9] Likewise godliness is clearly equated with "fear" when Watson quotes the Scripture, "*Job 28.28 The fear of the Lord, that is wisdom*" to support his claim that "Godliness is our wisdom." Thus, when the above terms appear in Watson's writings, there is a direct connection to his central theme of godliness.[10]

Watson's final two introductory maxims state that godliness is "glorious" and "permanent."[11] These maxims point towards the eternal outcome of godliness. It begins with God's work of regeneration, but culminates in glorification and communion with God. Later in *Godly Man's Picture*, Watson presents godliness as a transformation that occurs in the heart to make one like God and prepare the soul for the glories of eternity: "A godly man doth bear God's *Name* and *Image;* godliness is God-likeness."[12] The gloriousness of godliness is described thus, "Godliness is glory in the seed, and glory is godliness in the flower."[13] And the enduring quality of God's supernatural, regenerative work that produces godliness is conveyed through the phrase: "When godliness hath taken root in the soul, it abides to eternity."[14]

"The Godly"

When Watson speaks of "the godly," he often employs the term much the same way his fellow Puritans favoured. It serves as a shorthand reference to genuine Christians, defined according to Puritan thought. This raises the question of whether its usage was so general that its occurrences in Watson's writings do not necessarily shed light on the substance of godliness in his thought. But the reason "godly" was the favourite adjective for describing Puritan people lay precisely in the fact they had made godliness the defining feature of who they were.[15] John Spurr writes,

> Puritans were obsessed with the immorality and the religious apathy of their

8. *GMP*, iii.
9. *GMP*, 6. Tom Webster notes that in this period, "'Religion' had a primary meaning of 'attitude of worship' or 'way of being pious.'" Webster, *Godly Clergy*, 2.
10. *GMP*, iii.
11. *GMP*, 7-8.
12. *GMP*, 34.
13. *GMP*, 7-8.
14. *GMP*, 8.
15. See Webster, *Godly Clergy*, 4; Durston and Eales, 160; Spurr, *English Puritanism*, 15.

> neighbours and actively sought to distinguish themselves, the godly, from the formalists, the worldly and the profane. In their own words, the godly were identified by 'visible worthiness, which consists in competent knowledge, profession of piety, and immunity from scandal.'[16]

For Watson, "godly" is the appropriate descriptor for genuine Christians precisely because he ties the presence of godliness in the believer to their spiritual rebirth and ongoing sanctification, arising out of regeneration by the Holy Spirit. Thus, we could say his principle of godliness is thoroughly *evangelical* (particularly in the conversionist aspect).[17] Any true Christian has had their heart worked upon by God's Spirit and, thus, has the makings of godliness. Contemporaries who were assessed to be carnal or nominal professors of Christianity were ungodly by definition.

The biblical background for Watson's use of godliness: εὐσέβεια *and* חָסִיד

Watson's usage of godliness, piety and related terms drew on the relevant vocabulary of the Old and New Testaments. In a sermon on godliness, Watson gives his understanding of the New Testament term *eusebeia* (εὐσέβεια) and elaborates on its meaning. "The Greek word for Religion εὐσέβεια, signifies *a right worshiping.* This is Religion, when we not only worship the true God, but in that manner which he hath prescribed; by a right rule, from a right principle, to a right end."[18] Elsewhere he adds: "the Greek word for godly, signifies a right Worshipper of God: A godly man doth reverence Divine Institutions, and is more for the *Purity of Worship* than the *Pomp.*"[19] Thus, the manner of worship—along with requisite affectional attitudes—was a key element of biblical godliness from Watson's perspective. Most occurrences of eusebeia in the New Testament are in the Pastoral Epistles. Watson's interaction with verses that explicitly mention godliness reflects this. 1 Timothy 4:8 features in

16. Spurr, *English Puritanism*, 15. Collinson suggests, "'The godly' was the appellation preferred by those sixteenth-century Englishmen whose unsympathetic neighbours called them 'puritans', 'precisians'," *Godly People*, 1.
17. As famously described by David Bebbington in *Evangelicalism in Modern Britain: A History from the 1730s to the 1980s* (London: Routledge, 1989): 3, 5-10.
18. Watson, "How must we make Religion our business?" in *Morning Exercises at Cripplegate*, ed. Samuel Annesley (London: James Nichols, 1844): 1:527.
19. *GMP*, 39. The contrast between "pomp" and "purity" signals that Watson is interpreting eusebeia with his own religious context in mind. We will discuss his understanding of eusebeia over and against ceremonialism in the English church in more detail below.

the introduction of *Godly Man's Picture* to highlight the present and future benefits of godliness promised in the Scriptures.[20] This verse is revisited later in the work in support of the idea that godliness is a "profitable" endeavour.[21] 2 Timothy 3:5 is only explicitly cited once, though echoes of Paul's idea of a "form of godliness" can be heard throughout. The phrase "godliness with contentment is great gain" from 1 Timothy 6:6 is a key text for his earlier work *Autarkeia* (1653).[22]

Watson also incorporated a different biblical dimension of godliness into his teaching—when he interacted with the Hebrew word commonly rendered as godly or godliness in English translations of the Old Testament: *chasid* (חָסִיד). "The Hebrew word for godly [...] signifies *merciful*; implying, that to be godly and charitable, are [...], one and the same. A good man feeds the hungry, clothes the naked, *he is ever merciful*, Psal. 37. 6."[23] Here we see Watson deriving the idea from the Old Testament that godliness is always accompanied by essential qualities of character—in this case charitability. Watson's emphasis of the *chasid* aspect of godliness was necessitated by what he perceived to be an "unmerciful" culture in England, in which "Charity [was] never more cold."[24] As this study unfolds, it will be evident that Watson accentuates the New Testament idea of *eusebeia* more heavily than the Hebrew notion of *chasid*. However, it is clear that he believed that comprehension of both aspects was requisite for the practice of biblical piety.[25] True affections towards God would always lead to the manifestation of gracious social behaviour. Or, as Watson put it himself, "A good Christian makes Gospel Piety and Moral Equity kiss each other."[26] Key Psalms featuring the term chasid are prominent texts in *Godly Man's Picture*. Psalm 4:3, "But know that the Lord hath set apart him that is Godly for himself," serves as the header text for the whole treatise.[27] Psalm 32:6, "For

20. *GMP*, iii.
21. *GMP*, 291.
22. *Autarkeia*, i, 37, 230.
23. *GMP*, 248.
24. *APA*, iv; *Beatitudes*, 198
25. This has been identified as a common concern among English Puritans: "Always fearful that Reformed religion would turn inward, concentrate exclusively on the spiritual bond of God and man, to the grave neglect of earthly society, puritans insisted on outward charitable works as a manifestation of true belief." John Morgan, *Godly Learning: Puritan attitudes towards reason, learning, and education* (Cambridge: Cambridge University Press, 1986): 37.
26. *BPD*, 2:243.
27. *GMP*, ii.

this shall every one that is godly pray unto thee," is the preliminary text introducing the idea of the forgiven Christian seeking God.[28] When it comes to the theme of "fearing God," Malachi 3:16-18 is the critical text Watson uses to speak of piety in the times he found himself in and forms the substance of *Religion our True Interest.* While the New Testament is constantly engaged with in this work, the notion of "fear of the Lord" in Jewish Wisdom literature (e.g. Prov 10:27, 14:27, 19:23) appears to be Watson's main resource for describing Christian reverence.

Other key terms relating to godliness in Watson's works

Several other terms are pertinent to this theme in Watson's writings. *Sincerity* is not synonymous with godliness, but it describes an indispensable element of Watson's understanding of piety. This is evident in the way *hypocrisy* acts as a functional antonym of godliness across his writings. Watson's concern about the existence of widespread religious hypocrisy in the nation during his lifetime is evident in *Godly Man's Picture* and other key works.[29] This is a matter which receives further attention in Chapter 8.

The relationship between godliness and holiness in Watson's writings is more complex. On one hand, holiness for Watson is most clearly an attribute of God, namely: "the intrinsic purity of his Nature, and his abhorrence of sin."[30] The godly come to possess this same attribute through their relationship with God.[31] Watson regards divine holiness as "the most orient Pearl of the King of Heaven's Crown" and human holiness as "conformity to God's Will" and nature.[32] This suggests that holiness is the most important characteristic the godly person comes to share with God. On the other hand, when Watson describes "sanctification" (i.e. the process of becoming holy) in *Body of Divinity* he recycles six out of his seven introductory aspects of godliness in *Godly Man's Picture.* Sometimes there is little more revision than the substitution of the word "sanctification" for "godliness."[33] This suggests that Watson regarded godliness and holiness as inseparable and largely

28. *GMP*, 1.
29. See for instance *GMP*, 9-14; *RTI*, 10; *BPD*, 1:221.
30. *GMP*, 35.
31. *GMP*, 35.
32. *GMP*, 35.
33. Compare *BPD*, 1:139-140, with *GMP*, 5-8.

interchangeable. Yet he does not make them identical. The overlap, wherein the extent of their interchangeability lay, was that both realities were indispensable elements of a life being transformed by the Holy Spirit. Each aspect was contingent upon the believer's knowledge of, and relationship to, God. Beholding the holy, majestic, heavenly King produced an affectional, reverential esteem (godliness). Belonging to such a God necessitated the emulation of His moral purity (holiness).[34] To the extent that the two terms represent distinct spiritual realities, godliness has the priority in Watson's schema of spiritual theology as the primary, affective response of the heart towards divine holiness. Christian holiness as the emulation of divine holiness is a derivative and consequent effect of such godliness. For this reason, I will treat Watson's statements about holiness as pertinent to his understanding of godliness.

Summary

Watson's essential concept of godliness was a theologically-fuelled response towards God. Godliness was a true and proper regard for the holy and majestic God as He really is. It is inseparable from its affectional and active dimensions. Godliness is an essential element of true Christianity, as the godly are being transformed in preparation for the pure worship of God for eternity. Godliness therefore cannot be reduced to ethical behaviour or some sense of Godlikeness—even though both have their place in understanding what it entails for Watson. It distinguishes Watson's devotional approach from dry orthodoxy and moralistic religion by emphasising the affectional response of a regenerate heart. Only this kind of piety could bring glory to God. Therefore, godly reverence and living—in response to biblically accurate doctrine—were essential to true Christianity.

---

34. In terms of priority or causality, it can be argued that to the extent that the two terms reflect distinct elements of the Christian life, godliness comes before holiness in spiritual theology in much the same way that justification precedes sanctification in the ordo salutis. This matter will be revisited in more detail in the discussion of sanctification in Watson's systematic theology in Chapter 10 below.

Chapter 4
"Characters of Godliness:"*
Key spiritual qualities in Watson's piety

Watson's treatment of godliness as a multi-faceted spiritual phenomenon is a key part of what makes his approach noteworthy. Like a diamond, godliness could be viewed from different angles, allowing its facets to be appreciated more deeply than if beheld from a single perspective. *Godly Man's Picture* is an extensive anatomy of what godliness was for Watson. He devotes close to two-thirds of this treatise to exploring twenty-four distinct characteristics of a godly man.[1]

A godly man is...		
1. a man of knowledge	9. a lover of the Word	17. a thankful man
2. acted by faith	10. indwelt by God's Spirit	18. a lover of the saints
3. fired with love	11. a humble man	19. not indulgent in any sin
4. like God	12. a praying man	20. good in his relations
5. very exact ... about the worship of God	13. a sincere man	21. appropriately spiritual
	14. a heavenly man	22. thorough in religion
6. a servant of God (rather than men)	15. a zealous man	23. walk[ing] with God
	16. a patient man	24. an instrument for making others godly
7. a Christ-prizer		
8. an evangelical weeper		

* Title taken from *GMP*, 272.

1. It should be noted that Watson frequently uses non-specific male-gender terms in his writings to describe humanity in general—in line with typical English usage of the time. In no sense does he equate godliness with masculinity and thus his statements about what characterises a "godly man" should be interpreted as fully applicable to women.

Exploring these characteristics allows us to consider both Watson's exemplification of Puritan piety and his own distinctive contribution. While the list does not represent an attempt at a strict sequence in descending order of importance, the first few characteristics are critical to Watson's schema.

Knowledge

Watson is deliberate in beginning with *knowledge*. "The First Fundamental Sign is, a godly man is a man of Knowledge."[2] As stated above, godliness in Watson's mind requires living in consistency with one's theology. Therefore, some knowledge of God is essential to being godly. But Watson builds on this idea by making it clear that a certain kind of knowledge is needed: namely, a personal knowing of God. This is consistent with his conviction that godliness was only possible for the regenerate Christian. Godly knowledge includes the capacity to simultaneously discern the baseness of one's own spiritual state and appreciate the beauty of Christ.[3] Watson further describes this knowledge as "grounded," "appreciative," "quickening," "appropriating," "transforming," "self-emptying," "growing" and "practic[al]."[4] Godliness is grounded in the Word of God (i.e. it is doctrinal) and the work of the Holy Spirit in the life of the believer (i.e. it is experiential).[5] Watson compares the Christian's knowledge of God to the knowledge a jeweller has of a precious stone when they examine it to appraise its true value.[6] It is an impactful knowledge that has a discernible effect on the life, character, delights and priorities of the one who has it.[7] Watson's emphasis on knowledge is a clear response to his concern with widespread religious nominalism in the English context. "'Tis sad, that after the Sun of Righteousness hath shined so long in our Hemisphere, yet that persons should be under the power of ignorance ... Many Christians are no better than baptized Heathens."[8] He was concerned that many possessed an inadequate knowledge of God that was qualitatively inferior to the type he was promoting. For instance, the groundedness of godly knowledge in the "Word and Spirit" is contrasted with simply

2. *GMP*, 15.
3. *GMP*, 15-16.
4. *GMP*, 16-21.
5. *GMP*, 16-17.
6. *GMP*, 17.
7. *GMP*, 21-24.
8. *GMP*, 21.

"believing as the Church believes."[9]

Building on the fundamental characteristic of knowledge, Watson introduces the remaining characteristics of a godly person. Of these twenty-three characteristics, the vast majority could be considered to be affectional—describing an attitude or disposition of the heart towards God and religion. A number of them also describe a particular action or way of life that form part of the Christian's response to the kind of knowledge Watson has described. And one or two are more aptly described as qualitative, in that they better express the kind of person the godly Christian has become, without as strict a link to specific actions or affections (though these are always implicit in Watson's thought). We shall gain an appreciation for Watson's understanding of the characteristics of godliness by looking specifically at the first seven that follow knowledge. This will be supplemented by observing some of the more notable points from the remaining qualities.

Faith

Faith naturally follows knowledge in Watson's system of godliness, since he has already introduced the idea of "saving knowledge."[10] The knowledge that was fundamental to godliness was a kind which was married to faith. In much of the Reformed theological tradition faith is the primary action of the regenerate person in response to the knowledge they have gained via the revelation of God.[11] The believer comes to trust in God, His promises and His Son.[12] For Watson, the presence of genuine faith is a clear distinction between the godly and the spiritually dead. 'Faith is the vital artery of the

9. *GMP*, 16.
10. Watson explicitly makes knowledge the prerequisite to faith in his early work, *Charter*, 230-231.
11. For example, for a discussion of the relationship between faith and knowledge in the theology of Calvin, see Thomas H. L. Parker, *Calvin: An Introduction to his Thought* (Louisville: Westminster John Knox, 1995): 80-83. For Beza, see Jeffrey Mallinson, *Faith, Reason and Revelation in Theodore Beza, 1519-1605* (Oxford: Oxford University Press, 2003): 214-234.
12. In describing the breadth of descriptive language used by Puritans in relation to faith, Charles Cohen notes its affectional dimension. He cites examples of faith being described as a "disposition" or "an 'inherent principle' that activates the soul." Cohen, *God's Caress: The Psychology of Puritan Religious Experience* (Oxford: Oxford University Press, 1986): 96. He also suggests that faith "engenders" a range of other affectional responses, including fear and love, (101). This may further explain why faith follows knowledge in Watson's schema.

soul: 'The just shall live by his faith' (Hab 2:4). Such as are destitute of faith may breathe, but they lack life."[13] Faith is said to give rise to repentance, hope and patience and prevent sin.[14] It is clear that Watson sees it as another prerequisite for godliness. The presence of faith is essential if a person can be said to have gone from carnal to spiritual or to have been circumcised in the heart (to cite the language Watson has already used with respect to godliness). His treatment of faith again reflects a dismay with the spiritual state of England in his time. "In this Age there is scarce so much Faith to be found among men, as there is among the Devils, for *they believe and tremble.* James 2.19. It was a grave and serious speech of Mr. *Greenham*, that he feared not Papism, but Atheism would be *England's* ruin."[15] Making faith foundational, along with knowledge, directly challenged the prevalence of nominalism within England in the seventeenth century.

Love

Love follows faith as the other affectional response to the knowledge of God that holds utmost importance for Watson. "Faith and Love are the two Poles on which all religion turns."[16] The godly are "fired with love to God" in response to their knowledge of God as beautiful and superlatively good. "God is the Fountain and Quintessence of goodness, his beauty and sweetness lay constraints of love upon a gracious heart."[17] The godly possess a longing to be with God. He is their "Treasure and Centre"—worthy of more affection than anything else in the world.[18] Furthermore, He is worthy of more love than all His gifts and worthy of love even when He seems to withhold many blessings.[19] Given its importance, Watson's treatment of love in this work is surprisingly short. A fuller discussion can be found in the posthumous publication of his lectures on the WSC, including a more direct definition of his understanding of love as "an Holy Fire kindled in the Affections, whereby a Christian is carried out

13. *GMP*, 28.
14. *GMP*, 28-29.
15. *GMP*, 31.
16. *GMP*, 31. Elsewhere he calls love "the Soul of Religion" and "Queen of the Graces." *BPD*, 2:245.
17. *GMP*, 31.
18. *GMP*, 33.
19. *GMP*, 33.

strongly after God as the Supreme Good."[20] Love as an affection runs through several of the other characteristics Watson lists, including love for the Word of God, love for the saints and being good in relationships. Thus, love acts as a permeating characteristic in the lives of the godly.

Godliness as Godlikeness

Watson's declaration that "a godly man is like God" would appear to be the most purely qualitative characteristic of the set included in *Godly Man's Picture*. However, the following qualification elucidates what he means,

> He hath the same judgement with God; he thinks of things as God doth; he hath a God-like disposition; he *partakes of the Divine Nature, 2 Pet.* 1. 4. A godly man doth bear God's *Name* and *Image;* godliness is God-likeness. 'Tis one thing to profess God, another thing to resemble him.[21]

The reference to a "God-like disposition" suggests that the inclinations of a godly Christian's heart imitate God's own will and affections. This is supported by what Watson goes on to say about divine holiness.

> The Holiness of God is the intrinsic purity of his Nature, and his abhorrence of sin: A godly man bears some kind of Analogy with God in this ... The holiness of the Saints consists in their conformity to God's Will, which is the rule and pattern of all Holiness.[22]

The godly come to be like God in a qualitative manner, yet one of the chief manifestations of this Godlikeness is affectional. Abhorrence of moral impurity is a posture of the godly heart that mirrors God's own nature.[23] This holy "fire of zeal against sin" arises from the believer first perceiving God's holiness and then sharing in it.[24] Ongoing conformity to the divine will and character results in behavioural transformation in the life of the saint.[25] Watson is also

20. *BPD*, 2:245.
21. *GMP*, 34-35.
22. *GMP*, 35.
23. *GMP*, 36.
24. *GMP*, 37.
25. *GMP*, 36-38. Watson also here demonstrates how holiness is for him a characteristic of godliness—distinct from each other in some sense and yet with considerable conceptual overlap: "When piety is calumniated in the world, the saints will stand

quite clear that he sees no possibility for a relationship with God where holiness is absent.[26] He seems to have nominalism in mind again when he suggests that many participate in religious exercises, but lack the intimate relationship with God that comes through holiness.[27] It is also significant to note that the conceptualisation of holiness had been a key point of contention between the Puritan and Laudian parties within the state church in the first half of the seventeenth century. Their differing approaches remained unreconciled when *Godly Man's Picture* was written.[28]

Exactness in Worship

The next characteristic is the precision with which the godly treat the matter of worshipping God. I have already noted above that Watson renders the Greek *eusebeia* as pertaining to the true worship of God. This aspect is important for understanding Watson as a Puritan. It reflects a commonly held conceptualisation of godliness among many of his coreligionists. Concerning religious worship, Watson plainly states: "A godly man dares not vary from the *Pattern* which God hath shewn him in the Scripture."[29] The key departures from this Scriptural pattern of worship that he had in mind were undoubtedly Roman Catholicism and the Anglo-Catholic tendencies that existed within the state church. "Papists" are attacked explicitly in this section, while references to "outward commixtures in God's Worship" and "high Formalists" indict many in the religious establishment during the Restoration period.[30]

We shall discuss Watson's contentions with these religious approaches in greater detail in Chapter 8. But suffice it to say here that he is concerned with the challenge of promoting religion where the engagement of the heart is valued above form and ceremony. This addresses the dilemma posed by non-biblical (or *unbiblical* from the Puritan perspective) innovations in Christian worship or "traditions

---

up in the defence of it; they will wipe off the dust of a reproach from the face of religion; holiness defends the godly, and they will defend holiness; it defends them from danger, and they will defend it from disgrace." *GMP*, 36.

26. "Holiness is God's stamp and impress; if he doth not see this stamp upon us, he will not own us." *GMP*, 38.
27. *GMP*, 39.
28. The nature of this controversy is discussed further below.
29. *GMP*, 40.
30. *GMP*, 41.

of men."[31] A person's desire to respond to God sincerely from the heart would naturally be accompanied by a careful diligence to order their personal and corporate devotion around God's revealed will (as per the Scriptures). Whereas, those who replaced heart religion with mere formalism were likely to replace biblical worship practices with inventions of their own fancy.[32]

Serving God rather than people

This characteristic is a natural extension of the preceding one. For Watson and the Puritans, God was not simply the object of one's worship and service on a Sunday morning. Their emphatic commitment to *eusebeia* eliminates any suggestion that weekly, public worship services were not central to Puritan devotion. But the same ethos that characterised congregational gatherings was to extend to a saint's daily obedience to God as Master. This was one of the means of demonstrating the special relationship between God and the godly. They had turned from serving sinful desires and sinful people and bound themselves wholeheartedly to the command of one divine Master. The godly showed reverence for God in the lengths they were prepared to go to in order to follow Him. They actively sought His purposes and zealously defended His name against disparagement.[33] Watson's dichotomy between service oriented chiefly towards God and that which seeks to please people was biblical in origin. Yet at the time he penned *Godly Man's Picture*, it was a reiteration of the principle that he and other nonconformist ministers had applied in their pursuit of godliness with the costly effect of losing their parishes and clerical credentials only a few years earlier. Whether it was a choice between holiness instead of profane living, or a clean conscience instead of profit—Watson was convinced that godly fidelity in his day required a refusal to bend to the ungodly demands of others.[34]

Prizing Christ

This aspect of godliness is notable in its own right. Yet, as with many

31. *GMP*, 40.
32. *GMP*, 39-41.
33. *GMP*, 43-46.
34. *GMP*, 52.

of the characteristics to follow, it is to some extent a composite of some of the foundational characteristics discussed so far. "Prizing Christ" is a convergence of knowledge, faith, love and proper worship. Watson seeks to establish the foundational truth that Christ is precious due to the loveliness of His nature and the majestic glory of His Messianic offices (e.g. the *triplex munus* of Prophet, Priest and King). Watson maintained that those who had come to know Christ would naturally "have an honourable esteem" of Him.[35] Watson could distinguish between an "appreciation" of God (mainly relating to the human faculty of judgement that recognised intellectually that God was worthy of admiration) and "adoration" or "affection" (relating to the engagement of the heart in worship and love respectively).[36] But when speaking of "prizing" Christ there is no clear distinction in his thought. The godly "set an high estimation on Christ" in their minds and "prefer him in [their] judgements before other things," yet the affectional language of "complacency," "joy" and "delight" follows immediately in Watson's exposition of what it means for Christ to be prized.[37] This aspect of piety is the mind and heart of the believer acting in tandem in the cherishing of Christ. The crescendo of Watson's treatment of this characteristic comes with his declaration, "we cannot prize Christ at too high a rate."[38] The overvaluing of created things was a symptom of worldliness, whereas the realisation that Christ's worth exceeded the human capacity to truly appreciate it lay at the heart of godliness. Recognition of Christ's incomparable value was paramount.

Thus, this mark of the godly crystallises and synthesises the core elements of Watson's piety. This personal treasuring of Christ was not only the application of sincere faith and love to true knowledge. It formed the centre of singular devotion and service to one's heavenly Master and diligence in biblical worship. It was likewise a major incentive for the pursuit of holiness. For Watson, it is meaningless to speak of religious affections and derivative actions in the Christian life as godliness if they are not unmistakably characterised by this deep appreciation of Christ. He identifies several contemporaneous "sorts of persons who do not prize Christ" and are thus incapable of godliness.[39] These include Jews, Socinians, "Proud Professors"

35. *GMP*, 52.
36. *BPD*, 1:1-2.
37. *GMP*, 62, 64.
38. *GMP*, 68.
39. *GMP*, 59.

and "Airy Specularists."[40] While the first two are clearly identifiable religious groups (which receive further attention below), the latter categories would seem to mainly target trends within the English church again.

The negative aspects of godliness: Evangelical weeping and non-indulgence in sin

The reputation of the Puritans has long been tarnished by the popular perception that they had a penchant for "morbid introspection," woeful jeremiads and a generally negative approach towards life in the world.[41] On the one hand, this stereotype has frequently been challenged by scholars of Puritanism—especially those with a more sympathetic stance towards the spirituality of their subjects.[42] On the other hand, the dour aspect does exist and continues to be accentuated in some studies of the movement. For instance, after acknowledging the heights and joys that could be reached through Puritan piety, Bozeman is quick to remark "the morbid view [of Puritan spirituality] does not wholly miss the mark."[43] From this perspective, Puritan piety was a sombre affair, interspersed with oases of spiritual euphoria.

It is therefore notable that Watson's characteristics of godliness are overwhelmingly positive in nature. An exception is when he calls the godly "evangelical weeper[s]"—people who know how to shed tears over their spiritual corruption.[44] He sees this kind of crying as a manifestation of godly sorrow. Therefore, it is vitally connected to spiritual sincerity and true repentance.[45] A lack of this affective response to the seriousness of sin and the warmth of God's undeserved love is a sign to Watson that the heart, in all probability, remains spiritually dead. This aspect of Watson's piety

40. *GMP*, 60.
41. E.g. "The morbid introspection detectable in so many Puritan diaries." Paul S. Seaver, *Puritan Lectureships: The Politics of Dissent 1560-1662* (Stanford: Stanford University Press, 1970): 41. See also Perry Miller, *"The Jeremiad" in his New England Mind: From Colony to Province* (Cambridge: Harvard University Press, 1953): 27-39.
42. E.g. Packer, *Quest for Godliness*, 24-25; Ryken, *Worldly Saints*, 13-14, 18-19; Beeke and Jones, *Puritan Theology*, 917-918.
43. Bozeman, *Precisianist Strain*, 173.
44. *GMP*, 70.
45. *GMP*, 74-76. Schwanda remarks that "it would take a full article to explore the depth and variety of Watson's use of tears throughout his corpus." "Sweetnesse," 54.

is notable in the sense of it requiring spiritual sorrow that manifests itself in an external, physical reaction.[46] It is also significant that Watson regards it as transhistorical. Various historical Christian figures serve as touchstones for the importance of godly tears in his piety.[47] The other negative characteristic of the godly, which occurs later in the list, is non-indulgence in sin (#19). Awareness of God's omniscience and judgement of all sin is the prime reason put forward for why the godly will not indulge in certain kinds of sin in the way others might.[48] Together with weeping, this antipathy to sin in general fits with Watson's emphasis on the repentance, self-denial and the mortification of sin (as discussed further below).

A categorical survey of the remaining characteristics in Godly Man's Picture

Rather than giving a detailed summary of the remaining sixteen characteristics, I shall restrict my analysis to several important themes. This will provide a concise, if not comprehensive, overview of the nature of godliness in Watson's thought. As mentioned above, several of the subsequent characteristics share a close conceptual relationship to those already explored. Some even demonstrate something of a composite nature, synthesising certain emphases from the earlier marks. For example, doing "spiritual things in a spiritual manner" (#21) and being "thorough-paced in religion" (#22) are closely connected back to the idea of worshipping God in the correct manner.[49] In describing what "walking with God" (#23) means, Watson draws upon the composite elements of knowledge, faith and love. It is living with the knowledge that God is watching.[50] Furthermore, it is about fearing God. But this is a "fear springing

46. A conundrum is evident when we consider that there was always the possibility of tears without a godly, affective state (See *GMP*, 74-76). This meant that although the absence of tears was a grave sign, their presence could hardly provide assurance concerning someone's spiritual state. This makes Watson susceptible to the charge of promoting an excruciating state of self-analysis. See Ryrie, *Being Protestant*, 58-59. Compare Bozeman, *Precisianist Strain*, 102-107.
47. Concerning the place of tears in earlier generations of British Protestantism, Ryrie remarks, "Pious weeping ... had a long medieval history and was thriving amongst contemporary Catholics." *Being Protestant*, 187. See also, David D. Hall, *The Puritans: A Transatlantic History* (Princeton: Princeton University Press, 2019): 121.
48. *GMP*, 208.
49. *GMP*, 229, 238.
50. *GMP*, 251.

from affection" and "a fear joined with affiance."[51] Likewise, Watson's description of the godly as "heavenly" relates to their meditation upon the Scriptural presentation of heaven.[52] This is a means of directing their faith towards God and His promises.[53] The saint's delight in contemplating heavenly things is explicitly predicated on their choice to prize Christ above everything in the world.[54] When Watson employed darker hues to paint his portrait of a godly Christian, they served mainly to highlight the brighter qualities of godliness. Thus, sincerity (#13) is presented as a juxtaposition between a plain-hearted commitment to honour God and the hypocrite's "subtle subterfuges" and "dissimulation."[55] The zeal of the godly (#15) is a natural compound of their "love to God, and anger against sin."[56] And the godly quality of thankfulness (#17) is remarkable because the wicked are incapable of exhibiting it.[57]

Watson's presentation of many of these qualities conveys the sense that they are biblical and timeless. However, as with several of the characteristics discussed above, there are some indications of how the religious climate of his times impacted his teaching. Defects in Catholic piety and ethics serve as negative illustrations for Watson's teaching on humility and prayer.[58] However, consistent with what has been seen in this survey so far, many of his concerns appear to relate chiefly to the English church. In extolling the godly Christian's love for God's Word (#9) and their goodness in various relationships (#20), Watson criticises ministers with a predilection for lofty, inaccessible preaching and those who fail to address sin in the congregation.[59] In discussing the need for godly zeal, Watson repudiates anti-puritan allegations of "religious frenzy" or fanaticism and dismisses the "moderation," favoured by many in the established church, as "sinful neutrality."[60] There would seem to be a subtle allusion to Charles II in the treatment of the final characteristic of godliness. Watson suggests that rulers may drive their people

51. *GMP*, 256.
52. *GMP*, 142.
53. *GMP*, 142-143.
54. *GMP*, 142.
55. *GMP*, 131-134. See also *UMC* for another instance of Watson's representation of sincerity in this way.
56. *GMP*, 155.
57. *GMP*, 180.
58. *GMP*, 104, 120.
59. *GMP*, 86, 219-220.
60. *GMP*, 159-161, 270.

away from Christ by "Evil edicts" that compel them to sin.[61] When Watson stresses the love that the godly should exhibit towards other saints (#18), he decries both uncharitable divisions amongst English believers and those who "malign the godly."[62] This aptly captures a sense of the disquietude experienced by nonconformists in the Restoration. The pain arising from their costly inability to co-operate amongst themselves was still fresh and in part it had enabled the hateful persecution they were now experiencing.[63]

Watson appends two conclusions about the characteristics of the godly to his lengthy exposition of them. He seeks to encourage his readers to use the presence of these qualities in their lives as a "box of evidences" should they experience doubts about their spiritual standing or perceive the condemnatory activity of Satan in their lives. He also builds on his earlier remark "He who is godly is good all over; though he be regenerate but in part, yet it is in every part," by here declaring that "He who hath one of these Characters in truth, hath seminally all."[64] It will be observed below, when considering hypocrisy, that Watson shares a common Puritan concern to remove the false presumptions of nominal, religious pretenders. This leads him, in *Godly Man's Picture* and other works, to make a range of intense and exclusive declarations about the nature of godliness, which may have caused concern within the lukewarm and devout alike. Despite this, there is strong evidence here that his goal in thoroughly describing the characteristics of godliness was to bring comfort and assurance to godly believers who found any trace of them in their lives.

Godly Fear in Religion our True Interest

The most interesting omission from Watson's list of characteristics in *Godly Man's Picture* is one dedicated specifically to godly fear or reverence. "Fear" is typically used in a negative sense throughout the treatise and the "fear of the Lord" generally occurs only in passing references when treating other subjects. This holy, reverential kind of fear comes into focus the most in one of several subsections under the heading of the penultimate characteristic—concerning "walk[ing]

61. *GMP*, 267.
62. *GMP*, 199-200, 206.
63. See John Miller, "Restoration," in *HDSE*, 452.
64. *GMP*, 7, 272.

with God."[65] This is unusual precisely because Watson freely employs "fear of the Lord" as a virtual synonym for godliness in his introduction. Furthermore, the concept of reverential fear towards God clearly did have great importance for his concept of godliness, judging by the extensive treatment it receives in *Religion our True Interest.* There is no suggestion in the latter work that Watson was seeking to remedy a deficiency in his earlier treatise. It simply comes into the foreground due to his chosen text of exposition, "Then they that feared the LORD spake often one to another: and the LORD hearkened, and heard it, and a book of remembrance was written before him for them that feared the LORD, and that thought upon his name." (Malachi 3:16-18). Based on this text, Watson suggests that the general character of the godly is that "they are Fearers of God."[66] Against potential misinterpretations of the kind of fear he is referring to, Watson defines it as "the reverencing and adoring God's Holiness, and setting ourselves always under his Sacred inspection."[67] The following is a good example of Watson describing the nature of godly fear in contradistinction to other kinds of fear.

> This Holy Fear is the fixed temper and Complexion of the Soul; This Fear is not *Servile* but *Filial*; there is difference between *Fearing God,* and *being afraid of God*; the Godly fear God as a Child doth his Father, the wicked are afraid of God as the Prisoner is of the Judge.[68]

Watson makes extraordinary statements about this kind of fear. He declares it to be "the Sum of all Religion" and "the leading Grace, the first seed God sows in the Heart."[69] He adds that fearing God "goes to the very constituting of a Saint."[70] Since godly fear was the result of recognising "the infinite distance between God and us," there could be no talk of godliness without the reverential affections that were appropriate to this appreciation of God's immensity and superiority.[71] Fear of the Lord was as core to heart piety as faith and love. Indeed, Watson states that fear is "mixed" with both of them, making these three aspects the core godly responses of the heart towards true knowledge of God.[72]

65. *GMP*, 250-251, 255-256.
66. *RTI*, 2.
67. *RTI*, 15.
68. *RTI*, 16.
69. *RTI*, 15.
70. *RTI*, 16.
71. *RTI*, 15.
72. *RTI*, 16-17.

Negatively, Watson is clear "God interprets our not fearing him a slighting of him."[73] To fail to appreciate God's majesty and greatness was to regard Him as lesser than He was. This was the precise opposite of godliness. Watson blamed such an absence of holy fear on sinful ignorance of the Deity as He truly is.[74] "Did men know God in his immense glory, they would be swallowed up with divine amazement."[75] Those who failed to know God and fear Him appropriately would succumb to all kinds of sin, "Want of the fear of God is the innate Cause of all Wickedness."[76] I shall discuss Watson's perspective on the times in which he composed *Religion our True Interest* in Chapter 11. But it is appropriate to note at this point that he emphasised the fear of the Lord at a time when he felt it was in decline and when atheism and nominal religion were ascendant.[77]

On the other hand, those with proper reverence would live in a way that consistently honoured God and sought the good of their neighbours.

> The fear of God would influence all our actions. It would make us Good in both Tables. It would make us *Holy* towards God, and *Righteous* towards men. We would be true in our Promises, just in our dealings.[78]

Reverential fear can also be understood as one way the godly reflect in this life how things will be in heaven.[79] When the saints behold the fullness of God's heavenly majesty, Watson maintains that their glorified souls will respond with fear. "Though God hath so much beauty in him as shall cause love, and joy, in Heaven, yet this beauty is mixed with so much Majesty, as shall cause a Veneration in Glorified Saints."[80] Thus, despite not featuring as a distinct characteristic of godliness in *Godly Man's Picture*, holy reverence clearly forms part of the essential substance of godliness for Watson.

73. *RTI*, 19.
74. *RTI*, 23-24.
75. *RTI*, 23.
76. *RTI*, 22.
77. See *RTI*, iii-iv, 23.
78. *RTI*, 29.
79. *RTI*, 34-35.
80. *RTI*, 34-35.

Chapter 5
"Be diligent in the use of all means, that may promote godliness"*

Although Watson regarded godliness as impossible apart from the initial and ongoing work of the Holy Spirit in a person's heart, he believed that there were a range of divinely-ordained means of cultivating the affectional piety outlined above. Certain aspects of Watson's practical programme for growing in godliness have been emphasised in recent studies of his spirituality. My analysis of the various means which Watson regarded as essential for advances in piety will demonstrate that he had a more fully-orbed vision of spiritual duties and disciplines than what has been suggested by scholars focusing on his meditative or mystical inclinations.

The Foundation of the Word

The fundamental means of developing godliness were those which allowed the practitioner to make proper use of the revelation of God contained in the Scriptures. Watson takes it for granted that the majority of Christian knowledge is acquired via hearing the Word preached and personal Bible reading.[1] Engagement with the Scriptures was essential to piety: 'Reading of the word is the best way to usher-in the fear of the Lord.'[2] In fact, the reverential reading of God's Word is considered to be the only appropriate response to the dignity of the sacred writ and the majesty of its Author.[3]

* Title taken from *GMP*, 295.

1. Brown notes that daily Bible reading was encouraged by many of Watson's contemporaries and that Scripture memorisation was highly valued in anticipation of restricted access to Bibles. Brown, *Spirituality in Adversity*, 194, 198-199.
2. Watson, "How we may read the Scriptures with the most spiritual profit," in *Morning Exercises at Cripplegate*, ed. Samuel Annesley (London: Thomas Tegg, 1844): 2:58.
3. *BPD*, 1:18. Furthermore, the Scriptures themselves are to be cherished in an affectional

Likewise, biblical preaching was "the Quickener of Holy Affections."[4] The Puritan commitment to preaching is well-attested, but it was promoted in an environment where it was not appreciated by all.[5] J. S. McGee has suggested that Watson extolled preaching against a Laudian impulse for diminishing and suppressing it.[6]

Watson makes understanding the Scriptures the antecedent to the development of true affections: "the lamp of understanding must first be lighted, before the affections can be inflamed."[7] But he goes further, insisting that the mere reading of the Bible is useless in the cultivation of godliness.[8] "[It is not] enough to read the word of God, but it should be our care to get some spiritual emolument and profit by it, so that our souls may be ἐντρεφομενοι 'nourished up in the words of faith' (1 Tim iv.6)."[9] Watson urges his hearers to "leave not off reading in the Bible till you find your hearts warmed ... labour to be affected with it. Let it not only inform you, but inflame you."[10] Without this enflaming of the affections, there had been no meaningful encounter with God in the Word. Meagre reading precluded any progress in piety.

Despite understanding being vital for godly affections, Watson argues that human cognitive abilities of interpretation or mere logical comprehension of the Bible are unprofitable to true spiritual progress. The reader must be aware of their dependency on the Holy Spirit for illumination of the Word and application to the heart.[11] This connects naturally with Watson's beliefs about the necessity of spiritual regeneration being prerequisite for all godliness. It is also true to his strong convictions about the nature of Scripture as a divinely inspired document and the sovereignty of God in revealing Himself to people. Scripture alone was the source of theological

---

manner by God's people according to Watson in "How we may read the Scriptures," 63-65.

4. *BPD*, 2:342.
5. E.g. Julian Davies, *The Caroline Captivity of the Church: Charles I and the Remoulding of Anglicanism 1625-1641* (Oxford: Clarendon, 1992): 67-69, 126-127; Peter Lake, "The Laudian Style" in *The Early Stuart Church 1603-1642* ed. Kenneth Fincham (London: MacMillan, 1993): 169-170.
6. J. Sears McGee, *The Godly Man in Stuart England: Anglicans, Puritans and the Two Tables, 1620-1670* (New Haven: Yale, 1976): 243-244.
7. Watson, "How we may read the Scriptures," 60.
8. See for instance the comments on meditation in relation to "reading and hearing" below.
9. Watson, "How we may read the Scriptures," 59.
10. Watson, "How we may read the Scriptures," 68.
11. E.g. "We may read many Truths in the Bible, but we cannot know them savingly till God's Spirit doth shine upon us." *GMP*, 26-27.

illumination that formed the basis for piety. But reading and hearing Scripture did not stand alone in the cultivation of godliness. They must be accompanied by the other means explored below.

Catechesis

Catechesis has a rich heritage stretching back to the early church. Its ongoing significance in the Reformed tradition is evidenced by the production of key documents in the sixteenth century, including the Geneva Catechism (1545) and the Heidelberg Catechism (1563), and the Westminster Assembly's two catechisms published in 1648. Watson's magisterial *Body of Divinity* was the result of his own attempt to systematically catechise his congregation with the WSC. This was the practical expression of his conviction that catechising was the method by which people could be properly grounded in their faith (which he said was absolutely necessary for progress in godliness).[12] While in the introduction to *Body of Divinity* he could say of preaching: "[its] great end [is] to bring us to a Settlement in Religion," he later added:

> Catechising is the best Expedient for the Grounding and Settling of People. I fear one reason why there hath been no more Good done by Preaching, hath been because the chief Heads and Articles in Religion have not been explained in a Catechistical Way ... To Preach and not to Catechise, is to build without a Foundation.[13]

This gives great insight into Watson's understanding of the role pastoral ministry played in the cultivation of godliness amongst their congregants. To preach a weekly sermon from a biblical text was the minimal duty of the faithful minister. The pastor also needed to make use of additional opportunities to ingrain the most important truths of the faith into his people.[14] Only through being thoroughly schooled in the chief articles of the faith and their implications, could Christians "serve God aright," "worship Him acceptably," and avoid doctrinal errors that necessarily produced defective piety (as I will

12. "He can no more grow in Godliness, which is unsettled, than a Bone can grow in the Body that is out of joint." *BPD*, 1:ii.
13. *BPD*, 1:iv.
14. Raymond Brown has noted that catechising was a key means of sustaining the faith amongst nonconformists when government policy restricted the ability of ministers to freely preach to congregations. Brown, *Spirituality in Adversity*, 273.

discuss further in Chapter 8).[15] Watson's dedication to catechising in general and the WSC in particular makes him an exemplar of the widespread enthusiasm for catechesis amongst his fellow Puritans.[16]

Meditation

The main discipline that Watson insisted upon as a vital, personal means of engaging with biblical truths was meditation.[17] Watson defined this process as "the soul's retiring of itself, that by a serious and solemn thinking upon God, the heart may be raised up to heavenly affections."[18] He forcefully stated the need for meditation, in order to make Bible reading and hearing effective, when he said:

> Serious Meditation is like the engraving of letters in gold or marble which endure. Without this, all our preaching to you is but like writing in sand, like pouring water into a sieve. Reading and hearing without Meditation, is like weak Physic which will not work; want of Meditation hath made so many sermons in this age to have a miscarrying womb and dry breasts![19]

As already noted, the "meditative" or "contemplative-mystical" aspect of Watson's piety has received more scholarly attention than any other aspect of his theology or life. Neimeyer has argued strongly for the primacy of meditation in Watson's ranking of spiritual disciplines. This is based on his strong statements in *Christian on the Mount* such as, "[Meditation is] a duty wherein consists the essentials of Religion, and which nourisheth the very life blood of it,"[20] and "a good Christian is a meditating Christian."[21] Watson is often quoted in works treating Puritan approaches to meditation in general, or in works specifically looking at this discipline in the thought and practice of particular contemporary authors.[22] This demonstrates the

15. *BPD*, 1:iii-iv.
16. See Hambrick-Stowe, "Practical Divinity and Spirituality," 202-203.
17. See below for further discussion of Jennifer Neimeyer's thesis that meditation was the most important discipline in Watson's programme for spiritual growth.
18. *CM*, 61.
19. *CM*, 195.
20. *CM*, 58.
21. *CM*, 59; Neimeyer, "Thomas Watson," 173-174.
22. E.g. Joel Beeke, "The Puritan Practice of Meditation," in *Puritan Reformed Spirituality* (Grand Rapids: Reformation Heritage Books, 2006): 74, 78-79, 87, 92, 97; Keith Condie, "The Theory, Practice and Reception of Meditation in the thought of Richard Baxter" (PhD Thesis, Sydney: University of Sydney, 2010): 62fn, 66fn, 68, 71.

significance of his writings on this topic for understanding it generally. More recently, Schwanda has explored Watson's "contemplative piety" and demonstrated his indebtedness to Catholic devotional writers.[23] Both of these scholars have made a valuable contribution to our understanding of the relationship between meditation and growth in godliness. Schwanda suggests a strong similarity between Watson's approach to meditation and the *lectio divina* practice of Bible reading and reflection that was common amongst Catholic monastics and mystics.[24] While a distinction exists in this approach between "meditation" and "contemplation," Schwanda demonstrates that Watson uses the terms in a virtually interchangeable manner.[25] It is doubtful that Watson consciously adopted *lectio divina* as a model for his meditative spirituality, but his indebtedness to one of its most notable practitioners is undeniable. Schwanda shows how Watson was influenced by Bernard of Clairvaux (1090–1153) in how he viewed contemplation/meditation as a means of attaining a spiritual proximity to God and the heavenly realities (closely akin to the idea of "communion with God" employed by Watson, and others, elsewhere).[26] This kind of contemplation is supposed to continue until appropriate, godly affections are aroused in the heart of the practitioner.[27]

Neimeyer notes that the strong emphasis on meditation she has observed in key Watson works like *Christian on the Mount* and *Heaven taken by Storm*, is clearly evident in the guidelines for how to grow in godliness that he sets out in *Godly Man's Picture*. The eight guidelines Watson gives are listed in the table below.[28]

1. Be diligent in the use of all means that may promote godliness.
2. Take heed of the world.
3. Accustom yourselves to holy thoughts.
4. Watch your hearts.
5. Make spending your time a matter of conscience.
6. Think of your short stay in the world.

23. Schwanda speaks of the "contemplative heritage" of the Christian church, before seeking to demonstrate how Watson drew upon such devotional resources in developing his own approach. Schwanda, "Sweetnesse," 35.
24. Schwanda, "Sweetnesse," 45.
25. Schwanda, "Sweetnesse," 45.
26. Schwanda, "Sweetnesse," 45-47. For more on Bernard's influence on Watson, see the excursus in Chapter 7.
27. Schwanda, "Sweetnesse," 47.
28. Table compiled from *GMP*, 295-299. See Neimeyer, "Thomas Watson," 180.

7. Make this maxim your own—that godliness is the purpose of your creation.
8. Be often among the godly.

Neimeyer suggests that "at least half" of these directions "speak directly of meditation," nominating points 2–4 and 6.[29] But only points 3 and 6 explicitly call for meditation, while the other two may be thought of as enabled or enhanced by deeper contemplation of the relevant spiritual realities. Nevertheless, Neimeyer is correct that it is unsurprising to find Watson commending a meditative approach to those wishing to grow in godliness—given his emphatic commendation of it elsewhere.

Meditation was undoubtedly significant in Watson's programme of piety. However, it must be noted that Watson was capable of unapologetically promoting other things as crucial or fundamental to Christian life when they came into his focus. This will be apparent in the discussion of "self-denial" below. It would be foolish to discount the importance Watson places on meditation—especially (as Neimeyer argues) when it is done in conjunction with other means of grace (e.g. Bible reading, prayer). But we can avoid overstating its primacy by acknowledging that he could be similarly impassioned in describing other elements of Christian life. For Watson, meditation and contemplation derive the entirety of their significance from his goal for all spiritual disciplines: the increase of godliness. The truths Watson discovered in the Bible and inherited from his Reformed theological forebears were the fundamental ingredient for producing the godliness he understood God to require from every sincere Christian. The importance of meditation rested in its value as a means of applying these truths to the soul. This was to be carried out to the point that the affections (and even the nature or identity of the Christian) would be positively changed by the digested truths. Meditation was indispensable for Watson. Because he knew of no other practice that could exceed it in creating the reverent, affectional response towards God that formed the chief characteristic of the godly heart. Thus, it can be affirmed that meditation was vital amongst the spiritual activities Watson advocated. Yet, a fully-orbed appreciation of his programme for spiritual growth cannot be attained if the significance of meditation is allowed to eclipse other vital means of progress in piety.

29. Neimeyer, "Thomas Watson," 180.

Self-Denial and the Mortification of Sin

The potential for overstating the primacy of meditation in Watson's practice of piety is immediately evident when considering his equally impassioned statements about self-denial.

> Self-denial is the foundation of godliness; and if this be not well-laid, the whole building will fall. If there be any lust in our souls which we cannot deny, it will turn at length either to scandal or apostasy. Self-denial is the thread which must run along through the whole work of Religion.[30]

Elsewhere he adds: "I must profess I know not a more necessary point in *Divinity.* Self-denial is the first principle of Christianity; it is the life-blood, which must run through the whole body of Religion."[31] Here we find the same language of absolute necessity and "life-blood," used to argue for the primacy of meditation in Watson's practical piety. Yet here it is being employed by him in enthusiasm for a completely different discipline. Self-denial was so important to Watson, because he identified selfishness as "the reigning sin of the World."[32] Therefore self-denial served as a means of demonstrating sincerity in religion, in contrast to hypocrites: whom Watson regarded as spiritually incapable of renunciation of selfish, sinful desires.[33] He saw the denial of ungodliness and progress in godliness as two inseparable aspects of sanctification. This is evidenced by his treatment of Titus 2:11: "*Denying ungodliness and worldly lusts*; there is, being delivered from Evil; *that we should live soberly, righteously, and godly*; there is a progress in Piety."[34] Significantly, he did not regard suffering for Christ as something which only promoted godliness in the life of the persecuted or afflicted Christian. It also positively affected the lives of those who witnessed the suffering saint's resolve to follow Christ and resistance to evil.[35] Brown attests that this commitment to self-denial was a key component of nonconformist preparation for suffering in the reign of Charles II.[36] Watson's approach to persecution typifies this

30. *Beatitudes*, 427. See also *DSD*, 2.
31. *DSD*, Preface.
32. *DSD*, 51.
33. *DSD*, 51.
34. *BPD*, 3:860.
35. "Our sufferings for Christ propagate piety." *DSD*, 45. This topic is discussed further in Chapter 12.
36. Brown, *Spirituality in Adversity*, 178-189.

mentality.[37]

Thus, meditation shares its centrality with self-denial, in Watson's approach to godly growth. Both were indispensable for producing true affections born out of an appreciation of God. This is particularly the case when it comes to the practical discipline of dealing with the sinful desires and worldly temptations that the Christian encounters every day of their earthly existence. It is therefore unsurprising to find Watson, in his treatise on meditation, *A Christian on the Mount*, simultaneously exhorting believers to "mortification" (another term for self-denial) and "meditation."[38] Indeed, in doing so, he describes the act of meditating as part of the Christian's need to exercise self-denial (or "offer violence" to themselves) with respect to fleshly desires. This enables them to practise the other duties God has called them to perform.[39] Interestingly, Watson's work on self-denial lacks any references to meditation. On the other hand, *Heaven Taken by Storm*, his lengthy exposition on the idea of "holy violence" (derived from Jesus' statement in Matthew 11:12), joins the two together again. This text makes mortification the principle way in which Christians "offer violence to themselves" and meditation one of the duties requiring warfare against the flesh in order to succeed.[40] It is also noteworthy that some of the practices Watson commends which may seem to support the primacy of the meditation thesis are also closely related to the idea of self-denial or mortification of sin. For example, Watson's exhortation to "watch your hearts" in *Godly Man's Picture* and his calls to self-examination elsewhere are essential processes in the Christian's battle with the flesh.[41] In light of all of this, it is clear that Watson saw self-denial as an additional indispensable action to any advancement in godliness. This brings his advocacy of meditation into perspective. Meditation was his primary, positive means of growth in godly affections, while self-denial was pivotal in putting to death the sin that would hinder such growth.

Holy Conference

While meditation and self-denial were the major personal (or private)

37. E.g. *Beatitudes*, 422-423, 427-433.
38. *CM*, 211.
39. *CM*, 211.
40. *HTS*, 17-20.
41. *GMP*, 296.

ingredients for progress in piety, Watson also placed an emphasis upon corporate (or public) means of developing godliness. One of the most significant of these was "holy conference" or association with other godly people. He describes this practice as "learn[ing] the trade of godliness."[42] The company of the godly can have a strong effect on the affections and vitality of each individual.[43] Watson regarded this idea of godly discussion amongst God's people as both biblically commanded and the ancient practice of Christians.[44] Many of his Puritan contemporaries and predecessors agreed on this point.[45] In her recent work exploring conference as a significant Puritan devotional practice, Joanne Jung notes that despite the lack of previous scholarship dedicated to this discipline, "this communally practiced private means appears widely supported and promoted by the Puritans."[46] She proceeds to call upon a range of notable Puritan witnesses to the importance of the practice, including Richard Greenham, Richard Rogers, Richard Sibbes, John Bunyan and Richard Baxter.[47] Significantly, Watson is cited several times in this general work on the subject (especially with respect to the Scriptural basis for the practice and the seriousness of neglecting it).[48] This demonstrates that while this is a practice common to Puritanism, Watson's writings are valuable for understanding conference as a component of growth in godliness. Jung and Brown have both argued that this practice was a key means of expressing dissenting beliefs in a localised, lay setting when the government targeted nonconformist ministers or threatened to shut down certain kinds of religious meetings.[49]

Concerning neglect of conference, Watson was prepared to blame

---

42. "Be often among the godly; they are the salt of the earth, and will help to season you. Their counsels may direct their prayers may quicken: Such holy sparks may be thrown into your breasts, as may enkindle devotion in you: It is good to be among the Saints to learn the trade of godliness." *GMP*, 299.
43. "How doth Grace flourish by holy conference!" *DC*, 20.
44. *RTI*, 82, 94.
45. Arthur Dent's *Plain Man's Pathway to Heaven* (1601) exhorted Christians to "Keep company with the godly, and avoid the society of the wicked," which C. Haigh calls "the conventional counsel of godly preachers." *The Plain Man's Pathways to Heaven: Kinds of Christianity in Post-Reformation England* (Oxford: Oxford University Press, 2007): 102. Ryrie concurs, "The value of godly sociability was universally recognized." *Being Protestant*, 390.
46. Joanne J. Jung, *Godly Conversation: Rediscovering the Puritan Practice of Conference* (Grand Rapids: Reformation Heritage Books, 2011): chap. 5. Kindle Edition.
47. Jung, *Godly Conversation*, chap. 5.
48. Jung, *Godly Conversation*, chap. 5.
49. Brown, *Spirituality in Adversity*, 270; Jung, *Godly Conversation*, chap. 6.

deficiencies in godliness amongst Christians on the lack of proper spiritual conversation: 'I persuade myself one main reason of the decay of the Power of Godliness is want of Christian conference: people when they meet talk of Impertinencies, but God and Heaven are left out of their discourse!'[50] Watson reproves people who are either silent with respect to the things of God in their conversations, or who fill their conversations with idle, worldly or evil words and subjects.[51] On the other hand, he sees deliberate godly speech as a means of countering sin and inviting the presence of Christ, rather than that of Satan.[52] This is a sign that godly conference intersected with self-denial and mortification of sin in his thought. Speaking of things of spiritual substance was a way of practically overcoming evil, unprofitable inclinations with active expressions of godliness.

In *Religion Our True Interest*, Watson also demonstrates the connection between holy conference and meditation. Having delight in Christ, based on sound knowledge of Him is the key to being able to be speak of Him freely with others.[53] Watson argues that Christians can only converse genuinely about the holy things they have spent time pondering in their hearts. Conference can only occur when the affections have been appropriately stirred. This link is explicit in his description of the necessity of meditation, which immediately follows his section on holy conference: 'The Second Character of the Godly *in special* is, *they thought upon God's name*; these Saints when they were together did *speak* of God, when they were alone they did *think* of God.'[54]

Thus, it is clear that for Watson holy conference was to public, corporate Christianity, what meditation was to private devotion. This is significant to our understanding of his piety, as it eschews any notions of hyper-individualised spirituality.[55] Participation in communal Christian life is a pillar of personal piety on par with secluded contemplation. Watson's paragon of piety could not be reduced to the 'Christian on the Mount' seeking mystical, bilateral communion with God. She was also one of '[those] who feared the

50. *RTI*, 94.
51. *RTI*, 85-91.
52. *RTI*, 99.
53. *RTI*, 100.
54. *RTI*, 102-103.
55. Schwanda acknowledges the "importance of both communal and personal practices" in Watson's piety, but only gives the Lord's Supper as an example of the corporate element. "Saints' Desire," 90-91.

Lord,"[56] a Christian who lived and spoke publicly with her fellow-citizens of the "Jerusalem above."[57]

Prayer

Prayer has a vital place in piety across the whole breadth of Christian traditions. Yet this universality does not detract from its importance for the Puritans in general and Watson in particular, when it came to developing and practicing godliness. In *A Puritan Theology: Doctrine for Life* Beeke and Jones state that "Puritan piety was marked by a devotion to prayer."[58] They proceed to quote Iain Murray, who declared, "There was no duty higher in Puritan esteem than the duty of prayer."[59] With respect to Watson, Murray's assertion needs to be qualified in light of proper consideration of the other spiritual disciplines. And yet, our subject epitomises the Puritan concern with prayer by tying it to the efficacy of almost every other duty in the cultivation of godliness.

The relationship between prayer and the affections appears to be one of chicken and egg for Watson. Each is contingent upon the existence of the other. Proper prayer required godly affections like fervency and zeal to be effective. At the same time, prayer was a crucial means of developing the heart affections that were consistent with godliness.[60] At times, Watson presents affections like fear or love as the source out of which the godly person's prayers proceed.[61] In other passages he suggests that a spiritual stirring may occur during prayer, often in connection with some sort of mystical experience.[62] And elsewhere, a change or invigoration of the heart, mood and affections is presented as an after-effect of prayer or an answer to the believer's request to God for revitalisation.[63] While the saint can be held responsible for having these vital affections in prayer and seeking them through divine supplication, Watson's teaching

56. *RTI*, 1.
57. *RTI*, 1, 84.
58. Beeke and Jones, *Puritan Theology*, 787.
59. Iain H. Murray, *The Puritan Hope: A Study in Revival and the Interpretation of Prophecy* (Edinburgh: Banner of Truth Trust, 1971), 99, quoted in Beeke and Jones, *Puritan Theology*, 787.
60. For a brief discussion of this conundrum in British Protestantism, more broadly, see Ryrie, *Being Protestant*, 68-69.
61. *RTI*, 18, 43-44, 55-56; *BPD*, 1:142, 223; *BPD*, 2:423; *BPD*, 3:439; *GMP*, 124.
62. *GMP*, 120-121; *HTS*, 34-35.
63. *GMP*, 126; *Beatitudes*, 188; *BPD*, 2:248.

on prayer continues to highlight the Christian's dependence upon God. Specifically, the Holy Spirit is to be sought if pious affections are to be produced in their heart. "Implore the Spirit of God, *Jude 20. Praying in the Holy Ghost.* The Holy Ghost both indicts prayer, and inflames it ... pray *for* the Holy Ghost, that you may pray *in* the Holy Ghost."[64]

This understanding concerning prayer and piety relates to the picture of God as Majestic Sovereign, upon which Watson's concept of godliness depends.[65] Praying to God was one means of beholding Him through faith. This sight of the Almighty in His glory would have a profound effect upon any believer as they appreciated the magnitude of the divine splendour.[66] Prayer also expressed the saint's earnest desire to be with God and delight in Him. The ensuing communion with God through prayer was critical to the sustenance and progress of godliness.[67] Prayer also brought glory to God in the way that it demonstrated the believer's humble dependence on the Lord as Provider and Supplier of all necessary things.

Watson also saw prayer as pivotal to other key aspects of the believer's spiritual formation. If a person is not sure that they are one of the godly, they should pray for the Spirit to come and work in their heart in a manner that makes godliness possible.[68] Prayer for purity of heart and the ongoing spiritual work of sanctification are also cited as necessary, as are prayers for divine grace to enable the Christian life.[69] Watson also taught that several qualities he regarded as intrinsic to godliness—such as meekness, peaceability and love for God—should be sought from God by means of prayer.[70]

In *The Lord's Prayer*, Watson teaches that the petition "thy will be done" is a request to God for both the ability to live in obedience to His revealed will and the capacity to endure suffering as a Christian.[71] Indeed, since suffering has an important role to play in the Christian life it is appropriate for believers to pray that God would enable them to face it in a way that is fitting.

---

64. *GMP*, 130-131.
65. This topic is treated further in Chapter 9.
66. *GMP*, 123.
67. *Beatitudes*, 350.
68. *GMP*, 127-128.
69. *Beatitudes*, 294; *BPD*, 2:339, 422-423; *BPD*, 3:458ff; *BPD*, 1:26, 144, 218, 226; *HTS*, 108.
70. *Beatitudes*, 168, 323; *BPD*, 2:248; *HTS*, 38.
71. *BPD*, 3:512.

> It is a gift of God to be able to suffer, pray for this gift; do not think you can be able of yourselves to lay down life and liberty for Christ: Peter was overconfident of himself. John 13.37. *I will lay down my life for thy sake*; but Peter's strength undid him; Peter had habitual grace, but he wanted auxiliary grace; Christians need fresh gales from heaven; pray for the Spirit to animate you in your sufferings.[72]

Both affectional piety and godly action are impossible apart from prayer. This is well encapsulated by the following quote from *Godly Man's Picture*,

> A good Christian holds secret intelligence with heaven ... Private prayer keeps up the trade of godliness; when closet-holiness is laid aside, there is a stab given to the heart of religion.[73]

Watson also makes the success of several of the means for cultivating godliness dependent upon prayer. His general principle was that the performance of any religious duty required both "Examination and Ejaculation" [i.e. prayer] as proper preparation of the heart.[74] But his writings also give specific attention to the importance of prayer in relation to means of grace. Prayer for the ministers of the Word is essential if their ministry is to have an effect on others.

> God's Spirit must fill the sails of our ministry. It is not the hand that scatters the seed which makes it spring up, but the dews and influences of heaven: So it is not our preaching but the Divine influence of the Spirit that makes grace grow in men's hearts ... It is God's Spirit blowing in us that makes the Preaching of the Word by a Divine Enchantment allure souls to Christ.[75]

If someone finds that the preaching of the Word has little effect upon them, the problem may be attributed to their lack of prayer for the preacher.[76] Likewise, private Bible reading also must be joined to prayer in order to be spiritually profitable.

> Pray that the same Spirit that wrote the Word may *assist* you in the reading of it; that God's Spirit would show you the wonderful Things of his Law. *Go near*, saith God to *Philip, join thyself to this Chariot,* Acts 8.29. So when God's Spirit joins

72. *Beatitudes*, 456-457. See also, Ryrie, *Being Protestant*, 239-240.
73. *GMP*, 241-242.
74. *Beatitudes*, 280.
75. *Beatitudes*, 16.
76. *Beatitudes*, 17.

himself with this Chariot of the Word, then it becomes effectual.[77]

With respect to meditation, Watson urged Christians to pray for heavenly-mindedness and the ability to negate distractions and preoccupation with vain thoughts.[78] Concerning the mortification of sin and self-denial, it is prayer that "weeds out" and "purge[s] out sin" and believers are to "pray for mortifying grace" that will enable them to kill the sin within.[79] Watson makes prayer the key "spiritual weapon" for defeating sin. "The best way to combat with sin is upon our knees."[80] Prayer is needed for participation in effective holy conference—God must loosen the lips that "Satan hath locked up."[81] Watson saw prayer as the means for overcoming inhibitions that would prevent a Christian from speaking openly to others about Jesus.[82] Finally, the sacraments (which I will turn my attention to below), particularly the Lord's Supper were only approached correctly if preceded by prayer for God's blessing and the Spirit's activity.[83] Thus prayer was present at every turn in Watson's programme for progress in piety. It was essential in itself for the instigation of affections and the requisite ingredient for making the other means effectual in their respective roles.

Sacraments

The sacraments also had a vital role to play in cultivating and sustaining godliness. Brown has noted that for English nonconformists during the Restoration period, baptism provided a sense of belonging to Christ and the godly community, while the Lord's Supper also fortified their faith in the midst of difficult times.[84] Watson's sacramentology has attracted scholarly attention from historian Alec Ryrie. He regards it as a valuable, yet "atypical," example of how the ordinances could hold an important place in Puritan faith and practice.[85] Schwanda has observed, "Watson reveals some of his most contemplative-mystical themes in his discussion of the

77. *BPD*, 1:18.
78. *BPD*, 2:386-387, 423.
79. *GMP*, 128; *Beatitudes*, 346; *BPD*, 2:387.
80. *HTS*, 20.
81. *RTI*, 101.
82. *RTI*, 101.
83. *BPD*, 2:419.
84. Brown, *Spirituality in Adversity*, 234-238, 257-260.
85. Alec Ryrie, *Private and Domestic Devotion in Early Modern Britain* (Oxford: Routledge, 2016): 128-130.

Eucharist."[86]

It must be noted at this point that the Lord's Supper played a more significant part in Watson's thought on how to grow in godliness than Baptism. The reasons for this are readily comprehended. The supper was partaken of by believers on a regular basis. Watson does not specify how frequently, but he does insist it should be "often."[87] Baptism typically occurred during infancy and was an isolated event. Therefore, for the purposes Watson proposes the sacraments to have, the Lord's Supper was experienced *consciously* and *frequently* and therefore could have a direct effect upon the believer during the sacrament. Baptism, on the other hand, was personally *immemorial* and *distant* and could therefore only be experienced vicariously (in witnessing the baptism of others) or through reflective meditation upon what was intended and symbolised by the rite undergone in infancy.[88] Therefore, without dismissing baptism as insignificant to Watson's piety, the Lord's Supper is the major sacrament which demands greater attention.

As with prayer, Watson sees the sacraments as capable of nourishing godly affections.[89] Partaking of the supper can be a gateway to experiencing divine joy: "The Godly have in the use of the Ordinances, had such Divine Raptures of Joy and Soul-transfigurations, that they have been carried above the World, and despised all things here below."[90] In fact "the flourishing of joy" is said to be one of the "two grand ends of the Lord's Supper" (the other being the "strengthening of faith").[91] Another "end" mentioned elsewhere is "to work in us an endeared love to Christ."[92] In the Supper, the Christian is confronted by the love of the crucified Saviour, which should solicit an affective response of love from the beholder.[93] But the same beholding ought to also generate a real response of sorrow. "O Christian, when thou lookest on Christ in the Sacrament, remember how oft thou hast crucified him ... O remember Christ with Sorrow, to think thou shouldst make his

86. Schwanda, "Saints' Desire," 92.
87. *BPD*, 2:415.
88. See Wallace's similar observation about baptism's place in later English Puritan piety in *Spirituality*, xxvii.
89. For a recent treatment of this theme, see Schwanda, "Saints' Desire," 87-89.
90. *BPD*, 1:10.
91. *BPD*, 1:212.
92. *BPD*, 2:415.
93. *BPD*, 2:415, 420.

Wounds bleed afresh!"[94] While to some, the collective presence of these affections may seem to be incompatible, Watson elucidated the relationship between them: "the Soul oft comes Weeping after Christ in the Sacrament, and God sends it away Weeping for Joy."[96]

Watson believed that it was the Spirit who determined how the sacraments were effected. Yet he also believed that there was a need for preparation of both the heart and mind prior to partaking of the sacrament. Indeed an attitude of "reverence and solemn devotion" should already be present when coming to the ordinance. Watson warned his parishioners that "The Lord takes notice of the Frame of our Hearts when we come to his Table."[96] Watson speaks of a prerequisite "soul-dress[ing]" that must take place in order for the sacrament to be of real benefit.[97] This includes elements such as sincere repentance; "Holy Meditation and Heart-Consideration;" and a "vigorous" stirring of the heart leading to an appetite of "inflamed desires [for] Christ."[98] Only when the Lord's Supper is approached with this proper preparation could the participant expect to not only be blessed further affectively, but to have a meaningful encounter with Christ Himself.

This leads us to the special place of the Lord's Supper for Watson in the saint's relationship with God. When it came to its capacity for facilitating experiential communion with God and Christ, Watson was willing to say, "The Lord's Supper is the most Spiritual and sweet ordinance that ever was instituted."[99] This is clarified by his subsequent comparison with prayer.

> Here we have to do more immediately with the Person of Christ. In Prayer we draw nigh to God, in the Sacrament we become one with him. In Prayer we look up to Christ, in the Sacrament by Faith we touch him.[100]

It may be of surprise to some within the Reformed tradition that Watson ventures to make the Lord's Supper superior in this respect to the Word as well.[101] In the same passage of *The Ten Commandments*

94. *BPD*, 2:415.
95. *BPD*, 1:211.
96. *BPD*, 2:412.
97. *BPD*, 2:418-419.
98. *BPD*, 2:412, 419.
99. *BPD*, 2:412.
100. *BPD*, 2:412. For a similar emphasis in the wider Puritan movement, see Hall, *Puritans*, 123.
101. Schwanda, "Saints' Desire," 89.

he goes on to say: "In the Word Preached we hear Christ's Voice, in the Sacrament we feed on him."[102] Similar language is employed in his separate discourse on the Lord's Supper: "And herein the Sacrament excels the Word Preached. The Word is a Trumpet to proclaim Christ, the Sacrament is a Glass to represent him."[103]

This idea of the Lord's Supper as a potential communion-encounter with God or Christ intersects with his emphasis on godliness at an integral point. Any such encounter is a meeting with Christ that profoundly affects the soul and is a foretaste of the eternal beatific vision.[104]

> [I]f Christ be so sweet in an Ordinance, when we have but short glances, and dark glimpses of him by faith, Oh then, how delightful and ravishing will his presence be in heaven, when we shall see him *face to face,* and be for ever in his loving embraces?[105]

As a foretaste of the heavenly reward, an experience of the divine presence and a "glimpse" of Christ's glorious loveliness, the Lord's Supper aided the believer in their spiritual apprehension of God and spurred them on in a life of godliness.

The sacraments also had a valuable role to play in the believer's battle with sin. Remembering the significance of one's baptism confronted the godly with the claim that God had on their life and testified against the treasonous nature of sin.[106] Proper participation in the Supper could have a powerful effect against indwelling sin. "[The] end of the sacrament [is] the mortifying of corruption. To see Christ crucified for us, is a means to crucify sin in us."[107] Building on this theme, Watson urges Christians "to pray that this great Ordinance may be *Poison* to our Sins, and *Food* to our Graces" and calls the Supper "an Antidote to expel the Poison of Sin," which requires frequent administration.[108]

Based on the apostolic imperative "But let a man examine himself, and so let him eat" (1 Cor 11:28), Watson saw self-examination and confession of sin as an essential part of the "Soul-dress" required of

102. *BPD*, 2:412.
103. *Eucharist*, 2.
104. Schwanda, "Saints' Desire," 87-88.
105. *GMP*, 355; See also *BPD*, 1:123.
106. *BPD*, 2:411-412.
107. *BPD*, 2:415.
108. *BPD*, 2:415, 419.

those partaking of the Supper.[109] To come to the Table without this crucial step was perilous to the soul and would ruin any hopes of a spiritual enjoyment of Christ.[110] Thus, as often as the Supper was observed, it provided regular opportunities for dealing with "*Secret Corruption* in the Heart" that hindered the believer's growth in godliness.[111] Finally, the Supper was often the place where the godly became "evangelical weepers"—exhibiting the penitential mark of Watson's godly Christian.

> To think before we come to a Sacrament of our sins against the Bowel-Mercies of God the Father, the bleeding Wounds of God the Son, the blessed Inspirations of God the Holy Ghost, it is enough to broach our Eyes with Tears, and put us into an Holy Agony of Grief and Compunction.[112]

Thus, the sacraments—especially the Lord's Supper—had a multifaceted role to play in advancing godliness in the life of a believer. It is plain that Watson believed that a deficiency in piety would occur when proper use of these means was neglected.

Summary

While more could be said about each of Watson's proposed ways to cultivate godliness, the above survey brings us closer to a fully-orbed appreciation of how he saw the increase of piety as possible. Means involving the Word of God (i.e. private reading, listening to preaching) were foundational to everything in Watson's mind. Yet they were unprofitable if the Christian failed to combine them with other holy ordinances. Doctrinal instruction by means of catechesis was one such pillar that provided a sound theological basis for piety and protected the flock from heresy and defective devotion. Meditation in Watson's spirituality, as suggested by key scholars in this area of study, was a necessary means for generating genuine pious affections in response to received theological truths. Yet, the special place of meditation in Watson's spiritual regime is qualified by his emphasis on other disciplines. Self-denial is the most notable, but this is also true of holy conference, prayer and the sacraments.

---

109. *BPD*, 2:415.
110. *BPD*, 2:416-417.
111. *BPD*, 2:416.
112. *BPD*, 2:418.

Excursus
"Queen of days"
The Sabbath in Watson's piety

In line with the rest of Puritanism, the Lord's Day (alternatively referred to as the Sabbath) played a crucial role in the cultivation of godliness in Watson's schema of piety.[a] While not the same in nature as the individual means of grace I have discussed in this chapter, the sacred day of Sunday served as the locus in which most of their operations occurred. It was the weekly apex of participation in corporate piety for the Christian, but Watson also promoted it as a time for heightened personal and private expressions of devotion.[b] The godly were called to physically, mentally and spiritually leave their secular affairs and enter a phase of intense concentration on the divine. The essence and flavour of Watson's enthusiasm for Sabbath observance is expressed in his treatment of the fourth commandment,

> The business on the Week-Day makes us too forgetful of God and our Souls; the Sabbath brings God into our Remembrance. When the Dust of the World falling hath clogged the Wheels of our Affections, that they would scarce move towards God, the Sabbath comes and oils the Wheels of our Affections, and now they move swiftly in Religion: Therefore God hath appointed a Sabbath to ripen our Holiness. On this Day the Thoughts contemplate Heaven, the Tongue speaks of God, and is as the Pen of a ready Writer; now the Eyes drop Tears, now the Soul burns in Love. When the Heart was all the Week frozen, now on the Sabbath it is melted with the Word. The Sabbath is a friend to Religion, it files off the Rust of our Graces, it is a Spiritual Jubilee wherein the Soul is set to converse with its Maker.[c]

So vital was the Sabbath to piety that Watson could not conceive

a. This is a fairly uncontroversial point. See, for instance, Beeke and Jones, *Meet the Puritans*, 656.
b. *BPD*, 2:333.
c. *BPD*, 2:332.

of godliness apart from it. Such a position produces a mixture of consequences. Positively, there was a functional need for the observance of a set day for intensified religious devotion in Watson's vision for Christian spirituality. The gathering of saints to hear the Word, receive the Supper and confer about holy subjects required the allocation of time free from distraction—as did private sessions of prayer, Bible reading, meditation and self-examination. From this perspective, God had not only granted His children the means of growing in grace, but He had ordained a fixed time to ensure that they were experienced regularly. Neglecting the Sabbath was simply incompatible with progress in piety.

Yet, a potential negative consequence was that Watson appears to exclude from the ranks of the godly any Christian that did not share his particular understanding and practice with respect to the Lord's Day. Those guilty of "Sabbath profanation" were "sacrilegious" and would be condemned on the day of judgement and sentenced to the fires of hell.[d] Watson's writings on the subject suggest he has in mind some of his irreverent compatriots—perhaps those drinking in a raucous public house instead of church on Sunday morning, or playing a loutish game of football in the afternoon instead of leading their family in devotion. Left uncertain are the implications for the spiritual state of devout, moderate members of the English church who were not strict sabbatarians like Watson.[e] Likewise, one wonders if he might have given pause to reconsider some of his language if he looked beyond England to pious Lutherans and Reformed Christians on the Continent, who also fell short of the Puritan rigours for Sabbath observance.[f]

d. *HTS*, 70; *Mischief*, 59-61; *BPD*, 2:331; *Beatitudes*, 469.

e. Including, for instance, Calvinist, conformist clergy such as John Prideaux (1578-1650) and Samuel Ward (1572–1643). See John Prideaux, *The Doctrine of the Sabbath* (1634) (Oxford: TCP, 2003). http://ota.ox.ac.uk/id/A10094; Kenneth L. Parker, *The English Sabbath: A Study of Doctrine and Discipline from the Reformation to the Civil War* (Cambridge: Cambridge University Press, 1988): 193.

f. For Lutheranism see Mark Granquist, "Sunday and Sabbatarianism," *Dictionary of Luther and the Lutheran Traditions,* Timothy Wengart (ed.) (Grand Rapids: Baker, 2017): 708. A scholarly debate over the extent and strictness of Dutch Reformed sabbatarianism is ongoing. Often the continental view is presented as less stringent than the British perspective on the Sabbath. E.g. Carl Trueman, "Reformed Orthodoxy in Britain," *SBJT* 14:4 (2010): 8. For a recent work arguing against this idea, see Kyle J. Dieleman, *The Battle for the Sabbath in the Dutch Reformation: Devotion or Desecration?* (Gottingen: Vandenhoeck & Ruprecht, 2019): 21-26. See also Daniel Hyde, "Regulae de Observatione Sabbathi: The Synod of Dort's (1618–19) Deliverance on the Sabbath" *PRJ* 4:1 (2012): 161-163, 172-173, 177-180, 183. At the very least, there were devout, Reformed Christians on the Continent who were contemporaneous to Watson, yet did not share the view he propounded with respect to Sabbath observance. See Casey B. Carmichael, *A Continental View: Johannes*

Thus, the setting aside of the Lord's Day for pious devotion was a necessary component for the enactment of Watson's vision of godliness. Yet the strictness of his Sabbatarian prohibitions—particularly relating to matters of recreation—combined with his condemnatory assertions about Sabbath-breakers, ran the risk of spilling over into legalism and excluding genuine saints from his definition of godliness.

Cocceius's Federal Theology of the Sabbath (Gottingen: Vandenhoeck & Ruprecht, 2019): 7, 55, 140-141.

Chapter 6
"The End of Godliness:"*
The aims and outcomes of Watson's piety

Watson was convinced of multiple motivations for pursuing the life of affectional piety he advocated. Across his works, there are a number of aims, outcomes and benefits that can be attained by a Christian who possesses godliness and is growing in it.

The Glorification of God

Watson's *magnum opus* was a posthumous publication of his Sunday afternoon expositions of the WSC—a testimony to how important he regarded the theological framework of the Westminster Assembly of Divines.[1] The foundational statement of the WSC is well known:

> Q: What is the chief end of man?
> A: To glorify God and enjoy him forever.

It has been noted by Robert Swanton that the question itself and the theological outlook that stands behind it are indebted

---

* Title taken from *Beatitudes*, 64.

1. It appears as though Watson would have spent over 3 years working his way through the WSC, as the full three volumes of *Body of Divinity* consists of 176 separate lectures, which probably would have been delivered each Sunday afternoon at Watson's church (see *BPD*, 1:iv). There is a lack of clear historical evidence that can be used to establish a definite date for these lectures. The most likely period would be the Crosby Hall years (1672-86), where Watson had greater stability of ministry, compared to the "outlaw years" (1662-72) where he would not have had ease in delivering regular catechetical lectures. This period also saw a lack of published material compared to earlier in his life (the one work being published was Religion our True Interest in 1681, his final written work), which would suggest he was perhaps occupied with other matters during these years. Barker, "A Body of Divinity," 202-203.

to John Calvin and the catechism he produced almost a century earlier.[2] This principal question and answer also formed the starting point for Watson's practical divinity. But Watson's exposition of the catechetical opening show that he was not merely acting under the constraints he had placed upon himself by structuring his *Body of Divinity* along the model of this quintessential Presbyterian document. Watson shared the theological outlook of the Westminster divines and Calvin in regarding the glorification and enjoyment of God as the primary consideration in all matters of divinity. And this was relevant for understanding his goals in promoting godliness.

When Watson describes the nature of what it means to glorify God in *Body of Divinity*, it amounts to something similar to "being godly" in his thought, as expressed elsewhere.[3] He explains that on the one hand, God has an essential or intrinsic glory (the attribute being responded to by the godly), which cannot be added to or detracted from by any creature.[4] On the other hand, God is glorified by humans when they are "lifting up his Name in the World, and magnifying him in the eyes of others."[5] Watson nominates four aspects of glorifying God that echo his presentation of godliness as affectional, attitudinal and active. *Appreciation* is "to set God highest in our Thoughts, to have a venerable Esteem of him."[6] It is about admiring the attributes of God that one has come to see and know through the gospel.[7] *Adoration* is the rendering of appropriate reverence towards God as expressed in acts of worship.[8] It is almost identical in meaning to the Greek idea of godliness as "right worship" (*eusebeia*), as Watson emphasises the need for precision in worshipping God in the way He Himself has commanded.[9] *Affection* is the heart response of love towards God and the treasuring of him above all other delights. As Watson summarises beautifully, "He who is the chief of our happiness hath the chief of our affections."[10] Finally, *subjection* is the Christian's willing obedience and active service towards God in response to His glorious kingship. This

2. R. Swanton, "The Theology of Westminster," *Reformed Theological Review* (May 1943): 30.
3. Whereas glorification of God was the "chief end of man" in *BPD*, 1. Watson tells his readers, in *GMP*, that "godliness is the end of your Creation." *GMP*, 298.
4. *BPD*, 1:1.
5. *BPD*, 1:1.
6. *BPD*, 1:1.
7. *BPD*, 1:1-2.
8. *BPD*, 1:2.
9. *BPD*, 1:2.
10. *BPD*, 1:2.

is the practical, ordinary, day-to-day means of glorifying God by diligently following all of His commandments (in distinction from the honouring of God in set times of private devotion or public worship).[11]

Thus, the core components of glorifying God (as the "chief end of man") and being godly are essentially the same: appropriate regard for God in response to theological knowledge; precision in worship according to God's instructions; raising of the affections towards God and living in a way that displays what Watson called "exact harmony between holy Principles and Practises."[12] It is hardly an overstatement of the relationship between these two ideas to conclude that the goal of Watson's emphasis on godliness was the public glorification of God. The cultivation of godly reverence and affection was aimed at ensuring that God received the glory and honour He deserved. The individual believer glorified Him in their hearts and their subsequent, visible displays of genuine piety forced others to reckon with God's majesty, goodness and magnanimity. It is clear that Watson denied any mutability in God's intrinsic glory. Yet he believed, with the Westminster divines, that humanity's chief purpose was to increase the ascriptive glory of God through confession, praise and godly living that reflected God's glorious character.

Watson goes on to list seventeen ways people can glorify God and again there is plenty of overlap with his exhortations to godliness elsewhere.[13]

Christians may glorify God by the following ways:		
1. "when we aim purely at God's Glory"	7. "in working out our own Salvation"	13. "when we have an eye at God, both in our Natural and in our Civil Actions"
2. "by an ingenuous Confession of Sin"	8. "by living to God"	14. "by labouring to draw others to God"
3. "by Believing"	9. "by walking cheerfully"	15. "when we suffer for God"
4. "by being tender of God's Glory"	10. "by standing up for his Truths"	16. "when we give God the glory of all we do"
5. "by Fruitfulness"	11. "by praising of him"	17. "by an holy Life."
6. by being content where Providence places us	12. "by being zealous for his Name"	

11. *BPD*, 1:2.
12. *GMP*, iii.
13. *BPD*, 1:3-8.

Each means presupposes that the Christian has come to know something of God's glory before proceeding to glorify him appropriately. But the link between godliness and glorification is most clear in Watson's description of how believers glorify God by a holy life. "Though the main Work of Religion lies in the Heart, yet our *light must so shine,* that others may behold it ... when the Saints ... live as if they had seen the Lord with bodily eyes, and been with him upon the Mount, they adorn Religion, and bring Revenues of Glory to the Crown of Heaven."[14] Here it is explicit: proper appreciation of divine revelation produces godliness. This, in turn, glorifies God more fully by esteeming him before others through holy living. This is, for Watson, the most important outcome of increased godliness.

The Positive Impact of Godliness upon Others

Watson repeatedly emphasised the impact that godly living could have upon those who witnessed it in the lives of the saints. In a sermon entitled "The Good Practitioner," he remarks: "To be practitioners in Religion will not only do your selves good, but others: This will both honour Religion, and propagate it."[15] In terms of propagation, he argues that proper practice of piety is the most effective means of persuading others of the truth of Christianity and confirming people in the faith. Inconsistencies in religious devotion would send a harmful message that would produce the wrong conclusions about the genuineness of the Christian message.[16] This was an important dichotomy for Watson's understanding of godliness. Failure to live as though one's "holy principles" were true provided an excuse for people to make light of God. An earnest life, consistent with the glorious truths of the gospel, was able to promote a higher esteem for God and counteract the negative impressions some had of religion due to its false professors.[17] The ultimate characteristic of the godly in *Godly Man's Picture*, relates to being "an instrument of making others godly." Watson holds this to be necessary due to "the nature of godliness" itself. "It is like fire, which assimilates and turns everything into its own nature; where there is the fire of grace in the

14. *BPD*, 1:7-8.
15. "The Good Practitioner," *Beatitudes* (1660) (Oxford: EEBO, 2011): 645.
16. "The Good Practitioner," 646.
17. "The Good Practitioner," 646.

heart, it will endeavour to inflame others."[18]

A key extension of piety, which lifted the public estimation of biblical Christianity, was godly praxis—particularly acts of charity and mercy.[19] In *Body of Divinity*, this aspect of mercy is explicit: "The sum and definition of Religion is—Be *rich* in *works* of *Mercy*, be helpful to the Bodies and Souls of others. Scatter your *golden* Seeds; let *the Lamp* of your profession be filled with the Oil of Charity."[20] Watson revisits this theme later in his exposition of the WSC, by establishing a clear link between godliness and the showing of mercy and charity towards others.

> 'Tis our Excellency to be like God. *Godliness is God-likeness.* And wherein are we more like him than in Acts of Bounty and Munificence? ... The more helpful we are to others, the more like we are to God.[21]

Later in the same section, mercy appears again as the outworking of godly faith, which brings God glory in the eyes of others.

> To do good to others in Necessity, *keeps up the Credit of Religion.* Works of Mercy *adorn* the Gospel as the Fruit Adorns the Tree. When our *Light so shines* that others see our Good Works, this glorifies God, Crowns Religion, silenceth the Lips of Gain-sayers. *Basil* saith, Nothing rendered the True Religion more famous in the Primitive Times, and made more Proselytes to it, than the Bounty and Charity of the Christians.[22]

This citation of Basil points towards the ultimate goal of lifting the public esteem of God through godly living and benevolent actions. For Watson, the goal was not merely people speaking well of God and Christians because of positive publicity. It was to see people convinced of the magnitude of God and the truths of the gospel, so that they themselves might become regenerate, whole-hearted glorifiers of God.[23] Desiring the salvation of others and seeing the

18. *GMP*, 264.
19. For instance, Watson said of Job's advocacy for the poor: "This is that takes off the odium and obloquy from Religion, and makes others speak well of holiness, when they see good works, as hand-maids waiting upon this Queen." *APA*, 26.
20. *BPD*, 1:57.
21. *BPD*, 2:366.
22. *BPD*, 2:367
23. In fact Watson suggested that the conversion of the wicked was virtually impossible unless they were exposed to the influence of the godly: "The godly living among the wicked, by their prudent advice, and pious example have won them to the embracing of Religion; if there were not some godly among the wicked, how in a probable way

development of piety within their lives was a natural by-product of one's own godliness. Watson called it "a signal evidence of our salvation."[24] Failure to commend Christ to others signified a lack of appreciation for him in one's own heart.[25] In fact, for Watson, apathy concerning the salvation of others signified a hypocrisy that precluded godliness.[26]

But the goal of propagating godliness amongst family, friends and community was not restricted to a desire for their salvation. The genuine conversion of others to godliness through the gospel testimony and the living example of the saints achieves the primary Puritan goal for godliness I discussed above. God's ascriptive glory is increased in Christ.

> Tis a glory to Christ, when multitudes are born to him; every star adds a lustre to the sky, every convert, is a member added to Christ's body, and a jewel adorning his Crown. Though Christ's glory cannot be increased, as he is God, yet as he is Mediator, it may; the more are saved, the more Christ is exalted; why else should the Angels rejoice at the Conversion of a Sinner? but because now Christ's glory shines the more.[27]

Thus, for Watson, the more Christians living consistent, godly lives—the more likely others are to embrace the gospel and be encouraged in their own godliness. Any multiplication in godliness is an advance in the church's desire to see more of humanity glorifying God. In this, it realises the purpose it was created for.

The believer's preparedness for death and eternity

Godliness certainly carried personal benefits for the individual believer as well. For instance, Watson saw great pastoral value in the idea that true piety made the saint ready to face the end of their earthly life and to enjoy their eternal, heavenly life. Several scholars of Puritanism have observed the importance of this aspect within Puritan spirituality. For instance, Dewey Wallace writes, "A holy

without a miracle can we imagine that the wicked should be converted?" *Autarkeia*, 107.

24. *GMP*, 270.
25. *GMP*, 66.
26. *GMP*, 266.
27. *GMP*, 265-266.

death was for the Puritans the culmination of a holy life."[28] Gordon Wakefield devotes a chapter to the subject in his *Puritan Devotion*, remarking in the opening paragraph, "All spiritual writers devote much space to instructing their readers how to die well. Indeed, we may describe this as the purpose of all the Puritan guides to a holy life."[29] To have properly honoured and glorified God with one's earthly life was a source of comfort and confidence at the hour of death.[30] The Christian who has examined their life and found the true evidences of godliness can rest assured: "he is as sure to go to heaven, as if he were in heaven already."[31] By contrast, Watson states in the introduction of *Godly Man's Picture* that "To have only a pretence of godliness will yield no comfort at death."[32] Those who have not taken care to ensure they have genuine godliness deceive themselves in death.[33] Watson insists numerous times that many of the wicked will wish they had godliness at the hour of death. Moreover, every hypocrite and ungodly person will wish they possessed it immediately after death, as they experience eternal condemnation.[34]

This powerful contrast between the godly and the wicked at death permeates Watson's writings. It is therefore unsurprising to find him suggesting that the godly will often look forward to death due to the immense gains they are set to make the moment they leave this life.[35] The essential ingredient of godliness that is heavenly-mindedness, prepares the saint for death precisely because the object of their lifelong meditation is waiting on the other side of it.[36] The genuine Christian has the immense consolation that however painful, troubling or unexpected the circumstances of their death may be, this brief time of darkness will be swallowed up by the glorious light of the beatific vision.[37]

28. Wallace, *Spirituality*, 1.
29. Gordon Wakefield, *Puritan Devotion: Its Place in the Development of Christian Piety* (Eugene: Wipf & Stock, 1959): 143.
30. *BPD*, 1:233-234; *BPD*, 3:511; *GMP*, 310-315.
31. *GMP*, 271.
32. *GMP*, 12.
33. *BPD*, 1:141.
34. *GMP*, 293; *Mischief*, 29-30; *APL*, 15. See also *BPD*, 3:488-489, 503.
35. Powerful "foretaste[s]" of celestial felicity near the hour of death are well-attested among earlier generations of English Puritans. Ryrie, *Being Protestant*, 84-85.
36. *GMP*, 144-145; *BPD*, 1:234; Wakefield, *Puritan Devotion*, 152.
37. *Beatitudes*, 305-306. Wallace notes the consolatory value of heavenly mindedness amongst English Puritans more broadly. "Heavenly mindedness was the spiritual person's foretaste of the joys of heaven through meditation. This not only strengthened the soul for earthly trials but was one place in Puritan spirituality where the mystical

An appreciation of what heaven is like constitutes one of the motivations for godliness. It is part of what raises the affections and fills the heart with awe. Yet the circle is completed by godliness preparing the saint for their eternal habitation. It is clear in Watson's writings that through meditation and earnest desire, the godly have already come to heaven before their time.[38] Reverential awe and intense love toward God will characterise heaven. The majestic king will be worshipped and glorified in an endless, uninhibited manner. Therefore, those whose hearts already possess such a response towards God are preparing for what their eternal future will be like. Watson is clear that the closely related attribute of holiness is most necessary for anyone who intends to dwell in the presence of God eternally. '"Without holiness no man shall see the Lord.' God is an holy God, and he will suffer no unholy Creature to come near him ... It must be a clear Eye that sees a bright Object; only an holy Heart can see God in his Glory."[39] Thus, for Watson, the godly are the only people ready to face death, enter heaven and behold God in His glory.

The contribution of godliness towards the attainment of Happiness

Along with other serious students of human nature, Christian thinkers throughout history have recognised how important the quest for happiness is in the human experience. Thomas Watson was no exception. His opinion was that genuine happiness would come as a result of growth in godliness.[40]

---

element entered. The heavenly minded person was absorbed in divine things, weaned from earth, and advanced in communion with God because proleptically transported into that blessed state where the saints see God and enjoy his presence forever." *Spirituality*, xvii.

38. Note, for example, the title of his short work on communion with God, "A Christian on Earth, Still in Heaven" (appended to the larger *A Christian on the Mount*), which explicitly conveys this idea. Wallace has identified this as a common emphasis of later English Puritan spirituality in particular: "The holy and spiritually minded person was to think much of heaven, for he or she already lived there within the soul. Accordingly, 'heavenly mindedness' was one of the most prominent themes of Puritan spirituality in [the Restoration] era." *Spirituality*, xvi-xvii. See also Schwanda, "Saints' Desire," 87.
39. *BPD*, 1:141.
40. Other Puritans shared this notion of an essential relationship between happiness and godliness. S. Bryn Roberts, in his study of the pursuit of happiness as a theme in the theology of Watson's contemporary, Ralph Venning (c. 1621-1674), summarises his findings by saying of his subject, "for Venning, the puritan experience was the pursuit

> Happiness is the mark, and centre which every man aims at. The next thing that is sought, after *being,* is being happy; and surely, the nearer the soul comes to God who is the fountain of life and peace, the nearer it approacheth to happiness.[41]

This result of godliness has a direct link with that discussed directly above. The fullness of happiness can only be gained in heaven, in the eternal presence of God. This is the very goal the godly have been pursuing.[42]

Watson repeatedly uses variations of the following maxim to stress this relationship: 'Happiness is nothing else but the Quintessence of Holiness; Holiness is Glory militant, and Happiness Holiness triumphant."[43] He is clear that there will always be things that interfere with our enjoyment of godliness in this life. Yet, at the same time, he allows for the present enjoyment of God through the means of grace. Present enjoyment is also attainable by drawing on the sure promises of eternal felicity that every true believer possesses by grace through faith.[44] Of particular significance is Watson's contention that godliness allows for happiness in this world in the midst of affliction. Whereas the happiness of others seems to largely depend on their circumstances, the saints can rejoice in the darkest experiences of life. This is because their trials draw them closer to God—which is the key to all happiness.[45]

Happiness—beginning in this life and culminating into perfection in the age to come—as a result of godliness is a significant aspect in Watson's thought on the subject. It completes the second clause of the WSC's stated foundational purpose for humanity: to not only glorify God but *to enjoy him forever.* Thus, the goal and outcome of godliness in Watson's theological schema is very much connected to the realisation of the great end of human life. Proper reverence and genuine affections for God are essential means of glorifying Him in one's own heart and in the eyes and hearts of others. And a thorough appreciation of God's goodness and beauty attained through studying theological truth and meditating on revealed divinity allowed the beginnings of a presently imperfect enjoyment

---

and enjoyment of happiness through godliness." Roberts, *Puritanism and the Pursuit of Happiness*, 100.

41. *Charter*, 1-2.
42. *BPD*, 1:227, 230-232.
43. *BPD*, 1:49, 232. See also *BPD*, 3:384; *Beatitudes*, 280.
44. *BPD*, 1:36, 213-214, 232-233.
45. *BPD*, 2:262.

of God. This enjoyment would increase with spiritual maturity and culminate in eternity.

Summary of PART 2

The godliness that lay at the heart of Watson's thought, devotion and ministry was the appropriate, affectional response to God's revelation of Himself to the Christian—lying between principle (theology) and practice. The characteristic features of godliness that Watson provides in his focused studies of its nature are overwhelmingly affective dispositions of the heart towards God. These result from spiritual regeneration and are a response to spiritual knowledge the saints have acquired. Watson developed a schema of spiritual theology that was designed to progressively increase the quality of these godly affections. Progress was achieved through consistent use of the means God had appointed for spiritual growth. Regular diligence in these divine ordinances provided the Christian with deeper knowledge of God to which they could further respond affectively (e.g. via attending sermons, Bible-reading, catechesis). They raised the right affections while driving out ungodly passions and desires (i.e. the meditation/mortification dynamic). They could even lead to mystical experiences of God's presence that enabled a greater appreciation of Him (e.g. prayer and the Lord's Supper). I have observed that, for Watson, the possession of this kind of vital, affective piety was necessary for realising the chief goals of the Christian life. Proper regard and affection for God (and active living which demonstrated such) was what glorified Him and drew others to do the same. The cultivation of godliness prepared the Christian's heart not only for the joys of eternity, but for greater delight in God in this life.

Thus, for Watson, the essential marker of a genuine Christian life was a heart that directed appropriate affections—such as love, fear and gratitude—towards God. This concept of godliness dominated his entire vision of what today might be termed *Christian living.* It shapes everything from the daily practices of devotion to the ultimate goals and outcomes of a life following Christ. While Watson made a valuable contribution to seventeenth century devotional literature that specifically deals with the nature of godliness, he would not have regarded his own work as unique or innovative. He was merely communicating what he understood to be the consensus position on Christian piety among his Puritan co-religionists. It is the historical-theological context of his piety that requires further attention in the following chapter.

PART 3

Godliness in Watson's theological and historical *milieu*

As a representative figure of Late English Puritanism, the chief elements of Watson's perspective on godliness were shared with his Puritan contemporaries and predecessors. Yet, Watson's piety was also expressed in deliberate contradistinction to non-Puritan forms of devotion that he viewed as antithetical to the principles and practice of true religion. Watson's typicality in relation to his Puritan religious movement can be established by way of engagement with broader studies on the piety of English Puritanism and comparison with the devotional writings of key figures from this period. Doing so will not diminish Watson's contribution to our understanding of Puritan piety. While the same substantial understanding of godliness is found in other notable late English Puritans, Watson's extensive treatment of the subject is unmatched. I noted in the previous chapter how Watson not only drew from the Scriptures to formulate his approach to piety, but was heavily indebted to pivotal theological predecessors, including Augustine, Calvin and the earlier English Puritans. The latter group establishes his piety as *Puritan* (and not merely *late Puritan*), while his influences from earlier periods of Christian history were vital to Watson's sense that his understanding of godliness was transhistorical.

Watson was confident that Puritanism represented the contemporary expression that was most accordant with both Scriptural teaching and the best of historical Christian practice. In contrast, he did not see the same timeless commitment to biblical piety in the lives of rival religious groups. Rather, he perceived them as devotional deviants. This was either due to theological error or their betrayal of divinely-mandated worship for faulty human constructs. Appreciating Watson's concerns about these counterfeit pieties is crucial for situating his views on godliness in their historical and religious context. His polemics against such groups and their devotion contribute to the distinctively late English Puritan flavour of his piety. They are almost as important as the accord between his outlook and that of his contemporaries and predecessors on the positive aspects of piety.

Chapter 7
"Patterns of Piety:"*
Watson's Puritan peers
& pious predecessors

Watson's piety in consonance with his Late English Puritan peers

A picture of Watson as representative of late English Puritan piety emerges more clearly after observing how many of the themes in his works on godliness have been identified by scholars of Puritanism as generally true of the movement. This is further reinforced by direct comparison of Watson's vision of godliness to that of several of his most notable contemporaries. While there are many possible subjects that could be selected, I shall focus on John Owen, Richard Baxter and Stephen Charnock. Owen and Baxter are both widely recognised as individual Puritans who made an important contribution to the thought and practice of the movement. They serve as representative figures of Congregationalism and moderate Presbyterianism respectively.[1] Charnock serves as a notable Puritan theologian, who straddles the Congregational-Presbyterian divide, with the additional advantage of a close personal connection to Watson.[2]

While all Puritans used the language of godliness, like Watson they could utilise a range of terms to express closely-related ideas.

---

* Title taken from *GMP*, 188.

1. Although Baxter's theological quirks must be acknowledged. See for instance, Beeke and Pederson, 66. Geoffrey Nuttall refers to Baxter and Owen as the leaders of the "right wing" and "left wing" of "moderate Puritanism" respectively. *The Holy Spirit in Puritan Faith and Experience* (Chicago: University of Chicago Press, 1992): 10.
2. See L. Siekawitch, "Stephen Charnock's Doctrine of the Knowledge of God: A Case Study of the Balance of Head and Heart in Restoration Puritanism" (PhD Thesis, Bangor: University of Wales, 2007): 27-28.

For instance, Baxter shared Watson's willingness to alternate between godliness and holiness.[3] Owen displays a preference for holiness vocabulary over references to godliness across his works. His notable emphasis on "spiritual mindedness" overlaps significantly with Watson's focus on godliness. For Charnock, "Spiritual Worship" (derived from Jesus' words in John 4:24) is the topical heading under which he discusses much of the subjects that Watson relates to godliness. We should not dismiss the nuances that may be present in their respective choice of preferred terms. Yet, I will demonstrate below that their conceptualisations of Christian devotion were closely akin to one another.

The Foundation of Knowledge

Lovelace calls the idea that "knowledge is in order to godliness" a "Puritan principle."[4] He quotes John Dod in support, "An ignorant heart is always a sinful heart: and a man without knowledge, is a man without grace."[5] This suggests that Watson was operating under an established principle that was common to all Late English Puritans. Beeke and Jones, in their study of the knowledge of God in Puritan thought, also conclude that Watson's contemporaries believed proper regard for God and obedience towards Him is impossible for those who have not received His self-disclosing revelation:

> Saving knowledge is supernatural and comes through the Mediator, Jesus Christ. The Son reveals the Father to believers by the Spirit, so that they come to know God rightly, which is impossible to achieve by natural theology alone. Hence the need for supernatural theology and supernatural faith, produced by the Spirit, to believe and obey the Scriptures.[6]

Watson's co-pastor, Stephen Charnock, shared his emphasis on the knowledge of God as an experimental, appreciative knowledge which was essential to salvation as well as foundational to godliness.[7]

3. See Gordon Mursell, *English Spirituality* (Louisville: Westminster John Knox, 2001): 365.
4. Lovelace, "Anatomy of Puritan Piety," 301.
5. John Dod, *A Plaine and Familiar Exposition of the Ten Commandments* (1622), quoted in Lovelace, "Anatomy of Puritan Piety," 301.
6. Beeke and Jones, *Puritan Theology*, 26.
7. Siekawitch, "Stephen Charnock's Doctrine of the Knowledge of God," 139-140; Stephen Charnock, *Complete Works of Stephen Charnock* (Edinburgh: James Nichol, 1864): 4:42-49; *GMP*, 17, 23.

"Now it is impossible to honour God as we ought, unless we know him as he is; and we could not know him as he is, without divine revelation from himself; for none but God can acquaint us with his own nature."[8]

L. Siekawitch notes that Charnock regarded the right kind of knowledge as essential for realising the Puritan goal of glorifying God and enjoying him forever.[9] H. Lee argues that Charnock's approach to theology seeks to move beyond the speculative realm of knowledge to an "affectionate practice"—where the heart has truly been affected by the knowledge of God.[10] This is evident in Charnock's description of the nature of "spiritual worship:"

> Worship is an act of the understanding, applying itself to the knowledge of the excellency of God, and actual thoughts of his majesty, recognising him as the supreme Lord and governor of the world, which is natural knowledge; beholding the glory of his attributes in the Redeemer, which is evangelical knowledge; this is the sole act of the spirit of man ... It is also an act of the will, whereby the soul adores and reverenceth his majesty, is ravished with his amiableness, embraceth his goodness, enters itself into an intimate communion with this most lovely object, and pitcheth all his affections upon him.[11]

In *Saint or Brute* (1662), Baxter names "solid understanding of the substantial points of religion" as the first of several elements of "sound godliness."[12] He also describes, "The reception and observation of the true rule of Godliness; which is the will of God revealed partly in nature, and fully in the Holy Scriptures," as an essential component of what it means to be godly.[13] Baxter likewise regards such knowledge as foundational, yet insufficient for pious spirituality if left unapplied. He follows the quote immediately above by saying, "This [i.e. the reception and observation of the true rule of Godliness] must be in our very hearts."[14] He is even more explicit

8. Charnock, *The Existence and Attributes of God* (Grand Rapids: Baker, 1996): 1:208-209.
9. Siekawitch, "Stephen Charnock's Doctrine of the Knowledge of God," 146. Siekawitch further identifies religious affections as the proper outcome of accumulated knowledge, 141.
10. Hangsang Lee, "Trinitarian Theology and Piety: The Attributes of God in the Thought of Stephen Charnock (1628-1680) and William Perkins (1558-1602)" (DPhil Thesis, Edinburgh: New College, 2009): 44-45.
11. Charnock, *Works*, 1:298.
12. Baxter, *Saint or Brute*, 22.
13. Baxter, *Saint or Brute*, 12.
14. Baxter, *Saint or Brute*, 12.

when giving his practical directions for godliness, "See that your religion be principally seated in the heart. Understand it as well as you can (lest it be taken from you); but never think it is savingly your own while it is but in the brain."[15]

Carl Trueman notes that Owen's theology marries "true knowledge of God" with "proper worship" or "true godliness," in line with earlier Reformed theologians.[16] When describing "spiritual-mindedness" Owen differentiates between different kinds of thought based on the relevant Greek words:

> It is not so with respect unto speculation or ratiocination merely, which is διάνοια or σύνεσις but this φρόνησις is its power as it is practical, including the habitual frame and inclination of the affections also. It is its faculty to conceive of things with a delight in them and adherence unto them, from that suitableness which it finds in them unto all its affections. Hence we translate φρονεῖν sometimes to "think,"—that is, to conceive and judge, Rom. xii. 3; sometimes to "set the affection," Col. iii. 2,—to have such an apprehension of things as to cleave unto them with our affections; sometimes to "mind," to "mind earthly things," Phil. iii. 19, which includeth that relish and savour which the mind finds in the things it is fixed on. Nowhere doth it design a notional conception of things only, but principally the engagement of the affections unto the things which the mind apprehends.[17]

Like Watson and Baxter, Owen differentiates between notional knowledge and saving knowledge and sees the illumination of the mind by the Holy Spirit as the necessary precursor to regeneration.[18] Without these elements the truth of the gospel could not be apprehended and "approbat[ed]" in a manner that would produce genuine, pious affections.[19] This leads us to the subject of regeneration.

---

15. Baxter, *Saint or Brute*, 23.
16. Carl Trueman, *The Claims of Truth: John Owen's Trinitarian Theology* (Carlisle: Paternoster, 1998): 59.
17. Owen, *Works*, 7:269.
18. Owen, *Works*, 3:231-2, 251-2. Compare Walton, *Jonathan Edwards*, 111.
19. "What is that approbation of this way of holiness which we place as an evidence of saving faith? And I say ... it is a resolved judgment of the beauty and excellency of that holiness and obedience which the gospel reveals and requires." Owen, *Works*, 5:426. See also Owen, *ΠΝΕΥΜΑΤΟΛΟΓΙΑ* (1676) (Oxford, TCP, 2012): 236. http://purl.ox.ac.uk/ota/A53720; Walton, *Jonathan Edwards*, 110-111, 242-252.

Regeneration

Watson's belief that the Spirit needed to carry out a work of regeneration and stir up affections within the heart in order for godliness to be possible, was typical of English Puritanism. Beeke and Jones affirm Watson's representative stance on this spiritual theme, by using his emphasis on regeneration to introduce it as a common focus of the broader movement.[20] They go on to say, "Personal regeneration serves as the foundation of [the Puritans'] entire practical theology. Without regeneration, their practical and experimental exhortations would have made no sense."[21] Godliness was impossible apart from regeneration because without it, "[m]an is not fit for anything good and is not even willing to be so."[22] Wallace has suggested that Puritan spirituality in the period after the Restoration "intensified the new birth as an individual experience."[23] He concurs with Beeke and Jones, stating that, for Puritans in Watson's day, "inner religion and personal change began with conversion."[24] Lovelace is willing to speak of the necessity of regeneration to piety as a universal feature of Puritan devotional manuals: "There is always a full statement, usually at the beginning, of the necessity of regeneration and the path of life through faith in the doctrines of grace."[25]

Charnock regarded regeneration as the "foundation of all practical religion" and the "principal doctrine Christ, as a prophet, came to teach."[26] Regeneration was absolutely necessary for godliness, because,

> Our end was actively to glorify God in the service of him and obedience to him; but since man is fallen into this universal decay of his faculties, and made unfit to answer this end, there is a necessity he should be made over again, and created upon a better foundation, that some principle should be in him to oppose this universal depravation, enlighten his understanding, mollify his heart, and reduce his affections to their due order and object.[27]

---

20. Beeke and Jones, *Puritan Theology*, 465.
21. Beeke and Jones, *Puritan Theology*, 465.
22. Beeke and Jones, *Puritan Theology*, 466.
23. Wallace, *Spirituality*, xv.
24. Wallace, *Spirituality*, xv.
25. Lovelace, "Anatomy of Puritan Piety," 302.
26. Charnock, *Works*, 3:7.
27. Charnock, *Works*, 3:17.

Charnock also taught that "new birth is necessary in every part of the soul," mirroring Watson's emphasis that "He who is godly is good all over; though he is regenerate only in part—yet it is in every part."[28]

Baxter regarded regeneration as the key that made theological knowledge spiritually profitable.

> Till you are renewed you study in the dark, and without that internal sight and sense, by which the life, and spirit, and kernel, of all that you study, must be known ...You have only that light that will shew you the shell, and the dead letter, but not the soul, and quickening sense, of any practical holy truth.[29]

Elsewhere he makes regeneration's relationship to godliness even more explicit, "a heart and life made new by the Spirit of Jesus Christ, is absolutely necessary to true Godliness."[30]

Owen also linked foundational knowledge to regeneration, "An internal, efficacious work of the Holy Spirit must illuminate the minds of believers so that they not only recognize the divine authority of Scripture, but also embrace the truths contained therein."[31] Elsewhere he adds, "in our regeneration the native ignorance, darkness, and blindness of our minds are dispelled, saving and spiritual light being introduced by the power of God's grace into them."[32] For Owen, regeneration,

> consists in a new spiritual supernatural vital Principle or Habit of Grace infused into the Soul, the Mind, Will and Affections by the Power of the Holy Spirit, disposing and enabling them in whom it is, unto Spiritual, Supernatural, Vital Acts of Faith and Obedience.[33]

Like Watson, he regarded regeneration as the beginning of a restoration in men and women of Adam's capacity "to live to God, and to come to the enjoyment of him."[34] Elsewhere, in summarising 2 Peter 1:3-11, Owen states that God's creation of "a new spiritual nature" in the believer is what endows them with a "gracious ability

---

28. *GMP*, 7.
29. Baxter, *Practical Works*, 3:238.
30. Baxter, *Saint or Brute*, 20.
31. Beeke and Jones, *Puritan Theology*, 22.
32. Owen, *ΠΝΕΥΜΑΤΟΛΟΓΙΑ*, 186.
33. Owen, *ΠΝΕΥΜΑΤΟΛΟΓΙΑ*, 280.
34. Owen, *ΠΝΕΥΜΑΤΟΛΟΓΙΑ*, 280.

for the duties of a holy, godly, spiritual life."[35]

Characteristics

The collective attributes of godliness presented in *Godly Man's Picture* are not found listed in such extensive detail in the work of any other late English Puritan of comparable stature to Watson. Yet they appear separately or in shorter lists in the works of several contemporaries. Baxter held that those with their hearts and minds set on "the pleasing and glorifying of God" will love God, "For that is your God which you love most, and please best."[36] For Baxter, the goal of all Christian learning was "To know God, that we may love, and reverence, and trust, and admire, and honour him, and enjoy him."[37] *Saint or Brute* includes a number of qualities intrinsic to godliness. Many overlap with those present in Watson's writings, including: a desire for God's will (contained in Watson's treatment of holiness and patience); love of God's Word; love for the saints; prayerfulness; spiritual worship and service of God; seeking the sanctification of others; unrivalled esteem of Christ; humility; heavenly-mindedness; thankfulness; proper behaviour in relationships and duties to others; avoidance of sin and temptation; patience.[38]

Owen names several characteristics of "evangelical holiness." These include, "Meekness, Patience, Self-denial, Quietness in bearing Reproaches, Contempt of the World, Zeal for the Glory of God, Compassion to the Souls of men, Condescensions to the Weaknesses of all."[39] Charnock's description of the characteristics of spiritual worship also contains considerable overlap with Watson's picture of godliness. It must proceed from knowledge, understanding and a spiritual nature. Such worship is said to be: sincere; appropriately spiritual; marked by faith; acted in love; combined with a sense of mourning at one's spiritual deficiencies; full of thankfulness; joined with a "deep reverence" and "godly fear;" characterised by humility and holiness (expressly akin to "Godlikeness"); and undividedly

35. Owen, *ΠΝΕΥΜΑΤΟΛΟΓΙΑ*, 547.
36. Baxter, *Self-Denial*, 80.
37. Baxter, *Self-Denial*, 209.
38. Baxter, *Saint or Brute*, 15-19.
39. Owen, *ΠΝΕΥΜΑΤΟΛΟΓΙΑ*, 450. Kapic highlights these characteristics in his treatment of Owen's spirituality in "Evangelical Holiness: Assumptions in John Owen's Theology of Christian Spirituality," in *Life in the Spirit: Spiritual Formation in Theological Perspective*, eds. Jeffrey P. Greenman and George Kalantzis (Downers Grove: IVP, 2010): 113-114.

aimed at glorifying God.[40]

This survey of Baxter, Owen and Charnock suggests that Watson's leading contemporaries would have endorsed his presentation of godliness in *Godly Man's Picture* as a comprehensive treatment of the subject's importance to the Late English Puritan movement.

Means of cultivating godliness

Beeke and Jones list several of Watson's means for cultivating godliness in their general survey of Puritan methods. Attending sermons, Bible-reading, catechesis, meditation, prayer, conference, repentance (comparable to self-examination, self-denial and the mortification of sin) and appropriate participation in the Lord's Supper are all mentioned as typical Puritan practices.[41] The only sense in which Watson does not epitomise the characteristic means of developing piety listed here is that, so far as we know, he did not keep a spiritual diary.[42]

Wallace notes the importance of "reading, attendance at sermons, conferring with the spiritually mature, partaking of the Lord's Supper, prayer and meditation."[43] He also acknowledges that self-examination was a significant element of Later English Puritan spirituality. Lovelace notes the prominence of confronting inward sinfulness, the "foundational" nature of the Scripture, the Lord's Supper and prayer.[44] Hambrick-Stowe (though addressing the New England context) also identifies "the sacraments of baptism and the Lord's Supper ... the ministry of the Word (reading of and preaching from the Bible) ... and prayer" amongst other key public "means of grace."[45] Catechetical instruction, "devotional reading," "family prayer," "private conference," meditation, "self-examination" and "secret prayer" are attested to as further, common means of

40. Charnock, "Spiritual Worship," *Works*, 1:298-315.
41. Beeke and Jones, *Puritan Theology*, 849.
42. This is curious, since Watson's father-in-law John Beadle essentially wrote the handbook on Puritan journaling, according to Germaine Fry Murray, *A Critical Edition of John Beadle's A Journall or Diary of a Thankfull Christian* (New York: Garland, 1996): xxx. Watson does however recommend a Christian keep "two books" to record both their sins and God's mercies, which sounds analogous to diary-keeping. *GMP*, 185; *RTI*, 149-150. Compare Hall, *Puritans*, 124. See also Murray, *Beadle's Journall*, xxxiii-xxxiv.
43. Wallace, *Spirituality*, xxv.
44. Lovelace, "Anatomy of Puritan Piety," 311, 315.
45. Hambrick-Stowe, *Practice of Piety*, 93.

devotional piety.[46]

Matthew Barrett and Michael Haykin have shown that, for Owen, theologically-grounded, affectional piety is further developed through appropriately focused meditation.

> As to the subject of meditation, Owen stresses that especially the person and work of Christ must occupy first place. "If we are spiritually minded, we should fix our thoughts on Christ above, as the center of all heavenly glory," for it is in Christ that "the beatifical manifestation of God and his glory" is made for all eternity. Owen cautions believers, though, that such meditation on Christ must be according to the Word. "In your thoughts of Christ," he declares, "be very careful that they are conceived and directed according to the rule of the word, lest you deceive your own souls" and do not allow your "affections to be entangled with the paint or artificial beauty of any way or means of giving [your] love unto Christ which are not warranted by the word of truth."[47]

They go on to note that Owen believes that through meditation our spiritual state is improved in a way that can be "obtained only by a constant contemplation of the glory of Christ."[48] This kind of meditation also produces a side-effect on the believer regarding how they perceive themselves in contrast to the glorious brilliance of God in Christ.[49] Owen believed that a meditating Christian would naturally have a sense of self-abasement arising out of their contemplation of God's majestic holiness.[50] This is obviously connected to other prominent themes of Puritan spirituality, such as awareness of sin, humility and even self-denial and mortification of sin. On the other hand, for Owen, mortification of sin is necessary if a life of affectionate contemplation on spiritual things is to be possible for the believer.[51] Owen's works often delved into these aspects of

46. Hambrick-Stowe, *Practice of Piety*, 143, 150, 160-161, 168, 176.
47. Matthew Barrett and Michael Haykin, *Owen on the Christian Life: Living for the Glory of God in Christ* (Wheaton: Crossway, 2015): 223-224. Kindle Edition. David King also adds more on Owen's emphasis on meditation as part of what it means to be "spiritually-minded": "Owen defines spiritual mindedness as 'the actual exercise of the mind as renewed by the Holy Ghost, as furnished with a principle of spiritual life and light, in its conception of spiritual things and the setting of its affections on them, as finding that relish and savour in them wherewith it is pleased and satisfied." D. King, "Affective Spirituality of John Owen," *Evangelical Quarterly* 68:3 (1996): 229.
48. Barrett and Haykin, *Owen on the Christian Life*, 224.
49. Barrett and Haykin, *Owen on the Christian Life*, 224-225.
50. Owen, *Discourse of the work of the Holy Spirit in Prayer* (1682) (Oxford: TCP, 2005):190-191, cited in above.
51. See Owen, *Phronēma tou pneumatou or, The Grace and Duty of Being Spiritually*

the Christian life—perhaps most notably *The Mortification of Sin.* As Packer helpfully quotes:

> Constant self-abasement, condemnation, and abhorrency, is another duty that is directly opposed unto the ... rule of sin in the soul. No frame of mind is a better antidote against the poison of sin ... It is the soil wherein all grace will thrive and flourish. A constant due sense of sin as sin, of our interest therein by nature, and in the course of our lives, with a continual afflictive remembrance of ... instances of it ... is the soul's best posture ... To keep our souls in a constant state of mourning and self-abasement is the most necessary part of our wisdom ... and it is so far from having any inconsistency with those consolations and joys, which the gospel tenders unto us in believing, as that it is the only way to let them into the soul in a due manner.[52]

Owen's aphorism on mortification, "be killing sin or else it be killing you," is well known.[53] Watson expressed the same sentiment with a near identical statement, "Either kill thy sin or thy sin will kill thee."[54] The importance of this aspect of piety cannot be understated in both men's thinking and writing. Watson called self-denial the life-blood of religion and stressed the need for offering violence to one's self. Owen is so certain of the necessity of mortification that he names it alongside "universal holiness" as his "heart's desire" and calls it the "chief design of [his] life."[55]

Baxter shared with Watson an emphasis on heavenly-mindedness. This naturally leads to exhortations to meditate on heaven.[56] Whereas Watson makes heavenliness one of his characteristics of the godly man and names heaven and eternity as fit subjects for meditation in his *Christian on the Mount*, heaven is far more prominent as Baxter's recommended object for meditation.[57] Keith Condie's thesis, exploring Baxter's theory and practice of meditation, reveals

---

Minded (1681) (Oxford: TCP, 2012): 9. http://purl.ox.ac.uk/ota/A53719.

52. Packer, *Quest for Godliness*, 196. Taken from Owen, *A treatise of the dominion of sin and grace* (1688).
53. Owen, *Of the Mortification of Sin in Believers* (1668) (Oxford: TCP, 2006): 11. http://purl.ox.ac.uk/ota/A53715
54. Watson, "Souls Malady," *Beatitudes* (1660) (Oxford: EEBO, 2011): 481. It is possible that Watson picked up the phrase from Owen, as his sermon is probably later than Owen's Mortification, or they might have been drawing on a common source.
55. Owen, *Mortification*, vi. Owen also said "A despising of all things for Christ is the first lesson of the gospel." *Of Communion with God the Father, Sonne and Holy Ghost* (1657) (Oxford: TCP, 2012): 155. http://purl.ox.ac.uk/ota/A53713
56. Condie, "Meditation in the thought of Richard Baxter," 125-136.
57. Condie, "Meditation in the thought of Richard Baxter," ii, 16, 131.

not only how important Baxter regarded meditation, but how similar his understanding of it was to Watson's. For Baxter, "the activity of meditation aroused the affections and these stirred the soul to be resolute in its pursuit of godly living."[58] Condie also notes a link in Baxter's thought between self-denial and meditation:

> 'Without self-denial there will never be true reformation or unity,' said Baxter. He was clear about the means to acquiring qualities such as self-denial: 'The greatest help to self-denial is, to retire from the creature into God, and live in the love of him, and employ the soul continually upon him,' in other words, to meditate.[59]

Baxter makes it explicit in *Saint or Brute* that "It is essential to Godliness, and necessary to salvation, that this devotedness to God be with a true renunciation, resistance, and forsaking of three great contraries or enemies to God and us," namely the adversarial *troika* of "the devil," "the world" and "the flesh."[60] On the other hand, heavenly-minded meditation was itself the best way to deal with the sins and temptations that plagued a Christian in their spiritual walk, "A heart in heaven ... will be a most excellent preservative against temptations, a powerful means to kill thy corruptions, and to save thy conscience from the wounds of sin."[61]

Charnock's theology and piety also led him naturally towards meditation as a means of raising the affections towards God through focusing on spiritual truths.[62]

> Never, therefore, leave thinking of a spiritual subject till your heart be affected with it. If you think of the evil of sin, leave not till your heart loathe it; if of God, cease not till it mount up in admirations of him. If you think of his mercy, melt for abusing it; if of his sovereignty, awe your heart into obedient resolutions; if of his presence, double your watch over yourself. If you meditate on Christ, make no end till your hearts love him; if of his death, plead the value of it for the justification of your persons, and apply the virtue of it for the sanctification of your natures. Without this practical stamp upon our affections, we shall have light spirits.[63]

58. Condie, "Meditation in the thought of Richard Baxter," 134.
59. Condie, "Meditation in the thought of Richard Baxter," 133.
60. Baxter, *Saint or Brute*, 6.
61. Baxter, *Saint's Everlasting Rest* (1650) (Oxford: TCP, 2005): 610. http://purl.ox.ac.uk/ota/N17286; Condie, "Meditation in the thought of Richard Baxter," 148.
62. Siekawitch, "Stephen Charnock's Doctrine of the Knowledge of God," 35.
63. Charnock, *Works*, 5:308. Siekawitch cites this passage as evidence that Charnock "emphasiz[es] the priority and absolute necessity of the affections." 34-35.

Elsewhere we find,

> By meditation we enter within the veil and behold his glory. He meets those that humbly aspire to him; frequent ascents of the mind to God is the way to attain the manifestations of him ... But let our affections keep an equal pace with our meditations, that the heart may be inflamed with a divine love. Endeavour to have a savour of Christ's ointments. Cant. i. 3; we shall then profit more in the knowledge of God in a week, than, without blowing up our affections, we shall do in many years; for then God will communicate himself to us with a more cordial affection than we can embrace him.[64]

Charnock also has a place for holy mourning in his piety. In expositing Ezekiel 9:4 he speaks of the importance of mourning over the sins of others. He suggests that to do so—particularly at times when sin is rampant—is one way to show "a true affection to God."[65] And he shares Watson's emphasis on the cardinal importance of self-denial in piety.

> True piety is to hate ourselves, deny ourselves, and cleave solely to the service of God. To make ourselves our own rule, and the object of our chiefest love, is atheism. If self-denial be the greatest part of godliness, the great letter in the alphabet of religion, self-love is the great letter in the alphabet of practical atheism.[66]

Thus, the emphasis on meditation and self-denial is present in the piety of some of Watson's most notable contemporaries, while his other means of progressing in godliness are identified in scholarly surveys of Puritan spirituality.

Aims and goals of godliness

Watson's key aims of the godly life were also representative of his peers. In his survey of Late English Puritan spirituality, Wallace notes that "a holy death was ... the culmination of a holy life."[67] He later adds, "heavenly mindedness was the spiritual person's foretaste of the joys of heaven through meditation."[68] Baxter states that the

64. Charnock, *Works*, 4:108.
65. Charnock, "Mourning for other men's sins," *Works*, 9:97.
66. Charnock, "Practical Atheism," *Works*, 1:154.
67. Wallace, *Spirituality*, xvii.
68. Wallace, *Spirituality*, 1.

goal of godly living is "To be saved, and to Please the Lord, or to Glorifie God and enjoy him in Glory for ever."[69] The extent to which one has a "holy heart and life," determines the degree to which they realise these aims.[70] Those who wish to ensure they are "solidly godly," are exhorted to, "Be sure you take up with God alone, as your whole felicity."[71] Baxter also regarded self-denial and mortification as necessary for securing happiness. Human felicity came through recognising God as the source of all goodness and directing the soul to rejoice supremely in Him, as opposed to shallow happiness offered by creatures.[72] And like Watson, Baxter believed that one must set their chief affections upon God in this life, in the anticipation of full enjoyment of His goodness in the eternal state.[73] Elsewhere he called this "the intention of the true ends of Godliness," which included experiencing the "beatifical vision."[74] Baxter also expresses the effect that godliness has on others.

> What ornaments to the Church? and how excellently serviceable to God and man! Men would sooner believe that the Gospel is indeed a word of truth and power, if they could see more such effects of it upon the hearts and lives of men. The world is better able to read the nature of Religion in a man's life then in the Bible. They that obey not the word, may be won by the conversations of such as these.[75]

Owen establishes a strong link between love, Godlikeness and receiving happiness in God as the object of affection.

> The soul sees all goodness, and consequently all that is amiable and lovely, in God—the want of all which it finds in itself. The fruition of his goodness is that which it longs for as its utmost end, and conformity unto it as the means thereof ... For when [the principle of love] is duly affected with the excellencies of God in Christ, it fills the mind with thoughts and contemplations on them, and excites all the affections unto a delight in them. And where the soul acts itself constantly in the mind's contemplation, and the delight of the affections, it will produce assimilation unto the object of them. To love God is the only way and means to

69. Baxter, *Saint or Brute*, 11.
70. Baxter, *Saint or Brute*, 15.
71. Baxter, *Saint or Brute*, 20.
72. Baxter, "The Crucifixion of the World by the Cross of Christ," in *Practical Works*, 3:497.
73. Baxter, "Crucifixion of the World," 514.
74. Baxter, *Saint or Brute*, 5.
75. Baxter, *Gildas Salvianus, the reformed pastor* (1656) (Oxford: TCP, 2012): 73. http://purl.ox.ac.uk/ota/A26932

> be like unto him.[76]

After lamenting the state of Christianity in his time and the conduct of Christians that diminished the credibility of the gospel, Owen calls for the opposite.

> Could some see believers making it their business to be like Christ in the world–to deny themselves as he did–to do good to all as he did—to be patient under persecution and reproaches as he was—to be tender, pitiful, merciful, like him—to abide in faith and prayer as he did; what might we not expect, as to the advancement of the gospel amongst us?[77]

He follows this with a similar note in his conclusion,

> I wish they would seriously stir up and exhort one another to contend mightily for the crucifying of all their secret lusts and bosom sins—for heart purity and likeness to Christ in all things; that they would incite others, and draw all they can into their society and combination in all parts of the nation.[78]

Charnock echoes this idea of Godlikeness being linked to happiness, "[I]f our happiness consists in being like to God, we should imitate him in loving him as he loves himself, and as long as he loves himself."[79] The knowledge of God, which was foundational to piety, enables the possession of a happiness that is imperfect in this life and fulfilled in the eternal state.[80] In *Spiritual Worship* he details how affectional piety is perfected by God in heaven:

> The happiness of heaven consists in a full attraction of the soul to God, by his glorious influence upon it. There will be such a diffusion of his goodness throughout the souls of the blessed, as will unite the affections perfectly to him. These affections, which are scattered here, will be there gathered into one flame, moving to him, and centering in him. Therefore the more of a heavenly frame possesses our affections here, the more settled and uniform will our hearts be in all their motions to God, and operations about him.[81]

---

76. Owen, *ΧΡΙΣΤΟΛΟΓΙΑ, or, A declaration of the glorious mystery of the person of Christ* (1679) (Dublin: Richard Moore Tims, 1831): 153.
77. Owen, "Sermon XII," *Sermons of John Owen: Posthumous Sermons*, 2:164.
78. Owen, "Sermon XII," 167.
79. Charnock, *Existence and Attributes*, 1:308.
80. Charnock, "Knowledge of God," *Works*, 4:14.
81. Charnock, "Spiritual Worship," 341.

When Charnock describes holiness in his renowned *Existence and Attributes of God*, he treats it as a communicable attribute that must be emulated by God's people as a means of bringing him glory. He observes that "God seems to accept the glorifying this attribute, as if it were a real addition to that holiness which is infinite in his nature, and because infinite cannot admit of any increase."[82] This is akin to Watson's distinction between God's immutable essential glory and increasable, ascriptive glory. After an extended treatment of this topic, Charnock adds that when Christians are like God in holiness "it keeps up the reputation of God in the world and attracts others to a love of him."[83] This demonstrates an affinity with Watson's aim of increasing public godliness.

Earlier Puritan influences on Watson's piety (c. 1558-1638)

Watson's writings demonstrate familiarity with the works of earlier Puritan luminaries such as William Perkins, Richard Greenham, John Preston and Robert Bolton.[84] Richard Lovelace has noted that William Perkins (1558-1602) emphasised "the essential connection between godliness and correct theology," while his student William Ames (1576-1633) accentuated the significance of spiritual rebirth.[85] Lovelace claims that the Puritan devotional literature which emerged from 1600-1640 was "built on the theology of Perkins and Ames."[86] This literature would have been formative for Watson's piety. Indeed, I have already shown that the respective, key elements that Lovelace identifies in the piety of Perkins and Ames converge to constitute the essential starting point for godliness in Watson's thought. There is also correspondence between Perkins' list of key "sanctified affections" and those of chief concern to Watson.[87]

82. Charnock, *Existence and Attributes*, 2:202.
83. Charnock, *Existence and Attributes*, 2:202.
84. See for instance, *GMP*, 97, 242; *Beatitudes*, 243; *BPD*, 1:39; *BPD*, 2:332-4; *BPD*, 3:498, 872; *Mischief*, 70.
85. Lovelace, "Anatomy of Puritan Piety," 299.
86. Lovelace, "Anatomy of Puritan Piety," 299.
87. Perkins nominates "fear of God," submissive contentment, "love to God in Christ, and to Christ in man," "an high estimation of Christ and his blood above all things in the world," love towards one's neighbour and self-abasement towards personal sinfulness as sanctified affections. William Perkins, *A godlie and learned exposition upon the whole epistle of Jude* (1606) (Oxford: TCP, 2005): 10. http://purl.ox.ac.uk/ota/A09434. Elsewhere he lists "zeal for God's glory," "fear of God," "hatred and detestation of sin" and "joy of heart" as being of special importance. Perkins, *A*

The dual aspects of *eusebeia* and *chasid* in Watson's understanding of godliness and the primacy of the former over the latter, is present in Ames' *Marrow of Sacred Divinity.* Ames places "inward affections" and religious devotion towards God before "outward deeds" of "justice"—though he considers both indispensable to the Christian life.[88] Brad Walton notes that in Ames' thought, "the affections ... give rise to the 'outward deed,' and ... constitute the religious life understood principally in terms of holy practice."[89] Ames also saw each of God's attributes as having the capacity to "beget religion in us," with respect to both the affections and their resultant actions.[90] This anticipates what I will discuss in greater detail in relation to Watson's project of practical divinity in Part IV of this book. Significantly, Watson's fourfold description of glorifying God—adoration, appreciation, affection and subjection—are all represented in Ames' treatment of "Religion" in *Marrow of Divinity.* [91] This suggests he was operating within an established paradigm of piety when beginning his *Body of Divinity* with these categories. Charles Cohen has also identified a package of "godly sorrow," "hatred of sin" and repentance as a significant element of the piety promoted by Perkins and Ames.[92]

Richard Greenham has been identified by Theodore Bozeman as "the foremost architect of the first great awakening of Protestant piety."[93] Walton writes, "The Spiritual Brotherhood emanating from Greenham followed him in concentrating on, and further refining their understanding of, the nature of conversion and regeneration, the signs of genuine piety and the dynamics of hypocrisy and self-deception."[94] Watson follows Greenham's approach to pastoral and devotional writings on godliness by adopting the same concern with "the 'marks' and 'signs' of regeneration, and the distinction between

treatise tending unto a declaration whether a man be in the estate of damnation or in the estate of grace (1590) (Oxford: TCP, 2005): 71-76. http://purl.ox.ac.uk/ota/A09466; See also Walton, *Jonathan Edwards*, 77.

88. Ames, *Marrow of Sacred Divinity* (1642) (Oxford: TCP, 2005): 243-246. http://purl.ox.ac.uk/ota/A25291
89. Walton, *Jonathan Edwards*, 79.
90. Ames, *Marrow*, 246.
91. Ames, *Marrow*, 247-248, 268.
92. Cohen, *God's Caress*, 107.
93. Bozeman, *Precisianist Strain*, 69. Walton sees Greenham as "further develop[ing]" some of the emphases found in the piety of the English martyr John Bradford (see below). Walton, *Jonathan Edwards*, 65.
94. Walton, *Jonathan Edwards*, 69.

genuine and spurious conversion."[95] Greenham is an even earlier source than Ames for the relationship between vertical-horizontal aspects of religion. "[W]e must obey the first Table before the second, and piety must go before charity, and we must serve God before we serve man, and nature must give place to godliness."[96] Beeke and Jones have shown that Greenham and Preston promoted certain practices as "means of godliness"—including prayer, hearing and reading the Word and receiving the sacraments.[97] This makes them forerunners to Watson in this respect. It is also likely that Greenham's definition of meditation, stood behind Watson's own articulation of the practice. "Meditation is that exercise of the mind, whereby we calling to our remembrance that which we know, do further debate of it, and apply it to ourselves, that we might have some use of it in our practise."[98]

Watson's view of love as a crucial component of a godly response towards God is in line with many earlier Puritans. As Cohen observes:

> True 'natural love' includes, according to [Richard] Sibbes, a high esteem for the object, desire to be joined to it, contentment in the thing, and a desire to please the party loved; the Lord's excellency inspires the Saints to deepen these feelings beyond the norm. Since God determines what good comes to us, "we love Him more than our selves," [John] Preston averred "because our good depends upon him, more than on our selves." He is, in fact, the greatest good, deserving the greatest affection.[99]

The essence of Sibbes and Preston's view of love can readily be found in Watson.[100]

Watson also references a Latin expression—probably derived from Sibbes—to express the relationship between foundational

95. Walton, *Jonathan Edwards*, 65. Walton observes, "Greenham desired to identify the 'marks,' 'notes' and 'rules to know whether we have the Spirit.' Throughout he emphasises not externals, but the inward, affective disposition. He recommends that Christians consider their fundamental amative orientation toward holiness: 'what liking or misliking we have to sin.' It is not enough to reject sin. One must actively hate it as offensive to God," (67).
96. Greenham, *Works of Richard Greenham* (1612) (Oxford: TCP, 2004): 541. http://purl.ox.ac.uk/ota/A02178
97. Beeke and Jones, *Puritan Theology*, 425.
98. Greenham, *Works*, 22. Compare Watson's, "Meditation may be thus described; It is an holy exercise of the mind, whereby we bring the truths of God to remembrance, and do seriously ponder upon them, and apply them to ourselves." *HTS*, 42.
99. Cohen, *God's Caress*, 128.
100. See for instance, *BPD*, 2:245-246; *GMP*, 32-33.

knowledge and godly affections, *Claritas in intellectu, parit ardorem in affectu.*[101] Preston, along with Perkins, also stands behind Watson's definition of zeal as a compound of love and anger.[102]

Schwanda and Haukenfrer note that Watson would have spent considerable time reading the authors recommended by Richard Holdsworth—the master of Emmanuel College during his studies there.[103] From the prescribed list, the names of bishops Joseph Hall and John Davenant can be added to those already mentioned above.[104] Neimeyer observes that Hall's writings on meditation were read and appreciated by Watson. This suggests that the bishop contributed to some of his formative views on piety.[105] It is difficult to determine the extent to which Watson adopted the emphases of more recent predecessors without feeling the need to refer to them directly in any of his works. Neimeyer has demonstrated that there were, for instance, works by Puritan authors concerning meditation that preceded Watson's *Christian on the Mount.* Yet he shows no awareness of them in his writing.[106] This would also seem to be the case with godliness in general. Several authors senior to Watson wrote works dealing with similar themes to *Godly Man's Picture* and *Religion Our True Interest* prior to their composition.[107] Yet Watson does not interact with them and it cannot be assumed they were readily accessible for him.

Major Pre-Puritan influences on Watson's Piety: The ABC Strand

A wide range of Christian theological and devotional authors from

101. Rendered as "light in the understanding breedeth heat of love in the affections" by Sibbes in *The Bruised Reede and Smoaking Flax* (1630) (Oxford: TCP, 2005): 103. http://purl.ox.ac.uk/ota/A12171
102. Cohen, *God's Caress*, 130.
103. Schwanda, "Sweetnesse," 57; Haukenfrer, "Bellows of Affection," 13.
104. Schwanda, "Sweetnesse," 57; Haukenfrer, "Bellows of Affection," 13.
105. Neimeyer, "Thomas Watson," 169. It is noteworthy that Hall's own influences, with respect to meditation, included the late-medieval Brethren of the Common Life and, possibly, "contemporary Jesuit spirituality." Ryrie, *Being Protestant*, 113-114.
106. Neimeyer, "Thomas Watson," 169-170.
107. For example, Arthur Dent, *Plain Man's Pathway to Heaven* (1601); Lewis Bayly, *Practice of Piety* (1611); John Downame, *Guide to Godlynesse* (1622); select writings of Richard Greenham and Richard Rogers; John Ball, *Of the Power of Godliness* (1656). See Beeke and Pederson, *Meet the Puritans*, 73, 174, 188, 789. With respect to Downame's *Guide to Godlynesse*, it would seem that it did not enjoy wide distribution due to poor initial sales. Stephen Foster, *The Long Argument: English Puritanism and the shaping of New England culture 1570-1700* (Chapel Hill: University of North Carolina Press, 1991): 92.

earlier centuries stood behind Watson's approach to piety. Many of these are not so much intellectual influences upon his conceptualisation of godliness, as they are exemplars of what genuine Christian spirituality looked like in Watson's mind. Multiple references to the early post-Reformation English martyrs, Martin Luther and several early church fathers fall into this category.[108] Other notable figures are quoted in support of particular definitions or concepts that relate to Watson's explanation of piety, but do not appear to have impacted his understanding of the subject more broadly. Examples include Aquinas' definition of love, Beza's interpretation of self-annihilation and Ambrose on the Lord's Supper.[109]

While it is challenging to determine the breadth and depth of earlier Christian influences upon Watson, especially in relation to the concept of godliness, there are three notable figures—in the period stretching from the dawn of Christianity in the first century to the rise of Puritanism in the sixteenth century—who have left an unmistakable impression upon his piety. Augustine of Hippo (354–430), Bernard of Clairvaux (1090–1153) and John Calvin (1509–1564)—from the early, medieval and Reformation periods respectively—each eclipse their contemporaries in terms of their discernible influence upon Watson's piety. In order to trace the significance of this ABC strand of influences on Watson's piety, it is expedient to work our way upstream from Puritanism.

Calvin defined piety as *coniunctam cum amore Dei reverentiam, quam beneficiorum eius notitia conciliat*: the 'union of reverence and love to God which the knowledge of his benefits inspires.'[110] From the relevant passage in *Institutes of the Christian Religion*, it is clear that this reverence and love comes about in response not only to the knowledge of God's benefits, but also from an appreciation of the divine attributes.[111] As F. L. Battles notes, for Calvin 'knowledge of God (*cognitio Dei*) [is] the beginning of *pietas*.'[112] But, as noted in relation to Watson, the nature of piety itself was tied intrinsically to the idea of holy fear in response to such knowledge. This is

108. E.g. *GMP*, 105, 107, 127, 220; *Beatitudes*, 84, 289; *HTS*, 163; *BPD*, 3:437, 484, 522.
109. *BPD*, 1:61; *BPD*, 2:245, 288; *DSD*, 3; *Beatitudes*, 427; *Holy Eucharist*, 57, 100.
110. Calvin, *Institutio Christianae Religionis* (1536) (Paris: Cherbuliez, c. 1834): I.2.1. CCEL. https://www.ccel.org/node/19943 Accessed 02/12/16. English translation from Calvin, *Institutes of the Christian Religion*. trans. Henry Beveridge (Edinburgh: Calvin Translation Society, 1845). https://www.ccel.org/ccel/calvin/institutes.iii.iii.html Accessed 25/01/17..
111. Calvin, *Institutio*, 1.2.1.
112. F. L. Battles, *The Piety of John Calvin* (Philipsburg: P&R, 2009): 28.

further reinforced by an additional definition provided by Calvin in his *Institutes*, shortly after the phrase cited above.

> Such is pure and genuine religion, namely, confidence in God coupled with serious fear—fear, which both includes in it willing reverence, and brings along with it such legitimate worship as is prescribed by the law.[113]

Calvin disdained any notion of theological knowledge without an affectional response.[114]

Beeke's study of Calvin's piety identifies a range of vital characteristics in the Genevan reformer's approach to spirituality that I have noted as hallmarks of Watson's Late Puritan devotion. These include the indivisible nexus between theological principles and faithful practice; the primary goal of glorifying God; communion with God-in-Christ through the ministry of the Spirit; and an approach to cultivating piety which emphasised the necessity of hearing and meditating upon the Word, disciplined self-denial and approaching God through sincere prayer and reception of the Lord's Supper.[115] Michael Horton has demonstrated that Calvin placed considerable emphasis upon "meditation on the future life," coupled with continuous self-denial in one's life in the present age.[116] This is an important antecedent to the enthusiastic elevation of these disciplines, which I have noted in Watson's piety. Thus, Calvin set the standard for conceptualising godliness in the Reformed tradition as an appropriate affectional response to true knowledge of God. His Puritan successors expanded upon this essential definition of piety, but did not deviate from it. Watson stood in this same stream of piety and merely elaborated on some of Calvin's central emphases.[117]

Bernard has been described as "the most important and influential church leader of the West" during his lifetime.[118] The precedent for Watson's favourable reception of Bernard can be observed in the writings of Calvin and several, earlier Puritan figures.[119] The fact

113. Calvin, *Institutes*, 1.2.41. For an excellent, concise summary of the substance of Calvin's piety, see Beeke, "Calvin on Piety" in *The Cambridge Companion to John Calvin*, ed. Donald McKim (Cambridge: Cambridge University Press, 2004): 126.
114. *Horton*, Calvin on the Christian Life, 47, 55-56.
115. E.g. Beeke, "Calvin on Piety," 125-128, 131-135, 139-142.
116. Horton, *Calvin on the Christian Life*, 246-258.
117. Beeke and Jones, *Puritan Theology*, 848-849; Schaefer, *Spiritual Brotherhood*, 127-133.
118. Arie de Reuver, *Sweet Communion: Trajectories of Spirituality from the Middle Ages through the Further Reformation* (Grand Rapids: Reformation Heritage, 2007): 28.
119. De Reuver, *Sweet Communion*, 34-35. See also Ronald Frost, *Richard Sibbes: God's*

that Bernard was also one of the influences behind Richard Baxter's approach to meditative piety is a testimony to his special status among late English Puritans.[120] Anthony Lane suggests that Calvin extracted the best aspects of Bernard (from a Reformed perspective) but avoided engagement with many of the mystical aspects of his spirituality.[121] It is noteworthy then, that Bernard's approach to spirituality had a considerable impact upon, what Schwanda terms, Watson's "contemplative-mystical piety."[122] Schwanda highlights a shared interest between Watson and Bernard when it came to employing "bridal language" found in Song of Songs to describe the relationship between the Christian and her Saviour. They also shared an appreciation of the beatific vision as a focal point for present and future piety.[123] A strong relationship between the two is also evident when considering the importance of meditation in the Christian life.[124]

Bernard's place for tears and mourning for sin in his spirituality strongly resonated with Watson's own reflections on godly affections.[125] Watson agreed with Bernard that a true encounter with God via a particular means of grace would be evidenced by "a melting and mourning frame," resulting from awareness of sin.[126] For Bernard, "The tears of the penitent ... are sweeter than all worldly joy" and "the wine of Angels."[127] For Watson, the esteemed monk's

---

Spreading Goodness (Vancouver: Cor Deo, 2012): 268; Bozeman, *Precisianist Strain*, 78; Schwanda, *Soul Recreation*, 3, 6, 38, 122, 135. Watson cites Bernard more times in his corpus than Calvin does. See Anthony Lane, *John Calvin: Student of the Church Fathers* (Edinburgh: T&T Clark, 1999): 87.

120. Condie, "Meditation in the thought of Richard Baxter," 12, 154. Owen also quotes Bernard's sermons favourably, e.g. *ΠΝΕΥΜΑΤΟΛΟΓΙΑ*, 210, 221, 245. See also, Lovelace, "Anatomy of Puritan Piety," 296.

121. Lane, *John Calvin*, 100-101.

122. Schwanda, "Sweetnesse," 43-47.

123. Schwanda, "Sweetnesse" 41, 49-50, 58; Schwanda, "Saints' Desire," 85-89.

124. Schwanda, "Sweetnesse," 44-47. It is notable that Bernard equates *pietas* with *considerationi* in his *De Consideratione* and claims that it is the quintessential means of rendering worship to God. James D. Garrison, *Pietas from Vergil to Dryden* (University Park: Pennsylvania University Press, 1992): 12-13. Watson does not conflate the two to this extent in any of his writings, yet by making meditation so fundamental to progress in piety he displays affinity with this aspect of Bernard's spirituality.

125. Schwanda mentions tears as a theme in Watson, but does not explicitly connect it to the citations from Bernard. "Sweetnesse," 54-55.

126. *Beatitudes*, 103.

127. *Beatitudes*, 98-99; *Repentance*, 132. "This is the wine that gladdens man's heart, the wine that even the angels drink with gladness. In their thirst for men's salvation they rejoice in the conversion and repentance of sinners. Sinners' tears are wine

sayings on tears and mourning reinforced his own teaching that tears are "precious to God" and "mourning is the way to solid joy."[128] Watson's appreciation of this element of sanctified lowliness in Bernard's spirituality is also on display when he quotes him in *Godly Man's Picture.* Just as Watson considers humility an indispensable characteristic for the heaven-bound saint, Bernard declared that only the humble have the Spirit of God dwelling within them.[129] Watson saw Bernard's emphasis on humility as bolstering his own insistence on self-mortification as an essential aspect of godliness. "'Humility,' says Bernard, 'is *contemptus propriæ excellentiæ,*' a 'contempt of self-excellence,' a kind of a self-annihilation. This is the glory of a Christian. We are never so *lovely* in God's eyes—as when we are *black* in our own eyes."[130] Thus, Watson recognised an affinity with Bernard's spirituality in the positive component of raising the affections and drawing near to God. Likewise, they shared the negative requirement of putting sin to death and denying selfish desires.

Augustine defined true piety as *veri Dei vero cultu*: the true worship of the true God.[131] This is very close to Watson's understanding of the New Testament term *eusebeia.* It has been argued that Augustine redefined the common usage of *pietas* in his day to exclude a general sense of duty to others or acts of mercy (*misericordia*) and pertain "solely [to] the domain of religious life."[132] This, in turn, led to "the emergence of the idea that piety is an experiential devotion which is both the source and content of a private, individual Christian faith."[133]

It is evident from Watson's treatment of *chasid* that he did not divorce theocentric piety from humanitarian action. However,

---

to them; their sorrow has the flavour of grace, the relish of pardon, the delight of reconciliation, the wholesomeness of returning innocence, the gratification of a peaceful conscience." Bernard, "Sermon XXX: Mystical Vineyards and the Prudence of the Flesh," *Commentary on the Song of Songs*, ed. Darrell Wright (Internet Archive, 2008): 131. https://archive.org/details/StBernardsCommentaryOnTheSongOfSongs Accessed 12/06/18.

128. *Beatitudes*, 98-99.

129. *Non requiescit Spiritus Sanctus nisi super Humilem. BPD*, 1:224. Trans. "The Holy Spirit does not rest upon [any] but the humble."

130. *BPD*, 1:116.

131. Augustine, *De Civitate Dei* (Leipzig: BGT, 1877) V.19.230. English translation from *City of God*, Marcus Dods (trans.) (Edinburgh, 1871): 102.

132. Joseph Harp Britton, *Abraham Heschel and the Phenomenon of Piety* (London: T&T Clark, 2015): 26-27; Garrison, *Pietas*, 8, 12, 15. See Augustine, *De Civitate Dei* X.1.

133. Britton, *Abraham Heschel*, 26-27.

the nature of godliness in his thought is proximate to experiential devotion. It contains a private and individualised element, which is characteristic of the Puritans and their indebtedness to Augustine regarding piety. Perry Miller in his classic *The New England Mind* referred to the Puritan spiritual ethos as part of "the Augustinian strain of piety."[134] Miller identifies three essential Augustinian elements in Puritan piety: 1) A spiritual thirst for a true knowledge of God (which in practice comes by way of appreciating God through the sum of His attributes);[135] 2) Their doctrine of original sin and total depravity and the individual, even introspective, angst which characterised their practical response to the realities of spiritual corruption;[136] 3) The essential need for regeneration to make true piety possible.[137] This threefold Augustinian foundation is clear in everything discussed so far with respect to Watson's piety.

In terms of the affectional substance of godliness, Augustine appears to have significantly influenced the way in which Watson conceptualised and spoke of the Christian's love for God. In describing the importance of love for God as a characteristic of the godly, Watson quotes Augustine as saying "I would hate my own soul ... if I found it not loving God."[138] He immediately adds his own reflection: "A godly man loves God, therefore delight to be in his presence; he loves God, therefore takes comfort in nothing without him."[139] In *Beatitudes* Augustine is quoted as a witness to the "delectability" of God: *In Deo quadam, dulcedine delectatur anima, immo rapitur.*[140] Watson adds, "The love of God is an honey-comb which drops such infinite sweetness, and satisfaction into the soul, as is *unspeakable and full of glory*, 1 Peter 1.8."[141] Elsewhere Watson refers to Augustine's exhortation to love Christ "for Himself" or "for His loveliness," comparing this to a love of wine for its sweet taste.[142]

This is an appropriate note to conclude upon, as it is suggestive of the overall impact of this ABC strand on Watson's piety. The affective enjoyment of divine sweetness is a theme running

134. Perry Miller, *The New England Mind: The Seventeenth Century* (Cambridge: Harvard University Press, 1983): 4.
135. P. Miller, *New England Mind*, 8, 13.
136. P. Miller, *New England Mind*, 22.
137. P. Miller, *New England Mind*, 25-34.
138. *GMP*, 32.
139. *GMP*, 32.
140. *Beatitudes*, 27. Trans. "In God there is a certain sweetness which the soul is delighted—even raptured—by."
141. *Beatitudes*, 27.
142. *Beatitudes*, 438; *DC*, 87.

through the spirituality of Augustine, Bernard and Calvin, which saturates Watson's devotion.[143] This transhistorical testimony to the importance of spiritual delight in God stood behind Watson's sense of "the sweet savour of godliness" and his description of God as a "Hive of Sweetness."[144] Whatever the theological and contextual differences between Watson and these three notable forebears, theirs was the flavour of piety he wished to promote to his generation in contrast to the ceremonialism and nominalism that he loathed as defective.

It has been suggested that "Calvin saw [Bernard] as a witness to Augustinian truth during the Middle Ages."[145] Given that Bernard is the main influence upon Watson's piety from the era between Augustine and Calvin—it might be concluded that he adopted the same view of the medieval abbot. This strand of influences on Watson therefore reinforces Miller's argument for viewing Puritan spirituality as an Augustinian piety. But it also suggests that Bernard and Calvin were seen as the major torchbearers for Augustinian piety in their respective periods.

Conclusion

Watson clearly serves as a typical representative of Late English Puritanism. The fundamental need of knowledge and regeneration as prerequisites for godliness; the affectional nature of godliness; its various characteristics; the means of cultivating it and its goals and outcomes as described by Watson are all identifiable in the thought and ministry of his peers. This relationship between Watson's piety and that of his peers allows his presentation of godliness in *Godly Man's Picture* (and other key works) to serve as a legacy work that speaks for the Late English Puritan movement. Watson's distinctiveness lies in the fact that he produced the most comprehensive summary of what his contemporaries understood by godliness.

143. Schwanda, "Sweetnesse," 40, 48-55; See also I. John Hesselink, "Calvin, Theologian of Sweetness" *CTJ* 37 (2002): 318-332; Gordon Rudy, *The Mystical Language of Sensation in the Later Middle Ages* (London: Routledge, 2013): 61-65; Andrew Louth, "Augustine," in Cheslyn Jones, Geoffrey Wainwright and Edward Yarnold (eds.) *The Study of Spirituality* (London: SPCK, 1986): 139-140, 143-144; Lenka Karfikova, *Grace and the Will According to Augustine* (Leiden: Brill, 2012): 187, 203-204, 256-257.

144. *BPD*, 1:10; *BPD*, 3:449.

145. Lane, *John Calvin*, 98.

It is clear that the piety of Watson and his peers lay downstream from that of Perkins, Greenham, Ames, Sibbes and other, earlier English Puritans. The core elements of their approach to devotion were derived from these men, whom they esteemed as great masters of practical theology. These trailblazers of a distinctive kind of piety established the Puritan vision of godliness—rooted in regeneration, founded on theological truth and marked by key affections and characteristics. At the same time, from the beginning of the movement, Puritans maintained that their devotion was anchored in the biblical vision for spirituality and the best traditions from Christian history. Pious figures from the past—such as those constituting the ABC strand discussed above—provided Puritans with attestations to their conviction that vital, biblical godliness endured throughout the centuries. The late Puritans received this vision of godliness from their early Puritan forbears and were convinced by them that theirs was the biblical approach to questions of religious devotion.

This led Watson to determine that many contemporaneous religious groups did not exhibit the same fidelity to the teachings of Scripture on piety and he took it to be his solemn duty to refute their aberrant devotional practices in the course of promoting godliness.

Chapter 8
"False Devotion:"*
The polemical edge of Watson's piety

Watson's uncompromising dedication to his vision of godliness often led to him expressing it in contradistinction to rival forms of devotion that failed to meet his standards. Puritanism had always contained a considerable reactionary element. The nature of Puritan piety was clearer when articulated in light of its antitheses. Paul Lim goes as far as to remark that 'Puritan spirituality was as polemical as it was practical."[1] As an English deutero-Protestantism, Puritanism continued to protest the unbiblical doctrines and practices of Rome, while instigating a second, distinct push for reform within the partially reformed English Church. Eventually—like Luther and others before them—many Puritan reformers found themselves outside of the church they sought to change. Watson's earlier writings were composed while he was still a dissenting clergyman within the state church. But his major works on godliness were written following his experience of the Restoration and Great Ejection. Thus, his most detailed reflections on piety come in the historical context of his rejection by a church system that had repudiated all attempts at Puritan reform. In this context, Watson took pains to distinguish his vision for piety from the devotion of Roman Catholics and the Laudian or Arminian members of the English state church. He also censures heretical sects such as Socinians, Arians and Antinomians from the vantage point of his biblical, Reformed piety.[2] Non-Christian religions, including Islam and Judaism, do not escape his

* Title taken from *BPD*, 2:284.

1. Lim, *Mystery Unveiled*, 173.
2. John H. Leith notes that Puritan concerns with Roman Catholicism, Antinomianism, Arminianism and Socinianism were all evident in the proceedings of the Westminster Assembly in the 1640s. *Assembly at Westminster: Reformed Theology in the Making* (Richmond: John Knox Press, 1973): 42-3. Thus Watson is reflecting the alarm and outrage of his English Reformed heritage towards these theologies and their outcomes.

criticism either. But Watson's chief antithesis to godliness was not sectarian. Religious hypocrisy of all varieties was the archenemy to the sincere piety he was promoting.

Making "Ignorance the Mother of Devotion:" Roman Catholicism*

Papists were a prime target of the polemical edge to Watson's piety. *Romish* doctrine and practice frequently serve as negative foils when Watson establishes a key principle of piety.[3] In *Religion our True Interest*, Watson states "The fear of God is the *Sum* of all Religion," before establishing his doctrinal point, "it is an indispensable Duty incumbent on Christians, to be Fearers of God."[4] An attack on Catholicism follows, "[This] confutes the *Papists,* who hold that a Christian cannot have Assurance, because he is to serve God with fear."[5] The false, Catholic notion of fear unsettled confidence in one's relationship to God. This is juxtaposed with Watson's doctrine of godly reverence to illustrate where others err. Likewise, in *Doctrine of Repentance*, when elaborating on the meaning of repentance and "godly sorrow," Watson begins his application section by repudiating Catholic penitence:

> How far are they from Repentance who never had any of this godly sorrow! Such are 1. The *Papists,* who leave out the very soul of Repentance; making all penitential work consist in fasting, penance, pilgrimages; but there is nothing of spiritual sorrow in this; they torture their bodies, but their hearts are not rent. What is this but the carcass of Repentance?[6]

It is clear that Catholicism often functioned as the most obvious example of error and abuse in relation to what Watson was teaching about godliness. The reason Catholic transgressions were the first to come to mind is not difficult to deduce when one is sufficiently familiar with Watson's theological outlook. His contentions with Catholicism are part of the great Puritan struggle to see the English

* Title taken from *BPD*, 3:520.

3. Barker, "A Body of Divinity," 206. Notably, Trueman suggests that Catholicism was a distant third, behind Arminian and Socinian teaching, in terms of John Owen's polemical concerns. Trueman, *Claims of Truth*, 19. By contrast, Watson's concern is primarily with Rome.
4. *RTI*, 15.
5. *RTI*, 21.
6. *Repentance*, 24-25.

church reformed according to biblical principles. The alternative was seeing it *deformed* via a relapse into the corrupt traditions of the pre-Reformation church. Watson's concerns about Catholic abuses typify the Puritan casting of the Church of Rome as "public enemy number one" for gospel religion and the spiritual health of the realm.[7]

It has been suggested that Catholicism ceased to be the primary antagonist of Puritanism during its middle phase, being replaced by generic ungodly adversaries and the powerful Laudian party.[8] Renewed concern amongst Late Puritans can be explained by the resurgent Catholic influence at court. They faced a Catholic queen, heir presumptive and queen mother, along with the continual political strength of Rome on the Continent.[9] The Restoration had already returned a neo-Laudian, Anglo-Catholicism detested by Watson and his peers. An increase in Catholic influence—through official promotion or indulgence—suddenly seemed possible.[10]

Watson's fundamental problem with Catholicism was its violation of the Second Commandment. In *Godly Man's Picture*, Catholics are contrasted with the godly Christian who is characteristically careful in the worship of God. For Watson, Catholics violate the Second Commandment with human inventions (e.g. crucifixes and altars). They "introduce that into God's Worship which he hath not commanded" and "blot out that which he hath commanded."[11] Godliness is impossible amongst "Papists" because any reverence for God is compromised through superstition and idolatry.[12] Watson goes so far as to say that Catholics "hate God" through their image

7. See Peter Lake, "Post-Reformation Politics, or On not looking for the long-term causes of the English Civil War" in *The Oxford Handbook of the English Revolution* ed. Michael J. Braddick (Oxford: Oxford University Press, 2015): 29. This emphasis is consistent with the anti-Catholic rhetoric in documents signed by Watson including the *Solemn League and Covenant* (1643) and the *Seasonable Exhortation of Sundry Ministers* (1660).
8. Haigh, *Plain Man's Pathways*, 206-209.
9. See Alexandra Walsham, *Charitable Hatred: Tolerance and Intolerance in England, 1500-1700* (Manchester: Manchester University Press, 2006): 16; Alexander, *Religion in England*, 159, 221. Compare Schwanda's comments on the Morning Exercises at the Cripplegate in "Sweetnesse," 62.
10. See especially, *A Seasonable Exhortation* (1660). Greaves says of the 1660s "Religious convictions and fears were also responsible for the continuation of antipopish sentiments, the most serious form of which was the accusation that the king himself countenanced Catholicism." *Enemies Under His Feet*, 6.
11. *GMP*, 41.
12. *GMP*, 40-42.

worship.[13] Their piety is futile due to it being misdirected towards multiple objects of devotion, rather than being singularly focused upon God.[14]

Certain language that Catholics used in relation to the Eucharist was regarded as additional idolatrous transgressions. In *Holy Eucharist*, Watson clearly describes the practices of worship surrounding Catholic Mass as sin, idolatry and blasphemy.[15] We have seen that true knowledge is prerequisite for godliness in Watson's thought. It is therefore natural that he saw this mistaken devotion offered towards bread—as though it were Christ Himself—as false worship that precluded any true piety for those who participated in it. Watson is willing to recognise that Catholic zeal exists. But he holds it to be of no value since it is based on ignorance rather than true knowledge. 'The Papists make Ignorance the Mother of Devotion, but Christ makes Ignorance the Mother of Error."[16]

Catholic ungodliness was also clear in their behaviour. Watson considered Catholics selectively obedient to God's moral law—a sign that they did not take God or His Word seriously.[17] The popes were guilty of breaking the third commandment because they inappropriately affixed God's name to their denunciations of sincere Protestant Christians.[18] Church-supported violence against non-Catholics was an ungodly violation of the sixth commandment not to murder.[19] Likewise, Watson alleges that Catholics are also permitted to violate the ninth commandment, when their false statements further the Catholic cause.[20] The Church of Rome's dismal record with regard to permissive, clandestine sexual promiscuity is utilised by Watson to argue that they are an impure church where the seventh commandment against adultery has no bearing.[21]

Significantly, many of these charges are repeated in Watson's commentary on the first petition of the Lord's Prayer 'Hallowed be thy Name."[22] For Watson, this petition is of the utmost importance within the prayer and maintaining the sacred honour of God's

13. *BPD*, 2:284.
14. *BPD*, 2:282; *BPD*, 1:61.
15. *Eucharist*, 24.
16. *BPD*, 3:520.
17. E.g. *BPD*, 2:251.
18. *BPD*, 2:299.
19. *BPD*, 2:251, 362.
20. *BPD*, 3:452.
21. *BPD*, 2:251, 371-372.
22. *BPD*, 3:451-452.

name is fundamental to his understanding of godliness. Thus, when Watson brings extensive charges that the Pope's followers are guilty of instead dishonouring God's name through idolatry, immorality, blasphemy and lies—he leaves no room for his readers to conclude that there is any essential piety in the Catholic religion.

Watson presents godliness itself as the best preventative against a Christian falling into Roman error. He urges Christians to "get good principles" and "get love to God," in order to ensure they are not carried away by Catholic doctrine.[23] Other measures that the godly are to take, in order to limit the influence of Catholicism in their lives, include avoiding living with Catholics, associating too intimately with them and refraining from marrying them.[24] Watson regards mixing with those who impiously worship images to be greatly detrimental to one's growth in godliness. This is the negative counterpart to his emphasis on holy conference.

Thus, Roman Catholicism is for Watson the archetypal manifestation of religion that professes to honour Christ, but ultimately proves incapable of producing genuine piety. This is due to serious doctrinal error and the practical perversion of Scriptural worship. He does not deny that the faith and practice of Roman Christianity can produce a certain kind of religious affection or lead to positive behaviour from its adherents. However, he regards the theological aberrations of Rome to be too serious for piety based on Catholic religious instruction to bring any glory to Christ or any benefit to the individual. Such a position is curious if considered in light of Bozeman's suggestion that Watson's Puritan forebears (from Richard Greenham onwards) had not only drawn upon Catholic approaches to religious discipline, but had emulated enough aspects to be accused of "bringing in ... Monkery again," by other Protestants.[25] Watson's writings do not demonstrate any awareness that his predecessors were being indicted by their opponents as purveyors of the very kind of religion he detested. Nor is there any indication that Watson acknowledged the impact of Catholic devotional practices upon Puritan spirituality.[26]

23. *BPD*, 2:281.
24. *BPD*, 2:281.
25. Bozeman, *Precisianist Strain*, 74-83, 174. See also, Wakefield, *Puritan Devotion*, 87, 95.
26. Notwithstanding his positive reception of a monastic figure like Bernard (discussed in the chapter above), whose commonalities with the contemporary Catholic doctrines and practices that Watson despised were not highlighted. Cf. Hambrick-Stowe, *Practice of Piety*, 25.

It is possible that reflection upon either matter might have altered his presentation of Catholic piety. However, given his main concerns with Catholicism were doctrinal, it seems likely that Watson would have approved of the project undertaken by earlier Puritans to preserve or retrieve devotional practices and resources to the extent that they could be purified of Roman error.[27] Yet, because of his Puritan understanding of *true* worship Watson would always regard certain outward forms of Catholic worship to be corrupt and unbiblical. So much so, that biblical godliness would always be absent from Catholic devotion, so long as practices like image-worship and the veneration of the Mass were observed.

"Carnal Protestants:"[*] Arminianism, ceremonialism and nominalism

Alongside Catholicism, the other main aberration of Christian devotion Watson contended with in his promotion of piety existed within the church he was ejected from in 1662. The failure of state-sponsored ministers to promote biblical piety in their parishes was a serious blight on national spiritual health.[28] Watson's contention with some within the state church is disguised by a lack of direct references to "the Church of England."[29] Since "Anglican" lacked currency as a descriptor for people and congregations associated with the state church in the seventeenth century, it was absent from his vocabulary.[30] Neither does he opt for the "Laudian" adjective favoured by many historians of the period. This is not surprising when one considers that Laud's demise occurred prior to Watson's pastoral ministry and the prominence of the high church party associated with the executed Archbishop had ebbed significantly in the Civil War years. However, Watson did attack theological positions and devotional approaches within the established church that he considered incompatible with godliness, namely Arminianism, ceremonialism and formal or carnal Christianity.

27. See Schwanda, "Sweetnesse," 35-36; Wakefield, *Puritan Devotion*, 103.
* Title taken from *BPD*, 3:452.
28. E.g. *BPD*, 1:8-9; *BPD*, 2:363.
29. There are only two references in his entire corpus. The first occurs two years prior to the Restoration, when he was still a minister within the state church. *APA*, 21. The other occurs long afterwards during a repudiation of Anglo-Catholicism. *BPD*, 2:279.
30. See Davies, *Caroline Captivity*, 5.

Arminianism

Arminianism was the main theological position within the church that Watson attacked as detrimental to godliness. During Watson's youth, several prominent English Churchmen adopted Arminius' earlier complaints against Calvinism. Those who expressed a disdain for doctrines such as predestination and "limited atonement" within the Church, tended to be the same clergymen that favoured the retention of a Catholic identity for the English Church. This included the maintenance of the liturgical flavour which later came to be associated with the "high church" party within the established church.[31] Most of Watson's anti-Arminian references come during the post-Restoration period, when this party was experiencing a reascendancy to the dominance it had enjoyed until the demise of Laud in 1645.[32] Indeed, the majority of these references occur after Watson had been ejected from his ministry within the national church. For Watson, the Arminian party were guilty of promoting a serious heresy. He was willing to castigate Arminianism alongside antinomianism, Socinianism, Catholicism, Atheism and Islam.[33] This demonstrates the seriousness with which he regarded this teaching. Watson believed Arminians "Poison Souls ... with Error" by "advancing the Power of the Will" by which they "take off the Crown from the Head of Free-Grace."[34] In context, he is expounding on the sixth commandment and makes Arminian ministers (amongst others) "Soul-murderers," due to their destruction of the eternal happiness of their followers through deadly error.[35]

Why did Watson find Arminianism to be such a destructive teaching? It is clear that he regarded the Arminians' use of human reason to be a reproach to God. They misrepresented the divine attribute of justice.[36] Further, the prominence of human will in salvation for Arminians was not to be regarded as a simple point of disagreement with those who followed Calvin. To assert the sovereign power of the will with respect to salvation (as Watson understood Arminians to do) was to implicitly deny the need for

31. Spurr, *English Puritanism*, 86-87; I. Morgan, *Puritan Spirituality*, 18-19; Letham, *Westminster Assembly*, 20-21.
32. Spurr, *English Puritanism*, 129; Alexander, *Religion in England*, 220-221.
33. E.g. *BPD*, 1:131, 218; *BPD*, 2:363; *GMP*, 51.
34. *BPD*, 2:363.
35. *BPD*, 2:363.
36. *BPD*, 2:390; *Autarkeia*, 88.

divine intervention by the sovereign, saving power of God.[37] Watson also believed that "Such as advance the Power of their Will in matters of Salvation, without the Medicinal Grace of Christ, do absolutely put themselves under the *Covenant of Works*."[38] This rendered Arminian theology a disparagement to God and fatal to the souls of its adherents. Further still, for Watson, Arminian theology had a wrong view of justification and Christian perseverance. This stemmed from a defective understanding of Christ and His work. He argued that to believe that people united with Christ by faith could fall away from salvation was to suggest that Christ was imperfect. It provided no guarantee that any would be saved, potentially leaving Christ as "an Head without a Body."[39] Watson therefore rejected what he saw as a weakened understanding of justification, whereby Christ's work did not secure eternal benefits for those who believed. It was an unacceptable denigration of Christ.

Therefore, Watson's interactions with theological Arminianism portray it as a system with a wrong notion of God, Christ, grace, salvation and justification. In his mind, this set of doctrinal problems obscured the gospel to the point that a person's salvation was likely to be the casualty of Arminian teaching. With such an unstable theological foundation, true piety was impossible in the hearts of those who held to Arminianism.

Ceremonialism

These attacks on Arminianism are the most obvious examples of Watson reacting to the factions he opposed within the Church of England. But they are not his only statements about the issues he saw within the national church. Watson was concerned with problem of formal ceremonialism as an approach to corporate worship. In his formative years, during the Middle Puritan *milieu*, the religious faction led by William Laud championed a certain understanding of the biblical phrase "the beauty of holiness" (Ps 96:9). They accentuated lavish, external expressions of worship including ornate church buildings and services.[40] Watson wrote against this approach to corporate Christian worship during its resurgence in

37. *BPD*, 2:390.
38. *BPD*, 2:390.
39. *BPD*, 3:480.
40. Alexander, *Religion in England*, 153. See also John Morrill, "The Puritan Revolution," in *CCP*, 68; Wallace, "Puritan Polemical Divinity," in *CCP*, 214.

the Restoration years. He attacked this form of devotion as inimical to his own commitment to precise application of clear, Scriptural principles of worship as the necessary expression of sincere, reverent heart-piety. This is explicit in his treatment of the fundamental question "What is it to worship God in spirit?" Primarily, it meant "to worship him without ceremonies."[41] He added, "and if [we may] not use those *Jewish* Ceremonies which God did once appoint, then not those which he did never appoint."[42] The New Testament concept of *eusebeia*—as "right worship"—precluded the use of extrabiblical ceremonies that were inherited from Roman Catholic tradition. Ceremonialism was contrary to faithful piety. Watson elaborates on the reason for his perspective on ceremonies elsewhere: "Tis highly provoking to God to bring any Superstitious Ceremony into his Worship which he hath not prescribed; it is to tax God's Wisdom, as if he were not Wise enough to appoint the manner how he will be served."[43]

Those who were concerned with the outward, ceremonial elements of religion were those who not only lacked love for God's true people, but "became [their] oppressors."[44] Watson complained of those who showed great reverence for church buildings—as though they were temples of God—while not caring about those who were "spiritual temples," that is the godly.[45] He saw the pejorative use of "Puritan-Recusants" as a smear from people who did not honour those who sincerely sought to honour God.[46] All of these criticisms point towards the way anti-Puritan forces within the established church treated their nonconformist brethren.

41. *BPD*, 1:26.
42. *BPD*, 1:26.
43. *BPD*, 2:271.
44. *Two Witnesses*, 47.
45. "Mystical Temple," in Watson, *Doctrine of Repentance* (1668): 226. Google Books edition. https://books.google.com.au/books?id=ZSJlAAAAcAAJ. The context of these comments was the aftermath of the Great Fire of London, in which many church buildings were ruined, but nonconformists (including Watson) were holding services wherever they could (and often facing official harassment). Wilson, *History and Antiquities*, 332. See also, David J. Appleby, "From Ejection to Toleration in England, 1662-89" in *The Great Ejectment of 1662: Its Antecedents, Aftermath and Ecumenical Significance* ed. Alan P.F. Sell (Eugene: Wipf & Stock, 2012): 101; Greaves, *Enemies*, 160.
46. "Mystical Temple," 226.

Nominalism and "carnal" Protestantism

Watson was also deeply concerned about the spiritual state of England and the prevalence of Protestant nominalism around him. This was a perennial concern for the Puritan movement. Christopher Haigh demonstrates this with his social history of late 16th to early 17th century English men and women who exhibited many of the traits stereotyped by the early Puritan Arthur Dent (d. 1607) in his portrayal of the characters Asunetus and Antilegon in *The Plain Man's Pathway to Heaven* (1601). Asunetus and Antilegon were typical inhabitants of England who believed in God and observed religion to a certain extent, but found the Puritan zeal for godliness excessive and unwarranted.[47] The main difference between the two was that Asunetus' problem was gross ignorance (which could be corrected through proper instruction and persuasion by the godly), whereas Antilegon had a stubborn recalcitrance which was unlikely to give way to earnest pleading for piety.[48] While these religious dispositions could manifest open hostility towards Puritans and their principles at times, the main problem was their sheer prevalence among the populace. Those holding such sentiments vastly outnumbered their godly neighbours.[49] For Watson and his late Puritan contemporaries, the success of the Restoration in undoing any and all ecclesiological progress made by reformists before and after the Civil Wars and driving dissenters out of the national church, must have reinforced this sense of widespread malaise.[50]

Watson seldom gives an explicit indication that he is speaking specifically with the established church in mind. But it would be foolish to interpret Watson's warnings and lamentations about the spiritual malady of church and society independently of the state religion. Watson felt that there was so little love amongst professing Christians in the England of his day, compared to the early church. Thus, there could hardly be much true godliness in his nation.[51] He likened the spiritual climate of England to its natural, "torrid" climate and to the lukewarm church of Laodicea reproved by Christ in Revelation 3. He prays that God would instead "cause the fire of holy zeal to be always burning upon the Altar of our hearts."[52]

47. Haigh, *Plain Man's Pathways*, 59-60, 65, 68, 78-79, 97, 145-164.
48. Haigh, *Plain Man's Pathways*, 59-60, 145, 163-165, 218, 220-221, 223-224.
49. Haigh, *Plain Man's Pathways*, 165, 208-209.
50. McDermott, "Introduction," *Jerusalem's Glory*, 9.
51. *GMP*, 199.
52. *Eucharist*, 102.

Watson regarded England to be the most Christian nation on earth in terms of its expression "of the national part of religion."[53] But the English were "so far below the being inflamed with the divine and absolute part of religion that injustice and oppression is not removed from our hearts!"[54]

Watson was concerned that many churchgoers in London heard of Christ with their ears but lacked anything of Him in their hearts.[55] He warned his readers and hearers against carnal and nominal Protestantism. These lacked both the godly sorrow that generated true, transformative repentance and the godly zeal that was required to pursue true religion that glorified God.[56] These sketches are not imaginary or hypothetical. They represent real professing Christians that Watson had undoubtedly encountered in his life and ministry in London. The calamities his city experienced in the 1660s—the Plague and the Great Fire of London—were understood as God's judgement against the people's ungodliness and unfaithfulness.[57] Watson suggested that the only reason the nation was not overthrown altogether was because there were some true saints still in it. But England was in danger of losing the gospel from her midst. Indeed, it was already "under a cloud."[58] It was Watson's fellow Puritans who constituted the godly few that kept up true religion and gospel ministry. Thus, God's hand was deterred from bringing immediate and utter condemnation.

Heretical Sects

Catholics and compromised Protestants may have been the most significant religious groups in power and numbers in Watson's day and therefore warranted his attention when discussing matters of godliness. But they were not the only ones he expressed objection to in his promotion of piety. There were a range of departures from the historical, orthodox family of Christianity that Watson saw as heavily deficient in doctrine and piety.

---

53. *Two Witnesses*, 33.
54. *Two Witnesses*, 33.
55. *Christ All in All*, 652.
56. *Repentance*, 25; *GMP*, 306.
57. *BPD*, 2:348; *Repentance*, 165-166.
58. *Repentance*, 122.

Robbing Christ of His Divinity: Unitarian Heresies

Arianism and Socinianism were more prevalent on the Continent than in Britain during Watson's lifetime. However, there was enough concern over contemporary Christological deviations to provoke his response.[59] In 1655, at the behest of the Council of State, John Owen published repudiations of these theological systems. He particularly targeted the teachings of John Biddle, the so-called "father of English Socinianism."[60] Biddle's views had attracted the ire of English Presbyterians a decade earlier and he continued to be despised by many well after his death in 1662.[61] Owen claimed of Socinianism: "there is not a city, a town or scarce a village, in England, wherein some of this poison is not poured forth."[62] His reaction to this "poison" has been identified as a key polemical objective of many of Owen's theological projects.[63] Thus, there was a sense that this doctrinal diminishment of Christ's deity was a real enough danger to demand targeted opposition by Puritan leaders.

For Watson, Arianism and Socinianism alike "rob Christ of the best Jewel of his Crown, his Godhead."[64] Anyone who held such an "execrable opinion" was guilty of "blasphemously reproach[ing]" the "divinity of the Son of God."[65] True piety was impossible for those with such beliefs. This was because Arians and Socinians lacked an essential ingredient of godliness, namely "prizing Christ."[66] Because they refused to acknowledge the Son's full equality of being with the Father and the divine glory they shared, it was impossible for

59. English church leaders had been concerned about such teachings from as early as the mid-16th century and the establishment was still seeking to combat "antitrinitarian" views in the final months of Laud's arch-episcopacy. See Lim, *Mystery Unveiled*, 76-77; Church of England, "IV. Against Socinianisme," *Constitutions and canons ecclesiasticall* (1640) (Oxford: TCP, 2003). http://purl.ox.ac.uk/ota/A00089. James Ussher, *A copie of the proceedings of some worthy and learned divines* (1641) (Oxford: TCP, 2012): 2. http://purl.ox.ac.uk/ota/A32992

60. John Owen, *Vindiciae Evangelicae: or the Mystery of the Gospel defended and Socinianism Examined* (1655): 3. Google Books edition. https://books.google.com.au/books?id=zX4yAgAAQBAJ. Carole S. Fungaroli, "Unitarianism" in Gerald Newman (ed.), *Britain in the Hanoverian Age, 1714-1837: An Encyclopedia* (New York, Garland, 1997): 728.

61. See Lim, *Mystery Unveiled*, 38-68.

62. Owen, *Vindiciae Evangelicae*, 52.

63. See Tim Cooper, *John Owen, Richard Baxter and the Formation of Nonconformity* (Surrey: Ashgate, 2011): 33, 59-74.

64. *BPD*, 1:94.

65. *BPD*, 1:63; *Autarkeia*, 88.

66. *GMP*, 60.

these heretics to give Christ the honour He was entitled to receive.[67] Instead, the Socinians, in particular, were considered to be placing Christ's intrinsic dignity lower than that of the angels (since they held Him to be a human and humans are lower than the angels, cf. Ps 8:5).[68] In so doing, "they reflect dishonour upon the Lord of Glory."[69] Thus, the Socinians were devoid of salvation, for their failure to trust in Jesus as a truly divine and human Saviour. They were unable to bring God glory through their acceptance of the true gospel. As Watson summarised, "God never thinks his name to be hallowed, unless his Son be honoured."[70] The Arian denial of the Holy Spirit's divinity was likewise a severe error that precluded godliness and excluded people from eternal life.[71] Watson declared that "firm belief" in the Trinity was essential to proper Christianity and that all three persons must be reverenced equally in recognition of their equal divinity and glory.[72] Further, the Christian owed the Holy Spirit a "Tribute of Homage and Obedience," which was due to Him as God.[73]

Thus, Watson regarded the very beliefs of Arians and Socinians to be wicked departures from the truth revealed in the Scriptures concerning the Son and the Holy Spirit. These doctrines offered nothing but dishonour and injury towards their divine glory. Watson attributes to these groups an evil zeal in promoting their falsehoods about Christ.[74] The godly were to match or exceed this zeal in opposing heresies that dishonoured God.[75] Watson declares that a lack of zeal and indignation in the face of Socinian denials of Christ makes one "a traitor to the crown of heaven."[76] He lauds Athanasius as an exemplar of what the godly should be in the face of error, noting his persistent struggle against Arianism.[77] Thus, for Watson, one sign of true piety is a passionate opposition to those whose heresy renders them incapable of godliness.

---

67. *BPD*, 1:63-64.
68. *GMP*, 60; *BPD*, 3:449.
69. *BPD*, 3:449.
70. *BPD*, 3:449.
71. "They who would wittingly and willingly blot out the third Person, shall have their Names blotted out of the Book of Life!" *BPD*, 1:64.
72. *BPD*, 1:64.
73. *BPD*, 1:65.
74. *HTS*, 101-102.
75. E.g. *BPD*, 1:121.
76. *UMC*, 24.
77. *RTI*, 4.

"The Door to all Licentiousness:" Antinomianism, Libertinism and Enthusiasm*

Watson was also concerned by attitudes towards the Christian life that encouraged people to live according to their feelings and impulses. Such an approach to religion could be based on a doctrine of complete individual liberty, or the supposed leading of the Spirit. Groups which were charged with the former tendencies earned the moniker Antinomians or Libertines, while those emphasising the Spirit's leading were commonly labelled Enthusiasts. Each of these groups were denounced by Watson for their disregard of the Scriptures as God's authoritative Word.[78] He declared antinomians to be condemned for their rejection of the Old Testament and accused them of perverting Scripture so that it would seem to support their liberty to sin.[79] Their rejection of the law as a rule of life for Christians meant their prayers would be rejected by God. Indeed, Watson was bold enough to say: "They who will not have the Law to rule them, shall never have the Gospel to save them."[80] Watson certainly was not alone with respect to these concerns. Antinomians have been identified as a chief concern for Watson's contemporary, Richard Baxter in his polemics, practical theology and pastoral ministry.[82]

Enthusiasts—who claimed the personal leading of the Spirit as the central aspect of their approach to religion—were condemned by Watson as impostors who denigrated the Scriptures.[82] Watson firmly believed the Holy Spirit would not speak independently, let alone contrarily, to the Scriptures He Himself authored.[83] Therefore, those who treated the Bible as "a Dead Letter"—while regarding their own "Airy Notions" as "new Light"—were not only impudent, but more

* Title taken from *BPD*, 1:ii.

78. David Como notes that these terms were "hostile term[s] of abuse, often used imprecisely, sloppily or maliciously for polemical purposes." Yet at the same time, he acknowledges that, however laden with implied disapproval, such appellations described an identifiable suite of theological convictions. *Blown by the Spirit: Puritanism and the Emergence of an Antinomian Underground in Pre-Civil War England* (Stanford: Stanford University Press, 2004): 33-36.
79. *BPD*, 1:16; *BPD*, 2:250. See Hall, *Puritans*, 306.
80. *BPD*, 2:270.
81. Cooper, *Owen, Baxter and Nonconformity*, 74-83.
82. *BPD*, 1:17; *Beatitudes*, 174, 346. This category would likely include the Quakers, explaining why William Penn took objection to Watson's writings about his sect.
83. *Beatitudes*, 346-347.

likely influenced by Satan than the Spirit.[84] Here Watson reflects the common concern about enthusiasm that existed amongst his peers, as identified by Geoffrey Nuttall: "The claim [of the enthusiasts] that the Spirit which was in the apostles, as manifested in the written word, was also in themselves led inevitably ... to the further question, how men could discern God's Spirit within them from their own fancies."[85]

These groups could not produce the kind of piety Watson emphasised. Their disregard for the Word made it impossible for them to be properly grounded in the fundamentals of religion. It deprived them of an accurate revelation of God to respond to with heart-affection. Furthermore, they were unwilling to make proper use of God's ordinances—which was essential for growth in godliness.[86] David Como describes the attitude of one of these sects towards the programme of piety promoted by Puritans such as Watson: "Antinomians rejected this ferocious regime of moral oversight, claiming that the godly obsession with sanctification and holy duties compromised the Protestant message of free grace and seduced the people of God back into works righteousness and legalism."[87] Bozeman has argued that the very practices Watson advocated as means of godly growth, served as the precisionist provocation that gave rise to antinomian tendencies during the Middle Puritan period.[88] Therefore, while Watson saw antinomians as incapable of godliness, he would have faced the recrimination that his pursuit of piety through rigorous means obscured the gospel of grace.[89]

It is true that the Puritans' emphasis on obedience to the law and diligence in religious duties set them on a course which often sailed close to the rocky reef of legalism.[90] Watson's approach to piety was consistently demanding in the face of nominalism. But it was also simultaneously cardiocentric in

84. *BPD*, 1:17; *Beatitudes*, 174.

85. Nuttall, *Holy Spirit*, 35. To compare Owen's concerns with religious enthusiasm in his writings, see Kapic, "Evangelical Holiness," 105.

86. *Beatitudes*, 174.

87. David Como, "Radical Puritanism" in *CCP*, 249. See also Hall, *Puritans*, 303.

88. E.g. Bozeman, *Precisianist Strain*, 7, 184-186.

89. Bozeman, *Precisianist Strain*, 179-180. Mark Jones singles out *Heaven Taken by Storm* as an example of Watson doing precisely this. *Antinomianism: Reformed Theology's Unwelcome Guest?* (Phillipsburg: P&R, 2013): 99. Kindle Edition.

90. Indeed, Richard Baxter and others—in seeking to repudiate antinomianism—failed to avoid this danger and jeopardised the Protestant understanding of justification by grace with their legalistic position, commonly referred to as "neonomianism." See Packer, *Quest for Godliness*, 156-160.

eschewing the dangers of Pharisaic legalism and unapologetically committed to his programme of religious duties in response to antinomian criticism. Watson was aware that certain elements of his piety were dismissed by some antinomians as "legal doctrine."[91] But there is no indication that he adjusted his position or language in the face of such criticisms—rather he appears to have doubled down on these emphases in response. For instance, in *The Lord's Prayer*, after denouncing antinomianism as a satanic, carnal doctrine, Watson lays out the Scriptural texts that seem to demand godly hardship as an integral part of the Christian life, before extolling the duties of "meditation," "mortification" and "self-examination."[92] Significantly, he follows this with a treatment of the devil's opposite tactic. Christians may be driven to religious excesses—especially with respect to "humiliation," "mourning" and "repentance"—to the point that they collapse under the weight of condemnation and despair.[93] Thus, while Watson would not have wanted to cede any ground to the antinomian position—so staunchly resisted by the Westminster divines—he was aware of the spiritual danger of over-emphasising religious duties.[94] It is easy to imagine the stringent elements of godliness in Watson's schema producing the anguish that Puritan piety has been criticised for. Yet it is clear that he believed that such a response was a distortion of the outlook he was promoting and that a godly pastor had the resources to identify overscrupulousness and offer appropriate counsel to those affected by it.[95] Far from seeing

91. *BPD*, 2:401. We must note that any suggestion, from an antinomian perspective, that Watson was legalistic, must be considered alongside the accusation made by an established churchman that he was essentially an antinomian! See William Sherlock, *A defence and continuation of the discourse concerning the knowledge of Jesus Christ* (1675) (Oxford: TCP, 2005): 309-310. http://purl.ox.ac.uk/ota/A59809. Although Sherlock mainly targets John Owen in this treatise—making his views out to be substantially the same as the antinomian Tobias Crisp—it is clear that he wishes to implicate Watson in the same manner.
92. *BPD*, 3:842-843.
93. *BPD*, 3:844. See Hall, *Puritans*, 122.
94. See, for instance, Alan D. Strange, "The Imputation of the Active Obedience of Christ at the Westminster Assembly" in *Drawn into Controversie: Reformed Theological Diversity and Debates within Seventeenth-Century British Puritanism*, eds. Michael Haykin and Mark Jones (Gottingen: Vandenhoeck & Ruprecht, 2011): 38-39.
95. The extent to which Watson's pastoral counsel might have alleviated the spiritual struggles of those practicing the piety he commended is a matter that falls outside of my consideration of his interactions with antinomian ideas. It is also largely a matter of speculation, seeing as how any extant pastoral correspondence between Watson and his parishioners or readers is yet to emerge. However, Condie's discussion of the challenges faced by Richard Baxter, in providing pastoral care to several women who suffered angst as they sought to practice his regimen of spiritual disciplines, would

antinomians as Christians fatigued and deterred by the demands of Puritan piety, Watson believed they lived licentious lives because they were mistaken about God and about vital doctrines like justification. Watson took issue with their misapplication of the verse "He hath not beheld iniquity in Jacob," to suggest that God did not see any sin in his children.[96] He viewed this as the Antinomian's *carte blanche* for committing all kinds of sin without fear of God's response.[97] This is the polar opposite of Watson's teaching that the godly do not indulge in hidden sin, because they know God sees everything done in secret.[98] Thus, by blunting the effect of God's omniscient awareness of sin, the Antinomians confirm themselves in ungodliness, rather than godly fear that keeps the Christian from sin.

Watson also took issue with the Antinomian belief that believers are "justified from eternity."[99] He considered this a fatal error, for, as he reasoned, "what sins do they care they commit, so long as they hold they are *ab Aeterno,* justified whether they repent or no."[100] Because Antinomians failed to appreciate the seriousness of sin in their lives, they saw no need to practice repentance or exhibit sorrow for things in their lives that dishonoured God.[101] But for Watson, such things were both biblical and essential to godly living. Sin was a real problem for the believer and those who lacked repentance and contrition not only lacked godliness but grace itself.[102] Watson judged those who lived unrepentantly in sin—irrespective of their doctrinal grounds for doing so—as unconverted sinners.[103]

likely apply to Watson's pastoral ministry as well. See Condie, "Meditation in the thought of Richard Baxter," 343-370. This is further suggested by the fact that Condie focuses on the struggles of Mary Rich, Countess of Warwick, who, as we have seen above, was also a beneficiary and benefactor in relation to Watson's ministry.

96. This seems to occur chiefly in John Eaton, *The Honey-combe of Free Justification* (1642) (London: Supralapsarian Press, 2016): 39, 49-50. It has, however, been identified as a "hallmark of antinomian thinking." Jones, *Antinomianism*, 82.

97. *BPD*, 1:17.

98. *BPD*, 1:30-32.

99. *BPD*, 1:132. Significantly, there were notable Reformed figures who held to a form of eternal justification during Watson's lifetime, including no less than the prolocutor of the Westminster Assembly, William Twisse (1578-1646). See Robert J. McKelvey, "'That Error and Pillar of Antinomianism:' Eternal Justification" in *Drawn into Controversie: Reformed Theological Diversity and Debates within Seventeenth-Century British Puritanism*, eds. Michael Haykin and Mark Jones (Gottingen: Vandenhoeck & Ruprecht, 2011): 250-251.

100. *BPD*, 1:132.

101. *BPD*, 2:401.

102. *BPD*, 2:401.

103. *BPD*, 3:809.

Everything about their lifestyle suggested they lacked the new nature that was prerequisite for heart piety that pleased God. Instead of being godly Christians, they were deluded by Satan with false doctrines that promised fleshly comfort and an easy way to heaven.[104]

"*Atheistical Fools:*"[*] *Unbelief and Rationalism*

As an utter refusal to recognise God for who He is, atheism was in diametrical opposition to godliness. In Watson's day there were few vocal atheists, but in his observation "the world [was] full of Practical Atheism."[105] All ungodly behaviour could be attributed to a lack of belief that God would hold people accountable for their sins.[106] This point was important for Watson. He believed that proper consideration of hell and eternal punishment should produce fear and trembling and keep people from sin. But the lack of this response was a telling sign of an atheistic heart.[107] Those who lack the kind of godly fear that acknowledged judgement and kept them from sin were antithetical to Watson's picture of the godly. They were "worse than *brutish,* a Beast fears the fire, these fear not Hell Fire" and "worse than *Devils* for they *believe and tremble,* Jam. 2.19."[108]

On the basis of the above Scripture, Watson reasoned, "Sure[ly], none can be Speculative Atheists."[109] Deniers of God wished that He did not exist, rather than being intellectually convinced this was true. However, elsewhere Watson denies the possibility of intellectual atheism *unless* a person's conscience had been badly seared by sin.[110] Thus, the usual form of this severe impiety was to apprehend God's existence, but hate Him enough to desire His

104. *BPD*, 3:843. Of course, the antinomian retort was that the Puritan relationship to the law made them "unregenerate" and awaiting conversion, at best, or "legal Professors" at worst. Bozeman, *Precisianist Strain*, 195, 307.

* Title taken from *BPD*, 1:22.

105. *BPD*, 1:22. Haigh affirms this sense of "atheist" from earlier Puritan usage. "An atheist was then not a man who did not believe in God but a man who behaved as if there were no God and no divine retribution, a man without religion." *Plain Man's Pathways*, 68.

106. *BPD*, 1:22; *Mischief*, ii.

107. "Good Practitioner," 642-643; "Mystical Temple," 232; *The fight of faith crowned* (1678) (Oxford: TCP, 2004): 17, 21. http://purl.ox.ac.uk/ota/A65295

108. *RTI*, 23.

109. *BPD*, 1:22.

110. *BPD*, 1:20.

non-existence. The only way to wholeheartedly deny God's existence was to wholeheartedly destroy the conscience through wilful sin. Either way, the utter setting of the heart against God made the atheist "the wickedest Creature that is."[111] Watson warned that those who scoffed at God and piety would face "greater damnation."[112] He also noted that scoffers seldom repented and that unbelief prevented the Word of God from having the appropriate effect on many a sinful heart.[113] He allowed for miraculous intervention by God to rescue individuals from their hard-hearted atheism and sinful rebellion.[114] But at the same time, many in this position would be caught in Satan's "Draw-net" of unbelief and dragged into hell.[115] Watson's typical outlook on the fate of ungodly atheists is expressed in his terse statement: "They who will not believe a God, shall feel him, *Heb.* 10.31. It is a fearful thing to fall into the hands of the living God."[116]

In the opening of *Religion Our True Interest,* Watson says of Malachi 3:16-18, "The main design of this excellent Scripture, is to encourage Solid Piety, and confute the Atheists of the World, who imagine there is no gain in Godliness."[117] The godly and the atheists were in dispute primarily over the key question of whether a life of piety had any real value. The atheist chose ungodliness because they had concluded that there was no reward or benefit in honouring and living for God. Watson wrote his work to encourage believers to see the good effects and positive outcomes of living godly lives that honour God. He drew on the opening phrase of Malachi 3:16, "*Then those who feared the Lord talked with each other,*" to argue that when atheists remark that "It is *Vain to serve God,*" the godly must engage in holy conversation with one another in response.[118] This is consistent with the idea that the words of atheists were potentially dangerous to the godly.

Elsewhere, Watson calls atheists worse than thieves, because "they would take away our God from us, in whom all our Hope and

---

111. *BPD*, 1:22.
112. "The Fornace Heated Hotter" in *Mischief of Sinne* (1671 ed.): 208. Google Books edition. https://books.google.com.au/books?id=-pdkAAAAcAAJ.
113. *BPD*, 3:989-990.
114. "The Desperateness of Sinners," *Mischief of Sinne*, 128. Google Books edition.
115. *BPD*, 2:244.
116. *BPD*, 2:275.
117. *RTI*, iv.
118. *RTI*, 82.

Comfort is laid up."[124] Likewise, in *The Lord's Prayer* he notes that atheists say to the godly "You are too strict," but reasons with his hearers in response, "But who shall we believe, an holy God that bids us strive, or a profane Atheist that saith we strive too much?"[120] Thus, Christians must respond to a climate of atheism by intensifying their earnest pursuit of piety and encouraging each other in the hope of the gospel against the poisonous unbelief of scoffers.

Non-Christian Religions

To a lesser extent than the perceived departures from biblical Christianity discussed above, Watson also dealt with non-Christian religions in his writings. As with the above approaches to religion, Watson was prone to using non-Christian religions as examples of faulty piety. Yet, he was also capable of using the more virtuous qualities of these groups to exhort Christians to be even more diligent in their pursuit of the true faith.

Veiled Hearts:[*] Watson's reaction to Judaism

Watson's treatment of Jews and Judaism is complicated by the question of which "Jews" are in view. His writings deal with Jews as the people of God in the Old Testament and with their role and status in the New Testament. But they also include a Christian perspective on Jews in the post-biblical era. Jews were readmitted to England in 1656, after centuries of exclusion.[121] This accounts for why some of their theology and practices are targeted by Watson's corrections of contemporary religious groups. Overall, however, the English Christian's familiarity with biblical Jews grants them more prominence in his discussions of religion compared to any local, Jewish contemporaries.

Watson makes both positive and negative observations regarding the Jews as they appear in the Scriptures. The Jews and Israelites are often used for the purposes of negative illustration, due to their repeated disobedience towards God. For instance, Watson reflects

119. *BPD*, 1:22.
120. *BPD*, 3:506.
* Title taken from *GMP*, 22.
121. See Walsham, *Charitable Hatred*, 259.

on how their unfaithfulness brought reproach upon God's name instead of honour: "When the Heathens saw the *Jews,* who professed to be God's People, to be Scandalous, this made them speak Evil of God, and hate the true Religion for their sakes."[122] When exhorting Christians to zeal as a vital component of godliness, Watson again employs Old Testament Jews in a negative manner: "The *Jews* did spare no cost in their idolatrous worship, nay, *Jer. 32.35. They cause their Sons and Daughters to pass through the fire to Molech.* They were so zealous in their idol-worship, that they would sacrifice their Sons and Daughters to their false Gods."[123] On the other hand, when discussing the greatness of the divine name, he is happy to say "the name *Iohavah* was had in more Reverence among the Jews, than any other name of God."[124]

Watson particularly highlights the example of the New Testament Jews when warning Christians not to mistakenly suppose they have God for their Father. The New Testament challenged the Jewish notion that they were God's children by virtue of a godly pedigree—by being Abraham's children. This is used to warn Christians that they must be adopted by God through the grace of the gospel. They must not rely on the godliness of their parents for their standing before God.[125] Similarly, Christ's censure of the Jews in John 8:41, where he labelled them the children of Satan is used by Watson to make the following application: "*They who are of Satanical Spirits, and make use of their power to beat down the power of Godliness, cannot say God is their Father.*"[126] The Jews are also referred to negatively for their treatment of Jesus during His earthly ministry. However, Watson is willing to implicitly acknowledge a distinction amongst the Jews, when making a negative point about the unbelief of many. "All the Jews that saw Christ in the Flesh, did not see his God-head: all that saw the *Man,* did not see the Messiah."[127] He makes the distinction much more clear in teaching about God's forgiveness even for great sins: "Some of those *Jews* who had their Hands imbrued in Christ's Blood, were saved by that Blood."[128]

Watson also makes both commendatory and condemnatory statements about Jews as an ethno-religious group in his own

122. *BPD*, 2:295.
123. *GMP*, 162.
124. *BPD*, 2:252.
125. *BPD*, 1:136.
126. *BPD*, 3:428.
127. *BPD*, 1:95.
128. *BPD*, 2:287.

historical context. The faulty Jewish mono-personal understanding of God undercut any hope for salvation. A divine-human mediator was required to make satisfaction for sin and secure redemption.[129] The Jews cannot be godly, because they do not prize Christ or have true knowledge of God through the gospel. The veil remains on their hearts (2 Cor 3:15).[130] Instead of embracing Christ, they still await a Messiah. In the meantime they hate Jesus and all who are identified with Him.[131] Their piety can never be acceptable to God because: "God's name is dishonoured by the *Jews*; who give not equal Honour and Adoration to God the Son as to God the Father; they expect a Messiah yet to come, *seculum futurum*; they believe not in Christ; they blaspheme him, and slight Righteousness imputed; they vilify the Christian Sabbath."[132]

On the other hand, Watson employed examples of Jewish piety to urge Christians to do better. Watson speaks of "the more devout sort of the Jews" living out the Hebrew idea of godliness as *chasid* (mercifulness) by giving generously to the poor.[133] This illustrates how the godly man is "fruitful in good works"—part of what it means to be "thorough-paced in religion."[134] Elsewhere, when commenting on the same Jewish example, Watson remarks: "Now if the Jews are so devoted to works of mercy, who live without Priest, without Temple, without Messiah, shall not we much more profess our faith in the blessed Messiah!"[135] Jewish reverence for God's law, the Sabbath and their self-awareness with respect to sinful idolatry are all used positively and instructively in Watson's writings when he is exhorting Christians to take heed of such things themselves.[136]

"Turcism:" Watson's reaction to Islam*

Watson's knowledge of Islam is likely indirect. There is historical evidence to suggest that Muslims were in London during Watson's

129. *BPD*, 1:63.
130. *GMP*, 22.
131. *GMP*, 60. For a similar sentiment see Baxter, *A Christian Directory* (1673) (Oxford: TCP, 2004): 16, 108, 198. http://ota.ox.ac.uk/id/A26892
132. *BPD*, 3:451.
133. *GMP*, 248.
134. *GMP*, 248.
135. *Beatitudes*, 245.
136. *Repentance*, 84; *BPD*, 2:258, 333.
* Title taken from *HTS*, 111.

life and ministry.[137] But it is highly unlikely that he ever conversed with a Muslim personally (though it is not beyond possibility that he read an early translation of the Quran).[138] Alexandra Walsham (following Nabil Matar) argues that lack of personal interaction with Muslims during this period increased the propensity of English Christians to imagine the worst about them.[139] The Islamic Turkish Empire was also the best-known, non-Christian power among European Christians at the time. This explains the references to "Turks" and "Mahometans" in Watson's works.

Like Judaism, Islam is criticised for teaching a faulty, mono-personal understanding of God that makes salvation impossible. Like the Arians and Socinians, Watson accuses Mohammed of "pluck[ing] the Crown from Christ's Head, denying His Deity."[140] In this, the Turks, along with Catholics, Jews and ungodly Protestants dishonour God's name rather than hallowing it. He also alleges that Mohammed was "was of an impure, vicious life."[141] And like the Pope, Watson sees "the Turk" as Satan's agent in the world, in contrast to those who seek the advance of Christ's Kingdom. Disunity between Christians was seen as a direct or coincidental fulfilment of the Turkish prayer for variance amongst Christ's people.[142]

More unique to Islam is Watson's criticism of its perceived epicurean vision of heaven. For Watson, the eternal enjoyment of God was a strong motivation for persistence in godliness when life was difficult. Repenting of sinful, fleshly desires was incentivised by the much greater pleasures God offered to His people in the life to come, through the gospel. But he understood the Islamic concept of paradise to be one full of "Carnal Pleasures."[143] These included, "dainty dishes ... gold in abundance, silken and purple apparel, and ... red wine in silver cups, and golden plates."[144] Although Watson

137. See *A discovery of 29 Sects here in London* (1641) (Oxford: TCP, 2012). Cited in Nabil Matar, *Islam in Britain 1558-1685* (Cambridge: Cambridge University Press, 1998): 46.

138. Matar details the first translation of the Quran into English by Alexander Ross in 1649 and its impact upon British society in the third chapter of *Islam in Britain*, 73-119. He suggests that "thinkers from all sections of English society read Ross's 'Alcoran' and alluded to it." Matar, 81.

139. Walsham, *Charitable Hatred*, 121-122.

140. *BPD*, 3:451.

141. *BPD*, 3:451.

142. *BPD*, 3:460; *Mischief*, 74.

143. *BPD*, 1:11.

144. *BPD*, 1:11; *Repentance*, 111-112. For a brief discussion of the basis for this picture of Paradise in Islamic texts and Christian objections to it, see Mona Siddiqui, "Death,

makes no observations about how this might affect Islamic piety and ethics, he does reject this picture of heaven as wholly unsuitable for people to set the desires of their hearts upon. Delight in God Himself was to be the eternal reward of the godly. However, on a related note, Watson suggests that the Quran teaches "that God did not give men lustful desires to be frustrated."[145] This runs entirely counter to his emphasis on mortification of sin and self-denial as essential elements of Christian godliness.[146]

There are a few instances when Watson uses Muslims for more positive, illustrative purposes. As an illustration of the truth of God's omnipresence in *Body of Divinity*, Watson observes: "The Turks ... build their Temples open on the top to show, that God cannot be confined to their Temples or circumscribed, but is in all places by his Presence."[147] Similar to the Jews, the Islamic attitude towards almsgiving is cited positively on more than one occasion in Watson's writings. Twice, after noting the Quranic teaching on the goodness of charity, Watson implores his readers: "shall not a Christian's Creed be better than a *Turk's* Alcoran?"[148]

"Purblind Heathens:" Watson's reaction to polytheism*

Watson's references to "heathens" are sparse. But it is worth briefly noting that he used their example to exhort Christians to greater piety in a similar way to what I noted above with respect to his treatment of Judaism and Islam. In making his case for Sabbath observance in *Ten Commandments*, Watson reasons:

Resurrection, and Human Destiny: Qura'nic and Islamic Perspectives," in *Death, Resurrection, and Human Destiny: Christian and Muslim Perspectives*, eds. David Marshall and Lucinda Mosher (Washington: Georgetown University Press, 2014): 32.

145. *DSD*, 37. Significantly, Watson's marginal notes reveal that this impression was not gained through his own reading of the Quran, but based on the secondhand (and unreferenced) recollection of Sir Henry Blount in his *Voyage into the Levant* (London, 1636): 82. While this means that Watson was reacting to a popular English understanding of Islamic belief, rather than coming to these conclusions based on his own study of Islam, it should be noted that there is a substantial relationship between the Islamic concept of paradise and the fulfillment of human, bodily desires. See Aziz al-Azmeh, "Rhetoric for the Senses: A Consideration of Muslim Paradise Narratives" *Journal of Arabic Literature* 26:3 (1995): 215-231.

146. Richard Baxter also contrasts the perception of Islam as licentious with the Christian commitment to self-denial. Baxter, *Practical Works*, 11:82.

147. *BPD*, 1:27.

148. *APA*, 52; *Beatitudes*, 245.

* Title taken from *GMP*, 163.

> The very Heathens by the Light of Nature did set apart a whole Day in the Honour of their False Gods: *Macrobius* and *Scaevola* their High Priest did affirm, That the wilful Transgression of that Day could have no Expiation or Pardon. Whoever do rob any part of the Sabbath for servile Work or Recreation, *Scaevola* the High Priest of the Heathenish Gods shall rise up in Judgment against such Christians and condemn them.[149]

Elsewhere, when commenting on the importance of godly zeal towards God, Watson uses the example of heathen again:

> How far did the purblind Heathens go in their false zeal? [When] the Tribunes of *Rome* complained they wanted gold in their Treasuries, to offer to *Apollo,* the *Roman* Matrons plucked off their chains of gold, and rings, and bracelets, and gave them to the Priests to offer up sacrifice: were these so zealous in their sinful worship, and will not you be zealous in the worship of the true God?[150]

Watson also cites an anecdote about Titus Vespasian as an example of heathen charity that should provoke Christians to good works (as seen with Judaism and Islam above). He laments that professing Christians commit such "horrid impieties ... that [even] a modest heathen would blush at."[151] He further warns that ungodliness amongst Christians will cause the heathen to dismiss God, rather than reverence Him.[160] On the other hand, when Christians in the past exhibited love for their fellow saints, as one of the marks of true godliness, the heathen "wonder[ed]."[153]

Summary of Watson's treatment of non-Christian religions

It is evident that Watson adopts a threefold approach towards other religions when dealing with them in relation to godliness. The misguidedness of their piety is often highlighted to act as an illustrative foil in relation to a particular element of godliness. Commendable aspects of their devotion become tools for exhorting Christians to exceed such virtues as they follow the true God through biblical, Christ-centred piety. Finally, the diminished reputation of

149. *BPD*, 2:343.
150 *GMP*, 162-163.
151. *BPD*, 3:452.
152. *Two Witnesses*, 33-34.
153. *GMP*, 201.

God and Christ among non-Christians that results from deficiencies in Christian godliness is a sombre matter invoked by Watson to chastise those who fail to pursue piety in earnest.

"The worst sort of sinners:"* Hypocrisy as the antithesis of godliness

The above interactions have provided some historical and theological context for Watson's views concerning godliness and show how he engaged with other religious beliefs of his day. However, there is a category of people which, although not a defined religious group like those above, is nevertheless the most antithetical to Watson's vision of piety. As noted in Chapter 3, sincerity was a core component of Watson's picture of the godly. Because of this, religious hypocrisy was the most extreme opposite of godliness for Watson. Since godliness was an affectional heart-piety—any program of external morality or religious behaviour without true love and reverence was not only inadequate but offensive to God.

The essence of hypocrisy

In his *Doctrine of Repentance*, Watson gives a vivid description of what he means by hypocrisy:

> Hypocrisy is the counterfeiting of sanctity. The Hypocrite or (stage player) is gotten a step beyond the moralist, and doth dress himself in the garb of Religion: he pretends to *a form of godliness,* but denies the power, 2 *Tim.* 3. 5. The Hypocrite is a Saint in jest; he makes a majestic show, like an Ape clothed in *Ermine,* or Purple. The Hypocrite is like an house with a beautiful frontispiece, but every room within is dark: he is a rotten post fairly gilded: under his mask of profession he hides his plague-sores.[154]

While hypocrisy may be a universally familiar negative phenomenon, it is clear from the above quote that religious hypocrisy was particularly odious to Watson. He detested "the counterfeiting of sanctity" or "counterfeit piety" not simply because it was a lie.[155] The issue was that this kind of religion essentially divorced the vital

* Title taken from *GMP*, 138.
154. *Repentance*, 89.
155. *Repentance*, 89; *GMP*, 10.

relationship between pious affections and praxes. The hypocrite either acted devout without their heart being moved by affection towards God, or professed piety without obeying the commands of Christ.[156]

The real problem with the hypocrite, as opposed to the godly person, was that although they clearly saw value in living an outwardly religious life, their hearts had not been changed by God's Spirit.

> The illumination of Hypocrites is not virtual, it doth not leave an impression of Holiness behind; 'tis like weak Physic that will not work. The mind is enlightened, but the heart is not renewed. A Christian is all head, but no feet, he doth not walk in the ways of God.[157]

The unregenerate religious person lacked the change of heart in relation to God and sin that the godly possessed. For Watson, their culpability lay in their persistence in sinful masquerading despite hearing the Bible's calls to sincerity and warning against hypocrisy.[158]

The hypocrite's non-appreciation of God

If godliness for Watson centred around the right heart response to the truth about God, the fatal element of hypocrisy was the hypocrite's failure to properly appreciate who God was and what He required from his children. Watson particularly identified the hypocrite's problem as their failure to properly appreciate both divine omniscience and divine judgement. Like the atheist and the antinomian, the hypocrite indulges in sin either because he does not think God will see what he does, or that God will not judge all sin.[159] In some cases, the hypocrite's error might lie in their thinking that their pretence of religion had some value or that the things they did might somehow be enough to satisfy God's requirements. Watson criticises religious hypocrites for thinking God can be "put off" easily by their half-hearted observance: 'Hypocrites care not

156. See for instance the following quotes: "Hypocrites take God's Name in vain, their Religion is a Lie; they seem to Honour God, but they do not Love him, their Hearts go after their Lusts." *BPD*, 2:296; "Try an Hypocrite by Duties of the Second Table, Equity to his Neighbour, and there you find him Tardy." *BPD*, 2:271. See also, "Good Practitioner," 652.
157. *BPD*, 3:462.
158. *Anatomy*, 38-46; *GMP*, 138-139.
159. *BPD*, 1:31. *CM*, 75.

what Services they bring to God, they think to put him off with anything, they put no Cost in their Duties."[160] Similarly, hypocrites were mistaken in thinking that their partial and selective obedience to God's commands were of any value.[161]

The hypocrite's motivation for religious behaviour

Watson offered multiple explanations for why these pretenders to godliness might live and behave the way they did. If they performed religious duties, it was to look good in front of men: "Hypocrites, who have nothing of religion, besides the frontispiece, love to be seen."[162] If they refrained from sin it was to avoid public shame—but they would not cease from sinning when there was a minimal chance of discovery: "An Hypocrite may forbear *gross* sin, because of the shame; but not clandestine secret sin."[163] Likewise, a hypocrite could cease committing a certain sin, but still have an affinity for it: "An Hypocrite may leave Sin, yet love it; as a Serpent casts its *Coat* but keeps its *Sting:* but a sanctified Person can say, he not only leaves Sin, but loathes it."[164]

Watson acknowledged that hypocrites may have some shallow affections, but that these were qualitatively different to those found in the godly, regenerate heart. "An hypocrite may have affections of sorrow, as *Ahab;* affections of desire, as *Balaam,* these are sleight and flashy, and do not amount to real godliness."[165] If they had any sense of love for God—it was because of the good things he gives them. "Hypocrites love God because he gives them Corn and Wine: We must love God for himself; for those shining Perfections which are in him."[166]

The hypocrite's devotion did not stem from the heart, was not fuelled by a proper love and appreciation of God and was mainly aimed at gaining the approval of people. Watson thus regarded their religious façade as one of sheer convenience. He repeatedly states that they will only persist in their outward piety for as long as it is easy or gainful for them to do so. "Hypocrites may embrace the true

160. *BPD*, 3:518.
161. *RTI*, 204; *GMP*, 239; "Good Practitioner," 653.
162. *GMP*, 241.
163 *RTI*, 50.
164. *BPD*, 1:142.
165. *GMP*, 274.
166. *BPD*, 2:246. See Schwanda, "Saints' Desire," 72.

Religion in Prosperity, and court this Queen while she hath a Jewel hung at her Ear: But he is the good Christian, who will keep close to God in a time of Suffering."[167] "Hypocrites can sail in a Pleasure-boat, serve God in Prosperity; but when we can keep close to God in times of danger, when we can trust God when we have no Pawn, and love God when we have no smile; here is the trial of Sincerity!"[168]

Outcomes of hypocrisy

Watson unsurprisingly regarded hypocrisy as a completely futile exercise. "To pretend Holiness when there is none, is a *vain thing*."[169] Not only was the hypocrite sure to receive God's condemnation for their "counterfeit piety," but they were also likely to incur the hatred of their fellow man.

> The hypocrite is ... abhorred of all. Wicked men hate him because he makes a show, and God hates him because he doth *but* make a show: The wicked hate him because he hath so much as a mask of godliness, and God hates him because he hath no more ... The wicked hate the hypocrite, because he is *almost* a Christian, and God hates him because he is [but] almost.[170]

Resting in a false godliness—whether knowingly or ignorantly—was a severe form of "self-delusion" that would result in eternal loss.[171] In contrast to the godly, the hypocrite possessed no comfort at death. This was because their piety was ultimately hollow and their life had prepared them for hell rather than heaven.[172] The hypocrite's position on the precipice of damnation was compounded by the fact that they were so unlikely to truly repent. "None will find it more difficult to repent than Hypocrites; they have so juggled in Religion, that their treacherous hearts know not how to repent. Hypocrisy is harder to cure than frenzy. The Hypocrite's Imposthume in his heart seldom breaks."[173] Moreover, God would reserve a special degree of

---

167. *BPD*, 2:260.
168. *BPD*, 3:525; See also, "Hypocrites love a cheap Religion; they like a gospel that will put them to no charges." *Beatitudes*, 15. "Hypocrites will sooner renounce their Baptism, than take up the Cross." *Beatitudes*, 415.
169. *BPD*, 1:141.
170. *GMP*, 11.
171. *BPD*, 1:141. "The hypocrite deceives others while he lives, but deceives himself when he dies." *GMP*, 10.
172. *BPD*, 1:141; *GMP*, 12; *Repentance*, 91.
173. *Repentance*, 90-91.

judgement for the hypocrite,

> God's anger will fall heavier upon Hypocrites, they dishonour God more, and take away the Gospel's good name; therefore the Lord reserves the most deadly Arrows in his quiver to shoot at them. If Heathens be damned, Hypocrites shall be double-damned. Hell is called *the place of Hypocrites, Mat.* 14. 5. 1. As if it were chiefly prepared for them.[174]

Aside from all of these results of hypocritical religion, it was the reproach that hypocrisy brought to God and true piety which was extremely upsetting for Watson. 'Hypocrites are the worst sort of sinners, they reflect infinite dishonour upon Religion."[175] Therefore, the hypocrite not only failed to faithfully pursue humanity's great purpose of glorifying God, by seeking their own instead.[176] They in fact contributed negatively to the reputation of God and the gospel in the world. Thus, they were worthy only of eternal contempt.

Identifying Watson's "hypocrites"

Since the hypocrite is not associated with any externally identifiable religious group it is reasonable to ask whether Watson had any particular people in mind when writing against hypocrisy. Certainly, members of the established church would have been liable to such a charge if they persisted with an outward profession of Protestant faith, but did not prioritise the cultivation of genuine piety. Within the Puritan movement, Watson's debut publication, *God's Anatomy*, took aim at many among the Independent party for religious hypocrisy as an avenue for obtaining power.[177] There is nothing to indicate that Watson felt this way about all Independents or even the vast majority of them. But it is significant that he regarded hypocrisy as a grave danger during the period when Puritanism had the most political and social clout. There are no identifiable instances of Watson accusing fellow Presbyterians of hypocrisy in like manner. But since they would have constituted the main audience for his sermons and writings—and thus his warnings—there is little doubt that he believed this spiritual disease resided

174. *Repentance*, 91.
175. *GMP*, 138.
176. "'Tis the Note of an Hypocrite, he hath a squint Eye, he looks more to his own Glory than God's Glory." *BPD*, 1:3.
177. Trevor-Roper, *Crisis*, 308-309; Wilson, *Pulpit in Parliament*, 155.

within every congregation in the land.

Comfort for the godly in the face of doubts about their sincerity

Because Watson so emphasised the divide between the sincere, godly Christian and the outwardly religious hypocrite, it was natural that many of his readers and hearers would question the sincerity of their own piety. This was certainly common amongst the Puritans. Their adherents were well-known for spells of anxiety as to their spiritual state—and thus we find the earlier generation of Elizabethan Puritans already addressing such concerns.[178] Watson addressed this pastoral issue in a few different ways. In *Godly Man's Picture* he assures his readers that genuine believers may be blemished with some hypocrisy and yet not be classed as hypocrites. "[A]ll that have the risings of hypocrisy in them, are not to be judged hypocrites, for these may be the *spots of God's children.* But that which denominates an hypocrite, is, when hypocrisy is predominant, and is like a spreading humour in the body."[179] He goes on to lay down two chief indicators that someone is properly a hypocrite, namely "When one serves God for sinister ends" and "when there is some sin dear to a man, which he cannot part with."[180] Even if one fears they are under the power of hypocrisy, they ought to beg Christ for mercy and deliverance, rather than simply despairing.[181] But when a sincere Christian is aware of forms of hypocrisy within themselves, Watson makes this a preventative against spiritual pride. Even the godly cannot claim to have conquered all the insidiousness of insincerity in this life.[182]

In *Body of Divinity,* Watson notes that Satan often seeks to overwhelm Christians with condemnatory accusations of hypocrisy. "Satan would make us question our Interest in God, he tells us we are Hypocrites, and God doth not love us."[183] The antidote to these doubts is to seek assurance of salvation from God. The satanic thoughts were to be combated with the sure knowledge that "a real work of grace" has occurred in one's heart.[184] Watson likewise

178. See for instance, Beeke and Jones, *Puritan Theology*, 580, 588, 932-933.
179. *GMP*, 13.
180. *GMP*, 14.
181. *GMP*, 14.
182. *DC*, 60.
183. *BPD*, 1:203.
184. *BPD*, 1:203.

recalls the biblical story of Job being accused of hypocrisy by Satan. He extracts from it the principle that loyalty to God in the face of personal afflictions is another reassuring sign of godliness that disproves the charge of hypocrisy.[185] The other great testimony against the charge of hypocrisy is love for God. If a person loves God, they can be assured of their sincerity. Watson also exhorts Christians to labour to increase their love for God. Progressive growth in love was an even greater sign of sincerity over and against hypocrisy.[186]

Conclusion

Watson's concept of godliness precluded a casual attitude towards the religion of others. Since true piety was the appropriate response to true revelation from God, it could never be reduced to private religious practice based on personally held convictions. From Watson's perspective, all forms of piety must be evaluated according to their associated theology, religious affections and general practice.

The nature of the English and European religious landscape in Watson's time called for a strong and uncompromising presentation of Puritan piety amongst other variants. England was a nation which had been violently pulled back and forth in a seemingly apocalyptic struggle between Catholicism and Protestantism in the century before Watson's ministry. The threat of a Catholic resurgence continued to hang over the tenuous Protestant settlement of the Restoration period. Therefore, his attacks upon Catholic devotion as inferior to his own cannot be viewed as spiteful reminders of the failures of a vanquished foe. Rather, they convey an earnest concern to show his fellow English Christians a better way forward. Watson warned them against returning to life under Rome's influence through association, marriage or deception. Watson's most important texts relating to piety also come after Charles II had shattered the hopes held by many English Presbyterians that they might finally have their turn at shaping the nation's religious agenda.[187] Arminian theology and nominal Christianity were alarming symptoms of a church being deformed rather than reformed. Therefore, it was vital for proponents of Puritan piety to emphasise their vision of godliness in contradistinction with the state religion that was

185. *DC*, 33.
186. *DC*, 139.
187. Spurr, *English Puritanism*, 129.

passing as Protestantism.

Watson had confidence in God's faithfulness towards the godly. But this did not prevent him from seeing the need to promote biblical piety in existential terms. There was no guarantee, in his mind, that England would not become what we might today term a post-Christian society if it continued drifting away from biblical truth, piety and practice.[188] Such a drift would not, however, be perpetual. God would in all likelihood judge England. This could happen spiritually, by God removing the gospel, along with His favour and presence. Or it could occur temporally, as Watson believed had already taken place in the plague of 1665 and the inferno of 1666. Thus, the urgency that drove his preoccupation with godliness was due to the serious spiritual threat posed by the errors that deprived English religion of true piety.

Watson's engagement with atheism and non-Christian religions in his expressions of piety are less important than his contentions with broadly Christian groups. Yet it is not insignificant for understanding his context. Atheism was not only a disgracing of God, but a destructive influence to the community. It led to wavering in faith and piety and a moral laxity that brought the judgement of a very real God upon people, cities and kingdoms. Watson could foresee that godliness would always have to contend with godlessness. Yet he would be alarmed by how popular an opinion open atheism became in subsequent centuries and the effect it had upon the life of the nation. Watson's opinion of Islam, Judaism and polytheism is generally negative and all godliness is impossible apart from Christ in his thought. However, his use of their zealous, misdirected devotion as a goad to drive lax Christians into pursuing religion in earnest is notable. Watson could exhort believers to take note of the way non-Christians displayed reverence in response to what they believed what was true—even when nothing could be learned from them at the doctrinal level. This is insightful with respect to his approach to piety. Jesus had warned his disciples that their righteousness must exceed that of the misguided religious leaders if they were to enter the Kingdom of Heaven (Matt 5:20). Watson followed suit in urging Christians to ensure their zeal, love and devotion exceeded that of the pagans if God was to truly be glorified.

But parallel to all of these approaches to piety that were defective

---

188. See for instance, *Repentance*, 121-122. This subject is discussed further in Chapter 11.

due to their core doctrinal basis was the perennial problem of religious hypocrisy. This was present even in the most theologically pure communities. Defining godliness over and against hypocrisy was indeed timeless in some respects. It resonated considerably with the biblical emphasis expressed in that quotation which features prominently in both testaments, "This people honours me with their lips, but their heart is far from me" (Isa 29:13; Matt 15:8). But it did have special relevance in Watson's context due to the social advantages of appearing at least somewhat religious. Thus, the pedantic degree to which Watson and other Puritans emphasise sincerity of heart reflects their retrieval of a key Scriptural theme. They first examined the quality of their own piety, before proceeding to earnestly warn their neighbours not to trifle with God by feigning religion. Hypocrisy was a more pressing issue among Protestant and even Puritan communities. The more someone outwardly conformed to doctrinal orthodoxy and devout practice without appropriate, Godward affections, the greater the extent of their betrayal of piety. The appearance of godliness without the substance was the greatest antithesis of all.

Excursus
"How few Godly ones are to be found?"

The question of why "godly" was the preferred, shorthand descriptor for Watson and his co-religionists has been addressed, as has the issue of which religious groups were condemned by Watson for being incapable of godliness. A serious question remains as to the extent of the godly as a religious category in Watson's mind. Hypocrites were present in a range of Protestant denominations. But was the converse true—were there godly Christians to be found outside of Watson's theological tribe? The answer to this question matters because Watson leaves it somewhat unresolved in his writings. If one imagines Late English Puritanism as a bounded set—in which members of the movement held a clear consensus as to who was included or excluded—then it can be presumed that Watson had an understanding of "Puritan" (or, at least, "the godly") which extended beyond English and Scottish Presbyterianism.[a] But while it is clear that certain groups are completely excluded from the ranks of the godly in Watson's mind (e.g. Roman Catholics and non-Trinitarians) it is ambiguous as to how he views members of orthodox Protestant churches who differed with him on significant issues.

We noted in an earlier excursus on the Sabbath that Watson's strict expectations in relation to the Lord's Day may have called into question the piety of a range of devout Christians in England and Western Europe. There are no grounds for suggesting that his Sabbatarian polemics were ever intentionally targeting Lutherans, continental Reformed or pious conformists within the English Church. Instead it would appear that Watson generated an unintentional dilemma, of which he was seemingly incognizant. If his position on the Sabbath invalidated the devotion of Christians who likely shared many elements of his commitment to godliness,

a. I am borrowing the set analogy used by Albert Mohler in his chapter "Confessional Evangelicalism" in *Four Perspectives on the Spectrum of Evangelicalism* eds. A. D. Naselli and C. Hansen (Grand Rapids: Zondervan, 2011): 75-77.

Watson would come across as hyper-partisan—undercutting both his profession to be a "lover of peace" and his protestations against unnecessarily divisions in the church.[b] If, instead, he regarded devout members of these church traditions as godly brethren, then some of his Sabbatarian comments and the implications that they carry are too strong. I would suggest that the latter option better fits Watson's ecclesiological instincts, with the result that he has created an unwitting inconsistency in the practical impact of his Sabbatarianism. While he could have perhaps found a way to distinguish between impious Sabbath profanation and differing views on the Lord's Day within the Protestant tradition, he makes no effort to do so. This leaves him appearing more exclusionary in his understanding of godliness than he actually was.

The other area of ambiguity relates to those within the Puritan movement itself who were in disagreement with Watson on significant theological issues. I have noted that he regarded many in the Independent party during the Civil War and Interregnum as religious hypocrites. Still more of them were covenant-breakers in his mind, due to their neglect or abandonment of the SLC. And Watson was, for some time, in grave opposition to the Independent policy of religious toleration—regarding those who implemented it to be guilty of promoting heresy and ungodliness.[c] Calvinistic Baptists in England were fellow travellers with Watson on most important questions of theology and piety and yet his repudiation of credobaptism includes statements that would potentially impugn their status as godly Christians.[d] Did Watson's misgivings about these points of disagreement lead to an invalidation of the piety of men and women who were very close to him in much of their religious outlook?

Despite taking a strong stance on several of the points of contention that existed between them, it is highly implausible to propose that Watson excluded non-Presbyterian Puritans from the ranks of the godly. Earlier studies have pointed to his participation in the Hackney lectures of 1669 as evidence of Watson's positive collaboration with Independent ministers, along with his pastoral partnership with Stephen Charnock (who began his ministry as an Independent).[e] Such collegiality would have been impossible with men that Watson did not regard as genuinely pious. Within the

b. E.g. *Two Witnesses*, 6; *GMP*, 200-205.

c. E.g. *Beatitudes*, 86-87.

d. *BPD*, 2:410-411.

e. Haukenfrer, "Bellows of Affection," 22-23, 37; Bremer, *Congregational Communion*, 243.

Independent party in England, then, there were both saints and hypocrites—an assessment that would have applied equally to Watson's own Presbyterian circles. Significantly, while Watson did not regard his Independent partners at Hackney to be hypocrites, some of them, such as John Owen, would have been guilty of positions and actions which Watson had railed against previously (e.g. promotion of toleration; abandonment of the SLC; overthrow of the monarchy).[f]

In the case of the Calvinistic Baptists, it is harder to make a definitive conclusion, since Watson has nothing to say about either the group in general or his most notable contemporaries of that persuasion, such as John Bunyan, William Kiffin or Hercules Collins. Just as his assault on Sabbath-breakers appears to have had a particular kind of profane violator in mind and was not targeted at all who did not share his views, it is possible that Watson's denunciation of credobaptism was directed predominantly at Anabaptists rather than his Reformed brethren who refused to baptise infants. However, it is without question that Watson, as a minister in London, would have been aware of such Baptists who were active in the city. The argumentation against credobaptism in his catechetical lectures is worded in such a way that makes it difficult to avoid the conclusion that he was tarring all adherents of this theological position with the same brush, due to the practices of its most extreme proponents.

> The Baptizing of Persons grown up to Maturity, we may argue against *ab effectu*, from the Ill Consequences of it. They dip the Persons they baptize over Head and Ears in cold Water, and naked, which as it is Indecent, so it is Dangerous, and hath been often times the occasion of Chronical Diseases, yea, Death itself, and so is a plain Breach of the Sixth Commandment. And how far God hath given up many Persons, who are for the deferring of Baptism, to other vile Opinions and vicious Practices, is evident, if we consult with History: Especially if we read over the Actings of the Anabaptists in Germany.[g]

Thus, while the Anabaptists are named by Watson as the extreme example of this error, his comments here suggest that merely holding to the doctrine and practice of credobaptism is sinful and the gateway to heinous heresy. Therefore, Watson's Calvinistic Baptist contemporaries fall into a far greyer area with respect to his delineation of the godly. He was certainly not antagonistic towards

f. See Gribben, *Owen and English Puritanism*, 74-75.
g. *BPD*, 2:410-411.

them in the manner in which he expressed his utter disdain for other religious groups. And yet the complete lack of acknowledgement, let alone affirmation, of these brethren in his writings prevents us from assuming that he would have recognised the godliness of Baptists on the basis of their common theological vision and posture of piety. The introduction of the 1689 London Baptist Confession makes it clear that the English Calvinistic Baptists strove for Presbyterians and Congregationalists to recognise them as genuine members of the Reformed community. The drafters stated the Confession's purpose to be,

> for the information and satisfaction of those that did not thoroughly understand what our principles were, or had entertained prejudices against our profession, by reason of the strange representation of them by some men of note who had taken very wrong measures, and accordingly led others into misapprehension of us and them.[h]

This adds weight to the possibility that Watson maintained an uncharitable sentiment towards Baptists in general, which would have obscured his recognition of their piety being substantially the same as his. What seems certain is the Calvinistic Baptists would have sat very close to the boundary of the godly set—but the side on which they sat remains unclear.

In summary, "the godly," from Watson's perspective, were a devout minority in the superficially Christian England of the seventeenth century—the members of which were not confined to one church or sect. While Watson's hallmarks of godliness are intentionally exclusionary, he was seeking to draw a boundary between the sincerely pious and those with a more liberal disposition towards matters of religion, along with those with heretical doctrine or immoral lives. Orthodox Protestants who exhibited the characteristics of godliness and performed the necessary religious duties for spiritual growth would have satisfied Watson's criteria, even if there was considerable disagreement on certain points of doctrine. By today's standards, Watson's attitude towards other Christian groups was far from ecumenical, yet he was also not a factious fundamentalist excluding all but his own party from the Kingdom of God.

---

h. "Introduction" *Second London Baptist Confession* (1689): i.

Summary of PART 3

Watson's vision of godliness concurred with that of his Puritan contemporaries, was corroborated by the best historical witnesses to biblical piety and controverted all forms of devotion that did not correspond with his theology and practice. My survey of the secondary literature on Puritan spirituality and the writings of Baxter, Owen and Charnock has demonstrated that the substance of Watson's piety was common to late English Puritanism. Collectively, the writers of Scripture and the luminaries of Early-Middle English Puritanism including Greenham, Perkins, Ames and Sibbes were by far the most influential upon Watson's expression of piety. Yet, I have also highlighted the importance of Augustine, Bernard and Calvin as influences from the period between the first and seventeenth centuries.

Watson's contention with other religious groups can be distilled down to the evaluation of their faith and practice as departures from the ancient and biblical tradition of devotion. True piety would always have to be promoted in the context of widespread counterfeiting. This leaves Watson with an uncharitable appearance in relation to his theological opponents. However, this was a by-product of the Puritan conviction that worship must occur in strict adherence to God's revelation of Himself and His commandments concerning devotion. Roman Catholicism and general religious hypocrisy were the major targets of Watson's censure because of their antithetical relationship to sincere, biblical devotion from the heart. In the case of the former, misguided piety and practice arose from the obscuration of the biblical gospel. In the case of the latter, the correct form and motions of religion masked the insincerity of a heart that lacked genuine affections towards God.

Watson promoted what he believed to be the biblical approach to piety in a religious context where Roman Catholicism and Protestant hypocrisy were the greatest threats to this endeavour. The reversion of the English Church to Roman doctrine and practice was a live possibility in the reigns of the later Stuart monarchs (Charles II and James II). Pretentious religious devotion among the English elite (including clergy) was a perennial problem threatening the welfare of the national church. The necessity of the times required a clear and distinctively Puritan presentation of the nature of godliness. Watson sought to take on these threats directly by grounding people in biblical piety. Since this required firm instruction in Christian doctrine—he devoted much of his later pastoral ministry to that end.

PART 4

Practical Divinity: Watson's Catalyst for Godliness

The aim of Watson's catechetical project, posthumously published as *A Body of Practical Divinity*, was the advancement of godliness through theological instruction. The Westminster divines had an undeniable concern with the cultivation of piety.[1] Yet David Sytsma has recently noted a minimal focus on affectional piety in discussions of "dogmatic theology," by earlier generations of Reformed Christians.[2] He suggests that attention to the affections is often deferred until "the law and prayer sections of catechisms."[3] The Westminster documents are among the examples Sytsma gives of such a tendency.[4] Watson represents a late English Puritan corrective to this tendency in the Reformed tradition. The theological portion of the WSC forms the skeleton of the first volume of *Body of Divinity*. Watson exceeds the Westminster divines in the depth of his exposition of each doctrine. But *Body of Divinity* surpasses the WSC to an even greater degree, when it comes to elucidating the implications of each truth for practical piety.

In terms of systematic theology, Richard Muller has identified Watson as a representative figure of what he describes as the earlier phase of "high [reformed] orthodoxy" (i.e. 1640-1685).[5] This is true in the sense that his work explicitly "rests upon a confessional summation of faith."[6] But, whereas most of the other theologians from this period listed by Muller were university academics writing disputations in Latin, Watson was a pastor presenting doctrine in the vernacular and using imagery and phraseology designed to be accessible to the laity.[7] Watson was a capable and cogent theologian, but he lacked

1. See for instance WCF 21; WLC, Qs. 93, 95, 104-117, 157, 162, 167, 171, 175, 178-187, 190.
2. David Sytsma, "The Logic of the Heart: Analyzing the Affections in Early Reformed Orthodoxy," in *Church and School in Early Modern Protestantism: Studies in Honor of Richard A. Muller on the Maturation of a Theological Tradition*, ed. Jordan J. Ballor (Leiden: Brill, 2013): 472.
3. Sytsma, "Logic of the Heart," 472.
4. Sytsma, "Logic of the Heart," 472 n. 9.
5. Muller, *PRRD* 1:31, 49; *PRRD* 3:116.
6. Muller, *PRRD* 1:31.
7. The other exceptions are Stephen Charnock and Edward Leigh, both of whom—like Watson—wrote in English and did not hold a university office. Muller, PRRD 1:47-48. However, Charnock and Leigh nevertheless appear to have had more of an inclination towards engagement with theological issues of a more technical nature, than what is evident from Watson's writings. See Siekawitch, "Stephen Charnock's Doctrine of the Knowledge of God," 98-99; Ryan McGraw, *Reformed Scholasticism:*

a demonstrated interest or ability in the highly technical matters that were frequently discussed in more scholastic or speculative theology. Despite being more detailed in its discussion of individual theological points than the WSC itself, or Thomas Vincent's earlier commentary on the *Catechism*, Watson's *Body of Divinity* represents what one of his contemporaries described as the "succinct and brief" approach to theology.[8] From Watson's perspective, the Westminster standards had established a doctrinal consensus amongst English Presbyterians—one he had more interest in transmitting than reformulating. But it remained for an adherent of these articles to express a Puritan vision of spirituality that was clearly derived from them. Watson's significance lies in the fact that he was the figure to do exactly that. *Body of Divinity* represents the most substantial effort by a late English Puritan to draw out the connections between their confessional system of faith and their notion of godliness.

Understood as a project in later English Puritan spirituality, Watson's catechetical lectures developed the basic theological framework outlined in the WSC into a fully-fledged system of practical divinity. "Practical Divinity" is an intentional approach to doctrine geared towards an affectional or active response. Charles Hambrick-Stowe encapsulates this well when he says, "Every topic of theology relates to the call to 'live in accord with the will of God' in this life and the next—'all of which refer directly to practice.'"[9] In describing how Puritans executed this commitment in their preaching, Hambrick-Stowe offers the following model: "[It] began with the 'opening' (explication) of the text, moved to an examination of doctrines suggested by the text and concluded with 'uses' or application to the lives of those in the congregation."[10] *Body of Divinity* utilises this pattern consistently. Each topical treatment begins with theological exposition and clarification, before progressing to the "use" of the doctrine, along with any relevant "exhortations" and "reproofs."[11] Early on in *Body of Divinity,* Watson gives a key reason for gaining "knowledge of the grounds and principles of true religion."[12] Without these, he tells us, it is impossible to render God the "reasonable service" He requires of us.[13] Piety sits

Recovering the Tools of Reformed Theology (London: T&T Clark, 2019): 47-48.

8. Edward Leigh, *A Systeme or Body of Divinity* (1654) (Oxford: TCP, 2004): xiv. http://ota.ox.ac.uk/id/A47625
9. Hambrick-Stowe, "Practical Divinity and Spirituality," 193.
10. Hambrick-Stowe, "Practical Divinity and Spirituality," 195.
11. See for example "God is Spirit," *BPD*, 1:24-26.
12. *BPD*, 1:iii.
13. *BPD*, 1:iii.

at the crucial nexus of this matter. The Christian's reasonable service is only possible if the heart is moved with true affection towards God. This, in turn, is only possible if something of God has been revealed to the believer, in Christ, through the Scriptures.[14]

Watson drew upon the Westminster Assembly's doctrine of God to present his audience with a picture of an infinite and majestic Deity—convinced that a proper consideration of this God would naturally invoke a range of intense affections. The locus for beholding and contemplating the glories of God was Christ, who with the Holy Spirit also enabled the Christian to be restored to a frame of heart and mind that could render devotion to their King. This is intimately connected to Watson's utilisation of Westminster anthropology and soteriology to show how Christians—in undergoing the restoration of their humanity—experienced the Trinitarian God as a Saviour enacting their redemption. This culminated in the godly Christian's resurrection with Christ and glorification by God—enabling them to reflect, worship and enjoy God forever, in line with the purpose of their creation and redemption.

14. That this idea, of "reasonable service" being enabled by a solid theological foundation and appropriate disposition of the heart, was popular across the breadth of late reformed orthodoxy, is evident in Wilhelmus à Brakel, *The Christian's Reasonable Service* (1700) (Grand Rapids: Reformation Heritage, 1992): 3-5.

Chapter 9
Becoming "God-admirers:"*
The Trinitarian Core of Watson's Piety

A. "A Constellation of all Beauties:" Divine attributes that incite godly affections*

We have already argued that, for Watson, godliness was a theologically-fuelled response towards God. It was a true and proper regard for the holy and majestic God as He really is. Therefore, Watson's doctrine of God is indispensable to his understanding and promotion of godliness. A survey of Watson's treatment of the divine attributes will demonstrate that at the heart of his piety lay a picture of God as both a unique and incomprehensibly transcendent Being and a glorious, Almighty sovereign. When properly appreciated, these dominant aspects of Watson's perception of God incited love, reverence and the other heart responses that constituted the core affectional dimension of godliness. Each element of Watson's devotion was apposite to one or more aspects of the divine nature.

Adoration of the Unfathomable

> Q: What is God?
> A: God is a Spirit, Infinite, Eternal and Unchangeable in his Being, Wisdom, Power, Holiness, Justice, Goodness and Truth.
> WSC, Q4.

* Title taken from *BPD*, 2:284.

* Title taken from *BPD*, 1:1.

After a brief defence of God's existence, Watson progresses to speak successively of the divine attributes listed above.[1] There is no categorical division of these aspects of God's nature into incommunicable and communicable attributes, or any similar distinctions. But there is a clear break in the list at the *Being* of God. Those aspects introduced prior are all intended to describe both God's being and the subsequently listed attributes.[2] That is to say that God is, for example, infinite in both His being and His justice.[3] Therefore, these first four aspects (i.e. spirituality, infinity, eternality and unchangeability) function as a set of characteristics which emphasise the sheer immensity and uniqueness of the Being of God. The remainder are more relational and communicable in nature. These are qualities that might be possessed by a creature—with God possessing each in the superlative sense.[4]

The Attributes

Watson's treatment of God's spirituality focuses on His otherness and segues into an expanded discussion of His infinity. "God is a Spirit uncreate[d]," "immense" and "infinite," unlike other spiritual beings (such as angels).[5] He is distinct in kind from the human soul and incorporeal in contrast to embodied spirits.[6] "Infinite" best describes the "kind of Spirit" God is.[7] For Watson, divine infinity can best be understood in relation to omnipresence.[8] It is the lack of restrictions upon His divine Being which establishes God's

1. Muller has observed that treatments of the existence of God were the norm for early sections of Reformed orthodox systematic theologies. *PRRD*, 3:164. Watson's attention to this matter is driven by his later concern with widespread "practical atheism." *BPD*, 1:20, 22. However it is minimal compared to that given by his colleague Stephen Charnock. See *Existence and Attributes,* 1:23-88.
2. See for instance, *BPD*, 1:25.
3. *BPD*, 1:27.
4. See Muller, *PRRD*.III, 212-226, for comparison to other Reformed orthodox treatments of these attributes. For discussion of "incommunicable" versus "communicable" attributes see Michael Horton, *The Christian Faith: A Systematic Theology for Pilgrims on the Way* (Grand Rapids: Zondervan, 2011): 225.
5. *BPD*, 1:24.
6. *BPD*, 1:24. Muller notes that Calvin (in *Against the Libertines*) also emphasized this distinction between God and other kinds of Spirit. *PRRD*, 3:299.
7. *BPD*, 1:25.
8. *BPD*, 1:25. This way of describing divine infinity was common in earlier Reformed orthodox theological works. See, for instance, Ames, *Marrow*, 14-15; James Ussher, *A Body of Divinitie* (1645) (Oxford: TCP, 2005): 36-37. http://purl.ox.ac.uk/ota/A64622

transcendence—especially when viewed in contrast to the finiteness of creation.[9] Divine omnipresence would have been affirmed by most of Watson's theological adversaries.[10] Yet he attacks the Catholic doctrine of transubstantiation as a distortion of this attribute that wrongly extends a sense of unbound presence to the human body of Christ.[11] This is followed immediately by a denial of God's need for "Proxies" or "Viceregents" due to His immediate proximity to His entire domain.[12] Watson does not explicitly utilise this principle to invalidate the pontificate as Christ's supposed vicar —but the context lends itself to such an interpretation. This reinforces a sense of Watson's vigilance in identifying any defective doctrines in his *milieu* that might diminish God's glory by misrepresenting the divine attributes that incited piety.

This emphasis on divine infinity is extended to include a discussion on omniscience—an attribute not explicit in the text of the WSC.[13] Watson's understanding of omniscience reflects what has tended to be the standard view throughout Christian history. Laurence Wood notes that "perfect omniscience" was the "consensus of the Church down through the ages, particularly the theology of the Early Greek Church Fathers who formulated the standard doctrines of Trinitarian orthodoxy."[14] For Watson, God possesses full knowledge of all things, past, present and future—including the content of human thoughts. He is incapable of erroneous misapprehension or discovering something previously unknown to Him.[15] Watson's insistence that God "knows Future Contingencies" would appear to be a swipe at certain teachings that were circulating in his time, which queried the nature and extent of divine knowledge of the future.[16] For Watson, God's absolute knowledge establishes

9. *BPD*, 1:25. Watson's descriptions of God being unbound and uncontainable follow the treatments of divine infinity in earlier Reformed British theological treatises e.g. Ames, *Marrow*, 14-15; Ussher, *Body of Divinitie*, 27; Thomas Vincent, *An Explicatory Catechism* (1675) (Oxford: TCP, 2004): 18. http://purl.ox.ac.uk/ota/A64986

10. Perhaps not the Socinians, whose denial of divine infinity attracted the polemical attention of John Owen. See Carl Trueman, *John Owen: Reformed Catholic, Renaissance Man* (Aldershot: Ashgate, 2007): 39-42.

11. *BPD*, 1:27.

12. *BPD*, 1:28.

13. The related attribute of wisdom appears further down the list and Watson treats it separately in *BPD*.I.

14. He cites Irenaeus, Clement of Alexandria, Origen and Gregory of Nyssa to establish this point. Laurence Wood, *God and History* (Lexington: Emeth Press, 2005): 270.

15. *BPD*, 1:30.

16. For details of the Puritan contention with Socinians—and perhaps also Arminians—over this issue, see Trueman, *John Owen*, 57-66. See also, Muller, *PRRD*, 3:120-121.

His transcendence in relation to all other beings. "God's Knowledge is Primary. He is the Original, the Pattern and Prototype of all Knowledge; others borrow their Knowledge of him; the Angels light their Lamps at this glorious Sun."[17]

Watson presents God's eternality in a similar vein to his treatment of divine infinity and omniscience. It is contrasted with temporary creatures that have both beginning and an end (e.g. animals) and creatures which will live forever but had a definite beginning (i.e. humans and angels).[18] In treating this subject of eternality, Watson follows certain forebears in the Reformed tradition by honing in on the divine name as a communication of aseity and everlastingness.[19]

> [God] is *semper existens*, viz. from everlasting to everlasting; it is God's Title, a Jewel of his Crown. 1. He is called, The King Eternal, 1 Tim. 1.17. 2. Jehovah, a word that properly sets out God's Eternity; a word so dreadful, that the Jews trembled to name or read it ... Jehovah contains in it Time past, present, and to come, Rev. 1.4., which is, and which was, and which is to come; it interprets the word Jehovah. *Which is:* He subsists of himself, having a pure independent Being. *Which was:* God only was before Time. There is no searching into the Records of Eternity. *Which is to come:* His Kingdom hath no End. His Crown hath no Successors.[20]

Existing in perfection from and throughout all eternity, God was impervious to any alterations to His being or character, which would diminish His divine perfection. "In God there is nothing [that] looks like a Change, no better or worse, no better in him, because then he were not perfect, nor worse in him, for then he should cease to be perfect: He is immutably Holy, immutably Good; There is no Shadow of Change in him."[21] Again Watson is consistent with the Reformed tradition. Muller observes that the link between God's eternality and aseity and his immutability was present in the thought of Augustine and "remained at the heart of the doctrine in both the era of the Reformation and the era of orthodoxy."[22]

17. *BPD*, 1:30.
18. *BPD*, 1:33.
19. For a discussion of Calvin and other Reformed theologians' treatment of the Divine Name in relation to these characteristics, see Muller, *PRRD*, 3:248-251, 261. See also Ussher, *Body of Divinitie*, 30; Ames, *Marrow*, 11.
20. *BPD*, 1:33.
21. *BPD*, 1:37.
22. *PRRD*, 3:308. In summarising the Reformed orthodox position on this attribute, Muller offers "God's immutability is 'God's perfection according to which He remains what He is,' in all of his attributes and excellencies." *PRRD*, 3:313.

From this standpoint Watson criticises the lack of certainty in God's dealings with his people according to Arminian theology.[23]

The effect of these attributes on piety

Watson's proposed uses of each doctrine pertaining to an attribute of God provide us with a clear picture of what he understood to be the necessary, pious responses to the divine revelation received through the Scriptures. Since God is Spirit, Christians in response must seek to become more "spiritual" themselves and to worship God "in spirit" (as Jesus called for in John 4:24).[24] As I have noted in Chapter 7, this was also an important emphasis for Stephen Charnock.[25] For Watson, being spiritual means "To be Refined and Sublimated, to have the Heart still in Heaven, to be thinking of God and Glory, and to be carried up in a fiery Chariot of Love to God."[26] Worshipping God in spirit is "to worship him without ceremonies" and "[through faith in Christ] to worship him with the utmost Zeal and Intenseness of Soul."[27] We can see in these descriptions, Watson's emphasis on heart affections, meditation and a reiteration of his understanding of *eusebeia*. Christian spirituality was a response to God's essential spirituality. It necessitated spiritual engagement in worship, rather than the mere, external performance of religious duties. What I have already observed of Watson's contentions with Catholic and Anglo-Catholic approaches to worship are rehearsed in his treatment of this subject.[28]

The attributes which conveyed a sense of God's unmatched immensity and transcendence called for a heart response of sheer awe. This is evident in Watson's application of the doctrine of divine omnipresence.

> If God be Infinite by his Omnipresence, then see the Greatness and Immenseness of the Divine Majesty. What a Great God do we serve ... Well may the Scripture

23. *BPD*, 1:39.
24. *BPD*, 1:25-26.
25. Charnock proceeds from the Spirituality of God to the spiritual worship of God in his *Existence and Attributes*, 1:176-275.
26. *BPD*, 1:25.
27. *BPD*, 1:26. I have already noted, in Chapter 8, that this idea of worship without ceremony was a condemnation of Roman and Anglo-Catholic liturgicalism. This is made explicit by the fact that Watson attacks Catholic "image-worship" as an affront to the spiritual nature of God, before giving the above descriptions.
28. *BPD*, 1:26.

> display the Greatness of his Glory, who is Infinite in all places. He transcends our weak Conceptions, how can our finite Understanding comprehend him who is Infinite? He is infinitely above all our Praises, Neh. 9.5. Blessed be thy glorious name, which is exalted above all blessing and praise. O what a poor Nothing is Man, when we think of God's Infiniteness, as the Stars disappear at the rising of the Sun! O how doth Man shrink into nothing when Infinite Majesty shines forth in his Glory.[29]

In concluding his treatment of omnipresence, Watson introduces a phrase he will use with respect to God's attributes several times: "Adore/admire where you cannot fathom."

> If God be Infinite in his glorious Essence, learn to admire where you cannot fathom ... *Canst thou by searching find out God*? He is Infinite. We can no more search out his Infinite Perfections, then a Man upon the top of the highest Mountain can reach the Firmament, or take a Star in his hand. O have God-admiring Thoughts! adore where you cannot fathom ... In Heaven we shall see God clearly, but not fully, for he is Infinite; he will communicate himself to us according to the bigness of our Vessel, but not the Immenseness of his Nature. Adore then where you cannot Fathom.[30]

Contemplation of the incomprehensible aspects of God's nature facilitated two of the means Watson previously identified for glorifying Him: admiration (or appreciation) and adoration (or worship). There has always been a temptation amongst Christians to avoid giving serious thought to the nature of God, due to so much about it being beyond human comprehension. Watson encourages the opposite. The very fact that God is unfathomable is a reason to recognise His uniqueness as a Being and render worship to Him.

As noted already, divine omniscience stood behind the Puritan emphasis on sincerity and hypocrisy. Watson also uses it to reprove "baptized Heathen"—those nominal Christians who belong to the church but have the barest knowledge of God.[31] But Watson not only utilised the unlimited knowledge of God as a deterrent from secret sin and ignorance. He also provided a very positive application in relation to this doctrine.

> The setting ourselves, as under the Eye of God's Omniscience, would *cause*

29. *BPD*, 1:28.
30. *BPD*, 1:29.
31. *BPD*, 1:31.

> *Reverence in the Worship of God.* God sees the frame and carriage of our Hearts when we come before him: How would this call in our straggling thoughts? how would this animate and spirit Duty? it would make us put fire to the Incense ... To think God is in this place, he beholds us, would add Wings to Prayer, and Oil to the flame of our Devotion.[32]

Omniscience not only provided motivation to pursue religion in a lively manner. It also provided the assurance that just as surely as nothing evil would escape God's notice and punishment, so too nothing good done by the saints would go unnoticed and unrewarded.

> Christian, thou settest hours apart for God, thy Thoughts run upon him as thy Treasure, God takes notice of every good Thought ... When the Secrets of all Hearts shall be opened, God will make an honourable mention of the Zeal and Devotion of his People, and he himself will be the Herald of their Praises.[33]

Just as God's eternality reinforced the sense of his incomparable infinity, so it also called for the same kind of response, "it will make us adore where we cannot Fathom."[34] Proper appreciation of this attribute would serve as a corrective to sinful tendencies that interfered with godly esteem.

> The thoughts of God's Eternity would make us have high adoring thoughts of God. We are apt to have mean irreverent thoughts of him, *Psal.* 50.21. *Thou thoughtest I was such a one as thy self; weak* and *mortal.* But if we would think of God's Eternity, when all Power ceaseth, he is King Eternal, his Crown flourisheth for ever, who can make us happy or miserable for ever, this would make us have adoring thoughts of God.[35]

Finally, God's immutability induces great confidence in His character and promises. The godly should increasingly turn from reliance upon created things for security and joy and look to the one constant in the universe instead. When their circumstances changed for the worse, they were to cling to God's unchanging faithfulness and love and through their faith in Him, become unmoveable themselves.[36]

32. *BPD*, 1:32.
33. *BPD*, 1:32. Charnock echoes this idea in *Existence and Attributes*, 487.
34. *BPD*, 1:35.
35. *BPD*, 1:35. Compare Charnock, *Existence and Attributes*, 308.
36. *BPD*, 1:39. Compare Charnock, *Existence and Attributes*, 354-359.

Summary

God understood as a pure Spirit, infinite and perfect in His nature was fundamental to Watson's outlook on piety. An appreciation of the divine attributes which immeasurably distinguished the Creator from everything He created was key to producing the kind of awe that was integral to adorative devotion. Watson's treatment of God's infinite perfections demonstrates that he did accept limitations to human theological knowledge. His exhortation to adore the unfathomable indicates that the worship of the Triune God was a mixture between responding to what one knew about the Deity and marvelling at how much of the divine nature could only be comprehended in part. The mystery surrounding three divine persons who shared a common essence and were unlimited by factors pertaining to time and space, was crucial to Watson's concept of godliness. It was just as important as what could be apprehended and propositionally affirmed about God. But these attributes do not make God into an exclusively transcendent object of reverence-from-afar. Watson emphasises the sense in which God's omnipresence and omniscience make Him ever-immanent. He is the One who is always present and fully cognizant with respect to every aspect of the believer's life. This gives his piety a strong flavour of *coram Deo.* All public and private Christian conduct reflects the intimate proximity and knowledge of God in relation to His children and their activities. It explains why, for Watson and the Puritans, the concern with piety permeated the entirety of life. Awareness of the infinite God impacted every detail of every moment.[37]

God's Supreme Majesty

As I noted above, the final six attributes listed by the fourth question of the WSC are those which God possesses in a superlative sense and creatures possess in a derivative sense.[38] A creature can be relatively wise, powerful, holy, just, merciful and faithful, whereas God is absolutely wise, powerful etc.[39] Since these attributes are more relatable than the unfathomable ones discussed above,

37. Packer, *Quest for Godliness*, 23-24; Beeke and Jones, *Puritan Theology*, 848-849.
38. See n. 4 above.
39. See for instance, Muller, *PRRD*, 3:223.

they form a picture of God that is most analogous to that of a great king. Kings typically held more glory, honour, power and authority than any other person in the realm. One would likewise hope for their ruler to possess ample wisdom, justice, mercy and faithfulness. In like manner, God excelled in all of these qualities far beyond His natural subjects. Watson's conscious use of this dominant image is indicated by his repeated likening of these attributes to jewels in God's crown, as will be shown below. Before proceeding to develop Watson's use of these attributes to emphasise God's Supreme Majesty, it should be noted that he has already introduced this idea in dealing with the infinite aspects of the divine nature.[40] Therefore, this dominant picture is not confined to these attributes, though it becomes more accentuated as Watson deals with them.[41]

The Attributes

The way in which Watson describes divine wisdom appears to give it a transitional position in his discussion of God's attributes. It is closely related to divine omniscience, referred to as "one of the brightest beams of the Godhead" and an "infinite deep" which should be adored.[42] On the other hand, some of the language used in relation to this attribute is suggestive of kingship. For example, God is spoken of as having a "treasury" of wisdom; being sagacious in his superintendence of nature and society and delighting to outwit and "overthrow" the world's cunning political operators.[43] Wisdom is closely linked to the subject of God's Providence (which Watson discusses subsequently). This refers to His prudential capacity to "govern" the universe in the best manner possible, by "ordering all

40. For example, "If God be Infinite by his Omnipresence, then see the Greatness and Immenseness of the Divine Majesty." *BPD*, 1:28.
41. Muller has noted that in Reformed orthodoxy, "majesty" could often be used to refer to "a summation of all the attributions of eminence or perfections of God and, indeed, as a term for the unreachable and unsearchable height of the Godhead considered in its essence." Muller, *PRRD*, 3:541-542. There was also sometimes a distinction made between "majesty" as the "royal honour" of God as King and "glory"—pertaining to "all those perfections which render him infinitely superior to all other beings" (Venema). *PRRD*, 3:544. We are not suggesting that these nuances apply to Watson's usage of such words, but Muller's observations complement the idea that God could be considered through the prism of the infinite magnitude of His Being or as a lofty Sovereign.
42. *BPD*, 1:40, 42.
43. *BPD*, 1:40, 42.

Issues and Events of things after the Council of his Will to his own Glory."[44] This affirms Muller's summary of wisdom in the Reformed orthodox tradition, "Wisdom is the specific form of knowing according to which 'God knows what is necessary to be done, according to the circumstances of things, and in what order and manner it should be done; by what means he may best attain the end he designs, and thereby display his own glory.'"[45]

For the remaining attributes, the supreme majesty motif is more explicit. In describing God's power, Watson calls Him "Lord Paramount" and the "supreme monarch" from whom all other power and authority is derived.[46] The descriptions of His power that follow are styled as sovereign authority over all things, "O the infinite Power of Jehovah! Before his Scepter Angels vail, and prostrate themselves, Kings cast their Crowns at his Feet."[47] Divine omnipotence was crucial to God's grand roles of Creator, Saviour and Lord. To deprive Him of this attribute was a great travesty. "Take away a King's Power and we un-king him; take away the Lord's Power and we un-God him."[48]

Muller has described the role of holiness in the theology of Reformed orthodoxy as conveying "the inaccessible height of the divine majesty."[49] He also notes that "The divine holiness occupies a far more prominent place in Reformed orthodox discussion of the divine attributes ... than it does in the work of the Reformers themselves."[50] Watson illustrates this by calling holiness "the most sparkling jewel of [God's] crown."[51] He evokes the throne room scene of Yahweh exalted in holiness in Isaiah 6, by citing the cry of the seraphim from the prophet's vision. He considers holiness to be a necessary complement to divine power in order to establish the picture of heavenly majesty, "[God's] power makes him mighty, his holiness makes him glorious."[52]

Divine justice and righteousness are described as "another flower of God's crown" and Watson's treatment of this characteristic

44. *BPD*, 1:69.
45. *PRRD*, 3:386. Muller draws upon Benedict Pictet and Stephen Charnock in formulating this description.
46. *BPD*, 1:43.
47. *BPD*, 1:44.
48. *BPD*, 1:45.
49. *PRRD*, 3:498.
50. *PRRD*, 3:498.
51. *BPD*, 1:47.
52. *BPD*, 1:47. *PRRD*, 3:498.

is replete with references to regalia.[53] "*Psal.* 89.14. *Justice and Judgement are the habitation of thy Throne.* In God Power and Justice meet. Power holds the *Sceptre,* and Justice holds the *Balance.*"[54] God's supreme distribution of justice, determination of guilt and innocence and apportioning of rewards, punishments and clemency are all analogous to an earthly monarch's status as chief magistrate of their realm.[55] Interestingly, while Trueman has identified a concern to refute Socinianism in John Owen's writings on divine justice, Watson's discussion of this attribute is largely non-polemical—aside from his answering of a hypothetical objection about God's fairness in salvation that could have easily come from an Arminian opponent.[56]

In line with other Reformed orthodox figures, Watson views mercy as derived from God's essential goodness.[57] It too, was indispensable to his picture of God's supreme majesty.

> God is represented as a King, and a Rainbow was about his Throne, Rev. 4.2, 3. The Rainbow was an Emblem of Mercy. The Scripture doth oftener represent God in his white Robes of Mercy, then with his Garments rolled in Blood; oftener with his Golden Sceptre then his Iron Rod.[58]

Mercy is later called "one of the most orient pearls of [God's] crown."[59] This is followed shortly after by another of the comparative couplets of which Watson was so fond, 'His holiness makes him illustrious, his mercy makes him propitious."[60] That Watson interprets mercy to be God's "darling attribute" is vital for understanding what kind of king he perceives God to be. If this aspect of the divine character is diminished, we have a terrifyingly glorious and powerful heavenly monarch who would necessarily be unapproachable for sinful

53. *BPD*, 1:51.
54. *BPD*, 1:50.
55. *BPD*, 1:50-52.
56. See Trueman, *John Owen*, 42-46. *BPD*, 1:52.
57. Muller says of God's goodness, "Inasmuch as it is the primary characteristic of all divine relationships with the finite order, it also serves as the primary affection of the divine will. It is in this latter placement, in relation to love, grace, and mercy, that it is most typically found in Reformed theology." *PRRD*, 3:502. Later he presents Musculus as a sample, Reformed orthodox theologian who understood divine mercy as a derivative of God's goodness. *PRRD*, 3:576.
58. *BPD*, 1:54.
59. *BPD*, 1:54.
60. *BPD*, 1:54.

humans.[61] But Watson goes to lengths to ensure that his audience knows God as the king who invites His people into His presence on the basis of His mercy. "We are to look upon God in Prayer, not in his Judge's Robes, but cloth[ed] with a Rainbow, full of Mercy and Clemency ... *We are going to the Father of Mercy, who sits upon a Throne of Grace.* Go with Confidence in this Mercy."[62]

Finally, God's truth is called "one of the richest jewels of his crown."[63] This attribute is understood both in the reality of His being and His faithfulness to His word. Watson contrasts this with earthly rulers. "The word of a prince cannot always be taken, but God's Promise is inviolable."[64] Further, Watson compares God's willingness to be bound by His word in an inalterable manner to the "law of the Medes and Persians"—famously referred to in the Book of Daniel as the mechanism which prevented Darius from revoking his own royal decree.[65]

Before progressing to discuss the appropriate response to God's supreme majesty in Watson's scheme of piety, it is worth pausing to ask whether there exists any priority amongst the attributes with respect to this dominant picture of kingship? Gregg Allison has suggested that Watson's colleague Stephen Charnock elevates holiness above all the other divine attributes in his *Existence and Attributes of God.*[66] Did Watson share such a perspective? In answering this question, I must first reiterate that Watson was capable of using impassioned and even superlative language to describe any particular matter of importance that was his present concern.[67] This is not to say he contradicts himself through mutually exclusive enthusiasm. Rather he has the preacher's gift of being able to fully give himself to expressing the significance of the subject at hand. Thus, when we read his descriptions of the divine attributes,

61. *BPD*, 1:53.
62. *BPD*, 1:55.
63. *BPD*, 1:57.
64. *BPD*, 1:57. We may note here that Watson's experience with a human prince who did not keep his word would have been a fresh memory for him. Charles II's reneging on his undertaking to uphold and implement the *Solemn League and Covenant* was undoubtedly one of the great disappointments of Watson's life.
65. *BPD*, 1:57.
66. "If any, this attribute hath an excellency above His other perfections ... As it seems to challenge an excellency above all His other perfections, so it is the glory of all the rest; as it is the glory of the Godhead, so it is the glory of every perfection in the Godhead." Charnock, *Existence and Attributes of God*, 2:112-113. See Allison, *Historical Theology* (Grand Rapids: Zondervan, 2011): 222-223.
67. See the discussion of meditation and self-denial in Chapter 5.

Watson is dedicated to communicating the vitality and preciousness of each. However, his language does provide some clues as to which were most central to his picture of God as supreme monarch.

As noted above, holiness, justice, mercy and truth are all described as jewels or flowers on the crown of the heavenly majesty. Holiness though is singled out as the "most sparkling jewel" in contrast to the others.[68] It should therefore be taken as having special significance to God's regal splendour.[69] Mercy is called God's "darling Attribute which he most delights in."[70] Certainly Watson contends for a Scriptural priority of mercy over wrath (and perhaps, by implication, justice) and sees mercy as complementary to holiness.[71] Finally, God's sovereign power is so analogous to the royal authority of an earthly ruler that it forms a definitive component of this picture. While all attributes elucidated by Watson are indispensable to the Christian's understanding of God, these three appear to be the central characteristics of the kingly motif.[72]

Piety in response to the divine majesty

The primary affective responses to the picture of God as Supreme Monarch were fear and faith. Watson was explicit that an appreciation of God's unfettered power as Ruler would produce a response of such

68. *BPD*, 1:47.
69. This is consistent with Watson's earlier descriptions of divine holiness in *GMP*, 35 and *Beatitudes*, 255.
70. *BPD*, 1:53.
71. *BPD*, 1:53. Muller quotes Marcus Wendelin (1584-1652) on the relationship between divine mercy and justice: "Mercy and justice are equal in themselves and in God, [but] with respect to their effects and objects, mercy is the greater." *PRRD*, 3:580. Watson here appears to be bolder in suggesting the priority of mercy, even though he would have likely agreed with the notion of essential equality.
72. These attributes are also distinctly linked together as couplets, (i.e. "power makes him mighty, his holiness makes him glorious" and "his holiness makes him illustrious, his mercy makes him endearing"). We find a parallel passage in *GMP*: "Holiness is the most orient Pearl of the King of Heaven's Crown, *Exod. 15. 11. Glorious in Holiness.* God's power makes him Mighty, his mercy makes him lovely, but his holiness makes him glorious." *GMP*, 35. A possible objection against the priority of these three attributes could be made on the basis that Watson refers to "truth" as the "most orient pearl" of God or Christ in several places and more generically applies the same description to divine "glory." *BPD*, 1:121, 219; *BPD*, 3:457, 537. Elsewhere, justice appears in a couplet with power. *BPD*, 1:50. While this means we cannot be dogmatic about the significance of his language in relation to holiness, mercy and power, there is still a solid case for a special place for this triplet in Watson's piety.

great, reverential fear that it would "drive out all other base fear."[73] Divine justice also demanded fear.[74] Appropriate trembling at the thought of God's righteous punishment of sin was necessary for those wishing to avoid experiencing it. "Let us fear the threatening [of judgement] that we may not feel it."[75] Both God's pure hatred of sin (holiness) and His promise to judge the world in righteousness (justice) were matters that should constantly be on the mind of believers.[76]

God's wisdom and truth both induce trust from His subjects.[77] Faith in God's almighty power is crucial to progress in godliness for Watson. It is the believer's only real hope of defeating sin in the battle of self-denial and mortification. "The strong God can conquer thy strong Corruption; though sin be too hard for thee, yet not for him; he can soften hard hearts, quicken the dead."[78] Christians were also to have faith in His mercy and come into His presence to "touch the golden Sceptre of his Mercy, and live."[79] Mercy also plays a special role in inviting the believer's love.

> God's Justice may make us fear him, his Mercy may make us love him. If Mercy will not produce Love, what will? We are to love God for giving us Food, much more for giving us Grace; for sparing Mercy, much more for saving Mercy. Sure that Heart is made of Marble, which the Mercy of God will not dissolve into Love.[80]

Mercy makes the "Godhead appear amiable and lovely" and "sweetens all God's other attributes."[81] God, as king, is not only to be feared and obeyed like a fierce and powerful tyrant.[82] He should be cherished because of his supreme kindness and graciousness.

Since these kingly attributes are more easily relatable to qualities possessed by creatures, it is natural that Watson's pious response

73. *BPD*, 1:44.
74. *BPD*, 1:56.
75. *BPD*, 1:58.
76. *BPD*, 1:52-53.
77. *BPD*, 1:42-43, 58.
78. *BPD*, 1:45. So too Charnock, *Existence and Attributes*, 99.
79. *BPD*, 1:55.
80. *BPD*, 1:56. Love for God as a response to His mercy is also mentioned in Ussher, *Body of Divinitie*, 70.
81. *BPD*, 1:53-54.
82. Elsewhere, Watson uses the oppressive relationship between a Turkish master and slave as a negative contrast to the "ingenuous fear sweetened with love" the Christian ought to have towards God. *RTI*, 21.

to God's majesty includes the emulation of His character. Divine holiness, justice, mercy and truth are all to be imitated as part of the believer's response to God's revelation of Himself to them as these things. Divine wisdom and power are more to be relied upon than emulated, though (following biblical wisdom literature), Watson does present wisdom as something to be sought from God through prayer. There is no direct sense in which believers are to emulate God in the exercise of power—but rather they should beseech God to engage His power on their behalf.[83]

Imitation of holiness is the response most accentuated by Watson. His discussion of it is longer than the imitable aspects of the other three attributes combined. The Christian responds to God's holiness by being conformed to God's character and will.[84] For Watson this has the special sense of the believer coming to share several of God's qualities, in an analogous manner. But it also meant sharing His "disposition" towards things.[85] God's people come to "love what he loves, and hate what he hates."[86] This is significant for our understanding of godliness in Watson. He is effectively saying that the Christian comes to possess God's own affections, namely His "perfect loving of righteousness" and purity and his "abhorrence of evil."[87] Having this resemblance to God's moral character, sharing something of His outlook on the world and being willing to do whatever He wills are all indicative of the Christian being consecrated to her King. By extension, those who attacked the Puritans for their devout emulation of God's holiness were "devoted

---

83. *BPD*, 1:43, 45-46.

84. *BPD*, 1:48. Muller notes this to be a common feature among Reformed orthodox, concerning the applications of holiness. *PRRD*, 3:502. See for example, Charnock, *Existence and Attributes*, 199-206.

85. *BPD*, 1:48.

86. *BPD*, 1:48.

87. *BPD*, 1:47. This raises the question of whether Watson believed in divine impassibility and what implications that classic doctrine might have upon the notion of God possessing affections. Watson clearly affirms some sense of impassibility in *BPD*, 1:24-25, but limits it to God's incapability of "being hurt." Muller has clearly demonstrated that any notion of divine impassibility held by the Reformed orthodox tradition did not preclude God's possession of genuine affections such as love, joy and hatred. *PRRD*, 3:309-310. "[L]ike the Reformers the [reformed] orthodox assume that God has *affections* that characterize his relationship to the world and that some analogy can be drawn between these 'divine affections' and the affections that belong to human willing—with the major qualification that, unlike human affections, the divine affections do not indicate essential change in God and that they are permanent rather than transient dispositions." *PRRD*, 3:553. This is an apt summary of what we find in Watson's treatment of the subject.

to hell."[88] Watson likely has not only the profane sinner in mind, but also anti-Puritan oppressors within the ecclesiastical establishment.

Emulation of God's mercy is likened to children displaying their resemblance to their father.[89] Most of Watson's treatment of this topic consists in quotations from Ambrose: "The sum and definition of Religion is, Be *rich* in *works* of *Mercy,* be helpful to the Bodies and Souls of others ... Be merciful in giving and forgiving" and Luke's Gospel "Be merciful—as your heavenly Father is merciful."[90] This recalls his equation of godliness and "charitab[ility]" or mercy in *Godly Man's Picture* and *Beatitudes.*[91] Although Watson does not make direct mention of Christ's parable of the unmerciful servant (Matt 18:21-35), he seems to convey the same sense. Those who have experienced the vast mercy of their King naturally ought to display mercy to others.[92]

Imitation of God's justice and truth in one's dealings with their neighbour are, respectively, described by Watson as being adorned by a "graceful" robe and bearing God's "own image."[93] The Golden Rule is to function as the Christian's guide to emulating God's just dealings with men and women, whereas Watson warned, "By every unjust Action, you do deny yourselves to be Christians; you stain the glory of your Profession."[94] Saints are also to "labour" to be like God in truth.[95] "Be (I say) like God, be true in your Words, be true in your Profession [of religion]; God's Children are Children that will not lie."[96]

Summary

The picture of God as the majestic, heavenly King is fundamental to Watson's theocentric piety. An appreciation of the sense in which the divine attributes correspond to the regal splendour and sovereignty of an earthly monarch was necessary to produce key godly affections and behavioural patterns. Although all of these royal attributes were

88. *BPD*, 1:48.
89. *BPD*, 1:57.
90. *BPD*, 1:57.
91. *GMP*, 248; *Beatitudes*, 199.
92. *BPD*, 1:57. James Ussher refers to this passage and Luke 6:36 (see above) when making the same application in his *Body of Divinitie*, 70.
93. *BPD*, 1:52, 59.
94. *BPD*, 1:52.
95. *BPD*, 1:59.
96. *BPD*, 1:59.

important to Watson's piety, holiness, mercy and sovereign power held a priority among them as the core elements of this dominant picture. Watson's emphasis on this picture of God and these attributes was determinative for the flavour of his affectional piety. It was necessary in his view to appreciate these three key attributes as a theological package—if believers were to relate to God in an appropriate manner. The Heavenly King must be simultaneously recognised as possessing unlimited power, indescribable glory and unending goodness and mercy. Holiness was perhaps the most significant in terms of inducing adoration and emulation as means of worship. Mercy, though, was the key qualifier of awesome holiness and power. It made God "lovely" and approachable and guarded against the picture of an overwhelmingly strict and severe deity, which the Puritans are often charged with promoting.[97]

Appreciating God as a mighty, majestic and merciful monarch not only laid the foundation of the right knowledge of God. It also produced the leading affectional responses Watson expounded in *Godly Man's Picture*. God's power invited faith (#2), His mercy invited love (#3), His holiness called for emulation in holiness (#4) and exactness in worship (#5) and the overall picture of Him as King called for devoted service to Him above all others (#6). Thus, Watson's attention to these attributes of God served to aid his parishioners (and later readers) in becoming the godly Christians he had envisioned earlier in his ministry.

Tri-Unity

The final aspects of God's Being and attributes elucidated in *Body of Divinity*, which require attention here are the unity of God's essence and the relationship of the three divine Persons. Beeke and Jones have commented that "the typical, oversimplistic distinction

97. For instance, Ryken cites William Rogers' statement "I serve a precise God" in his evaluation of Puritan strictness. *Worldly Saints*, 5. The severity of Puritan life in response to the idea of a severe God has also been suggested by some scholars. E.g. Albena Bakratcheva, *Visibility of the Invisible: The Poetic Discourse of American Transcendentalism* (Amsterdam: Rodopi, 2013): 18. Watson did acknowledge God's severity as a reality in relation to sin and His enemies. See *BPD*, 1:101. But in describing God's mercy he says, "Acts of Severity are rather forced from God; Justice is his strange Work, Isa. 28.21. Therefore the Disciples ... wonder[ed] when the Fig-tree was Cursed and Withered, because it was not Christ's manner to put forth acts of Severity." *BPD*, 1:287.

between a Western focus on one divine essence and the Eastern focus on the relationship between the three persons breaks down when it comes to analyzing the doctrine of the Trinity in Puritan thought."[98] This is true of Watson, who gives a close-to-equal treatment of both dimensions of the Godhead. The understanding of divine tri-unity, established by the Cappadocian Fathers and the early ecumenical councils, was central to the theology of the Westminster Assembly and the practical divinity of Watson which derived from it.[99] Watson's preference for pastoral and practical theology, rather than the scholastic or speculative, is evident in his treatment of the Trinity. His goal is to provide enough explanation to stimulate worship and clear up any errors amongst his congregants and he avoids the more detailed discussions of intra-Trinitarian relations one might find in the works of Ussher, Leigh or Ames.[100]

Watson uses the divine unity to qualify some of the previously discussed attributes. For example, he states that there can only be one infinite and all-powerful God in existence.[101] He emphasises the equality of essence and dignity of the three divine persons, and describes them as distinct from one another. All the while he maintains the truth of their unity as one God. Watson's treatment of this aspect of theology is one of his most polemical. The contentions between him and Jews, Muslims, Socinians and Arians, discussed in Chapter 8, all surface in his robust defence of the orthodox doctrine of the Trinity.[102] While these religious perspectives were not as prevalent or prominent a threat to Watson's practical divinity as Catholicism or Arminianism, he regarded their denial of the Trinity as even more perverse.

---

98. Beeke and Jones, *Puritan Theology*, 90.
99. Robert Letham notes that the concise nature of the Assembly's treatment of the Trinity in the WCF "demonstrates the divines' acceptance of the Council of Constantinople's resolution of the fourth-century Trinitarian controversy." Letham, *Westminster Assembly*, 164. There is no evidence that Watson regarded the matter any differently. Later, in his discussion of Christology, Watson cites the "Apostolical, Nicene [and] Athanasian Creed" as authoritative witnesses to Christ's deity against views he considered heretical. *BPD*, 1:94. It is clear therefore that he accepted these creeds as standards of orthodoxy when it came to core questions of theology.
100. See Ussher, *Body of Divinitie*, 76-88; Leigh, *Body of Divinity*, 208-215; Ames, *Marrow of Divinity*, 16-21. I am indebted to Ryan McGraw for suggesting this line of inquiry and comparison.
101. *BPD*, 1:60.
102. *BPD*, 1:63-64. Socinians receive the lengthiest rebuttal in this section, suggesting that Watson may have shared John Owen's perspective that adherents to this theology were the chief antagonists against the orthodox doctrine of the Trinity. Trueman, *John Owen*, 47-50.

This was because he viewed the unity and triune nature of God as fundamental to understanding Him as the object of worship. This constituted the very basis for godliness. The unity and uniqueness of God demands singularity in the aims and affections of people towards the only true Deity. The goal of Christian life should be the pleasing of God alone and the godly heart should be enamoured with God above all other things.[103] Christians should also be unified in their affections when it comes to the one true God: "though there are several Christians, yet there should be one sweet harmony of Affection among them."[104] Thus, while Watson does not use the exact words, he conveys the sense that there is not only one God, but one godliness amongst all who know Him.[105] This common expression of heartfelt devotion towards God amongst Christians is the key to increasing God's ascriptive glory, by drawing more people to worship Him. "There is nothing [that] would render the true Religion more lovely, or make more Proselytes to it, than to see the Professors of it tied together with the heart-strings of love."[106]

The Tri-personality of God is of great practical and devotional importance, because Christians are to "give equal reverence to all the persons in the Trinity" and "Obey all the persons in the blessed Trinity, for all of them are God."[107] Paul Lim has demonstrated how John Owen articulated his piety in response to the threats he perceived to be posed by non-trinitarian theologies. By presenting the Christian life as "Communion with God the Father, Son and Holy Ghost," the pre-eminent late English Puritan theologian sought to expose the fatal deficiencies of Socinianism (and similar theological departures) and counter them directly with a robust, Trinitarian system of devotion.[108] The effect of Watson's approach to practical divinity is markedly similar. He declared godliness impossible whenever the divinity of the Son or Spirit is diminished. Each Person of the Trinity must be worshipped for God to be glorified—the godly must "Adore Unity in Trinity."[109] The Trinitarian character of Watson's piety can be seen even more clearly when considering the indispensable role of the divine

103. "If there be but one God, who is *above all,* Ephes. 4.6. then he must be loved above all. 1. We must love him with a love of *Appreciation*; set the highest estimate on him who is the only Fountain of Being and Bliss. 2. We must love him with a love of *Complacency*." *BPD*, 1:60-61.

104. *BPD*, 1:62.

105. He does come close to this with the phrase, "if there be but one God, there is but one Religion." *BPD*, 1:60.

106. *BPD*, 1:62.

107. *BPD*, 1:65.

108. Lim, *Mystery Unveiled*, 183-203.

109. *BPD*, 1:65.

Son and Spirit in his system of practical divinity, which I will consider below.

B. Christology: Christ as the Mediator, Object and Enabler of Godliness

Watson calls Jesus "the sum and quintessence of the gospel"[110] and names "the doctrine of redemption by Jesus Christ" the "marrow and quintessence of the gospel."[111] His piety was not only theocentric and Trinitarian, but Christian in the fullest sense. All of the glorious attributes of the Godhead described above were incarnated in the person of Jesus and mediated through Him to the believer. For Watson, Christ serves as the Mediator of deity, the object of piety and the enabler of godliness.Christ's role as Mediator is chiefly redemptive. It describes the bridging of the divide between the holy God and sinful humanity:

> The Greek word for Mediator signifies a middle Person, one that doth make up the breach between two disagreeing Parties. God and we were at Variance by Sin, now Christ doth Mediate and Umpire between us; he reconciles us to God through his Blood, therefore is called the Mediator of the New Covenant. There is no way of Communion and Intercourse between God and Man, but in and through a Mediator: Christ takes away the Enmity in us, and the Wrath in God, and so makes Peace.[112]

Christ is uniquely able to act in this capacity between God and humanity because of His divine and human natures.[113] But Christ's mediation also has a revelatory aspect to it. Christians are to understand Christ as "the Effigies of His Father."[114] They "look upon Christ's *Divine Nature*" in order to appreciate Him properly and render Him appropriate worship as God.[115] On the other hand, Christians are exhorted to "look upon his human nature, as incarnate," appreciating the truth that: "Christ took our Flesh that the same Nature which sinned might suffer; and [...], *The word made flesh,* that through the Glass of his Human Nature

110. *BPD*, 1:93.
111. *BPD*, 1:121.
112. *BPD*, 1:93-94.
113. *BPD*, 1:93-94.
114. *BPD*, 1:94.
115. *BPD*, 1:94.

we might look upon God."[116] This aspect of beholding God in the incarnated Word is a significant point here for Watson (which he develops further in his section on the humiliation of Christ). God can only be known and related to by fallen humans in a manner that is mediated by the humanity of Christ.[117] As he goes on to say: "Were it not for CHRIST's Manhood, the sight of the Godhead would be formidable to us: but through Christ's Flesh we may look upon God without Terror."[118] Thus, Christ as the Divine-Human Mediator is pivotal to godliness. Without the ability to see God in Christ there would be no divine revelation that could be appreciated and responded to with the appropriate affections. The main response to Christ as Mediator is one of admiration (again, one of Watson's four key aspects of glorifying God). Specifically, this regards His dual nature and His love in humbly assuming our lowly human nature.[119] Again, Watson speaks of seeing God's glory in Christ, through His human nature.[120] He also presses the need for every saint to "have Jesus Christ written in his heart."[121]

Christ's roles as Prophet and Priest can be seen as extensions of this theme of mediation. Christ as Prophet brings the revelation and knowledge prerequisite for a relationship with God.[122] Trueman identifies this as a key component of John Owen's contention against the Socinians: "the divinity of Christ secures his knowledge of the Father's will, [while] it is his humanity which is necessary for the communication of that knowledge to other human beings."[123] This applies to Watson's perspective as well. Christ acts as a Priest "to mediate between a Guilty Creature and an holy God."[124] In

116. *BPD*, 1:94.

117. Kelly Kapic has identified the same dynamic in the thought of Owen. *Communion with God: The Divine and the Human in the Theology of John Owen* (Grand Rapids: Baker, 2007): 76. Trueman notes that, "for Owen the resurrected humanity of Christ is the medium through which the saints will gaze upon God for eternity." *Claims of Truth*, 62.

118. *BPD*, 1:94.

119. *BPD*, 1:95-96.

120. "All the Jews that saw Christ in the Flesh, did not see his God-head: all that saw the Man, did not see the Messiah. The Temple of Solomon within was embellished with Gold: Travellers, as they passed along, might see the outside of the Temple, but only the Priests saw the Glory which sparkled within the Temple; only Believers, who are made Priests unto God, Rev. 1.6. see Christ's glorious inside, the God-head shining through the Manhood." *BPD*, 1:95.

121. *BPD*, 1:96.

122. *BPD*, 1:99.

123. Trueman, *Claims of Truth*, 171.

124. *BPD*, 1:100-101. Trueman notes that Owen discusses the priesthood of Christ at

so doing, He further reveals divine "mercy," "justice" and "love."[125] The response to Christ's sacrificial death must be one of deep and heartfelt affection. It must lead to a love that is willing to suffer for Jesus and produce "the Fruits of Humility, Zeal, Good-works ... unto the glory and praise of God."[126]

Watson's treatment of Christ's kingly office and exaltation are also inseparable from His role as mediator. But these aspects shift the focus more to His role as the object of Christian piety. The image of Christ as King is presented in the context of explaining His mediatorial role, but it also correlates closely to the dominant image of God as King which I observed above. The same aspects of the divine nature Watson highlighted in his discussion of God's kingship are true of Christ. Watson describes Jesus as a monarch with absolute power over and above all earthly rulers.[127] He uses this regal power to deliver and defend His people and to shatter His enemies.[128] He is a holy king, commanding His subjects to live in holiness and "a King full of Mercy and Clemency."[129] Christ's supreme majesty is further conveyed in Watson's discussion of His exaltation. The Saviour has been elevated by God to "the highest part of the *Empyrean Heaven*" and is "next ... to God the Father in Dignity and Honour."[130] In His exalted majesty, Christ becomes the proper object of godliness. His people are to praise, adore and obey Him and reflect His glorious holiness by the earnest pursuit of consecrated living.[131] It was not only God-as-King, but Christ-as-King, which served as the focal point of godliness.

Christ's role as mediator—especially as expressed in the *triplex munus* (the three offices)—also played a part in enabling godliness in the life of believers. As Prophet, Christ "teacheth the heart," providing

far greater length than his prophetic or kingly offices. This is contrasted against a contemporary Socinian emphasis upon Christ's prophetic function. Trueman, *Claims of Truth*, 168. Elsewhere he notes that Catholicism and Arminianism, along with Socinianism, were perceived to be undermining this aspect of Christ's mediation. Trueman, *John Owen*, 87-88. Watson also focuses on the priestly office to a far greater extent, devoting more words to his discussion of it in *Body of Divinity* than the other two offices combined. His main theological concern appears to be the problems that Catholicism posed to this doctrine. *BPD*, 1:101-102, 106-107.

125. *BPD*, 1:100-101.
126. *BPD*, 1:103.
127. *BPD*, 1:108.
128. *BPD*, 1:109-110.
129. *BPD*, 1:109.
130. *BPD*, 1:118-119.
131. *BPD*, 1:121.

not only "the light of the truth" but also "the love of the truth."[132] According to Watson, Christ has the unique capacity to enable His learners to "savour" the word; incline their will to His teaching; and "animate" those He "illuminates."[133] As Priest, Christ's blood deals with the sinful "corruption" that hinders the godly in their devotion.[134] His prayers as their Intercessor sustain them in their walk with God despite their many failings.[135] Positively, the duties of the godly that fell short of being acceptable to God on their own were transformed by Christ. "Christ purifies and sweetens [our] Services, mixing the sweet odours of his Intercession with them, and now God accepts and Crowns them. What would become of our Duties without an High Priest?"[136] As King, Christ "rules the Will and Affections, His Power binds the Conscience: he subdues Men's Lusts."[137] The saints depend on the power of their king to conquer sin. This makes Christ the key to the essential practice of mortification. In these ways, Christ served not only as a mediator of godliness and object of devotion, but the one who enabled the saints to come to a proper knowledge of God. He alone could overcome the sin that hindered their piety.

Summary

In both a systematic and practical sense, Watson's schema of piety centres on the Person and work of Jesus Christ. The Son shares in the Father's position as the divine object of piety. But he also shares in the role of enabling godliness—primarily the purview of the Holy Spirit (which I turn my attention to immediately below). But the incarnated and exalted Messiah uniquely mediates the revelation of the divine nature to human believers and facilitates their pious communion with God Himself. Charles Wesley's famous line "Veiled in flesh the Godhead see! Hail the Incarnate Deity!" captures the core of Watson's Christological piety.[138] Without mediation of divine revelation through the Person of Jesus, God's people could not know Him adequately enough to respond with pious affections. There was no godliness divorced from the revelation of God-in-

132. *BPD*, 1:97.
133. *BPD*, 1:97.
134. *BPD*, 1:105.
135. *BPD*, 1:105.
136. *BPD*, 1:105.
137. *BPD*, 1:109. Compare Owen, *ΠΝΕΥΜΑΤΟΛΟΓΙΑ*, 562.
138. Charles Wesley, "Hymn for Christmas Day," *Hymns and Sacred Poems* (London: William Strahan, 1739): 207.

Christ. This reinforces what was observed in Chapter 8 concerning the inability of groups with unorthodox Christology to produce genuine godliness.[139] The crucifixion of the divine-human Saviour also conveyed a special sense of God's love, mercy and justice. The atoning death of Christ was thus a crucial catalyst for piety itself. Watson's schema of godliness was consummately Christocentric.

C. Pneumatology: The Holy Spirit as the Instigator and Sustainer of Godliness

Watson lacks a detailed section on pneumatology in *Body of Divinity*, reflecting the absence of a proper treatment of this doctrine by the WSC itself. While the WSC refers to the Holy Spirit several times, it does not provide any detailed instruction as to how the person and work of the Spirit are to be understood and believed. The *Larger Catechism* (WLC) contains more references to the work of the Holy Spirit than the WSC, yet it also lacks a section dedicated to the Christian understanding of the Spirit. Robert Letham has sought to defend the Westminster documents against the charge by T. F. Torrance that the lack of a specific treatment of the Holy Spirit was a '"grave omission."[140] After a lengthy survey of references to the person and work of the Spirit in the Confession and WLC, Letham summarises: 'For Torrance to complain that a chapter on the Holy Spirit is lacking from the Confession is to overlook the way the divines see the Spirit and his work pervading the whole of creation, active at every stage in grace, and undergirding the entire Christian life."[141] The pervasive role of the Spirit is evident in Watson's theology as well, as argued above. However, notwithstanding Letham's protestations, the lack of pneumatological exposition in the WSC and WLC should be viewed as a deficiency. Because Watson replicates this structural omission in *Body of Divinity*, the importance of the Holy Spirit in his spiritual theology of godliness must be ascertained by a survey of the references to the Spirit across the entire work.[142] The Holy Spirit acts as the originator or instigator of godliness in the lives of

139. Compare Lim's treatment of Owen's attitude toward Socinian piety on account of their defective Christology. *Mystery Unveiled*, 186.
140. T. F. Torrance, *Scottish Theology: From John Knox to John McLeod Campbell* (Edinburgh: T&T Clark, 1996): 141. Quoted in Letham, *Westminster Assembly*, 171.
141. Letham, *Westminster Assembly*, 173.
142. For an earlier treatment of the role of the Spirit in Watson's piety, see Schwanda, "Saints' Desire," 75-76.

Christians. It was the Holy Spirit who made true piety possible by means of His regenerative work on the hearts of sinners.[143] But the Spirit did more than simply initiate godliness: "God's Spirit doth not only quicken us in our Regeneration, but leads us on till we come to the end of our Faith, Salvation. It is not enough the Child have Life, but he must be led every step by the Nurse."[144] Watson saw the Spirit as the divine agent whose initial and ongoing works of renewal in the believer were the very thing that produced piety in them.

> [T]he Spirit of God dwells in the Elect as their Guide and Comforter. The Spirit possesseth the Saints; God's Spirit sanctifies the Fancy, causing it to mint holy Thoughts; it sanctifies the Will, putting a new Bias upon it, whereby it is inclined to Good. He who is sanctified, hath the Influence of the Spirit, though not the Essence.[145]

In his brief description of the Holy Spirit in *Body of Divinity*'s section on the Trinity, Watson says the Spirit's work "is to illuminate the Mind, and enkindle sacred Motions."[146] These are the very things I have identified as intrinsic to godliness: enlightened knowledge of God, accompanied by contingent, Godward affections. Thus, it is the "enlightening, sanctifying, quickening Spirit" who "inflames" the hearts of believers and enables them to "move more vigorously in the Sphere of Religion."[147]

The Spirit is said to redraw the image of God that was defaced in sinful men and women, when He does His work of sanctification and restoration in the godly.[148] Moreover, the Spirit makes the redeemed "partake of the divine nature (2 Pet 1:4)," making the soul of the saint "to be holy, and to resemble God."[149] Significantly for Watson, "partaking of the divine nature" is not simply a matter of the Spirit

143. *BPD*, 3:430.
144. *BPD*, 3:430.
145. *BPD*, 1:142.
146. *BPD*, 1:63.
147. *BPD*, 1:26.
148. *BPD*, 1:68.
149. *BPD*, 1:105. Watson appears to eschew any notion of deification in his discussions of pneumatology and anthropology—consistently interpreting participation in the divine nature as the possession of holiness (see *GMP*, 34-35). His distinction between the believer's possession of the influence of the Spirit, rather than the essence (see above), bears some similarity with patristic and Eastern Orthodox paradigm of essence *versus* energies. See Horton, *The Christian Faith*, 689-703 for a useful discussion of this topic in the Reformed and Orthodox traditions.

uniting believers to the Son or enabling them to worship the Father "in Spirit." Christians are to think of themselves as temples of the Holy Spirit. They should render proper worship to the God who dwells within them. "To him belongs, Divine Worship; our Souls and Bodies are the *Temples of the Holy Ghost,* 1 Cor. 6.19. in which Temples he is to be worshipped."[150]

The Spirit who dwells in the hearts of believers also works through the ordinances that God has appointed for the growth of godliness. This is what makes such means effectual.

> This sweet enjoying of God is, when we feel his Spirit co-operating with the Ordinance, and distilling Grace upon our Hearts: 1. When in word the Spirit doth quicken and raise the Affections, Luke 24.32. Did not our hearts burn within us? 2. When the Spirit doth transform the Heart, leaving an impress of Holiness upon it, 2 Cor. 3.8. We are changed into the same Image, from glory to glory. 3. When the Spirit doth revive the Heart with Comfort, it comes not only with its Anointing, but its Seal, it sheds God's Love abroad in the Heart, Rom. 5.5. this is to enjoy God in an Ordinance. 1 Joh. 1.3. Our fellowship is with the Father and his son Jesus. In the Word we hear God's Voice, and in the Sacrament we have his Kiss; this is enjoying of God: And what infinite Content[ment] doth a gracious Soul find in this? The Heart being warmed and inflamed in a Duty, this is God's answering by Fire.[151]

The Christian is not to look to the Spirit solely for the warming of their hearts. They are also to look to Him to produce godly sorrow for sin. This produces true repentance—another crucial element of authentic piety.[152] Likewise, Christians are to look to the Spirit when seeking assurance that promises of God-in-Christ are theirs.[153]

Summary

On the one hand, the fact that *Body of Divinity* was chiefly an exposition of the WSC explains Watson's choice not to dedicate at least one afternoon out of his three-and-a-half-year catechetical lecture programme to a specific lesson on the person and work of the Holy Spirit. But on the other hand, we must acknowledge that

150. *BPD*, 1:64.
151. *BPD*, 1:9-10.
152. *BPD*, 2:404.
153. *BPD*, 1:64.

on occasion he broke with an exact replication of the Catechism's topical structure to teach on an important subject, such as his inclusion of omniscience in his treatment of God's attributes (which is not mentioned in the relevant list in the WSC). Thus, Watson has maintained the approach of his Presbyterian forebears in discussing the Spirit in the context of other doctrines (e.g. the Trinity; regeneration; sanctification). This is in contrast of the pneumatological approach of leading Independent divine, John Owen. Despite producing a confession that reproduced the WCF's references to the Holy Spirit without significant addition, Owen penned a roughly three hundred thousand word treatise that focused specifically on pneumatology. There is nothing comparable in Watson's corpus, suggesting that he either did not see the topic as warranting a separate treatment, or he did not regard himself as the best author to undertake such a task. Given the importance of the subject and the fact that both the Son and Father receive extensive, focused attention in volumes one and three of *Body of Divinity* respectively, the absence of a detailed discussion of pneumatology is an unfortunate lacuna in a project aiming to ground Christians in the fundamentals of religion.

None of this nullifies Watson's recognition of the vital role played by the Holy Spirit in godliness and sanctification. We have seen that each and every expression of godly affection or action was predicated upon the regenerative work of the Spirit. Such expressions were enabled by His ongoing activity and influence. Thus, everything pertaining to godliness depended upon the Spirit of God. Though the third Person of the Trinity was typically only the focal point of adoration when the Father and Son were simultaneously in view, it was critical that the saints maintained a constant awareness of the Spirit's presence and operations in their lives of devotion.

Chapter 10
"Restored to God's Image:"*
Godliness in light of Christ's redemption

Next to the doctrines pertaining directly to the Holy Trinity, Watson's theological anthropology and soteriology played the most important role in relation to godliness in his practical divinity. As noted in Chapter 8, erroneous soteriology could preclude piety. A biblical view of human nature, sin and salvation was necessary if people were to see their need for divine redemption and develop a healthy approach to the Christian life. These truths determined how the godly should relate to God and appreciate His redemptive work in their lives. They do not constitute the primary object of piety. Justification cannot serve as the focus of affectional devotion in the same manner as the Person of Christ. Yet they did play an important, secondary role in producing godly affections. The redeemed grew in gratitude, love and awe toward the God who was active in saving them and restoring them in His image.

Azure brightness to midnight darkness: Humanity's innocence and fall*

Watson's practical divinity portrays godliness as a gradual recovery of the disposition towards God that humanity possessed in the state of innocence. *Body of Divinity* contains the language of a quest when discussing the practical implications of the doctrine of humanity's original creation.

> Did God create our Souls after his Image, but we lost it, let us never leave till we

* Title taken from *BPD*, 2:68.

* Title taken from *BPD*, 1:83.

> are restored to God's Image again ... As the Sun to the World, so is Holiness to the Soul. Let us go to God to repair his Image in us: Lord! thou hast once made me, make me anew, Sin hath defaced thy Image in me, O draw it again by the Pencil of the Holy Ghost.[1]

This emphasis on the glory of humanity in its prelapsarian state was foundational to Watson's biblical anthropology. Only with this in place could Christians appreciate how far men and women have fallen and what they should in fact be. Indeed, Adam's original condition is described in terms superior to that of his descendants.

> [Man] was full of Holiness; Paradise was not more adorned with Fruit, then Adam's Soul was with Grace. He was the Coin on which God had stamped his lively Image; Light sparkled in his Understanding, he was like an Earthly Angel, his Will and Affections were full of order, tuning harmoniously to the Will of God.[2]

Adam is presented as being capable of a kind of piety that fallen humanity is now incapable of imitating.

> Adam was a perfect Pattern of Sanctity. Adam had intimacy of Communion with God, and conversed with him, as a Favourite with his Prince. Adam knew God's Mind, and had his Heart. He not only enjoyed the Light of the Sun in Paradise, but the Light of God's Countenance.[3]

This high presentation of Adam in humanity's original condition anticipates the discussion of sin and salvation in the following sections of *Body of Divinity*. 'Sin hath blotted God's Image, and stained the orient brightness of the Soul.'[4] Sin's effect upon men and women is described in stark terms. 'We have lost that excellent quintessential frame of Soul which once we had. Sin hath cut the lock of original purity where our strength lay ... it hath turned the azure brightness of our Souls, into a midnight darkness.'[5] Sin was not merely transgression, impurity or corruption. Watson speaks of it as the polar opposite of godliness. 'Sin strikes at the very Deity. *Peccatum est Deicidium.* Sin would not only unthrone God but un-

1. *BPD*, 1:68. Note here the pencil drawing language, which is similar to that used in *GMP.*
2. *BPD*, 1:75.
3. *BPD*, 1:75.
4. *BPD*, 1:76. Owen held a similar perspective. See Trueman, *Claims of Truth*, 126.
5. *BPD*, 1:82-83.

God him. If the sinner could help it, God should no longer be God."[6] Describing sin in this manner highlights its opposition to the pious reverence of God. It is a hateful denigration of God that would denude Him of His divinity.

The greatest impediment to people entering a holy state was original sin. It has corrupted the image of God in humanity since Adam's transgression. It is also the greatest source of interference to those who seek to grow in sanctification. "Original sin retards and *hinders* us in the exercises of God's worship. Whence is all that dullness and deadness in Religion? It is the Fruit of Original sin."[7] Proper awareness of the presence and activity of original sin in the lives of the godly is essential to any discussion of godliness, since original sin has "diffused itself into all the *parts* and *powers* of our Soul."[8] It affects the heart, will and affections of every person—even those redeemed by Christ.[9] Since the affections are so important to our consideration of godliness in Watson's thought, it is notable that original sin is blamed for the misdirection of the affections. The result is that even Christians "have impure Lustings instead of holy Longings."[10] The Christian life of the godly is tainted by original sin, affecting both their "duties" and "graces," so that "the best works of the godly have sin cleaving to them," and "there is some Unbelief mixed with Faith, Lukewarmness with Zeal, Pride with Humility."[11]

This distinguishes Watson's view of godliness, as a progressive repristination of the human heart's posture towards God, from the Arminian understanding of obedience. In *A Display of Arminianism*, John Owen attacks Arminians for teaching 1) that Adam was created innocent of sin, but with an inclination to transgress;[12] 2) that original sin is not imputed to Adam's descendants, but people are born in the same state of innocence with the same inclination to sin;[13] 3) that people are able to return to this state of innocence, wherein they are subject to temptations to sin, but not to the ongoing effects of corruption derived from original sin.[14] Thus, the

6. *BPD*, 1:77.
7. *BPD*, 1:84.
8. *BPD*, 1:83.
9. *BPD*, 1:83.
10. *BPD*, 1:83.
11. *BPD*, 1:84.
12. Owen, *A Display of Arminianism*, (1643) (Oxford: TCP, 2006): 85-90. http://purl.ox.ac.uk/ota/A90293
13. Owen, *Display of Arminianism*, 70-77.
14. Owen, *Display of Arminianism*, 68-69, 85-86.

Puritans understood their Arminian opponents to be promoting a vision of sanctification that was neither a return to perfect piety (for Adam never possessed singular, heart-devotion to God), nor a sincere struggle of devotion that would always be partially tainted by sinful corruption (because Christians were not affected by original sin). Watson held that "we cannot do any holy action without sinning, as wanting a Principle of Original Righteousness."[15] This was significant when the dominant party in the established church was teaching that such a principle was not lacking in the Christian, who could freely choose to do good towards God. For Watson, it is Christ's atoning work that makes the believer's duties acceptable to God. Indeed, God's purpose in permitting original sin to remain in the regenerate is said to be related to evangelical humility. The result is a great longing for heaven and complete freedom from corruption.[16]

Summary

The doctrine of humanity's creation and fall into sin is important to a spiritual theology of godliness, precisely because the WSC frames "Man's chief end" as the eternal glorification and enjoyment of God. It was necessary for Christians to appreciate the incredible extent to which God created human beings with the capacity to fulfil this purpose. The pathetic inability of sinful men and women to bring any glory to God in their state of corruption was an equally striking reality. The Christian's volitional and affectional renewal and restoration in the image of God was critical to Watson's understanding of godliness. Resisting the ongoing effects of sin—which hindered the progress of restoration—was a vital, daily duty of Christian life.

Redemption Begun:*[*] *Antecedents to the life of godliness

Following the structure of the WSC, Watson proceeds from outlining the effects of sin to describing God's redemptive plan as the merciful, divine response to human rebellion. He mentions election and begins his discussion of the "application of redemption" in the Christology

15. *BPD*, 1:84.
16. *BPD*, 1:85.
* Title taken from *BPD*, 1:122.

section of *Body of Divinity.*[17] There is a detailed exposition of the nature of faith, explaining its role in the Spirit's application of Christ's redemption to the life of the believer—as per WSC Q. 30.[18] Since we have already considered faith in relation to godliness in Chapter 4, we will not revisit this subject here, but instead focus on Watson's treatment of effectual calling and justification.

The Effectual Calling of God's Elect

Watson concurs with earlier Reformed thinkers in referring to effectual calling as the beginning of the application of Christ's work of redemption to the elect, through the ministry of the gospel and work of the Holy Spirit.[19] He condenses the WSC's definition to "a gracious work of the Spirit, whereby he causes us to embraceth Christ freely offered to us in the gospel."[20] Watson understood this doctrine as covering both the external ministry of the Word (i.e. the proclamation of the gospel and invitation to trust Christ) and the internal ministry of the Spirit, whereby God "works grace" in the subject and "the heart is renewed."[21]

There is a clear link here between Watson's systematic soteriology and spiritual theology of godliness. These outward and inward components of the effectual call correspond with the core, dual prerequisites to godliness identified in Chapter 4: 1) revelation or theological knowledge to which the subject responds (here the presentation of the gospel) and 2) spiritual regeneration (here the inclining of the heart towards Christ by the Spirit). Through the call, the Spirit addresses the ungodliness of fallen humanity, discussed above. Christians are called out of the "darkness" of "Ignorance and Unbelief" and enabled to perceive enough of God's goodness to respond to Him in faith.[22] Through regeneration a

17. This is consistent with J. V. Fesko's observation that "for most Reformed theologians, the doctrine of election is never considered abstractly; it is never a bald choice on God's part. Rather, election is always coordinated with the other loci, such as Christology, pneumatology and soteriology." "John Owen on Union with Christ and Justification," *Themelios* 37:1 (2012): 10.
18. *BPD*, 1:124-127.
19. See for instance, Calvin, *Institutes* 5.24; WCF 10.1; Beza, *A briefe declaration of the chiefe points of Christian religion set forth in a Table* (1613) (Oxford: TCP, 2006): 28-32, 65-68. http://purl.ox.ac.uk/ota/A68592
20. *BPD*, 1:127. Cf. WSC Q. 32.
21. *BPD*, 1:128.
22. *BPD*, 1:128.

person's fallen status as a "God-hater" is nullified and they are drawn into the transformative and restorative work of the Spirit.[23] Watson saw clarity on this doctrine as important in the face of Arminian teaching that God's work in human conversion was limited to "*Moral Persuasion.*"[24] He summarises their position as "God in the Conversion of a Sinner, doth only *morally persuade,* and no more. He sets his Promises before them, to allure them to Good, and his Threatenings to deter them from Evil; and here is all he doth."[25] This teaching undercut godliness by diminishing the need for regeneration and obscuring God's glory as the one responsible for the sinner's conversion.[26]

By contrast, because divine election lay behind the effectual calling, understanding how God drew His chosen people to Himself was vital to those embarking on a life of godliness. For Watson, it is those who recognise they've been effectually called by the Spirit—through their subsequent pursuit of holiness—that can be confident about their eternal destiny. "Calling is an *earnest* and *pledge* of Glory. 2 Thess. 2.13. *God hath chosen you to salvation through sanctification.* We may read God's predestinating love in the work of Grace in our heart."[27] Clear signs of sanctification and purity in the Christian's life were the surest sign that they were numbered among God's elect.[28] God certainly never elected anyone on the basis of any inherent holiness, yet holiness always bloomed in the elect.[29] The elect and the godly were one in the same. This was not only because godliness was impossible apart from election, but because, for Watson, those who could discern true signs of godliness and holiness in their lives could rest in the assurance of their election.[30]

23. *BPD*, 1:129.
24. *BPD*, 1:129.
25. *BPD*, 1:129.
26. *BPD*, 1:129. Owen also disputes "moral persuasion" in *A Display of Arminianism*, 141-142. This demonstrates that it was a chief point of contention between Puritans and Arminians. For evidence of this in earlier generations, see Baird Tipson, *Hartford Puritanism: Thomas Hooker, Samuel Stone, and Their Terrifying God* (Oxford: Oxford University Press, 2015): 184.
27. *BPD*, 1:130.
28. *BPD*, 1:142; *DC*, 179.
29. E.g. *BPD*, 1:39, 142.
30. *BPD*, 1:130, 142; 201; *GMP*, 271-273.

Justification and Adoption

Following the pattern of Romans 8:30, "and *those* whom he called, these *he* also justified," the WSC and *Body of Divinity* both proceed from effectual calling to a discussion of justification. The WSC calls justification "an act of God's free grace, whereby he pardons all our sins, and accepts us as righteous in his sight, only for the righteousness of Christ, imputed to us, and received by faith alone."[31] Watson's doctrinal treatment of the subject is very typical of Protestant thought. He echoes Luther's famous statements in his introduction to the topic in *Body of Divinity*, saying "Justification is the very hinge and pillar of Christianity. An error about justification is dangerous, like a crack in the Foundation."[32]

It is clear that Watson saw the biblical understanding of justification as under attack from all quarters.[33] Arminians, Socinians, Antinomians and, predictably, "Papists" are named as antagonists towards this cardinal truth of Protestantism. For Watson, they each denied the gospel through faulty teaching on justification—by discouraging either repentance or complete reliance upon the finished work of Christ.[34] It has been suggested that the Westminster Assembly perceived antinomianism as the main contemporary threat to justification.[35] But Watson devotes more attention to the older Protestant contentions with Catholicism on this issue than he does refuting antinomians—reflecting his own priorities.

Against these errors, Watson sought to ground Christians in the Protestant perspective of justification as a forensic concept, concerning the pronouncement of righteousness and absolution of guilt. Its basis is in the free grace of God and the atoning sacrifice of Christ and it occurs by means of the imputation of righteousness through faith.[36] Watson's perspective concurs with much of J. V.

31. WSC Q. 33.
32. *BPD*, 1:131.
33. Significantly, there was an impassioned, published debate concerning justification raging in England around the time the catechetical lectures that constitute *Body of Divinity* are likely to have been delivered. Christopher, Haigh, "'Theological Wars': 'Socinians' v. 'Antinomians' in Restoration England," *Journal of Ecclesiastical History* 67 (2016): 341. Quoted in Tim Cooper, "John Owen, Richard Baxter and the Battle for Calvin in Later-Seventeenth Century England," *SBJT* 20.4 (2016): 65-66.
34. *BPD*, 1:132.
35. Shawn D. Wright, "Justification by Faith Alone: The Perspectives of William Kiffen and John Owen," *SBJT* 20.4 (2016): 31.
36. *BPD*, 1:131. For a discussion of Luther's understanding of justification in like manner, see Mark Mattes, "Luther on Justification as Forensic and Effective" in Robert Kolb

Fesko's analysis of Owen's doctrine of justification.[37] In addition to the aspects we have already mentioned, Owen and Watson both make the believer's righteous status before God dependent upon the alien, "imputed" righteousness of Christ, rather than anything "inherent[ly]" righteous about the individual.[38] Fesko contrasts Owen's view with that of the Catholic church, Arminians and his rival Richard Baxter "all [of which] hold that justification is an ongoing process where the believer's sanctification plays a role in their final justification."[39] While Watson often makes statements which exclude those who lack holiness from heaven, he is abundantly clear that sanctification is the evidence of one's justified status rather than a contributing cause to it.[40] This is starkest when he offers comfort to the godly in cases of insufficient obedience to God.

> Though Believers should be humbled under their Defects, yet not despond, they are not to be justified by their Duties or Graces, but the Righteousness of Christ. Their Duties are mixed with Sin, but that Righteousness which justifies them, is a perfect Righteousness.[41]

This serves as a counterbalance to his strong emphasis on having assurance about election and effectual calling when signs of holiness were identifiable. Thus, Watson is more aligned with Owen, over and against the positions of Baxter and heterodox groups, in "distinguish[ing] between the nature and essence of justification and the manifestation or declaration of it."[42]

The foundational nature of justification to Watson's understanding of godliness is clearest in *Godly Man's Picture*. Watson prefaces his discussion of godliness with a short exposition of Psalm 32:6, highlighting the need for divine pardon before one can be godly.[43] The relationship between justification and godliness in Watson's systematic theology is more interesting. Godliness refers to the Christian's *right* regard of God. Justification refers to God graciously regarding the Christian as *right*. The godly

---

et. al., *The Oxford Handbook of Martin Luther's Theology* (Oxford: Oxford University Press, 2014): 264-271.

37. See Fesko, "Owen on Union with Christ," 12-15.
38. *BPD*, 1:132; Fesko, "Owen on Union with Christ," 13-14.
39. Fesko, "Owen on Union with Christ," 14.
40. *BPD*, 1:132.
41. *BPD*, 1:133.
42. Fesko, "Owen on Union with Christ," 15.
43. *GMP*, 1-5.

have been transformed by the Spirit so they behold God as He really is in Christ and render Him worship. The righteous have been united with Christ by the Spirit through faith so they may be viewed by God with divine pleasure. The problem that requires redemptive godliness and justification is the same. Sin keeps people from seeing God clearly and responding with reverence and love. It likewise prevents God from looking upon sinners without holy wrath. Christ's mediation resolves both issues by returning God to His rightful status in the eyes of the godly and granting the justified sinner a righteous status in the eyes of God. This provided comfort to the godly when they were held in low esteem by their ungodly neighbours. Knowing that they would be "publicly" vindicated "at the Day of Judgment" brought consolation whenever their reputation was denigrated by their adversaries.[44]

The saints could also take comfort in their royal status as God's adopted children.[45] This adoption also took part at the beginning of the Christian life. Like justification, it occurred by means of faith.[46] It complements the justificatory aspect of a righteous status before God by granting the believer a threefold freedom "from the Dominion of Sin, the Tyranny of Satan, the Curse of the Law."[47] Additionally, justification and adoption are inseparable from the Spirit's transformation of a person's nature.[48] This clearly correlates with Watson's emphasis on godliness.[49] But it is also a response to what he identified as the ill effects of the Fall. God's justified and adopted children were able to begin the life of reverent obedience—that was made impossible by Adam's sin—through the inner workings of the Spirit.[50]

> It is not enough that the Child have Life, but it must be led every step by the Nurse: so the adopted Child must not only be born of God, but have the Manuduction of the Spirit to lead him in a Course of Holiness ... the adopted Ones need God's Spirit to lead them, they are apt to go wrong. The fleshy Part inclines to sin, the Understanding and Conscience are to guide the Will, but the Will is imperious and rebels, therefore God's Children need the Spirit to check Corruption, and lead

44. *BPD*, 1:133.
45. *BPD*, 1:134-135.
46. *BPD*, 1:135.
47. *BPD*, 1:135. Compare Owen, *Communion with God*, 243-246. See also Ussher, *Body of Divinitie*, 201.
48. *BPD*, 1:132, 134-135.
49. Compare above references with *GMP*, 5.
50. See also Ussher, *Body of Divinitie*, 201.

them in the right way.[51]

The impact of these doctrines upon affective piety

The function of soteriology in Watson's *Body of Divinity* was not to provide abstract propositions that could serve as a litmus test for orthodoxy. His goal was for the Christian to encounter God and behold Him at work in the saving of souls. This allowed the truths pertaining to salvation to play a part in generating the affectional responses befitting godliness. Those with grounds for confidence in their election and calling were required to appreciate what an august privilege it was to be chosen by God when others were passed over.[52] These doctrines were a window to God's goodness, mercy and love and should incite gratitude and love in the believer's heart.

> How should they that are called be affected with God's discriminating Love; how should the Vessels of Mercy run over with Thankfulness; how should they stand upon Mount Gerizim, blessing and praising God: O begin the work of Heaven here! Such as are Patterns of Mercy, should be Trumpets of Praise: Thus St. Paul being called of God, and seeing what a Debtor he was to Free-grace, breaks forth into Admiration and Gratulation, 1 Tim. 1.13.[53]

Thankfulness of heart was in turn conducive to holiness of life. The effectual calling is a summons to "embrace Christ," but also a call to come away from sin, the dangers of hell and worldliness and go after "holiness" and "glory."[54] Watson describes it as a "high calling," "because we are called to *high Exercises of Religion*."[55] This intersects with several key aspects of godliness, including self-denial, faith and love towards God and the praise and enjoyment of the divine. The chosen status of the godly required them to live in a manner distinct from the ungodly and act in accordance with their identity as "consecrated persons" and "temples of the Holy Ghost."[56] Appreciation of justification also produced a response of affectional worship.

---

51. *BPD*, 1:138.
52. *BPD*, 1:130.
53. *BPD*, 1:130.
54. *BPD*, 1:127-128.
55. *BPD*, 1:129. The specifics of this calling are thus described, "To be crucified to the World, to live by Faith, to do Angels Work, to love God, to be living Organs of his Praise, to hold communion with the Father and the Son, 1 *John* 1.3."
56. *BPD*, 1:130.

> The end [of justification] is that God may inherit praise. "To the praise of the glory of his grace." Hereby God raises the everlasting trophies of his own honour. How will the justified sinner proclaim the love of God, and make heaven ring with his praises![57]

As did adoption,

> See the amazing Love of God in making us his Sons ... 1 Joh. 3.1. Behold, what manner of love the Father hath bestowed upon us, that we should be called the sons of God! It is an *Ecce Admirantis*, a Behold of Wonder. [58]

Therefore, while we have observed that salvation involved restoration to the qualities and piety that humanity possessed before the Fall there is a sense that the relationship believers have to God is greater than that enjoyed in Eden. "Extol and magnify God's Mercy who hath adopted you into his Family ... Adoption is a greater Mercy then *Adam* had in Paradise; he was a Son by Creation, but here is a further Sonship by Adoption, to make us thankful."[59] Redemption goes beyond restoration and provides God with a special praise He would not have received from prelapsarian humanity. Those who have been appropriately impacted by the incredibility of justification will "adore the infinite Wisdom and Goodness of God to find out such a way to justify us, by *rich Grace* and *precious Blood*."[60] This demonstrates how Watson shifts from soteriological doctrines (justification/adoption) back to the divine attributes (wisdom and goodness) to produce a suitable affective response to God's revelation of Himself in salvation. Understanding what God has done for His children in justifying and adopting them "should fill us with wonder and love."[61]

Summary

We have seen that Watson's teaching on the branch of soteriology incorporating the process of divinely-enacted salvation had a dual function in relation to his piety. First, an understanding of all that

57. *BPD*, 1:132.
58. *BPD*, 1:135.
59. *BPD*, 1:138. Compare Ames, *Marrow*, 137.
60. *BPD*, 1:133.
61. *BPD*, 1:133. Compare Owen, *Communion with God*, 248.

occurred up to, and including, a person becoming a Christian was useful for avoiding misapprehensions about salvation that would lead to defective piety. The approach that Christians took to godly living would be shaped by their recognition that God had begun restoring them to His original design for humanity. Secondly, election, calling, justification and adoption were all displays of God's love and mercy as Saviour. This revelation of His character made these soteriological doctrines a secondary focal point for Watson's affectional piety. Seeing God in action as Saviour and experiencing the benefits of His grace took the godly beyond intellectual comprehension of the divine attributes. It invoked deep affection and gratitude in response.

Godliness expressed and enjoyed: Sanctification and its benefits

The relationship of Watson's systematic teaching on sanctification to his devotional emphasis on godliness is characterised by a different dynamic to the doctrinal areas considered above. Sanctification is in effect the process of becoming holy. We have noted the close—and somewhat overlapping—connection between godliness and holiness in Watson's writings. It is therefore little surprise that the approach taken to the subject of sanctification in *Body of Divinity* is more descriptive and instructive in relation to affectional piety, than it is incitative. In other words, Watson's exposition of sanctification describes godliness and its outcomes more than it contributes to producing them.

Watson's definition of sanctification differs slightly from that found in the WSC. Watson describes it as "a Principle of Grace savingly wrought, whereby the Heart becomes holy, and is made after God's own heart. A sanctified Person bears not only God's Name, but Image."[62] The WSC has, "Sanctification is the work of God's free grace, whereby we are renewed in the whole man after the image of God, and are enabled more and more to die unto sin, and live unto righteousness."[63] The significance of Watson's different selection of words should not be exaggerated. Yet it should

62. *BPD*, 1:139. Owen also uses the "principle of grace" description for sanctification. *Communion with God*, 196. Leigh gives a similar description to Watson of the nature of sanctification, "Christians … have God's Image repaired in them, which consists in righteousness and true holiness. Holiness is a conformity of the frame of the heart to the will of God." *Body of Divinitie*, 533.

63. WSC Q. 35.

be noted that the wording of this statement appears more closely connected to the regenerative emphasis of his spiritual theology, while the WSC's phraseology is more suggestive of a progressive process of sanctification.[64] Watson's focus on the heart certainly fits well with his pervading emphasis upon affectional piety. The renewed bearing of God's image is again key to understanding redemption as the process of rectifying the damage done by Adam's sin. As we have already seen in *Godly Man's Picture* and *Body of Divinity*, holiness was about reflecting God's character once more.[65]

Another remarkable link with Watson's earlier works is his recycling of the key characteristics of godliness listed in *Godly Man's Picture* to elucidate the nature of sanctification here in *Body of Divinity* (See Appendix A). Sanctification is described as being "intrinsical," "supernatural," "extensive" and "intense"—with portions of the corresponding texts in *Godly Man's Picture* being reused verbatim with minor edits and additions. There are two other slightly altered pairings between the relevant sections of each work: godliness is "glorious" and "permanent," while sanctification is "beautiful" and "abiding."[66] Curiously, this only leaves one unique statement about godliness and sanctification in the respective texts in which they are discussed. Watson's first aspect of godliness is that it is "real," while his final description of sanctification is that it is "progressive."[67] While this sole difference cannot be explained definitively, a plausible reason can be proposed. In *Godly Man's Picture*, Watson contrasts his ideal of godliness with religious "enthusias[m]."[68] Unlike the baseless religion of enthusiasts, the "reality" of godliness was based on revelation that had emanated from God Himself.[69] The ongoing aspect of sanctification is instead being distinguished from the settled and fixed nature of justification. In the context of his systematic theology, Watson was more concerned with erroneous teaching that conflated these two aspects of salvation and created confusion that would interfere with healthy Christian growth. Against the dangers of discouragement

64. Watson himself certainly believed in "progressive sanctification," as demonstrated by the last of his subsequent seven "positions" on sanctification. But it is noteworthy that these propositions begin with a regenerative focus before moving onto other aspects. *BPD*, 1:140.

65. *GMP*, 34-39; *BPD*, 1:48-49. For some brief observations on the same theme in Owen's approach to holiness, see Kapic, "Evangelical Holiness," 106.

66. *BPD*, 1:140; Compare *GMP*, 7-8.

67. *BPD*, 1:140; Compare *GMP*, 5-6.

68. *GMP*, 6.

69. *GMP*, 6.

at lingering sinfulness or the delusion that sin no longer posed a problem, Watson assures Christians that God's restorative work in their lives occurred over their lifetime.[70]

The similarities between sanctification in *Body of Divinity* and godliness in *Godly Man's Picture* continue in each work's treatment of insincere religiosity. One form of pseudo-sanctification was hypocrisy—reflecting Watson's abiding concern with this widespread problem.[71] Other forms nominated by Watson, which we have also discussed, include moralism and Catholic devotion.[72] Watson discredits these religious expressions due to their failure to sufficiently address the problem of humanity's corrupted nature. The superficiality of external religious observance precluded the restorative redemption that the Spirit was working in the godly.

Watson is far more restrained in his selection of "signs of sanctification" compared to his detailed characteristics of godliness in *Godly Man's Picture*. However, the brief list of signs he does nominate correlate almost entirely with things he had said previously about godliness. Several of these features illustrate a transformation from the unregenerate person's corrupt inability to respond to God's will to the Christian's capacity to glorify Him and pursue good. These include the indwelling presence of the Holy Spirit; hatred of sin; heart-piety; "a well-ordered Life;" and a "steadfast resolution" to persist in the ways of holiness.[73]

While Watson's "inducements" to sanctification are akin to various statements about godliness, some of them do not have explicit correspondence to passages in *Godly Man's Picture*. The differences between equivalent sections in *Body of Divinity* and *Godly Man's Picture* are illustrated in the table below.

70. See *BPD*, 1:85, 231.
71. *BPD*, 1:140-141. Cf. *GMP*, 9-14. See also Leigh, *Body of Divinitie*, 532.
72. *BPD*, 1:140.
73. *BPD*, 1:142.

Chief Inducements to Sanctification[74]	**Motives to persuade people to godliness**[75]
1. "It is the Will of God that we should be Holy"	1. The Misery of remaining in an ungodly state
2. "Jesus Christ hath *died for our Sanctification*."	2. The rarity of the godly
3. "Sanctification makes us *resemble* God."	3. The rationality of striving for godliness
4. Sanctification is what God loves	4. The qualitative excellence of godliness
5. Sanctification distinguishes from the wicked	5. The scarcity of the godly
6. It is shameful to lack sanctity as a Christian	6. The vanity and contemptibility of ungodliness
7. "Sanctification fits for heaven."	

Watson is not recycling material here in the same manner we witnessed above. The leading motivations for pursuing sanctification are not identical to those for seeking after godliness. It appears as though Watson again takes a different approach in his discussion of sanctification due to its place in his schema of practical divinity. Whereas the motives for godliness appear towards the end of a work dedicated entirely to expounding on the nature of godliness, the inducements to sanctification come in the midst of his systematic, catechetical project and his reasoning appears to build upon material he has already covered.[76] For example, the will of God as a motivation relates back to his theology proper and the death of Christ to Christology. The motivation of resembling God explicitly connects with anthropology and sin: 'It was *Adam*'s sin that he aspired to be like God in Omniscience, but we must endeavour to be like him in Sanctity."[77] Ironically, we have noted that Adam did originally possess holiness after God's likeness.[78] Thus, the godly seek to attain the very thing their ancestor lost through his improper pursuit.[79]

Watson's means of attaining sanctification reiterate what we have seen concerning the cultivation of godliness. They include growth in knowledge of the Word; faith in Christ; vital spirituality; holy conference and prayer as methods for developing holiness.[80] Given its importance in cultivating godliness, one would expect

74. *BPD*, 1:143-144.
75. *GMP*, 275-294.
76. *BPD*, 1:143.
77. *BPD*, 1:143.
78. *BPD*, 1:75.
79. Edward Leigh paints the same picture of sanctification as simultaneously regaining what humanity lost through Adam's fall and being conformed to the image of the holy God. *Body of Divinitie*, 531.
80. *BPD*, 1:144.

meditation to feature as a means of sanctification. However, it is virtually omitted from the whole chapter in *Body of Divinity*.[81] Self-denial and mortification of sin feature in other parts of the chapter on sanctification. But they are not included in the list of means by which it may be attained—which is another curiosity in comparison to Watson's earlier works.[82]

This is an appropriate junction to reconsider whether godliness can be distinguished from holiness in Watson's spirituality and systematic theology. Is there a simple solution to the conundrum which arises from the significant overlap between the two concepts on one hand and the existence of two distinct terms on the other? Delineating between the two in a broader manner than that which Watson himself is willing to do explicitly, comes with the risk of proposing a distinction which he himself would not have recognised. And yet, he has left enough hints as to what he considered the nuanced difference to be. Thus, my analysis would be deficient if I did not attempt to outline the relationship between these two aspects of the Christian life. There is an identifiable nuance between godliness and holiness in Watson's thought. Godliness is an appropriate, affectional heart-response towards the glorious revelation of God. Holiness is moral purity, religious consecration and an antipathy toward sin. We can argue that, in the life of the believer, godliness precedes holiness according to Watson's spiritual theology. This is due to the nature of each aspect. The Christian cannot emulate God in his holiness without first beholding God-as-holy and responding to Him with awe and reverence. As this in turn affects the believer's character and behaviour they demonstrate the holiness of God in their own lifestyle and actions. Godliness is an appreciation of God's character and nature—holiness is a reflection of His character and nature. In terms of their place in the redemptive restoration of humanity, godliness restores the capacity to worship God from the heart, while holiness restores our image and likeness of God. Sanctification allows Christians to live in emulation of the God they have come to adore.

The WSC lists five benefits that arise as the result of sanctification (along with justification and adoption): "assurance of God's love,

81. Only one phrase that could be interpreted as possibly implying meditation appears in the whole exposition of sanctification. "God's Spirit sanctifies the Fancy, causing it to mint holy Thoughts." *BPD*, 1:142. The absence can probably be ascribed to brevity, but is nonetheless striking in contrast to its prominence elsewhere.

82. *BPD*, 1:139, 142.

peace of conscience, joy in the Holy Ghost, increase of grace, and perseverance therein to the end."[83] Together with the Westminster divines, Watson sees these five elements of the Christian life as things which naturally proceed from the believer's status as a justified and (progressively) sanctified person. But Watson expands upon the significance of each one, beyond the bare outline provided by the WSC. Their derivation from sanctification links these elements inseparably to his understanding of piety and spiritual theology. Assurance, peace, joy etc; can all be viewed as products of sanctification which are brought about in the Christian's life by the work of the Holy Spirit (much like regeneration). But, once present, they become means of propelling believers to greater advancements in piety.

The impact of these doctrines upon affective piety

Assurance of God's love amplified the believer's own love and praise of God in response.[84] The confidence that it brought to Christians also enabled them to wholeheartedly devote themselves to obedience in spiritual duties.[85] Watson also exhorted those with assurance to "admire" and "adore" God's mercy, "be endeared in Love to God" and "improve it for God's glory" (which includes, among other things, setting one's affections upon heavenly things).[86] Peace gained through serving God "revive[s] the Soul, and bear[s] it up from sinking."[87] It "fires the Heart with Love to Christ," because of what He did to secure it by His blood.[88]

The effect of joy in the Spirit upon the believer is profound: "Divine Joy is Cordial Water, which doth not only Comfort, but Cleanse; it makes a Christian more Holy; it causeth an Antipathy against Sin; it infuseth strength to do and suffer ... the Joys of God do not only refresh the Soul, but strengthen it, The Joy of the Lord is your strength."[89] It also enhances the saint's religious experience by eliminating dreariness from duties:

83. WSC Q. 36.
84. *BPD*, 1:206.
85. *BPD*, 1:203.
86. *BPD*, 1:206-207.
87. *BPD*, 1:209.
88. *BPD*, 1:210.
89. *BPD*, 1:212. The strengthening aspect of spiritual joy and its effect against sin are both noted in Leigh, *Body of Divinitie*, 546.

> Because Spiritual Joy carries the Soul through Duty cheerfully; the Sabbath is a Delight, Religion is a Recreation. Fear and Sorrow hinder us in the Discharge of Duty: But a Christian serves God with Activity, when he serves him with Joy. The Oil of Joy makes the Wheels of Obedience move faster.[90]

In this manner, joy has a medicinal function for the soul hindered in piety by original sin. Furthermore, the believer's experience of spiritual joy now serves to spur them on to the inexpressibly greater joy they will receive in heaven.[91] Growth in grace naturally entails "a more Spiritual frame of heart" with greater quality of affections and duties and greater hatred of sin.[92] Zeal and reverence are the natural companions of any spiritual growth.[93] The idea that God should sustain believers in the face of many obstacles to their final perseverance should "provoke in the Saints everlasting Love and Gratitude to God."[94] They are to marvel at His amazing power in keeping His children and pray for it to be continually at work in their lives.[95] Finally, Watson urged Christians to draw encouragement from the lives of previous generations who "Persevered in Religion."[96] Their attainment of the object of their piety served to provide hope to those who continued to strive toward the end.[97]

Watson was alert to whatever false teachings he perceived would hinder godliness by rendering the possession of these benefits difficult, or impossible. Arminians and Papists alike were enemies to assurance and perseverance and needed to be firmly refuted.[98] The lax attitude of nominal Christians was a dangerous influence which would prevent growth in grace.[99] While antinomians are not mentioned directly in this section of *Body of Divinity*, Watson's teachings on sanctification and its benefits clashed with their understanding of the Christian life at several key junctions.[100] Discrediting these perspectives on the

---

90. *BPD*, 1:213.
91. *BPD*, 1:213-214.
92. *BPD*, 1:217.
93. *BPD*, 1:217-218.
94. *BPD*, 1:221.
95. *BPD*, 1:221-222.
96. *BPD*, 1:224.
97. *BPD*, 1:224.
98. *BPD*, 1:203, 218, 220-222. See also Leigh, *Body of Divinitie*, 224.
99. *BPD*, 1:216-217.
100. These include the idea that sanctification is evidence of a person's justification and election; that God's love increases towards Christians as they grown in holiness and grace; that growth and enjoyment in relation to sanctification and its derivative benefits is partially dependent on the believer's unrelenting warfare against indwelling sin; and that a believer's assurance is derived from their progressive sanctification

Christian life was vital to ensuring that people could have clarity about the products of salvation and not be deceived out of a settled spiritual state that was conducive to ongoing growth.

Summary

Watson's teaching on sanctification incorporates much of his earlier work on godliness. It carries over his emphasis of Christian spirituality "[lying] chiefly in the heart;" being enabled by the Spirit; permeating the whole life; demanding an affectionate response; being pleasing in God's sight and enduring into eternity.[101] While godliness clearly runs throughout *Body of Divinity* as a major concern, it is clear that its inseparable affinity with holiness makes the treatment of sanctification the section to deal most explicitly with Watson's signature theme. We have acknowledged that the distinctions between godliness and holiness are initially confusing. But there are clear nuances present in Watson's use of the two terms to describe adoration and emulation of divine holiness respectively. This leads to the benefits of sanctification being clearly inseparable from evidence of and progress in godliness. The Christian's possession of assurance, peace and joy were all contingent upon the existence of godliness in their hearts and their enjoyment of these benefits depended on the vitality of their piety. Watson's teaching on "growth in grace" consolidated his earlier writings about how to cultivate godliness. Watson allowed for the possibility of spiritual retardation or regression. But the steady increase of sanctification was the normal pattern of life for the saint being restored in the image of God.

Perfect Piety Realised: Death, Glorification, Resurrection and Final Judgement

In Chapter 6, we noted that preparedness for death and eternity formed a key element of the goals and outcomes of godliness. In Watson's catechetical project the end of the Christian's earthly life and beginning of their eternal blessedness is once again a major concern of his practical and pastoral theology. The Christian's death

and "humiliation for sin." See *BPD*, 1:141-143, 145, 205-206, 210, 216-217; Jones, *Antinomianism*, 10-11, 82, 98-99.

101. *GMP*, 6; Compare *BPD*, 1:139.

and subsequent resurrection brings the full realisation of everything they sought through piety.[102] God's restoration of His image in them will be completed.[103] The godly will possess "a full knowledge of God;" their faith will become sight; they will love God as they ought; they will attain immaculate holiness; they will worship and serve God alone forever and in seeing the Christ they have prized and adored, they will be satisfied.[104] Prayer, the Scriptures and the sacraments are superseded by direct communion with God; meditation upon God and heaven are replaced by enjoyment of the reality; mortification and self-denial are made redundant by the permanent eradication of sin and holy conference will be more fully enjoyed in "the sweet Society of glorified Saints and Angels."[105]

For Watson, heaven is not chiefly a regaining of Eden's Paradise by escaping the effects of the Fall. It is the restoration to the relationship humanity first enjoyed with God. "We are apt to think the Happiness of Heaven is in being free from Pain and Misery, but the very ... Quintessence of Happiness, is the Enjoyment and Fruition of God."[106] The hope of bodily resurrection serves positively as the means of the godly receiving their reward and glorification from God and negatively as an escape from the eternal condemnation of the wicked at the great judgement. "Their Bodies shall be raised up to Glory, and shall be openly acquitted at the day of Judgment, and crowned with the full and perfect Enjoyment of God to all Eternity."[107] The bodies of the saints will be "Illustrious and Glorious" in stark contradistinction to the contemptible state of the wicked in their resurrection.[108] Just as we saw in Chapter 6 (and will observe again in Chapter 10), a *post-mortem*, divine adjudication that rectifies the unjust disparities between the godly and ungodly is an important outcome of faithful piety. This naturally leads to Watson's discussion

102. See Chapter 6, n. 36-38.

103. It is worth reiterating here that this did not amount to human deification in Watson's view. He believed that even the glorified human nature of Christ remained distinct from His deity and that the Christian's eternal experience of the divine nature was mediated through Christ's humanity. *BPD*, 1:119, 226. Yet, intriguingly, he employs the metaphor of sunbeams to describe the procession of divine glory from God *via* Christ's humanity. This is the same imagery commonly associated with *theosis* in Eastern Orthodoxy (see Horton, *Christian Faith*, 690) and that which Watson employs elsewhere in describing godliness, *GMP*, 6.

104. *BPD*, 1:231-234.

105. *BPD*, 1:226.

106. *BPD*, 1:231. Compare Leigh, *Body of Divinity*, 870-871.

107. *BPD*, 1:241.

108. *BPD*, 1:237.

of the final judgement, the topic with which he concludes the first volume of *Body of Divinity*. The public shaming and sentencing of the wicked who obtained and retained their worldly status by sinful means is a major aspect of Judgement Day. So too is the vindication and reward of the godly who were slandered and persecuted in the world for their righteousness.[109] The reversal of the worldly fortunes of the godly is a significant source of encouragement to them in their perseverance. "Those whom the World scorned and looked upon as Precisians and Fools, Christ will take by the Hand, and openly acknowledge them to be his Favourites."[110] The permanent distinction is vividly described as the sinner's descent into eternal fire and a "Sea of Wrath," while the righteous experience a "Day of Jubilee," inherit the Kingdom and enter into eternal joy.[111]

The impact of these doctrines upon affective piety

Positively, Christians were to meditate on their future "Celestial Glory," "thus might you by a Contemplative Life, begin the Life of Angels here, and be in Heaven before your time."[112] Negatively, they were to meditate seriously upon the day of judgement, as a means of producing sincerity. They would soon need to give an account to God for their whole person (rather than hiding behind their public persona).[113] Likewise, they should reckon seriously with their own sins. God would hold them to account for any wrong they had left outstanding or undenied.[114] In a similar vein, they were to pursue humility through self-annihilation and take care not to violate their consciences.[115]

It is noteworthy that Watson concludes this first section of his catechetical project with the exhortation: "If you would stand acquitted at the Day of Judgment, get an entire Love to

109. *BPD*, 1:238.
110. *BPD*, 1:239. For further discussion of this theme in *Religion Our True Interest*, see Chapter 11.
111. *BPD*, 1:239.
112. *BPD*, 1:234. This theme appears in the works of Watson's Puritan contemporaries, sometimes briefly (e.g. Leigh, *Body of Divinity*, 869) and sometimes at great length (e.g. Baxter, *Saint's Everlasting Rest*, 686-848).
113. *BPD*, 1:240-241.
114. *BPD*, 1:241. "[A]ccusing ... judging and even punishing" one's self were important aspects of Protestant repentance, with a view to avoiding final judgement for particular sins. Ryrie, *Being Protestant*, 54.
115. *BPD*, 1:241.

the Saints."[116] This is of course the eighteenth characteristic of the godly man in *Godly Man's Picture.* The fact that Watson concludes with this application is suggestive of its immense importance to his practical divinity. He considers this love to be "A Blessed Evidence that you shall be acquitted in the Day of Judgment" because it serves as the "truest Touch-stone of Sincerity."[117] Seeing and loving grace in other believers is the fruit of the Spirit's indwelling of the saint.[118] Watson also speaks of delighting in the brightness of God's image in others.[119] It is significant that this is the final application given in this volume—as it caps his soteriological emphasis on the Christian's restoration in God's image. Those who have come to understand God's workings of salvation in their lives should respond by cherishing every person experiencing the same spiritual transformation. Thus, in concluding, Watson draws together a number of the qualities of godliness in the manifestation of this love and offers Christians confidence that "we have passed from Death to Life, because we love the Brethren (1 John 3:14)."[120]

Summary

For Watson, matters of death, resurrection, final judgement and eternity are not merely the last logical topic to be treated in a systematic theology. The reality of these last things shapes every day, every decision and every duty in the present life of the godly Christian. For beyond the hour of death lay the reality of all they had prepared and strove for; the resolution of all that they had struggled with; and the restoration of their corrupted souls into God's image.

116. *BPD*, 1:241.
117. *BPD*, 1:241.
118. *BPD*, 1:241.
119. *BPD*, 1:241.
120. *BPD*, 1:241.

Summary of PART 4

I noted in my discussion of Catechesis in Chapter 5, that the goal of Watson's exposition of the WSC was the "grounding and settling" of believers in the fundamental articles of religion, in order that they might "serve God aright" and "worship [Him] acceptably."[1] As a project in Puritan practical divinity this work was aimed at kindling increased affectional piety in response to thorough theological instruction. With respect to theology proper, Christology and pneumatology, instruction is intended to culminate in adoration. The nature, attributes and offices of the three divine persons are all subjects that should be studied for the purpose of appreciating God enough to love and reverence Him. The redemptive work of Father, Son and Holy Spirit and the study of soteriology provides a helpful framework for the believer to understand their relationship to the triune God. But knowledge of these doctrines was a gateway to the adoration of God as the merciful and powerful Saviour. It produced holy living in response to divine holiness and thankfulness for God's work of salvation. Watson's soteriology charted the restoration of the redeemed to the image of God marred by the Fall. It was through this restoration that Christians came to fulfil the purpose of humanity—to glorify God and enjoy Him forever.

Watson's massive catechetical undertaking was no slavish transmission of official Presbyterian doctrine promulgated by the Westminster Assembly divines. He actively improved upon the basic theological answers provided in the WSC with further doctrinal

1. *BPD*, 1:iii.

exposition and vivid illustrations—all with the goal of seeing a solid foundation in religious instruction culminate in an increase of godliness. He left no doubt as to how each doctrine should apply to the saint's spiritual affections and practical actions. Thus, his project of practical divinity served his preoccupation with godliness and the glorification of God.

Excursus
The Ten Commandments and *The Lord's Prayer*

Time and space have not permitted the inclusion of a detailed treatment of the second and third volumes of Watson's *Body of Divinity*—dealing with the Ten Commandments and the Lord's Prayer—in this study. However, it is worth highlighting, in brief, how some of the main themes in these volumes contribute to Watson's central emphasis on godliness.

Before commencing with a detailed commentary on each of the Ten Commandments, Watson discusses the foundational importance of obedience and love towards God. Obedience, for Watson, was not mere compliance with God's commands, but a "cheerful," "sincere," "devout and fervent" embracing of the goodness in the divine laws.[a] He is explicit that "it is Fervency [that] makes Obedience acceptable."[b] Here, as always, the accent is placed upon the heart's response to God—even when matters of practical obedience are being discussed. Watson's treatment of love here is considerably more extensive than the discussion it receives as a characteristic of the godly in *Godly Man's Picture*. He defines it as "Holy Fire kindled in the Affections, whereby a Christian is carried out strongly after God as the Supreme Good."[c] The intensity of the affection is further conveyed by the types of words Watson uses to describe it: e.g. it must be whole-hearted, "vehemen[t]," "industrious," "superlative" and "constant."[d] There is an earnest yearning for spiritual intimacy with God, which is inseparable from the saint's relating to Him through the means of grace.[e] By stressing the affectional nature of the obedience and love required in relation to God before dealing with the requirements of particular commandments, Watson lays down his affectional piety

a. *BPD*, 2:242.
b. *BPD*, 2:243.
c. *BPD*, 2:245.
d. *BPD*, 2:245-246.
e. *BPD*, 2:246-248.

as the basis of his approach to Christian worship and ethics.

Although the Decalogue in its entirety is important to the *praxis* of godliness for Watson, it was the first four commandments that contributed the most to his understanding of the substance of *eusebeia*. Since we have already discussed the Sabbath briefly in an excursus above, we shall limit discussion here to the significance of the first three commands. Watson calls the first commandment, "the foundation of all true religion" and defines it as "sanctify[ing] God in our Hearts, and giv[ing] him a Precedency above all created Beings."[f] The homage that was given to God by His people was to proceed from a sincere soul that had come to know Him.[g] This very personal worship of God was marked by the kind of affectional responses we have noted in Watson's piety numerous times already. Particularly noteworthy is his reiteration of the twin importance of fear and love: "in the Godly, Fear and Love Kiss each other."[h] In showing how this commandment might be violated, Watson propounds a wide definition of idolatry that would be familiar to many Christians from before his time up to the present day, "To trust in [or love] anything more than God, is to make it a god."[i] This naturally fits with his emphasis on heart religion—one did not need to bow to a physical idol to be an idolater—only to forsake God internally for something inferior. When Watson taught on the second commandment, a similar theme emerges. Worshipping God through images was *anathema* for Christians, who were to "conceive of God Spiritually... in his attributes—his Holiness, Justice and Goodness—which are the Beams by which his Divine Nature shines forth."[j] As he unpacks the text of the second commandment, he returns to the theme of love, stressing its vital importance to piety again, "We must love God ... [for] those intrinsic Excellencies wherewith he is crowned ... [a sincere Christian] cannot but love God for the Beauty of his Holiness."[k] Watson's discussion of the third commandment flows out of what he has already established. The God who is to be reverenced, loved, trusted and obeyed must not be represented—in speech or action—in a manner unbecoming of His "infinite Majesty."[l] While dishonouring God through flippant invocations of His name was the most obvious example of this, it was by no means the

f. *BPD*, 2:272.
g. *BPD*, 2:273-274.
h. *BPD*, 2:274.
i. *BPD*, 2:276.
j. *BPD*, 2:281.
k. *BPD*, 2:289.
l. *BPD*, 2:295.

only way the command might be violated. Watson classes external expressions of worship that do not engage the heart in the same category, based on Isaiah 29:13.[m]

Watson explicitly states that the third of the Ten Commandments and the first petition of the Lord's Prayer, "Hallowed be thy name," are two sides of the same coin.[n] This idea of God receiving the sacred reverence that was his due—not only within the church, but throughout the world—reiterates Watson's earlier discussions of godliness and glorifying God. Many of the ways the Christian hallows God's name correspond with the means of glorifying God that were outlined at the beginning of the first volume of *Body of Divinity*. Again, the focus is on increasing the ascriptive glory of God.[o] Likewise, the link with godliness is explicit after Watson outlines these ways of hallowing God's name, "See the true note and character of a Godly Person; he is a sanctifier of God's Name."[p] This required "holy and spiritual worship" towards God on the part of believers, with an accent upon an intense, affectional response to God.[q] Thus, this opening portion of the Lord's Prayer was an invocation of God the Father to bring about godliness in the heart of the believer and magnify His name throughout the world.

The second petition, "Thy kingdom come," receives the most extensive treatment in Watson's commentary on the Prayer. In line with the dominant picture of God that we observed above in *Body of Divinity*, Watson commences with an extended reflection on God as King, which recapitulates some of the key divine attributes and calls for an appropriately pious response.[r] But even more attention is given, in the opening of this volume, to the significance of God's fatherhood in relation to believers, encapsulated in the invocative phrase, "Our Father" at the beginning of the Prayer. Knowledge of God as one's heavenly Father produces a "filial disposition" that is expressed in various affections befitting this relationship.[s] Everything that follows in the Lord's Prayer proceeds from this consciousness of God as King and Father and a desire to see His name treated as sacred everywhere.

The ethical teaching contained in Watson's exposition of the remaining commandments and the implications of the petitions,

m. *BPD*, 2:296.
n. *BPD*, 2:295.
o. *BPD*, 3:446.
p. *BPD*, 3:450.
q. *BPD*, 3:447.
r. *BPD*, 3:455-458.
s. *BPD*, 3:428-429.

"Thy will be done" and "lead us not into temptation, but deliver us from evil," is extensive enough to warrant a separate study. Suffice it to say that there are a number of features that stand out about this subject matter, in relation to this study's focus on Watson's affectional piety. In shifting to the so-called Second Table of the Law, which incorporates the laws pertaining to love for one's neighbour, Watson describes adherence to these commands as "walk[ing] Righteously towards man," which corresponds to "walk[ing] Religiously towards God."[t] This framework creates a number of parallels between Watson's theocentric piety and the social implications that flow out of it. For instance, in expounding the fifth commandment, he calls for the same "fear mixed with love" towards one's parents that he elsewhere calls for in relation to God as Father.[u] Shortly afterwards, it is as though Watson cannot help returning to matters of piety, as he names the honouring of God as Father as the primary application of the commandment.[v] Watson follows the precedent set by Jesus in his exposition of the commandments beyond their plainly accepted meaning, to incorporate a range of related behaviours and, of course, attitudes of the heart.[w] Significantly, Watson is committed to providing positive obligations as correlations to God's prohibition of particular sins. The prohibition of murder necessitates positive works of charity that preserve life; the prohibition of adultery promotes a positive embrace of marriage and conjugal duties; the prohibition against false testimony calls for defending the name and reputation of others against slander, etc.[x] At times, Watson invokes an attribute of God he has previously discussed in *Body of Divinity* to press its relevance to the commandment under discussion, e.g. "As the Holiness of God sets him against Uncleanness, *Thou shalt not commit Adultery*, so the Justice of God sets him against Rapine and Robbery, *Thou shalt not steal.*"[y] As we have observed in an earlier chapter, Watson's implications for each commandment frequently included attacks on religious groups he considered to be impious, giving his ethics a polemical edge. Roman Catholics were the main target of Watson's condemnations—he charges them with breaking at least six of the

---

t. *BPD*, 2:349.

u. *BPD*, 2:354.

v. *BPD*, 2:356-357.

w. E.g. *BPD*, 2:359-361, 376-378.

x. *BPD*, 2:366, 369, 374, 382. This approach has its origin in the Westminster Shorter Catechism, but, as is often the case, Watson is far more extensive in drawing out the possible positive implications of each command.

y. *BPD*, 2:376.

Ten Commandments.[z]

Eventually, his treatment of the commandments and the principle of doing God's will leads him back to "evangelical obedience"—an idea he had introduced previously in works such as his *Beatitudes* and *Godly Man's Picture*.[α] This is his attempt at a solution to the problem posed by the failure of even the godliest Christians to live in perfect accordance with the laws of God. It consisted of an attitude of approval and delight towards God's law in general; a sincere desire and effort to observe each commandment to the greatest possible extent; and considerable distress in response to shortcomings in obedience.[β] Watson assures believers that where this disposition and diligence towards the law is present, the imputation of Christ's righteousness will fill the chasm between actual and desired obedience and render the saint's obedience perfect in God's sight.[γ] As a loving Father, God accepts these imperfect attempts to do His will and keep His commandments, the way a parent accepts their children's efforts at obeying their instructions or making a present out of filial love—even though they lack the capacity to do the thing well.[δ]

---

z. *BPD*, 2:252, 259, 280, 297, 362, 370, 380; *BPD*, 3:451-452.

α. *Beatitudes,* 419-420; *GMP*, 250. For a discussion of the closely related idea of "evangelical holiness" in the piety of John Owen (and William Twisse), see Kapic, "Evangelical Holiness," 100-101, 112-114.

β. *BPD*, 2:391; *GMP*, 249.

γ. *BPD*, 2:391; *GMP*, 250.

δ. *BPD*, 2:391; *BPD*, 3:434.

PART 5

"Divine Consolation:"* Sustaining godliness through trials

* Title taken from *BPD*, 3:528.

Chapter 11
Assessment of Watson's outlook in light of his historical situation

Introduction and initial assessment of Watson's pastoral objectives

A key challenge for Watson as a Puritan pastor in the Restoration period was how to promote and preserve godliness amongst his fellow saints in a hostile environment. The harsh realities of the political and religious landscape in the latter twenty-five years of Watson's ministry precluded ethereal notions of piety that lacked the robustness to endure various kinds of suffering. Watson's main pastoral goal in this historical setting was the sustenance of godliness among the saints in the face of persecution and marginalisation.[1] The previous chapters have sought to demonstrate the centrality of godliness in Watson's thought and ministry—examining this theme through the lenses of spiritual, historical and systematic theology. Since Watson's approach to theology, piety and action was always conjoined we have interacted with matters of practical and pastoral theology at several junctions.[2] This chapter explores the relationship of the dominant motif to Watson's pastoral theology. In particular we will consider how his production of consolatory literature is connected to his central concern with godliness. We are concerned with Watson's pastoral method and the theological resources he employed to buoy the afflicted spirits of his spiritual kin.

Like godliness, themes of contentment and consolation feature prominently in Watson's earlier works—but become even more accentuated in his later writings, following the Restoration. At

1. Till names "the sufferings of the elect" as a "recurring concern" for Watson. Till, "Watson," 5.
2. E.g. Chapters 5-6; the discussion of hypocrisy in Chapter 8; and Chapter 10.

a cursory glance, Watson's sermons and treatises that deal with peace, comfort and hope in the life of a believer might appear to adopt a different focus to the preoccupation with godliness we have seen across his other works. But they are in fact derivative of this emphasis. Watson understood himself as a member of and minister to a godly afflicted minority. Combined with his assessment of the times he found himself in, this necessitated a pastoral programme of exhortation and encouragement to fortify the godly to face adversity.[3] He approached this task with confidence that the Scriptures spoke to every difficulty he and his fellow Christians experienced. He also worked hard to apply biblical truths and promises to various, afflictive situations to aid believers in escaping dejection and avoiding compromise or apostasy. Watson came to see persecution and general trials as necessary elements in the Christian life for progressing in sanctification and achieving his stated goals of godliness. On the one hand, this attitude was necessitated by the times Watson found himself in. On the other hand, he drew his perspective from an important Scriptural theme and a Christian tradition of suffering for godliness that stretches back to Christ and the faithful remnant of Yahweh in the Old Testament.

Watson's great pastoral challenge

Watson's nomination of twin pastoral challenges in his *A Divine Cordial* provides a great insight into his overall pastoral approach.

> Here are two things, which I have always looked upon as difficult: The one is, to make the *Wicked sad* ... The other puzzling difficulty, is, to make the *Godly joyful* ... dejection in the Godly, ariseth from a double Spring; either because their inward comforts are darkened, or their outward comforts are disturbed."[4]

Watson's negative goal of making the wicked sad, is consistent with what we have already seen in his writings about sin, repentance, self-denial and conversion. No one would ever be converted unless they were first brought low by God and self-denial was indispensable to godliness. But his positive goal of making the godly joyful, particularly in cases where "their outward comforts are disturbed" encapsulates his primary pastoral objective in *A Divine Cordial* and extends to much of his other consolatory literature.

3. Wallace, "Watson," 266.
4. *DC*, v.

In the preface to *A Divine Cordial*, Watson goes on to add:

> To know that nothing shall hurt the godly, is matter of comfort; but to be assured that all things which fall out, shall co-operate for their good, that their crosses shall be turned into blessings the bloody showers of affliction shall water the withering root of their Grace, and make it flourish more; here is that may fill their hearts with joy till they run over.[5]

This provides a sample of Watson's pastoral method. He carefully selected Scriptural truths and promises to bring consolation and encouragement to godly Christians facing hardships. Watson did not proffer superficial solutions to the experiences of suffering among the godly. He skilfully applied his theology to address particular kinds of affliction that were being endured. Even though he had already published consolatory and hortatory works in the years from the Restoration to the Great Ejection, Watson found the political, social and religious climate of 1663 (just months after his ejection from the ministry) to be ripe for a thorough exposition of Romans 8:28.[6] *Divine Cordial* highlighted the reality of God's sovereignty and goodness in the midst of the unpropitious circumstances which the Late Puritans and early nonconformists found themselves in.

Almost two decades later, in his last publication while living, *Religion our True Interest*, Watson sets out to "encourage solid piety" with the text of Malachi 3:16-18, while "confut[ing] the Atheists of the World, who imagine there is no gain in Godliness."[7] He posits the question, "Will the World or men's Lusts give them such noble Recompenses of Reward, as God bestows upon his Followers?" before answering, "Surely, it is *Holiness* [that] carries away the Garland."[8] The goal of confuting the atheist, in this work, bears some analogy to his previously stated goal of saddening the wicked. But Watson's primary goal in confuting opponents was the promotion of piety. *Religion Our True Interest* represents the synthesis of two of Watson's main pastoral concerns. It exhorts believers to constancy in piety, while drawing out consolation from the Scriptures for those experiencing hardship on account of their walk with Christ. This is clear in his closing paragraph,

5. *DC*, v-vi.
6. Beeke and Pederson, *Meet the Puritans*, 606.
7. *RTI*, iv.
8. *RTI*, iv.

> Be encouraged therefore, O ye Saints of God, to persist in a course of Holiness; though now ye seem to be lower-most, yet in the Resurrection ye shall be uppermost, *Psalm* 49.14. *The Righteous shall have Dominion over them in the Morning*; They shall have Dominion over the Wicked in the Morning of the Resurrection. They shall then *Laugh the Wicked to Scorn,* Psalm 52.6. Then shall the difference be seen *between the Righteous and the Wicked, between him that Served God and him that Served him not.*[9]

Watson follows this up with an appendix based on Psalm 119:65, entitled "A Consolatory in Affliction"—reinforcing the nature of the overall work.[10]

The above serves as an initial demonstration of Watson's conceptualisation of his pastoral role. He sought to bring comfort, joy and contentment to the godly in their times of distress. And he led them by exhortation and example as they pursued piety in the face of adversity. His application of these guiding principles will be examined in more detail below. But first, it is fitting to consider Watson's personal trajectory of identification with a marginalised religious cause and community. The context of his pastoral concerns is also best understood in light of his bleak assessment of the religious environment in England during his lifetime.

Watson's personal trajectory of religious marginalisation

We have already acknowledged the uncertainty surrounding Watson's earliest affiliation with Puritanism. But it is highly plausible that his time at Emmanuel College during the Laudian arch-episcopate crystallised a sense of solidarity and self-identification with like-minded Christians that was common to the movement.[11] Shortly after his graduation from Cambridge and throughout his ministry thereafter, Watson's hearty commitment to the *Solemn League and Covenant* helped define his political and religious hopes and disappointments. He shared a desire with many fellow Presbyterians, in accordance with the SLC, to see the English Church presbyterianised and thoroughly reformed, while remaining under the rule of the king. He was alarmed at the regicidal inclinations of the Rump Parliament

9. *RTI*, 214.
10. *RTI*, 215.
11. See Ryken, *Worldly Saints*, 12.

and Independents in the Army. And he continually protested against the religious and political direction the Grandees were taking the country in, culminating in his participation in the Love Plot. The plot itself seems to have developed as a result of the future Charles II signing the SLC in Breda in 1650. Watson therefore likely hoped that a restored monarchy would bring about church reform in favour of Presbyterianism.

It would appear that Watson adopted a stance of political quietism in the decade between his imprisonment and ejection—focusing his energies on pastoral ministry.[12] He seems to have recognised that provoking the regime once again with political activity might mean his death. The petition for mercy he made to Parliament (which resulted in his release) does not appear to be extant. However, his co-conspirator William Jenkin made a similar petition which included an acknowledgement that the change of regime was God's will.[13] If Watson used similar language, he may have simply been keeping true to his word by not interfering with the government again.[14] He may well have shared the hopes of many Presbyterians that Charles would follow through on his pledge to uphold the SLC upon his return to England. But these hopes were quickly dashed. Even at the time of his ejection from the ministry, Watson still prayed for the welfare of the king and the good governance of the land.[15] But in a farewell sermon he contrasted the accusations of disloyalty levelled against him for not submitting to the Act of Uniformity with his earlier monarchist activism: 'Some indeed say we are disloyal, we are seditious. Beloved, what my actions and sufferings for his Majesty hath been is not unknown to a few of you."[16]

Watson's identification with the Ducklings within the Presbyterian movement during the post-Restoration period is strongly suggestive of Watson's resignation with respect to achieving reform within the state church through political and ecclesiastical means. Instead, he and other likeminded Presbyterians had prioritised the freedom

12. Elizabeth Clarke accuses him of "preach[ing] a quietist piety dependent only on a sense of God's personal favour." *Politics*, 180.
13. William Jenkin, "The Humble Petition of William Jenkin" (1652) (Oxford: TCP, 2009). http://purl.ox.ac.uk/ota/A46808
14. There is perhaps a hint at this in the following phrase in a later work, "What King will pardon that man, who after he hath confessed his treason, practiseth new treason?" *Repentance*, 32.
15. Watson, "Mr. Watson's Prayer at Walbrook," *An Exact collection of farewel sermons preached by the late London-ministers* (1662) (Oxford: TCP, 2005): 33. http://purl.ox.ac.uk/ota/A31961
16. *APL*, 6.

to practice gospel ministry without official interference.[17] Watson remained disturbed at the religious state of the nation and alarmed by the proliferation of erroneous doctrine and practice. But the presbyterian system—seen as the solution to these problems—could never be imposed from the top the way it had been in Scotland. This left those who advocated for it to apply presbyterianism locally and regionally and leave the state church and religious sects to their own devices. We can conclude that, in line with Wallace's thesis, Watson focused on faithfully maintaining piety as part of a godly minority—having lost hope in the mechanisms for national reform. This self-identification was further solidified by the circumstances surrounding the Restoration and Ejection. However, it was already present from the time of the Laudian period, throughout his monarchist plotting and then in the Protectorate period.

Summary

PERIOD OF MINISTRY	OUTLOOK/GOALS
English Covenanter Period *Protestation Oath* (1642) – Love Plot (1651)	Sought the national establishment of Presbyterianism under the Stuart monarchy.
Quietist Period Release (1652) – Restoration (1660)	Focused on preaching/writing ministry (perhaps due to his earlier undertakings in petitioning his release).
Restoration (1660-1662)	Perhaps retained some hope of established Presbyterianism under Charles II. Expressed disdain for toleration.
Outlaw Period (1662-1672)	Became disillusioned with restored monarchy.[18] Abandoned hopes for comprehension. Shifted towards Toleration.
Crosby Hall Period (1672-1686)	Considered the religious, political and social situation in England to be grave. Sought to sustain the godly.

17. This brought them closer to the Independent position. Compare that of John Owen in Crawford Gribben, *An Introduction to John Owen: A Christian Vision for Every Stage of Life* (Wheaton: Crossway, 2020): 101, 149.
18. See Greaves, Enemies *Under His Feet*, 124.

We have seen that Watson held an influential ministry in London and had some notable connections. Yet he was never a true insider when it came to the political and religious establishment of England. His opposition to the usurpation of royal and parliamentary power by the Army and Rump Parliament, along with his involvement in the Love Plot did not ingratiate him to the Cromwellian regime.

While he could carry out gospel ministry without hindrance from 1652 to 1662, he was clearly troubled by the spiritual state of the nation both during the Interregnum and at the Restoration. The reign of Charles II brought a climate of marginalisation and persecution that some have described as "even worse" than the Laudian archepiscopate.[19] Certainly for Watson, the loss of his office and the deprivation of a meeting place made ministry for some years more difficult than ever before. The ongoing interference, harassment and persecution that he faced would have crystallised his identity as godly preacher to a godly minority, afflicted by an ungodly establishment. Many significant Puritans of this period had their taste of power and privilege during the Interregnum, but were marginalised under the restored monarchy. But Watson did not fall from the favour of officialdom into the mire of persecution. He merely continued further on a trajectory of godly suffering that he had been on for his entire ministry.

Being godly in a "profligate age:" Watson's perspcctive on his times*

In his biographical sketch of Thomas Watson, Barry Till suggests that Watson maintained an "apocalyptic" outlook.[20] Such an attribution must be properly qualified in order to accurately represent his general perspective. While divine judgement of the sinful world was an important theme for Watson, for much of his ministry, he was far more focused on the imminent danger of English society incurring God's wrath than on the final judgement at Christ's second coming.[21] As we will see below, his writings drip with foreboding of national calamity and divine judgement for the

19. E.g. Lee, "Thomas Watson," 5; See also Spurr, *English Puritanism*, 129-130; Spurr, "From Puritanism to Dissent," 236.
* Title taken from *RTI*, 8.
20. Till, "Watson," 5.
21. The example from Watson's works that Till quotes would support this interpretation. "Watson," Till, 5.

sins of church and kingdom.[22] But Watson is far less interested in familiar eschatological topics such as the antichrist, the nature of the millennium described in Revelation 20 and the timing of events awaiting prophetic fulfillment.[23]

There is certainly a sense in Watson's writings that the godly would always live among the "perverse generation" repeatedly spoken of in the New Testament (Matt 17:17; Luke 9:41; cf. Acts 2:40; Phil 2:15).[24] Towards the end of his ministry, he expounded the New Testament idea of "the world" as evil. The various elements of this evilness included its corrupting influence upon Christians; its capacity to tempt, discourage, deceive and dull the affections of God's people; and the way in which it injured the godly through affliction and disparagement.[25] Those following Christ would never receive a welcome reception from the world, nor have an easy passage through it. This reflected the experience of the Lord Himself during His years on earth.[26] This led Watson to a dual view of the times in which the godly Christians of seventeenth century England found themselves living. On the one hand he saw himself and the godly community in continuity with the persecuted and marginalised saints of the past. This included the *remnant* (רְאָשׁ) of the Hebrew Scriptures, the Christians of the pre-Constantinian period and the early Protestant martyrs of England and the Continent.[27] The idea of an evil age meant there was a sense of timelessness applied to the godly minority that endured throughout the centuries. On the other hand, at any given time in his ministry, we find Watson troubled by particular aspects of the state of religion in England, which require his urgent attention. Wallace has suggested a post-Restoration shift amongst English Puritans from earlier chiliastic hopes to a different kind of eschatological outlook emphasising personal anticipation of Christ's return.[28] While Watson does not embody this description exactly, there is some correlation with the trajectory of his outlook. By the end of his ministry his earlier hopes for lasting, national

22. David Hall has noted that a dismal perspective of a society in moral decay was already gaining popularity amongst English Protestant writers in the mid-16th century. *Puritans*, 146-149.
23. Contrast this, for instance, with the eschatological method of Thomas Goodwin. Beeke and Jones, *Puritan Theology*, 803-818.
24. Compare Haigh's description of an earlier Puritan outlook in *Plain Man's Pathways*, 165.
25. *BPD*, 3:877-879.
26. E.g. *Beatitudes*, 446.
27. E.g. *GMP*, 293; *Paramythion*, 37; *RTI*, 8; *Beatitudes*, 396.
28. Wallace, *Spirituality*, xxi.

religious reform through the SLC had dissipated and we instead find him emphasising perseverance amongst members of a godly minority who will receive their vindication and reward on the Last Day.[29]

Early Ministry

As we do not have any published works of Watson's that pre-date his sermon before the newly-configured Rump Parliament, we must begin with his concerns in the Civil War period. This was when his Presbyterian party was being marginalised by the Independents, who had the strength of the nation's military behind them. In addressing the Parliament as perhaps the sole Presbyterian in the chamber, Watson opened with a lamentation about the state of post-war England, '"Was there ever need to lie in *sackcloth,* then when the Kingdom almost lies in *ashes.* Or to shed *tears,* then when the Nation hath shed so much *blood?*"[30] Watson suggests that the religious humiliation that was intended to accompany the parliamentary fast day is entirely appropriate given the deplorable, sinful pride that abounded in the nation. He proposes a possible diagnosis for the spiritual problem behind the country's political chaos,

> These days are called in Scripture, *Soul-afflicting days,* Lev. 23. 29. *For whatsoever soul it be that shall not be afflicted in that same day, he shall be cut off from among his people.* And certainly, that may be one reason why there is so much State-affliction, because there is so little Soul-affliction.[31]

We have already noted the seriousness with which Watson regarded the abandonment of the *Solemn League and Covenant* by the new regime. Suffice it to say here that he saw this as a moral and religious failure by the parliament, which provoked God to judge England for the treachery of her leaders. The failure to use the powers of state to pursue the reform of the church spoke volumes about the character of the men who had seized control of the government. Watson accused many members of the government of being disingenuous in their campaign against '"popery" and '"mak[ing]

29. See Wallace, *Spirituality*, xiii, xxi.
30. *Anatomy*, 2.
31. *Anatomy*, 2.

Religion a Cloak for their Ambition."[32] He was also distressed about the way the ministry was being treated,

> Oh what a sad change is there in our days! Those that once would have *counted our feet beautiful,* that would have been ready to have pulled out their eyes for their Minister, are now ready to pull out their Minister's eyes; and what is the quarrel? Even this! *Am I become your enemy because I tell you the truth?*[33]

Thus, the Parliamentary victory in the First and Second English Civil Wars was not viewed by Watson as a catalyst for religious reform and spiritual revival in England. He was frustrated by the political failure of English Presbyterians to achieve the kind of religious results their brethren in Scotland had managed to implement.

Interregnum (1649-1659)

Although Watson's remarks in *God's Anatomy* demonstrate his unhappiness with the state of affairs following the first two civil wars and Pride's Purge, the period between the reigns of Charles I and II was nevertheless an improvement on the antebellum status quo. It would also prove to be better than what came after the Restoration. We therefore find Watson less vocal about the evils of the times during this period. Yet, he was by no means silent, as we will see below.

In *Autarkeia* (1653), Watson sounds warnings about the sin of murmuring,[34] and the general prevalence of ungodly discontentment.

> Never certainly since the Creation did this sin of discontent *reign,* or rather *rage,* more than in our times; never was God more dishonoured; you can hardly speak with any, but the passion of his tongue betrays the discontent of his heart: every one lisps out his trouble, and here even the stammering tongue speaks too freely and fluently.[35]

He also addresses the issue of widespread heresy across the nation, 'We live in times wherein there is a sluice open to all novel opinions,

32. *Anatomy*, 41-42.
33. *Anatomy*, 31-32.
34. "'Tis a ripening sin; this, without God's mercy, will hasten *England's* funerals." *Autarkeia*, 135.
35. *Autarkeia*, 56.

and every man's *opinion* is his *Bible*."[36] The reference to an open sluice that conducts, rather than holds back theological error should be understood as a tacit criticism of Independent religious policies of toleration.[37] In the paragraph which follows this remark, Watson seems to lend credence to the idea that the saints alive during this time live in a generally impious society—but he does not elaborate.[38]

Also from this period, comes a warning in the sermon *The One Thing Necessary*, invoking the imagery of Revelation 1-3, "*England's* golden hour will soon run out; Gospel-blessings are very sweet, but very swift. *Now they are hid from thine eyes, Luk. 19 42.* We know not how soon the *Golden Candlestick* may remove."[39] The context suggests that Watson anticipates the departure of the gospel from England due to a particular sinful neglect by the people. The "golden hour" is not therefore the period of the Protectorate, but the longer period in which the gospel has been (and will be) in England. The failure of the English to take hold of the gospel and respond with serious reform was a symptom of the deep spiritual neglect that Watson was concerned about.

Watson is much more alarmed in tone on the eve of the Restoration. "The whole Axle-tree of the Nation is ready to break under the weight of sin; what an inundation of wickedness is there among us? Mourn for the *hypocrisy* of the times."[40] Watson was particularly concerned with the proliferation of theological error. He takes this to be an intrinsic consequence of religious policies of toleration.

> Mourn for the Errors and Blasphemies of the Nation; there is now a free Trade of Error: toleration gives men a Patent to sin. What cursed opinion that hath been long ago buried in the Church, but is now digged out of the grave, and by some worshipped! England is grown as wanton in her Religion, as she is antic in her Fashions. The Jesuit's Exchange is open, and every one almost is for an opinion of the newest Cut. Did men's faces alter as fast as their judgements, we should not know them.[41]

36. *Autarkeia*, 100.
37. Generally speaking, the Puritans were divided over the question of religious toleration, with Independents in favour and Presbyterians opposed. See Greaves, *Enemies Under His Feet*, 143.
38. *Autarkeia*, 102.
39. *One Thing Necessary*, 54.
40. *Beatitudes*, 86.
41. *Beatitudes*, 87. Alexandra Walsham attributes this attitude towards toleration as an Augustinian legacy. "Religious unity was crucial to the political stability and social

Although more than a decade had passed since his sermon to Parliament and the political *status quo* in England was being reversed, Watson returned to the themes of "Covenant violation" and "the Pride of the Nation" as deadly problems facing the English in 1660.[42] He sums up the terminal state that the nation appears to be in, in his *Beatitudes*.

> Methinks I hear *England's* Passing bell go, let us shed some tears over dying *England*; let us bewail our intestine divisions. *England's* divisions have been fatal; they brought in the *Saxons*, *Danes*, *Normans*; if *a Kingdom divided cannot stand*, how do we stand, but by a miracle of free-grace? Truth is fallen, and peace is fled.[43]

Later he adds,

> How fatal intestine divisions have been to this Land! *Cambden* and other learned Writers relate, our discerptions and mutinies have been the scaling ladder by which the *Romans*, and the *Normans* have formerly gotten into the Nation. How is the bond of Peace broken! We have so many Schisms in the body, and are run into so many particular Churches, that God may justly unchurch us, as he did *Asia*."[44]

While Watson clearly implicates the whole nation in this despondent state, he does not identify the godly as the main perpetrators of this sin.

> If Peace-makers are the children of God, then Peace-breakers are the children of the Devil. Heretics destroy the truth of the Church by Error; and Schismatics destroy the peace of it by division ... There are too many make-bates in *England*, whose sweetest Music is in discord; who never unite but to divide ... These are the persons God's soul hates. *Prov. 6.19 Sowers of discord among brethren* ... If there be a Devil in man's shape, it is the Incendiary.[45]

order of a state as well as to its spiritual welfare. Unity of faith was supposed to be the best antidote to sedition and subversion and a preservative against internal dissolution, both being indirect manifestations of the wrath of the Almighty against iniquitous nations. Accordingly, toleration was anathema, a recipe for chaos and anarchy, if not an invitation to apocalyptic destruction. Any country that permitted religious pluralism was thus committing an act of corporate suicide." Walsham, *Charitable Hatred*, 2.

42. *Beatitudes*, 87.
43. *Beatitudes*, 89.
44. Watson refers here to Christ's warning to the churches of Asia Minor, in the opening chapters of Revelation, that they risked having their "lampstand removed"—an allusion to their loss of status as the church of Christ. *Beatitudes*, 326.
45. *Beatitudes*, 325.

The godly were those who continued to seek peace and truth in a nation that had already felt the sword of war due to its sinful divisions and which was soon to feel the sword of God's wrath in greater judgement still—failing prompt repentance.[46] Such divisions brought the Christian religion into disrepute and provided fertile ground for atheism.[47] Yet the godly also needed to be prepared to face great hardship and persecution for their convictions. Watson's treatment of the final beatitude is replete with examples from the New Testament and early church of faithful suffering for Christ's sake.[48] The spread of error and culpability of the incendiaries, along with a general lack of reform and religious peace are all matters of concern to Watson which continued to demonstrate his commitment to the ethos of the SLC. All of those concerns are present in the text of that document. Charles II's Parliament would condemn the SLC and order its repudiation just months after Watson aired these concerns in *The Beatitudes*.

The Restoration and the Ejection of Nonconformist Ministers (1660-1662)

In 1662, the year Watson lost his position within the state church along with the other Black Bartholomeans, he wrote the consolatory work, *Paramythion*. In this text, designed to bring comfort to the godly in a tumultuous time for the church and nation, it is not surprising to find ample material relating to Watson's assessment of the times he was living in. Watson identifies "Nine sins which drive God out of a Land" and invite divine judgement.[49] He speaks of them not as hypothetical possibilities, but with the implication that they are already present in the land. The list includes: "idolatry," "oppression," "uncleanness," "covetousness," "apostasy," "weariness of God's ordinances," "perjury," "hatred of Reformation" and "incivilities" towards gospel ministers.[50] The last five vices are particularly telling of Watson's perspective. In treating "apostasy" he remarks with his usual flair, "There are many who courted the Queen of Religion when she had a Jewel hung at her ear, but when she is in her night-dress, and her Jewels of preferment are pulled off,

46. *Beatitudes*, 89-90.
47. "Confident I am, *England's* divisions have made many turn Atheists." *Beatitudes*, 327.
48. E.g. *Beatitudes*, 396, 399, 403, 409, 411.
49. *Paramythion*, 23.
50. *Paramythion*, 23-29.

now they desert her."[51] This appears to be a pointed reference to the changed religious circumstances under Charles II.

When outlining the problem of gospel weariness, Watson laments, "How sad is it for any Nation, when their *Seers* are blind!"[52] This appears to be an anticipation of a great decline in gospel preaching and faithful teaching of Scripture following the ejection of nonconformist preachers from the ministry. Discussing "Perjury" leads to the following warning, "When a people play fast and loose with God, breaking their Solemn Vows and Obligations, whether Sacramental or other, this is a God provoking sin, it will make the Lord go away from a Nation, and though they cry after him, he will turn a deaf ear."[53] The abandonment of the SLC, first by the Independents and then by Charles II, was clearly on Watson's mind when he penned these words. This demonstrates that he still considered this a grievous transgression against God for which the nation would be judged.[54] The idea of England as a covenanted nation is further implied in Watson's description of what it means to hate religious reform, "Hath not God called to us to be an holy reformed people, but are there not those found among us, who hate Holiness, and cry down Reformation?"[55] Finally, it would be hard to imagine that Watson was not referring to the Ejection itself when he decried the ungodly mistreatment of gospel ministers as a sin inviting national calamity.[56] He rounds out this bill of sins with a sober warning, "Let us take heed of these sins, which will cause God to depart from the Nation."[57]

But all was not gloom. In dealing with the possibility that judgement might be unavoidable and that England stood as-good-as-forsaken already, Watson provides "six seeds of hope" that indicate this is not in fact the case. The primary reason for hope is that there remains "a generation of righteous persons in the Nation."[58] As

51. *Paramythion*, 25.
52. *Paramythion*, 27.
53. *Paramythion*, 27.
54. David J. Appleby has noted that Watson and several other key figures known for their subscription to the *Solemn League and Covenant* make no mention of the word "covenant" in their farewell addresses in 1662. Appleby, *Black Bartholomew's Day: Preaching, Polemic and Restoration Nonconformity* (Manchester: Manchester University Press, 2007): 28. This is noteworthy, however Watson's comments in *Paramythion* suggest this may be more a sign of tact than acquiescence.
55. *Paramythion*, 28.
56. *Paramythion*, 28.
57. *Paramythion*, 29.
58. *Paramythion*, 32.

Watson goes on to explain,

> Were the godly, (who are the Chariots and Horsemen in Israel) removed, the Lord would make quick work with the Nation; he would destroy the weeds, were it not for the Corn. The Ship of Church and State would soon be drowned, if the Elect were not in it. The Saints stay God's hand when he is going to strike.[59]

Among the other reasons for hope given are the prayers of the saints ("Prayer staves off wrath from a Land") and the idea that "there have been many sins committed *in* the Nation, which are not the sins *of* the Nation."[60] This is significant for the discussion at hand, regarding Watson's approach to piety within his perceived context of a perverse age and decaying nation. It demonstrates that the fidelity of the godly was not merely a matter which concerned their own relationship with Christ. They were preserving the entire nation in the face of impending judgement.

Decade in Exile (1662-1672)

1666 was a significant year for Watson, marking the mid-way point of his forty years of pastoral ministry and the publication of *Godly Man's Picture.* Watson's assessment of this period includes a lament over the lack of love amongst Christians in England.[61] He contrasts this with an earlier period in which "England was once a fair garden where the flower of love did grow."[62] It is unclear which historical period serves as Watson's supposed halcyon days.[63] He was also concerned with a general decline in piety, speaking of Christians "wavering in Religion" and "*fall[ing] from that godliness which once they seemed to have.*"[64] Watson's treatment of this issue suggests that there was a real incentive to abandon godliness for a compromised, toned-down version of Christianity to avoid the loss of liberty or property.[65] It is significant that he cites several passages from Hebrews during this discourse. This suggests that he saw himself giving counsel to Christians facing similar pressures and temptations to the Jewish believers of the first century.[66] There is

59. *Paramythion*, 32.
60. *Paramythion*, 33, 36.
61. *GMP*, 200.
62. *GMP*, 200.
63. The latter part of Henry VIII's reign through to the accession of Mary is a possibility.
64. *GMP*, 299-300.
65. *GMP*, 301-303.
66. E.g. Heb 6:6, 10:38, 3:12, 2:10, 13:9. *GMP*, 301-303.

a conceptual connection between reversion to Judaism in the *Sitz im Leben* of Hebrews and abandonment of evangelical or Puritan religion for comfortable conformity in Watson's milieu. Watson viewed both as spiritually deadly apostasy. *Godly Man's Picture* also contains an identification of Watson's godly contemporaries with the biblical remnant motif,

> This may prevail with us to be godly, if the number of the Saints be so small, how should we labour to be found among these pearls? *Rom. 9. 27. but a remnant shall be saved:* it is better going to Heaven with a few, than to Hell in the crowd.[67]

Watson also draws a connection between the ungodly aspersions cast upon the saints during his time and the similar contempt experienced by the early church.

> Though godliness be the object of the worlds scorn and hatred (as in *Tertullian's* days, the name of a Christian was a crime) yet be not ashamed to espouse godliness; know, that persecuted godliness, is better than prosperous wickedness.[68]

In 1668's *Doctrine of Repentance*, we find stark warnings again about England's spiritual state and impending judgement. "What horrible impieties are chargeable upon the Nation! We see persons daily listing themselves under Satan. Not only the banks of *Religion,* but *Civility* are broken down."[69] "*England* is an Island encompassed with two Oceans, an Ocean of *water,* and an Ocean of *wickedness;* O that it might be encompassed with a third Ocean, namely, repenting tears."[70] Watson calls for national repentance in the face of dry "formality" of religion and, again, the threat of the gospel disappearing from the land—which naturally precludes future opportunities to repent.[71] As we have already noted, the calamities of the plague and the fire were "afflictive providences," which warned of greater judgements to come. [72] The only appropriate response from Londoners and English people was to weep for their sins and turn away from them.[73] The urgent need for sincere repentance is conveyed in the following quote, "if we repent not now, we stand in

67. *GMP*, 293.
68. *GMP*, 273.
69. *Repentance*, 83.
70. *Repentance*, 84-85.
71. *Repentance*, 96.
72. *Repentance*, 165.
73. *Repentance*, 165.

a contempt of God, and do interpretatively bid God do his worst; and such a *climax* of wickedness will hardly be pardoned."[74] Clearly, at this time, Watson saw England as a wayward nation that risked reaching the "climax of wickedness" and therefore liable to experience the worst imaginable judgements.

A few years later, Watson begins his *Mischief of Sinne* with yet another diagnosis of England's spiritual state.

> The excess of impiety which hath broken down the Banks of common Civility & Modesty, did at first lead my thoughts to these subjects ensuing. The Spirits of men are leavened with Atheism, and their lives stained with debauchery. I know not what to call them, but *Baptized Heathens.* Not long since there was a complaint that the Springs grew low: Sure I am the floods of sin are risen, even to a Deluge. There is a Generation among us, of whom I may say, as *Oecumenius*, they *militate* against Religion; they are so prodigiously profane, that they esteem the Bible a Fable and would jeer all Holiness out of the world![75]

Perhaps such a pessimistic outlook is to be anticipated from a treatise on sin. However, Watson's particular highlighting of national and social sin shows that this remained an ongoing concern for him. He continued to expect divine judgement to come upon England. Against the background of the English exceptionalism in Christendom explicit in his earlier writings,[76] Watson now believed the sins of other nations were rife within England.[77] This would lead to the onset of the same judgements that came upon other ungodly nations. "Sin hath brought other Nations low, and do we think to scape better than they?"[78] Watson again lists the sins he determines to be particularly problematic in the nation. Pride, "Covenant-violation" and "abuse of the Gospel" feature yet again, with Watson making special mention this time of "neglect of Family worship."[79] Coupled with this is "Barrenness under the Means of Grace"—failure to bear spiritual fruit despite having ample access to the divine ordinances.[80] Watson notes that this was the reason given

74. *Repentance*, 168.
75. *Mischief,* iv-vi.
76. Example, "God hath fed this Nation with the finest of the wheat, even the bread of life, we have had the Cream of Ordinances, God hath come down to us in a golden shower of blessings, the Vintage of other Nations, hath not been so good as the gleanings of England." *Paramythion*, 26.
77. "The sins of *Denmark, Spain, France, Italy* are translated into English." *Mischief,* 49.
78. *Mischief,* 52.
79. *Mischief,* 62, 64-65.
80. *Mischief,* 68.

by those escaping the Marian persecutions for why they believed their circumstances had come upon them.[81] This is a significant reference since he viewed this generation as more pious and faithful than his own. Widespread swearing and sexual immorality are also identified as national problems. Watson concludes by again expressing dismay at disunity and unloving behaviour amongst Christians as a serious symptom of the nation's problems.[82]

The remnant motif once again appears in an appendix to this work. Watson refers both to the idea of God sparing a nation from judgement because of a righteous minority and to His preservation of persecuted prophets during the time of Elijah.

> Perhaps the reformation of a few may help to keep off wrath from the Nation. Jer. 5.i. *Run ye to and fro and see if ye can find a man that seeketh the truth, and I will pardon it* ... if by this word, *Man*, we understand *few*, yet that shews us, that sometimes the repentance of a few may help to save a Nation ... The Lord knows in a storm how to hide his jewels. God hid *Jeremy* in Captivity; he hid an hundred Prophets in a Cave, 1 Kings 18.13. He hid several under his wings in the Marian Persecution.[83]

The coupling of the Old Testament cases of deliverance with the experience of Protestants under Mary's severe reign creates a more recent link between Watson's readers and the ancient, biblical examples. It also reinforces the idea that the nonconformist experience under Charles II was relatable to what the English martyrs had endured a century earlier. Mary Tudor served as the default historical example of a tyrannical oppressor in Watson's time, in much the same way Adolf Hitler or Joseph Stalin have been invoked since the mid-twentieth century. However, Raymond Brown notes,

> In reality, however, far more innocent Protestants died in squalid prisons in the reign of Charles II than at the stake under Mary. Additionally, under Charles thousands were robbed of goods, money, livelihood, security, freedom and health, which cannot be said for life under the Catholic queen.[84]

81. *Mischief*, 69.
82. *Mischief*, 74-75.
83. "The Desperateness of Sinners," 171-173.
84. Brown, *Spirituality in Adversity*, 16.

Watson's final years

Towards the end of Watson's life we find yet another bleak assessment of the religious climate. "It is an unhappiness that in these Luxuriant times, Religion should for the most part run either into *Notion* or *Ceremony*; The Spirits of Religion are evaporated."[85] *Religion our True Interest*, the last work published by Watson before his death, is essentially a manual for surviving and thriving as godly people in "evil times."[86] He openly states in the introduction that Malachi 3:16-18 has the capacity "to encourage Solid Piety, and confute the Atheists of the World, who imagine there is no gain in Godliness."[87] It is clear that Watson sees the social, political, intellectual and ecclesiastical environment in England as hostile to biblical piety two decades on from the Restoration. He was not alone in this opinion. Crawford Gribben has documented John Owen's dismal perspective on the sins of the nation and infirmities of the church from the mid-1670s to 1680s.[88] He notes that in 1679, Owen declared England guilty of "atheism and profaneness, blood and murder, adultery and uncleanness, and pride" and the next year was gravely concerned with a possible relapse into state-sanctioned Catholicism.[89] Richard Greaves has shown that John Bunyan was affected by considerable anti-Catholic angst during the same period, accompanied by "a sense of impending danger."[90] Bunyan also believed that the English churches had been in spiritual decline since the Great Ejection of 1662.[91]

In Watson's earlier works, piety is presented as a potential means of preserving the nation from destruction. In this final work, the focus shifts to godliness being an opportunity to glorify God in contrast

85. *RTI*, v.
86. Watson uses a range of synonymous descriptors for the times he lived in, including "a time of common infection," "times of degeneracy," "times of general defection," "an adulterous generation," "a profligate age," "worst times," "times of apostasy" and "corrupt times." See *RTI*, 4-9, 13.
87. *RTI*, iv.
88. Crawford Gribben, *John Owen and English Puritanism Experiences of Defeat* (Oxford: Oxford University Press, 2016): 255-258. Kindle Edition.
89. Gribben, *Owen and English Puritanism*, 256.
90. Greaves, *Glimpses of Glory*, 362-363, 371.
91. Greaves, *Glimpses of Glory*, 443.

to the general ungodliness of the nation. Being consistently godly in unfavourable conditions glorifies God to a greater degree than a situation where there is less opposition and difficulty. This is not to suggest that Watson has ceased anticipating temporal judgement for the nation's sins. He warned '"May not we fear some portentous calamity should bring up the rear of former Judgments?"'[92] His fellow lamenters, Owen and Bunyan, certainly saw national ruin through Catholicism or a cataclysmic event as imminent possibilities that would manifest God's wrath against the English people.[93] But Watson does appear to shift to a greater emphasis on eschatological judgement where the distinction between the godly and the wicked will be most clear.[94] In this context, we also find another association of the godly with the biblical remnant motif.

> To be holy in times of General defection is that which God is Greatly pleased with. The Lord was much taken with the holy conferences and dialogues of these Saints in the Text. When others were inveighing against the Deity, that there should be a parcel of holy Souls speaking of Glory and the Life to come, their words were Music in God's ears. [95]

Summary

It is clear that Watson maintained the notion that he and his religious fellow-travellers were living in an ungodly age throughout his forty years of ministry. This general sense of national sin and a degenerate culture was his constant concern before, during and after the Puritan revolution and Interregnum. It does, however, appear to have been exacerbated by the religious and social developments that occurred during and after the Restoration of the Stuart monarchy. While particular sins and religious problems came into his focus at different points during his ministry, some remained constant. The idea that England was an impious society, rampant with heresy, hypocrisy, formalism and immorality, is a consistent one. Likewise, the breaching of the *Solemn League and Covenant* and subsequent repudiation of it by Parliament were viewed by Watson as a form of national infidelity towards God. Such actions amounted to the

92. *RTI*, 25-26.
93. Gribben, *Owen and English Puritanism*, 257-258; Greaves, *Glimpses of Glory*, 370-371.
94. E.g. *RTI*, 68-73, 210-214.
95. *RTI*, 7.

abandonment of religious reformation in favour of compromise.

Watson continually held out the dual options for the nation. For years he maintained there was an urgent choice between continued rebellion resulting in judgement (and perhaps loss of the gospel or the Church from England) and repentance on the part of sinners—combined with steadfast piety on the part of the godly. The latter choice would potentially lead to reformation and revival, or at least stay God's hand from executing his wrath upon England. By the end of his ministry Watson shifted his focus to exhorting the godly to maintain their piety in the face of gross ungodliness as a means of glorifying God. While, even before the Restoration, Watson expressed the view that the end of all things was very near (a view he appears to have maintained throughout his ministry), he was haunted by the fear that Christian England might come to an end first.[96] His shift to a more explicitly eschatological hope for the godly in his final years was perhaps due to his surprise that God had not brought utter catastrophe upon the nation after so many years of dereliction and sin.

Throughout this entire period, Watson implicitly identified himself and at least a segment of his congregants and readers with a godly minority in the midst of an ungodly nation. It was true that the godly were implicated in some of the sins of the nation and needed to take care to repent of any known transgressions or impiety. But they were never the ones who bore primary guilt. Instead they were analogous to the remnant of the Old Testament—those who maintained devotion towards Yahweh when the majority defected to idolatrous practices.[97] The saints needed to persist in godliness for the glory of God, the sake of the nation and for their own future inheritance. Ensuring that this happened was Watson's goal throughout his ministry. This was particularly so in the upheaval of the Restoration and Great Ejection and increasingly so towards the end of his ministry.

96. "Day of Judgement," 444-445. Compare *BPD*, 1:238.
97. *GMP*, 293; *RTI*, 5; *Paramythion*, 36-37; *Righteous Man's Weal*, 8.

Chapter 12
"Steadfast in Godliness:"* Pastoring an afflicted, religious minority

Watson's pastoral method in exhorting and comforting the godly

Watson's trajectory of self-identification with an afflicted, godly minority and his sense of perversity regarding the times in which he found himself ministering, has been established. We return to the question of how he operated pastorally in light of these perceptions. An examination of some of the major themes in Watson's consolatory literature reveals that he drew on a range of biblical themes and historical Christian examples to provide encouragement to the suffering saints whose piety he was seeking to sustain. As we will see below, there is also a strong link between the goals or outcomes of godliness that we identified in Chapter 6 and the grounds for consolation in the midst of suffering that Watson develops.

Suffering to the glory of God: the preciousness of afflicted godliness

The greatest encouragement to the godly in the midst of persecution and affliction was the capacity for their suffering to contribute to the first two great goals of godliness. Christian suffering could glorify God and benefit others. Nowhere is this clearer than in Watson's list of means for glorifying God in the first chapter of *Body of Divinity*:

> We glorify God in an high manner when we suffer for God, and Seal the Gospel with our Blood ... God's Glory shines in the Ashes of his Martyrs, Isa. 24.15. *Wherefore glorify the Lord in the fires. Micaiah* was in the Prison, *Isaiah* sawn

* Title taken from *GMP*, 301.

> asunder, *Paul* beheaded, *Luke* hanged on an Olive-tree, thus did they by their Death glorify God. The Sufferings of the Primitive Saints did Honour God, and make the Gospel famous in the World: What would others say, See what a good Master they serve, and how they love him, that they will venture loss of all in his Service.[1]

Enduring suffering for God's sake communicated a sense of His infinite worth to the watching world. This had the effect of increasing His ascriptive glory in the world and potentially winning people to the cause of the gospel. Watson elsewhere compares the honour that Christ receives from His followers' willingness to endure harsh ordeals for Him, to the credit Caesar received to his reputation from the loyal tenacity of his troops on their difficult campaigns.[2] He goes on to note that this capacity for bringing Christ glory in hardships made some of the early Christians more willing to endure suffering than to be immediately relieved of it.[3] For Watson, the basic principle could be summed up as: 'He who is divinely qualified, is so zealously ambitious of God's glory, that he cares not what he loseth, so God may be a gainer."[4] Thus, suffering hardships as a member of a godly minority in a perverse age was a means of achieving the Christian's chief end of bringing God glory.[5]

Regarding the impact that suffering for righteousness' sake might have upon other people, Watson encouraged the saints with his conviction that this was in fact the great means of seeing true religion multiply in their society.

> God hath always propagated Religion by sufferings ... Saints under their persecutions, hath much added both to the *growth* of Religion, and the *Crown. Basil,* and *Tertullian* observe of the Primitive Martyrs, that diverse of the Heathens seeing their zeal and constancy, turned Christians. Religion is that *Phoenix* which hath always revived and flourished *in the ashes* of holy men.[6]

Brown attests to this being a common perspective amongst Puritans in this period, citing examples in the writings of Thomas Brooks, Joseph Alleine and John Bunyan, amongst others.[7] Cosby reinforces

1. *BPD*, 1:7.
2. *Beatitudes*, 429.
3. *Beatitudes*, 411, 448.
4. *Beatitudes*, 419.
5. See also Lee, "Thomas Watson," 9, 11.
6. *Autarkeia*, 112-113.
7. Brown, *Spirituality in Adversity*, 79.

this emphasis with the following summary of John Flavel's perspective. "The saints' bearing witness to the reality of the gospel and the glory of God before a watching world ... is one of the reasons God ordains suffering."[8]

Elsewhere, Watson displays a fondness for phrases such as "Sanguine showers have always made the Church grow the more" and *sanguine fundata est ecclesia sanguine crevit*, which he renders "The Church is founded in blood and by blood it increases."[9] Watson clearly desires suffering saints to press on through their trials, with the knowledge that even fatal persecution will be used by God to draw more people to Christ. This had occurred throughout the history of the church and God's people should expect to see it taking place again as a result of their own sufferings.

Identification with Christ and the long list of martyrs

As we have already noted in Chapter 7 (and in the segment directly above) Watson frequently drew upon past Christian figures as exemplars of the kind of piety he was promoting. Those who had suffered for their godliness were particularly favoured. For Watson, the suffering of the *church militant* was a means of identifying with innumerable saints who now constituted the *church triumphant* after themselves enduring various trials while on earth.[10] More important still, suffering as a Christian was a crucial means of identification with Christ Himself—the paragon of persecuted piety.[11]

Brown has noted that the example of Christ's suffering was a pertinent motif in nonconformist devotion during the persecutions of the 1680s.[12] We find Watson emphasising this theme many years earlier, most notably in his *Beatitudes*. Based on its publication date it is probable that Watson penned his reflections on the final beatitudes—pertaining to persecution—in the opening days of the Restoration. It is in this context that Watson presents the relationship between Christ's suffering and that of the believer.

8. Brian H. Cosby, *Suffering and Sovereignty: John Flavel and the Puritans on Afflictive Providence* (Grand Rapids: Reformation Heritage, 2012): chap. 4. Kindle Edition.
9. *Paramythion*, 21. *Beatitudes*, 448.
10. *BPD*, 1:224. Compare *BPD*, 3:528-529; *Beatitudes*, 55.
11. Brown says the same thing of nonconformists more generally, "Persecution provided a unique context for identification with Christ." Brown, *Spirituality in Adversity*, 173. See also Lee, "Thomas Watson," 9.
12. Brown, *Spirituality in Adversity*, 182-185.

'While we suffer for Christ, we suffer with Christ. *Rom. 8. 17. If we suffer with him,* &c. Jesus Christ bears part of the suffering with us."[13] Here the identification is personal, spiritual and almost mystical. Christ assists the believer in carrying the burden of their trials. But there was also a sense in which suffering for Christ's name was a logical consequence of receiving salvation through His suffering. It was certainly a necessary aspect of following His example. Watson asks his readers eleven questions about what kind of suffering they face—including poverty, reproach, slander, unjust treatment, betrayal and death—and shows how Christ Himself has already suffered the same.[14] He rounds this passage out with the appeal,

> Did the Lord Jesus endure all this for us, and shall not we suffer persecution for his Name? Say as holy *Ignatius, I am willing to die for Christ, for Christ my love was crucified*! Our cup is nothing to the cup which Christ drank; his cup was mixed with the wrath of God; and if he did bear God's wrath for us, well may we bear man's wrath for him.[15]

Given what followed for Watson and his peers in the reign of Charles II, these remarks appear preparatory, if not prescient. Other passages in *Beatitudes,* and later in *Body of Divinity,* reinforce the idea that the Christian's attitude towards suffering should proceed out of the recognition of what Jesus has already done on her behalf. Suffering was part of God's continued outworking of salvation in the believer's life. 'Christ's Kingdom is Regnum Crucis, this is the way God hath always gone in, such as God intends to save from Hell, yet he doth not save from the Cross; the consideration of this should quiet our Minds in Affliction, and make us say, *Thy Will be done.*"[16] Watson repeatedly emphasises this need for affliction as part of the Christian's identification with Christ's earthly suffering. 'Religion gives no Charter of exemption from suffering; to have two heavens, is more than Christ had. Was the head crowned with Thorns, and do we think to be crowned with Roses!"[17] The encouragement of this aspect came from the role of afflictions as a means of making the godly more Christlike. 'Now the more our Wills are subject to God's

13. *Beatitudes*, 451.
14. *Beatitudes,* 446-447.
15. *Beatitudes*, 447-448.
16. *BPD*, 3:529.
17. *Beatitudes*, 413. Watson rejects the idea of the Christian having "two heavens" (i.e. peace in this life and the next) on multiple occasions. E.g. *BPD*, 3:529.

Will in Affliction, the nearer we come to Christ our Pattern; is it not our Prayer we may be like Christ? by holy Submission we imitate him: His Will was melted into his Father's Will."[18] Thus Watson sees godly suffering as a participation in Christ's own suffering. It solidifies the believer's inward and outward identification with their Saviour. "Martyrs are not only Christ's *Followers*—but his *Ensign-bearers*."[19] Cosby locates a similar emphasis in Watson's fellow Presbyterian, John Flavel. "One of the best expressions of this communion with Christ comes through the experience of suffering. God ordains suffering so that the believer ultimately might enjoy greater communion with Jesus, who has experienced suffering."[20]

Brown has observed that a sense of connection with historical martyrs and confessors was one of the hallmarks of the Late English Puritan attitude towards suffering.[21] Watson typifies this, by stressing solidarity with previous generations who had borne Christ's ensign amidst adversity. Those experiencing hardships now could take comfort and encouragement from the fact that their godly predecessors were now enjoying Christ in heaven—just as they themselves soon would.

> Set often before your Eyes the noble Examples of those who have Persevered in Religion; *quot Martyres, quot Fideles in Coelis jam Triumphant*? What a glorious Army of Saints and Martyrs have gone before us? How constant to the Death was St. *Paul, Acts* 21.13. How Persevering in the Faith were *Ignatius, Polycarp, Athanasius*? These were Stars in their Orb, Pillars in the Temple of God. Let us look on their Zeal and Courage, and be animated *Heb.* 12.1.[22]

In *The Lord's Prayer*, Watson also catalogues the sufferings traditionally ascribed to several of the apostles. He follows with the exhortation, "Why should we think to tread only upon Roses and Violets, when Prophets and Apostles have marched through the Briars to Heaven?"[23] *Beatitudes* features another catalogue of godly suffering, ranging from the Old Testament prophets Micaiah, Jeremiah and Isaiah, to early Christians not wavering whilst being tortured and killed. It goes on to cite the bold confessions of Jan Huss, Polycarp, Laurence Saunders and several anonymous martyrs

18. *BPD*, 1:534.
19. *Beatitudes*, 445.
20. Cosby, *Suffering and Sovereignty*, chap. 4.
21. Brown, *Spirituality in Adversity*, 51-52.
22. *BPD*, 1:224.
23. *BPD*, 3:529.

as they faced execution.[24] These examples are used to fortify the confidence Watson's readers have in God to sustain them through the worst imaginable trials. 'These suffering examples we should lay up, God is still the same God; he hath as much love in his heart to pity us, and as much strength in his arm to help us."[25] This assurance that Watson's godly contemporaries had the same God as noteworthy figures who suffered martyrdom at the hands of the Roman church in the preceding centuries and the Roman state in antiquity is an indication of what kind of climate he anticipated would transpire in Restoration England.[26]

Watson believed that these accounts of godly suffering in the lives of saints now with Jesus had a special power in the lives of those suffering presently, 'The Holy Spirit shews us the blood of Saints and Martyrs, to infuse a spirit of zeal and courage into us."[27] But he was also happy to use negative examples from church history as a warning to his readers against turning from identifying with Christ. "*Erasmus* highly extolled *Luther's* doctrine; but when the Emperor threatened all that should favour *Luther's* cause, he unworthily deserted it. Hypocrites will sooner renounce their Baptism, than take up the Cross."[28] By making a reference to a hostile anti-Protestant ruler in the opening days of the Restoration, Watson may have been sending a warning to his contemporaries about his worst fears of what might lie ahead. There was a true and lasting reward that came as a consequence of identifying with Christ in severe afflictions (which I will turn my attention to more fully below), "As the sufferings of the Godly have raised their Fame and Renown in the World—the Zeal and Constancy of the Martyrs in their Suffering have Eternized their Name."[29] Those who earnestly sought Christ's glory—perhaps even to the point of death—would themselves receive glory as a result of their testimony.

Thus, Watson's use of the suffering saint's identification with Christ and their confessing forebears as an encouragement and exhortation is clear. Those who have benefited from Christ's own suffering and death now endure hardship, persecution and perhaps

24. *Beatitudes*, 443.
25. *Beatitudes*, 444.
26. This is supported by the dire warnings about religion and state issued in *A Seasonable Exhortation of Sundry Ministers in London* (1660), to which Watson subscribed his name.
27. *Beatitudes*, 443.
28. *Beatitudes*, 415.
29. *BPD*, 3:864.

death as they follow Him. But their suffering is a participation in His death. Those who participate in His death will also share in His glory (as per Romans 8:17). As believers bear the cross in this life, they are made more Christlike through the sufferings they experience for His name. Past examples of suffering for Christ served as reminders that Watson's contemporaries were not an unusual case in the history of the church. If they held fast to their confession (Heb 10:23) as earlier generations had, they would soon gain the same glory, honour, life and rest that those saints now had.

The Great Reversal: the wicked judged and saints vindicated

Another of Watson's key pastoral resources for comforting the godly in the face of suffering and persecution was closely related to the role godliness played in preparing the believer for death (which we also examined in Chapter 6). Watson frequently sought to encourage his fellow-sufferers with the hope they could have in their reward after death. This reward not only made their perseverance in piety worthwhile. It stood in sharp contrast to what their adversaries would receive as their eternal recompense.

Watson's understanding of the general attitude believers should have towards their trials is heavily shaped by the words of the apostle Paul in 2 Corinthians 4:17, "For our light affliction, which is but for a moment, worketh for us a far more exceeding and eternal weight of glory" (AV). This perspective that temporal suffering is beneath comparison with eternal joy—is recurrent in Watson's encouragements to the godly.[30] It features prominently in the "Blessed are the Persecuted" section of his *Beatitudes*,

> Affliction is light in comparison of glory; the *weight of glory* makes persecution light; 'If,' says *Chrysostom*, 'the torments of all the men in the world could be laid upon one man, it were not worth one hour's being in heaven;' and if persecution be light, we should in a manner set light by it; let us neither faint through unbelief, nor fret through impatience.[31]

This message also constituted some of Watson's final words to his congregation before he was ejected from the ministry of the state church.

30. It was also shared by some of his notable contemporaries. See Cosby, *Suffering and Sovereignty*, chap. 7.
31. *Beatitudes*, 450 (compare 455).

> The thoughts of eternity would make us slight and contemn all the things in the World ... as not to over value, so not to over-grieve at the loss of them; what are these sufferings, they are but for a while, 1 *Phil.* 5. 10. and what is that to eternity? our suffering may be lasting, but they shall not be everlasting; our greatest afflictions are not worthy of that Eternal weight of glory.[32]

Each of these excerpts demonstrates the contrast between immeasurable, celestial glory and measurable, earthly suffering. Faith in how wonderful heaven and the resurrection would be was the only means of enduring what seemed to be unbearable.[33] Watson also taught that the more one experienced suffering as a witness for Christ, the greater their glory would be in eternity.[34]

But it was not only thoughts of their heavenly reward that sustained the afflicted saints. Watson repeatedly sought to deepen his readers' appreciation of the greatness of their salvation and lightness of their trials by conveying a grave sense of the punishment that awaited their persecutors. The contrast between the eternal fate of the oppressed godly and their ungodly oppressors was a key pastoral resource for English nonconformists to draw comfort from in seasons of adversity. Bunyan and Flavel each make use of it in their writings.[35] The discouragement of the godly when the wicked obtain power and prestige was an ancient problem—one which the Scriptures addressed directly.[36] But Watson's trajectory of marginalisation and affliction gave him an acute awareness of the need to put the temporal privileges of their adversaries in eternal perspective.

Autarkeia warns that those who enjoy ungodly prosperity now will soon experience the penalty for their sins. 'When the wicked

32. *APL*, 9.
33. For this theme in other nonconformist writers, see Brown, *Spirituality in Adversity*, 89.
34. "Christ's suffering Saints shall have greater degrees in glory, Matth. 19.28. God hath his highest seats, yea, his *Thrones* for his Martyrs; it is true, he that hath the least degree of glory, a door-keeper in heaven, will have enough; but as *Joseph* gave to *Benjamin* a double mess above the rest of his brethren, so God will give to his sufferers a double portion of glory; some orbs in heaven are higher, some stars brighter. God's Martyrs shall shine brighter in the heavenly Horizon." *Beatitudes*, 455.
35. Bunyan, *Seasonable counsel, or, Advice to sufferers* (1684) (Oxford: TCP, 2012): 217. http://purl.ox.ac.uk/ota/A30202. Cosby, *Suffering and Sovereignty*, chap. 7.
36. "The prosperity of the wicked is a great stumbling block: This made *Averroes* deny a Providence, and made *Asaph* say, *Surely I have cleansed my heart in vain, Psal.* 73.12." *BPD*, 3:482.

have eaten of their dainty dishes, there comes in a sad reckoning which will spoil all. The world is first musical and then tragical; if you would have a man fry and blaze in hell, let him have enough of the *fat of the earth*."[37] In a passage of *Beatitudes* dealing with persecutors, Watson quotes Revelation 16:6 to remind his readers of the fate of such people. "*They have shed the blood of Saints and Prophets, and thou hast given them blood to drink, for they are worthy*."[38]

Most frequently, Watson juxtaposes the outcomes of godliness/suffering and wickedness/persecution as a warning and exhortation to those undergoing hardships for Christ. Sanctifying refinement is contrasted with hell, "God hath two fires; one where he puts his gold, and another where he puts his dross; the fire where he puts his dross is hell fire; the fire where he puts his gold, is the fire of persecution."[39] The present power-balance will be reversed, "The wicked first reign and then suffer; the godly first suffer, and then reign."[40] The choice between immediate and lasting gratification was stark. "*When a man hath been virtuous the labour is gone but the pleasure remains; when a man hath been wicked, the pleasure is gone, but the sting remains*."[41] And the ignominious status of the godly in society would be applied to the wicked for eternity.

> So though now God's People are low and despised, and the Wicked Insult over them, yet when the *Critical-day* comes, there shall be a final Separation made between the Righteous and the Wicked: the one shall be Dignified, the other Damned, *Mat.* 25.46.42

For these reasons, the godly should "pity" the wicked rather than "envy" them.[43] Further, they must ensure that they do not turn their backs on piety and its reward in an attempt to abate their present sufferings.[44] It made no sense for the saints to wish themselves in the position of their oppressors, since Watson strongly believed that

37. *Autarkeia*, 98.
38. *Beatitudes*, 416.
39. *Beatitudes*, 446. Watson expresses a similar idea using the biblical imagery of wheat and chaff, "If God thresh his Wheat, he will burn the Chaff. If the Godly suffer Castigation, the Wicked shall suffer Condemnation. If he mingle his Peoples Cup with Wormwood, he will mingle the Wicked's Cup with Fire and Brimstone." *BPD*, 2:262.
40. *Beatitudes*, 456.
41. *Weal*, 26.
42. *RTI*, 214.
43. *Autarkeia*, 97.
44. *Autarkeia*, 97.

'There is a time coming when the wicked would be glad to have some of that Holiness which they now despise.'[45] He uttered those words in a farewell sermon to his St. Stephen's congregation, at a time when religious differences in England were being sharply accentuated once again. Nearly twenty years later, when Watson was distressed by the direction the nation had taken, he reiterates this theme. 'Sinners shall be convinced *with a Vengeance,* that the State of the Righteous and Wicked is different: They shall see the Righteous advanced to a Kingdom, and themselves cast into a Fiery Prison.'[46]

The Blessedness of Persecution

In Chapter 6, we noted that, while full felicity could only be attained in the age of glory, Watson considered happiness possible in this life. It came through growing one's appreciation of God and the future hope believers had in Christ. We have also encountered the happiness-holiness connection in Watson's writings—the idea that greater sanctification leads to deeper joy. While it is counterintuitive that persecution and suffering would contribute to a Christian's happiness, it is not surprising to see Watson develop an idea that features in the two final beatitudes of Christ's Sermon on the Mount. For Watson, Christian suffering serves as a kind of negative, passive means of cultivating godliness.[47] This is in contrast to the positive means one would actively and voluntarily utilise, such as those examined in Chapter 5 (e.g. Bible reading; meditation; prayer). Suffering contributes to happiness negatively by assisting the believer to practice self-denial and be purified from sin. By extension, it makes a positive contribution by enabling a deeper development of godly affections and a greater dependence upon God for comfort and joy.[48]

There are two important observations to make before delving

45. *APL,* 15.
46. *RTI,* 211.
47. See also Brown, *Spirituality in Adversity*, 174 for a distinction between "passive" endurance of reproaches and "active" cross-bearing.
48. See also Lee, "Thomas Watson," 9-11. Brown has demonstrated a widespread conviction amongst Watson's contemporaries that suffering could have this kind of effect on Christians. E.g. Brown, *Spirituality in Adversity*, 63, 89. Cosby's summary of this perspective in John Flavel is particularly insightful, "By affliction, Flavel argues, Christians are made partakers of Christ's holiness; sin is removed, and happiness is perfected." *Suffering and Sovereignty*, chap. 7.

into the negative role of suffering on the path to greater sanctification and happiness. First, Watson recognised personal sinfulness and the general fallenness of creation as potential causal factors behind the suffering experienced by the godly. While my main focus below will remain upon persecution and innocent suffering, there is some overlap between Watson's pastoral treatment of these different kinds of suffering. He certainly believed that any kind of affliction could be used by God for the sufferer's sanctification.[49] Second, it should be noted that Watson saw self-denial as a necessary prerequisite to enduring suffering as a Christian.[50] However, as we will see below, this fundamental need for self-denial did not preclude the role of suffering in advancing sanctification. Affliction often led to further self-denial and mortification of sin.

Watson employs a range of rich metaphors for the effect of persecution and suffering on the sinful heart.[51] There is the medicinal, such as a "physic" to treat "ill humours," a blade or lance to deal with an "imposthume" and a "purgative" medication to "Tympany of pride, the Fever of lust, the Dropsy of covetousness."[52] And there is the fire to "refine and purify," along with the "corrosive to eat out the proud flesh."[53] Each carries the unmistakable sense of benefiting the believer's spiritual health by curing or cleansing them of indwelling sin.[54] God is always sovereign with respect to the type and timing of the believer's suffering. He always intends for it to accomplish His sanctifying purposes. This brings us back to the idea of suffering as a kind of negative means of cultivating godliness. Positive means are things God reveals to the believer as good and necessary to participate in for their spiritual health. By contrast, affliction is God's means of bringing about the aforementioned effects in the Christian's life with respect to sin.

God's role in the saints' experience of suffering should shape their attitude towards it. "Consider First, Whence doth Affliction come? even from a Wise God, who prescribes whatever befalls us. Persecutions are but like Apothecaries, they give us that Physic

49. See for instance, *DC*, 24-33.
50. E.g. "[T]hey who cannot deny themselves, if sufferings come, they will deny Christ." *Beatitudes*, 432.
51. For a survey of similar metaphors in contemporary literature, see Brown, *Spirituality in Adversity*, 60-61.
52. *Beatitudes,* 453; *BPD*, 2:262; *Weal*, 9; *Repentance,* 29.
53. *BPD*, 1:51; *Beatitudes*, 453.
54. Cosby has identified a similar emphasis in Flavel. *Suffering and Sovereignty*, chap. 4.

which God prescribes."[55] Watson also reasoned with his readers who may have been struggling with doubts about God's goodness in permitting suffering to come upon them. "Is it any Injustice in God to put his Gold into the Furnace to purify it? Is it any Injustice in God by afflicting his People, to make them *partakers* of his Holiness?"[56] As Watson himself faced the trials and uncertainties connected to his ejection from the ministry, he assured his congregation of the positive outcomes in sanctification that God would bring through their afflictions. "The rod of God upon a Saint is but only God's pencil whereby he draweth his Image more lively on the soul; God never strikes the strings of his Viol, but to make the Music the sweeter."[57] In sum, Watson's outlook was that the godly should take comfort in the midst of their painful trials that this expunging of sin from their hearts and refining of their souls was itself a form of blessedness.[58]

The spiritual-medicinal effects of affliction were the necessary antecedent to a far more positive experience of blessedness. Both *Divine Cordial* and *The Lord's Prayer* testify to a pattern that progresses from the purging of sin and extinguishing of worldly lust and comfort to a deeper enjoyment of God. In *Divine Cordial*, under the heading "Shewing that the evil of affliction works for good, to the Godly," Watson details how afflictive circumstances show Christians their sinfulness, make their hearts "upright," increase their Christlikeness, destroy their indwelling corruption and "loosen [their] hearts from the world."[59] But after this foundation, he encourages his readers with the assurance that their afflictions will lead to comfort and closeness to God.[60] Comfort may come through an affectional increase of joy, "God sweetens outward pain, with inward peace. *Joh.* 16.20. *Your sorrow shall be turned into joy* ... The Saints in affliction have had such sweet raptures of joy, that they have thought themselves in the borders of the Heavenly *Canaan*."[61] The ultimate source of felicity is an increased sense of spiritual intimacy with God.

55. *BPD*, 2:262. For a similar thought in Bunyan, see Greaves, *Glimpses of Glory*, 494.
56. *BPD*, 1:51.
57. *Weal*, 7.
58. *Beatitudes*, 453.
59. *DC*, 24. See also Brown, *Spirituality in Adversity*, 76. Again, such a perspective is present in Watson's fellow Presbyterian, Flavel. Cosby, *Suffering and Sovereignty*, chap. 4.
60. See also Brown, *Spirituality in Adversity*, 71.
61. *DC*, 30-31.

> How do afflictions make us happy? Answ. In that afflictions being sanctified, bring us nearer to God. The Moon in the full is further off from the Sun: so are many farther off from God in the full Moon of prosperity: affliction brings them nearer to God.[62]

In *The Lord's Prayer*, answering the question "What profit is in affliction?" Watson again lists several positive spiritual outcomes of affliction, including: coming to self-awareness of one's sins, purgation, being removed from worldly delights and purification.[63] Shortly afterwards he comforts believers with the reliability of God's "gracious supports in affliction" and "divine Consolation."[64] In describing the comfort that God administers by the Spirit, Watson emphasises the extraordinary, affectional nature of such consolations. "Some of the Saints have had such ravishing Joys in Affliction, that they had rather endure their Sufferings, than want their Comforts."[65] This subsection of *The Lord's Prayer* climaxes with Watson again answering the question: "How do afflictions contribute to our happiness?"[66] First, he repeats that afflictions should lead to increased spiritual intimacy. "[T]hey are a means of bringing us nearer to God. The Loadstone of Prosperity doth not draw us so near to God as the Cords of Affliction."[67] Second, a "cheerful ... submi[ssion]" to God's will is possible, by recognising that the hardship one is facing is leading them to the eternal joys of heaven.[68] "Afflictions make us happy, as they are Manuductions to Glory. The Storm drives the Ship into the harbour: Happy is that Storm which drives the Soul into the Heavenly harbour."[69]

Several of Watson's other consolatory sermons and writings also contain encouragements to believers that their experiences of suffering may prove to be a gateway to greater enjoyment of God and lively affections. *Paramythion* is primarily a sustained exposition of the biblical promise to afflicted Israel in Psalm 46:5 "God is in the midst of her." The more affliction God's people suffer the more they are to trust in the reality that He is with them.[70] While in *Paramythion*, much of the evidence of God's presence is

62. *DC*, 32.
63. *BPD*, 3:526.
64. *BPD*, 3:527-528.
65. *BPD*, 3:528.
66. *BPD*, 3:528.
67. *BPD*, 3:528.
68. *BPD*, 3:528.
69. *BPD*, 3:528.
70. *Paramythion*, 3, etc.

linked to His provision for and deliverance of His people—there is also an important spiritual sense of this aspect. If the church continues on faithfully in the biblical ordinances throughout their suffering, they will be strengthened through "God's quickening, sanctifying, comforting presence; the smiles of his face, the kisses of his lips."[71] The harshness of the times was also an opportunity for professing Christians to ensure that the God who remained with the church corporately also dwelt within them personally. "This should be our wisdom and ambition, not only to have the *presence* of God with us, but the *Spirit* of God in us."[72] In the second sermon in the posthumous collection *Seven Sermons*, Watson reminds his hearers that discipline was a sign of love they could take comfort in when experiencing affliction.

> God spares the Rod in anger. God's hand is heaviest when it is lightest. God punisheth most when he doth not punish; but now God smites, that he may save his People; and is not that love? And the Love of God doth allay and take off the smarting power of the Rod, and gives the Soul comfort. Let me feel God's hand, so I may have his heart.[73]

But the circumstances of affliction were used by God to communicate comfort to the believer and bring about affections of joy in place of sorrow.

> God's Rod upon his Children doth not only make way for comfort; but, which is more, this Rod distils comfort into the Soul. Even as the Fire causes sweet Water to drop from the Still: So out of Affliction, God stills the sweet Water of Consolation. A clear Instance for this, 2 Cor. 1.4. Who comforteth us in all our tribulations. Here is the Rod of God comforting. When the Saints Trials have been sharpest, their Comforts have been sweetest. Behold here Honey at the end of the Rod, John 16.22. Your sorrows shall be turned into joy.[74]

In the sixth sermon in the same collection, "Light in Darkness," Watson suggests that experiences of divine "desertion" in times of trial are used by God to propel the saint towards Him in more earnest, prayerful seeking. The temporary lull in the Christian's enjoyment of God's presence precedes a greater enjoyment of His

71. *Paramythion*, 5.
72. *Paramythion*, 17.
73. "Sermon II," *Seven Sermons*, 34.
74. "Sermon II," *Seven Sermons*, 35.

presence thereafter.[75] In this sermon, Watson gives a detailed description of the relationship between the saint's suffering and the spiritual enrichment that comes from God during such times. It is worth quoting at length.

> God sometimes causes a light of spiritual joy and consolation to arise in the dark and disconsolate Soul: And truly this light of spiritual joy, it is the very glimmering of the light of Heaven, *Isa* 12.1. *Thine anger is turned away, and thou comfortest me*. This light of spiritual comfort, it is sweet and ravishing; it as far excels all other joys, as Heaven excels Earth. Thus you see in the midst of darkness or black clouds, God makes light to arise and shine unto the godly: It is only God himself that can make it lightsome, when the Soul is in a dark disconsolate condition. As when the Sun is set, none can make it rise but only God: So when it is Sun-set in the Soul, and the dew of tears drop, none can make day-light in that Soul, but God himself: others may preach comfort to us, while it is God that must make us feel comfort: others may ring a Cordial to us, and set it to us, and by us; but it is God that must pour in this Cordial, Psal. 4.7. *Thou, Lord, hast put gladness in my heart.*[76]

Deeper joy and enjoyment of God during and after periods of affliction form the substance of Watson's encouragement to the godly in a range of other passages across his corpus.[77] As he summarised his outlook in one place: "if Affliction make a Christian happy, they cannot denominate him miserable."[78]

Conclusion

Watson's pastoral aim of "making the godly joyful," when their comforts were threatened, involved demonstrating how their suffering contributed to their attainment of the goals of godliness. The fact that their endurance of hardship brought God glory was of primary importance. But Watson taught that it even held the potential to increase their spiritual enjoyment of Him in this life. When considering Watson's use of these aims to bring encouragement to embattled believers it is significant to recognise the balance between eternal and temporal outcomes. When it came to the fruition of their glorification of God, identification with Christ and reward

75. "Sermon VI," *Seven Sermons*, 131-133.
76. "Sermon VI," *Seven Sermons*, 135-136.
77. See for instance *Beatitudes*, 445; *BPD*, 3:529, 864; *Weal*, 7-8.
78. *BPD*, 2:262.

for fidelity, the godly were required to suffer and wait in faith—drawing hope from the certainty of their eternal future. And yet for those who earnestly sought to attain vital spiritual affections and communion with God during this life there was good news in Watson's conviction that suffering would become their servant in this quest. Their trials allowed them to further die to the world and possess more of the heavenly bliss here and now. This was a piety refined for the dark times Watson and his friends found themselves living in.

Summary of PART 5

Watson's increasing sense of being sidelined by an ungodly society which rejected his party's religious priorities created his strong self-identification as a minister to a godly, afflicted minority. This came to characterise his pastoral ministry. As a pious Presbyterian, Watson was part of an influential section of seventeenth century English religious life which consistently failed to gain the power necessary to implement its desired reforms to the doctrine, devotion and organisation of the national church. This was a source of frustration which led to a gradual shift in his outlook and goals. Moreover, his perennial, foreboding anticipation of divine judgement for national failings in religion did not dissipate throughout his ministry. We have, however, suggested that it was accentuated at particularly bleak points in the life of the nation. Furthermore, it appears to have shifted from a temporal expectation to an eschatological one by his later years.

This outlook was constantly reinforced by the sufferings Watson and his community endured from the malicious authorities. It contributed significantly to his pastoral priorities and the manner in which he sought to promote his vision of godliness. Watson's pastoral consolations and exhortations in the face of suffering were aimed at the furtherance of his vision of godliness. He was convinced that affliction served the goals and objectives of the godly. It was often God's means of dealing with sin and worldly attachments in the saints. It paved the way for greater enjoyment of Him. In particular, the godly could take comfort in knowing that persecuted piety was precious to God. It glorified Him in a peculiarly Christlike way that was impossible under tranquil circumstances. The nonconformist experience of marginalisation, shame and loss was countered with the gospel promise of an eternal, exalted status over their adversaries. These enemies would experience a just relegation to a misery which was worse than what they had inflicted upon the godly. The grief, anxiety and discouragement that accompanied their mistreatment in the Restoration period were ameliorated by the prospect of enhanced spiritual affections following the time of trial.

Thus, Watson's main technique for pastoral consolation was to assure the godly that their suffering was in fact conducive to their present and permanent happiness. It was an opportunity to shine more brightly in piety.[79] This serves as a valuable example of how a Presbyterian Puritan figure sought to cope with the unrealised hopes for national reform which ran high in the 1640s and the dire change in fortunes for those of dissenting faith in the wake of the restored monarchy and episcopal system. We unfortunately have no records to indicate the extent to which Watson's approach was found to be helpful or encouraging to members of his community. But we do have a clear picture of how he carried out his pastoral ministry in line with his chief goal of promoting godliness.

79. *RTI*, 8; *GMP*, 314; *Beatitudes*, 401.

PART 6

Conclusion

Conclusion

Thomas Watson emerges as a prime example of a Late English Puritan whose thought and ministry were dominated by the godliness motif. He distinguishes himself amongst the devotional writers of his period for his ability to convey a thorough picture of the nature of piety in this tradition, which goes on to pervade the entirety of his corpus. The study of *Godly Man's Picture* has provided an affectional picture of godliness. Most of the characteristics of godliness identified by Watson involve responsive dispositions of the heart. These responses are directed towards God and enabled by the work of the Holy Spirit. Affections such as love, fear, gratitude and zeal demonstrated the right regard for God that lay at the core of the New Testament idea of *eusebeia*. These affections enabled the believer to worship Him as they ought. They were never divorced from the pious actions which emanated from them. Yet Watson lays the accent upon the adorative and reverential reaction of the heart to the revelation of divine glory. This is important for understanding godliness in Late English Puritanism, as I noted at the beginning of the study that despite its widely acknowledged significance as a key Puritan theme, scholarly analysis of its precise nature has remained underdeveloped. Watson offers an opportunity to progress beyond cursory, generic or assumed references to godliness in Puritan literature by providing such an extensive anatomy of what he and his peers understood by this watchword.

Godliness was nurtured by a fully-orbed, practical programme of piety, which depended upon several indispensable disciplines or duties. While previous studies of Watson's spirituality have focused upon the meditative dimension of his devotion, we have demonstrated that he does not elevate it to primacy at the expense of other means of grace. Neimeyer's claims for the priority of meditation could not be sustained when evaluated in light of Watson's superlative language about self-denial and enthusiastic endorsement of prayer, conference, the Lord's Supper and other means. Meditation, like the other duties, was a means to Watson's great end of godliness. Diligent use of the ordinances either consolidated the Christian's appreciative knowledge of God or nourished the affections in response to what was already known. On one hand, duties such as meditation, prayer and the Lord's Supper opened the possibility for a mystical, spiritual encounter with God. This could have a profound and lasting impact on the piety of the heart. On the other hand, the ongoing battle of soul-examination, self-denial and the mortification of sin dealt with the impediments to greater godly affection. They allowed the believer to set their hearts upon heaven. Crucially, we have also shown that while there is an undeniable mystical element to Watson's piety, he eschewed any notion of an internalised, isolated and individualistic spirituality. The church provided key means of spiritual nourishment and growth that private prayer, meditation and Bible reading alone could not. Thus, while we should expect to see Watson's name continue to appear in studies of the meditative elements of Puritanism, this book has demonstrated that his contribution to Late English Puritan piety is too extensive for him to be relegated to discussions of mystical spirituality. Watson further contributes to our understanding of Puritan spirituality by presenting several goals of the Christian life that were only obtainable through the cultivation of godliness. Religion driven by vital affections glorified God; increased the public credibility of biblical Christianity; prepared the believer for their eternal future as an unencumbered worshipper; and provided a foretaste of heavenly joy that could be enjoyed in the present. Thus, godliness was the "grand errand" of human life.[1] It culminated in maximal, personal satisfaction through the rendition of loving service to God and neighbour.

*

The congruity between Watson and some of his most notable contemporaries on the nature, means and goals of godliness attests that his essential understanding of piety was standard for Late English Puritanism. At the same time, we have argued for a distinctive place in the movement for Watson, based on the unmatched extensiveness and accessibility of *Godly Man's Picture's* presentation of the characteristics of mature Puritan piety. In order for this claim to be contested, future research would need to demonstrate that a

1. *GMP*, 298.

Late English Puritan of comparable renown to Watson produced a treatment on godliness that excels *Godly Man's Picture* in these respects. We have also seen how Watson's devotional outlook was deeply influenced by the preceding generations of English Puritans. His emphasis on godly affections—arising from a regenerate heart in response to the revelation of divine glory—built upon the works of Perkins, Ames, Greenham, Sibbes and others from the early and middle phases of English Puritanism. This further establishes his importance as a figure representative of the movement's spirituality and invites future studies of Puritan spirituality to engage with Watson in a more substantial manner than has often been the case previously. Earlier figures, especially Augustine, Bernard and Calvin reinforced Watson's sense of the transhistorical importance of elements such as contemplation, the mortification of sin and affectional delight in Christian piety. It remains for another study to examine whether this ABC strand of influences had the same degree of impact on Watson's late English Puritan peers that it had upon him. Research on this question would enhance our understanding of the reception of earlier Christian figures by Puritans in formulating their approach to piety.

Watson was also representative of Puritan spirituality in expressing his piety with an eye to the polemical concerns of his religious milieu. The most prevalent threats to biblical piety that have emerged from reading Watson in his context were Roman Catholicism in English society and the Arminian or neo-Laudian party within the English Church. Watson saw these systems as incapable of producing godliness, because doctrinal error led to defective devotion. He understood *eusebeia* as worship in accordance with Scripture. This led him to condemn such groups due to their ceremonialism and liturgical innovation. Watson applied the same principles to his assessment of all other contemporary religions and indeed irreligion. All the while, he emphasised the cruciality of honouring God through sincere affections and holy living in response to theological truth. Hypocrisy was especially condemned as an insidious problem for Christian communities, since it involved the pretence of subscription to orthodox beliefs, with no genuine, affective response. Hypocrites dishonoured God through the maintenance of external morality before people, while privately indulging in sin. While spiritual sincerity was a hallmark of Puritan piety, it is clear from Watson's early sermon *God's Anatomy upon a Man's Heart* that he was concerned by hypocrisy within the movement.

Christianity—even the Reformed branch of it—enjoyed a privileged position in English society and it was seen as advantageous to be an adherent. This made hypocrisy a perennial problem that Puritan piety with its emphasis on sincerity set out to address. For Watson, duplicity in religion was more noxious to his vision of godliness than faulty piety built on erroneous doctrine. Recent scholarship has highlighted the competing anti-Socinian and anti-Antinomian motivations—of Owen and Baxter respectively—to create a vivid juxtaposition in Puritan polemical priorities.[2] While we have seen that Watson also wrote and preached with these heresies in mind, his polemics are far more coloured by a threefold concern with the more pervasive enemies of popery, Laudian-Arminianism and hypocrisy. Watson's divergent concerns caution against organising the wider Late English Puritan movement around the totemic *bêtes noires* of its two most prominent figures.

*

We have demonstrated that Watson's sustained promotion of affectional piety through his lengthy, catechetical project was not a banal transmission of the doctrinal propositions outlined in the Westminster Shorter Catechism. In unpacking the affectional and practical responses required by each doctrine, Watson transformed the skeletal outline of Presbyterian tenets into a fully-fledged, robust practical divinity. His friends and fellow travellers recognised this in publishing these lectures as *A Body of Practical Divinity* several years after his death. There is no sense that Watson set out to produce the definitive applicational commentary on the Catechism to emerge out of Late English Puritanism and high reformed orthodoxy. Yet that is the distinction of what became his greatest literary legacy. We have seen that the system of piety that grew out of the Catechism's doctrinal foundations was characterised chiefly by a sense of the unfathomable immensity of God's nature and His majestic, kingly glory. This portrayal of God called for the greatest possible adoration. The absolute grandeur of God was the theological centre of Watson's notion of godliness. The essential place of Christ and the Holy Spirit in his schema of piety, detailed in Chapter 9, made his devotion both distinctively Christocentric and Trinitarian in nature. We have also noted how Watson situated godliness within a theological framework of Reformed anthropology and soteriology. Godliness was a progressive restoration of Adam's

2. See, especially, Cooper, *Owen, Baxter and Nonconformity*, 33, 55-56, 59-83.

original, spiritual disposition towards God in the Christian man or woman as they experienced Him in salvation. But the joy and gratitude birthed out of this redemptive experience of God led to an eternal piety that exceeded that of humanity's first parents in their Edenic state. Because Watson bases his theology on that of the Westminster Assembly and can correctly be described as "standard seventeenth century Calvinism" or representative of high orthodoxy—there are many other writers from the period that scholars could look to and find expressions of the same theology.[3] But any future studies considering the relationship between Westminster theology and Puritan spirituality cannot afford to overlook the significance of Watson and his *Body of Divinity* to our understanding of this subject.

One of the recurring themes that has arisen from this exploration of Watson's theology is the relationship and overlap between godliness and holiness. On the surface, godliness and sanctification were counterparts in Watson's spiritual and systematic theologies, respectively. Both were contingent upon election, effectual calling, justification, conversion and concerned with the present state of Christian life. However, we have gone beyond this level of analysis to posit a nuanced understanding of the difference between the two terms in Watson's theological vocabulary. Godliness was an affectional response of the heart towards the reality of God's holiness. Christian holiness or progressive sanctification is derived from this godliness, as the believer emulates the object of worship. The extent to which such a distinction applies to the usage of these terms amongst Watson's contemporaries requires further exploration—since previous scholarship has identified a seeming lack of distinguishability or preference for other terms in several of his notable peers. But the fact that this distinction is evident in Watson's thought requires scholars of Puritan spirituality to treat these terms more carefully than has often been the case and consider how they might each be conveying distinctive aspects of an author's spiritual theology.

Another recurring theme we have seen in Watson's theology and piety is the essential role of godliness in preparing the soul for everlasting life and joy in the presence of God. This aspect functions as one of the goals or benefits of godliness; the end point of the dogmatic component to Watson's practical divinity; and one of the sources of comfort for the godly enduring afflictions. It is

3. Barker, "A Body of Divinity," 206; Muller, *PRRD*.I, 49.

understandable that Watson took death seriously when we consider that he witnessed his nation being struck by deadly wars and disease, buried several of his children and came very close to execution in the aftermath of Love's Plot. The Christian needed confidence to face death and only his vision of godliness could provide it. Watson does not match Baxter's emphasis on heavenly-mindedness, but he is another witness to its importance in the Late English Puritan ethos—as previously identified by Wallace.

*

Finally, Watson's chief pastoral goal, after the promotion of godliness, was to sustain it in the lives of those facing hardship. This is particularly true of his focus in the Restoration years. It is apparent that Watson's own personal experience of marginalisation and his bleak assessment of the times in which he lived, drove him to comfort his godly brethren and exhort them to persevere in piety in the midst of adversity. While Watson's concerns with the spiritual state of England persisted throughout his ministry—including, notably, during the Independent-dominated Interregnum—the Post-Restoration period clearly exacerbated his sense of English Christianity being in dire straits. In this climate we see him produce his major works on godliness—after his hopes for cultivating piety through ecclesiastical reform had been diminished. Because Watson's emphasis on godliness was already present in works before this period, he authenticates Wallace's thesis that Late English Puritans intensified their focus on piety after the Restoration and Great Ejection, without altering its substance. However, the most detectable shift in Watson's outlook during this phase was from his emphasis on the preservative power of piety against God's judgement of the nation to his late focus on the value of godliness when juxtaposed against an ungodly culture. This does not appear to occur until twenty years after the Restoration, but characterises the thrust of his final antemortem work *Religion Our True Interest.* While scholarship on the eschatological outlook of Puritans in post-Restoration England exists,[4] further studies focused on how changing political, social and religious realities affected the eschatology of Watson's peers and, in turn, coloured their approach to devotion, would be beneficial to our understanding of the piety of

4. See particularly Warren Johnston, "The Patience of the Saints, the Apocalypse, and Moderate Nonconformity in Restoration England," *Canadian Journal of History* (Dec 2003) 38:3, 505-520.

the movement in this period.

Despite this shift in perspective towards the end of his life, Watson was consistent in viewing the godly as a maligned and marginalised minority in England. This shaped the course of his pastoral ministry. Watson's hortatory and consolatory writings demonstrate his deliberateness in encouraging his congregants and readers to view their adversity and afflictions as means for glorifying God. Trials also helped them realise the other outcomes of godliness we identified within his works. Thus, the circumstances that seemed to pose the greatest threat to late English Puritan piety were interpreted as providentially subservient to the achievement of its goals. There was of course biblical precedence for such thinking, but this should not diminish our appreciation of Watson's genius in presenting an indefatigable vision of godliness that could withstand the vicious opposition it faced in the reign of Charles II.

*

Watson's stated goal in writing *Godly Man's Picture* was '"that all into whose hands this Book shall providentially come, may be enamoured with Piety."[5] It is evident that Watson possessed the passionate preoccupation with godliness he commended to his readers. He considered his subject too wonderful for an author to adequately describe it. 'So sublime is *Godliness,* that it cannot be delineated in its perfect radiance and lustre, though an Angel should take [up the] Pencil.'[6] Yet Watson manages to outshine his contemporaries with his masterpiece portrayal of godliness, the hues of which imbue the gallery of works he left as his legacy.

5. *GMP*, iii.
6. *GMP*, iii.

Appendix A

"GODLINESS" in *Godly Man's Picture*	"SANCTIFICATION" in *Body of Divinity*
2. Godliness is an *intrinsical* thing It lies chiefly in the heart. Rom. 2. 29. Circumcision is that of the heart. The dew lies on the leaf, the sap is hid in the root. The Moralists Religion is all in the leaf, it consists only in Externals ... but godliness is an holy sap which is radicated in the soul. Psalm 51. 6. in the hidden part, thou shalt make me to know wisdom. The Chaldean expounds it, In the close place of the heart.	**2. Sanctification is an *intrinsical* thing** It lies chiefly in the *heart.* It is called *the adorning the hidden man of the heart,* 1 Pet. 3.4. The Dew wets the Leaf, the Sap is hid in the Root; the Religion of some consists only *in externals,* but Sanctification is deeply rooted in the Soul, *Psalm* 51.6. *In the hidden part thou shalt make me to know wisdom.*
3. Godliness is a *supernatural* thing By nature we inherit nothing but evil. Rom. 7. 5. When we were in the flesh, the motions of sin did work in our members: we did suck in sin, as naturally as our Mothers milk; but godliness is the wisdom from above, James 3. 17. it is breathed in from heaven. God must light up the Lamp of Grace in the heart: Weeds grow of themselves, flowers are planted. Godliness is a Celestial Plant, that comes from the New Jerusalem: Therefore it is called a fruit of the Spirit, Gal. 5. 22. A man hath no more power to change himself than to create himself.	**1. Sanctification is a *supernatural* thing** 'Tis divinely infused; we are naturally polluted, and to cleanse God takes to be his Prerogative, Lev. 21.8. I am the Lord that sanctifieth you. Weeds grow of themselves, Flowers are planted. Sanctification is a Flower of the Spirit's planting, therefore it is called, The Sanctification of the Spirit, 1 Pet. 1.2.

4. Godliness is an *extensive* thing	**3. Sanctification is an *extensive* thing**
It is a sacred leaven that spreads itself into the whole soul. 1 *Thess. 5. 23. The God of peace sanctify you wholly.* There is light in the understanding, order in the affections, pliableness in the will, exemplariness in the life. We do not call a Blackamore white because he hath white teeth: he is not godly who is good only in some part. Grace is called *the new man,* Col. 3. 10. not a new eye, or tongue, but a new man: he who is godly is good all over; though he be regenerate but in part, yet it is in every part.	It spreads into the whole Man: 1 Thess. 5.23. The God of peace sanctify you wholly. As Original Corruption hath depraved all the Faculties, the whole head is sick, the whole heart faint, no Part sound, as if the whole mass of blood were corrupted; so Sanctification goes over the whole Soul. After the Fall there was Ignorance in the Mind, now in Sanctification we are light in the Lord, Eph. 5.8. After the Fall the Will was depraved, there was not only impotency to Good, but obstinacy; now in Sanctification there is a blessed pliableness in the Will, it doth symbolize and comport with the Will of God. After the Fall the Affections were misplaced on wrong Objects, in Sanctification they are tuned into a sweet order and harmony, the Grief placed on Sin, the Love on God, the Joy on Heaven. Thus Sanctification spreads itself as far as Original Corruption. It goes over the whole Soul: The God of peace sanctify you wholly. He is not a consecrated Person who is good only in some part, but who is all over sanctified. Therefore in Scripture Grace is called a New Man, Col. 3.10. not a new Eye, or a new Tongue, but a new Man. A good Christian, though he be sanctified but in part, yet in every part.
5. Godliness is an *intense* thing	**4. Sanctification is an *intense* ardent thing**
It doth not lie in a dead formality and indifferency, but is vigorous and flaming, Rom. 12. 11. Fervent in spirit. We call water hot, when it is so in the third or fourth degree. He is godly whose devotion is inflamed, and his heart boils over in holy affections.	Rom. 12.11., fervent in spirit. Sanctification is not a dead Form, but is inflamed into Zeal. We call Water hot, when it is so in the third or fourth degree. He is holy whose Religion is heated to some degree, and his heart boils over in love to God.

6. Godliness is a *glorious* thing	5. Sanctification is a *beautiful* thing
As the Jewel to the Ring, so is Piety to the Soul bespangling it in God's eyes. Reason makes us Men, Godliness makes us earthly Angels; by it we partake of the divine nature, 2 Pet. 1. 4. Godliness is near akin to Glory, 2 Pet. 1. 3. Glory and Virtue. Godliness is glory in the seed, and glory is godliness in the flower.	It makes God and Angels fall in love with us, Psalm 110.3. The beauties of holiness. As the Sun is to the World, so is Sanctification to the Soul, beautifying and bespangling it in God's Eyes. Chrysostom. That which makes God glorious, must needs make us so. Holiness is the most sparkling Jewel in the God-head; Exod. 15.11. Glorious in holiness. Sanctification is the First fruit of the Spirit; it is Heaven begun in the Soul. Sanctification and Glory differ only in degree; Sanctification is Glory in the Seed, and Glory is Sanctification in the Flower. Happiness is the quintessence of Holiness.
7. Godliness is a *permanent* thing	**6. Sanctification is an *abiding* thing**
Aristotle saith, denominations are given from the habit. We do not call him sanguine that blusheth, but who is of a ruddy complexion 1 Sam. 17. 42.A blush of godliness is not enough to denominate a Christian, but godliness must be the temper and complexion of the soul. Godliness is a fixed thing: There is a great deal of difference between a Stake in the Hedge, and a Tree in the Garden; a stake rots and moulders, but a tree having life in it, abides and flourisheth. When godliness hath taken root in the soul, it abides to eternity. 1 John 3. 9. his seed remaineth in him. Godliness being engraven in the heart by the Holy Ghost, as with the point of a Diamond, can never be raced out.	1 *John* 3.9. *His seed remaineth in him.* He who is truly sanctified, cannot fall from that *state.* Indeed *seeming* Holiness may be lost, Colours may wash off, Sanctification may *suffer an Eclipse,* Rev. 2.4. *Thou hast left thy first love*; but true Sanctification is a *blossom* of *Eternity,* 1 John 2.27. *The anointing which ye have received abideth in you.* He who is truly sanctified, can no more fail away then the Angels which are fixed in their heavenly Orb.

N.B. Numbering indicates the order of appearance in the respective texts.[†]

† Table compiled from *GMP*, 5-8; *BPD*, 1:139-140.

Bibliography

PRIMARY SOURCES

Works by Thomas Watson

Books/Treatises (in order of original publication)

Watson, Thomas. *The Christian's Charter of Privileges* (1652). Oxford: TCP, 2005. http://ota.ox.ac.uk/id/A65287

——— *Autarkeia* or *The Art of Divine Contentment* (1653). Oxford: TCP, 2005. http://ota.ox.ac.uk/id/A65276

——— *The Saint's Spiritual Delight to which is annexed a treatise of meditation* (1657). Oxford: TCP, 2013. http://ota.ox.ac.uk/id/A96109

——— *The Beatitudes* 2nd edition. (1671) (originally published in 1660). Google Books edition. https://books.google.com.au/books?id=mAo8AQAAMAAJ

——— *Jerusalem's Glory* (1661). Fearn: Christian Focus, 2002.

——— *Suffering for the Law and the Gospel or Two Witnesses Anatomized* (1661). Coconut Creek: Puritan Publications, 2009.

——— *Paramythion, or A Word of Comfort for the Church of God* (1662). Oxford: TCP, 2005. http://purl.ox.ac.uk/ota/A65306

——— *A Divine Cordial or The transcendent priviledge of those that love God and are savingly called* (1663). Oxford: TCP, 2005. http://purl.ox.ac.uk/ota/A65292

——— *The Godly Man's Picture, Drawn with a Scripture-Pensil, Or Some Characteristical Notes of a Man that shall go to Heaven.* (1666). Oxford: TCP, 2004. http://purl.ox.ac.uk/ota/A65296

——— *The Doctrine of Repentance: Useful for these times* (1668). Oxford: TCP, 2005. http://purl.ox.ac.uk/ota/A65293

——— *The Holy Eucharist, or The Mystery of the Lord's Supper briefly explained* (1668). Oxford: TCP, 2004. http://purl.ox.ac.uk/ota/A65300

——— *Heaven Taken by Storm or The holy violence a Christian is to put forth in the pursuit after glory* (1669). Oxford: TCP, 2005. http://purl.ox.ac.uk/ota/A65299

——— *The Mischief of Sinne it brings a person low* (1671). Oxford: TCP, 2004. http://purl.ox.ac.uk/ota/A65303

——— *A Plea for the Godly person* (1672). Oxford: TCP, 2004. http://purl.ox.ac.uk/ota/A65308

——— *The Duty of Self Denial briefly opened and urged* (1675). Oxford: TCP, 2004. http://purl.ox.ac.uk/ota/A65294

——— *Religion our True Interest* (1681). Oxford: TCP, 2005. http://purl.ox.ac.uk/ota/A65309

——— *A Body of Practical Divinity* Vol. I-III. (1692). Oxford: TCP, 2005. http://purl.ox.ac.uk/ota/A65285

Sermons (in chronological order)

Watson, Thomas. *God's Anatomy Upon Man's Heart* (1649). Oxford: TCP, 2005. http://purl.ox.ac.uk/ota/A65297

——— *The One Thing Necessary* – Phil 2:12 (1656). Oxford: TCP, 2005. http://purl.ox.ac.uk/ota/A65304

——— *The Crown of Righteousness* – 2 Tim 4:8 (1656). Oxford: TCP, 2008. http://purl.ox.ac.uk/ota/A96098

——— "Christ's Loveliness" (1657). In *Discourses*. Google Books edition. https://books.google.com.au/books?id=IOdLAAAAYAAJ

——— *The Upright Man's Character and Crown* (1657). Oxford: TCP, 2008. http://purl.ox.ac.uk/ota/A96110

——— *A Plea for Almes* – 1 John 3:17/Ps 112:9/Ps 41:1 (1658). Oxford: TCP, 2008. http://purl.ox.ac.uk/ota/A96106

——— *The Holy Longing, or, The Saint's Desire to be with Christ* – Phil 1:23 (1658). Oxford: TCP, 2008. http://purl.ox.ac.uk/ota/A96103

——— "How must we make religion our business? – Luke 2:49" (1659). In *Morning Exercises at Cripplegate* Vol. I. Edited by Samuel Annesley. London: James Nichols, 1844.

——— "The Day of Judgement Asserted – Acts 17:31" (1659). In *The Morning Exercise Methodized.* Edited by Thomas Case. London: R.W., 1676.

——— "The Beauty of Grace – 1 Pet 1:2." In *Beatitudes* (1660). Oxford: TCP, 2011. http://purl.ox.ac.uk/ota/A96093

——— "The Good Practitioner – John 13:17." In *Beatitudes* (1660). Oxford: TCP, 2011.http://purl.ox.ac.uk/ota/A96093

——— "The Heavenly Race – 1 Cor 9:24." In *Beatitudes* (1660). Oxford: TCP, 2011. http://purl.ox.ac.uk/ota/A96093

——— "The Perfume of Love – 1 Pet 1:22." In *Beatitudes* (1660). Oxford: TCP, 2011. http://purl.ox.ac.uk/ota/A96093

——— "The Preciousness of the Soul – Matt 16:26." In *Beatitudes* (1660). Oxford: TCP, 2011. http://purl.ox.ac.uk/ota/A96093

——— "The Soul's Malady and Cure – Luke 5:31-32." In *Beatitudes* (1660). Oxford: TCP, 2011. http://purl.ox.ac.uk/ota/A96093

——— "The Spiritual Anchor – Titus 2:13." In *Beatitudes* (1660). Oxford: TCP, 2011. http://purl.ox.ac.uk/ota/A96093

——— "The Spiritual Watch – Prov 4:23." In *Beatitudes* (1660). Oxford: TCP, 2011. http://purl.ox.ac.uk/ota/A96093

——— "The Trees of Righteousness – Phil 1:11." In *Beatitudes* (1660). Oxford: TCP, 2011.http://purl.ox.ac.uk/ota/A96093

——— *Weal to the Righteous but Woe to the Wicked* – Isa 3:10-11 (1662). Oxford, TCP, 2004. http://purl.ox.ac.uk/ota/A65311

——— "Mr. Watson's Prayer at Walbrook." In *An Exact collection of farewel sermons preached by the late London-ministers* (1662). Oxford: TCP, 2005. http://purl.ox.ac.uk/ota/A31961

——— "Love One Another – John 13:34" (1662). In *Sermons of the Great Ejection.* Edinburgh: Banner of Truth, 2012.

——— "Parting Counsels – 2 Cor 7:1" (1662). In *Sermons of the Great Ejection.* Edinburgh: Banner of Truth, 2012.

——— "Farewell Sermon – Phil 4:9" (1662). In *Sermons of the Great Ejection.* Edinburgh: Banner of Truth, 2012.

——— "Ὕπαρξις, or, The Substantial Excellency of Spiritual Things – Prov 3:14." In *Doctrine of Repentance* (1668). Google Books edition. https://books.google.com.au/books?id=ZSJlAAAAcAAJ

——— "The Mystical Temple – 1 Cor 3:17." In *Doctrine of Repentance* (1668). Google Books edition. https://books.google.com.au/books?id=ZSJlAAAAcAAJ

——— "How God is His People's Great Reward – Gen 15:1" (1674). In *Morning Exercises at Cripplegate* Vol. III. Edited by Samuel Annesley. London: James Nichols, 1844.

——— *Time's Shortness* – 1 Cor 7:29 (1676). Oxford: TCP, 2005. http://purl.ox.ac.uk/ota/A65312

——— *The fight of faith crowned* – 2 Tim 4:7-8 (1678). Oxford: TCP, 2004. http://purl.ox.ac.uk/ota/A65295

——— *Light in Darkness or, Deliverance proclaimed unto the church in the midst of all her despondencies and discouragements* – Ps 112:4 (1678). Oxford: TCP, 2005. http://purl.ox.ac.uk/ota/A65301*

* N.B. This work also appears as "Sermon VI" in the *Seven Sermons* collection.

——— "Sermon I – Job 14:14." In *Seven Sermons* (1689). Oxford: TCP, 2004. http://purl.ox.ac.uk/ota/A65313

——— "Sermon II – Ps 23:4." In *Seven Sermons* (1689). Oxford: TCP, 2004. http://purl.ox.ac.uk/ota/A65313

——— "Sermon III – John 16:33." In *Seven Sermons* (1689). Oxford: TCP, 2004. http://purl.ox.ac.uk/ota/A65313

——— "Sermon IV – Ps 2:12." In *Seven Sermons* (1689). Oxford: TCP, 2004. http://purl.ox.ac.uk/ota/A65313

——— "Sermon V – Ps 112:7." In *Seven Sermons* (1689). Oxford: TCP, 2004. http://purl.ox.ac.uk/ota/A65313

——— "Sermon VII – John 10:14." In *Seven Sermons* (1689). Oxford: TCP, 2004. http://purl.ox.ac.uk/ota/A65313

——— "How we may Read the Scriptures with the most Spiritual Profit – Deut 17:19." (n.d.). In *Morning Exercises at Cripplegate* Vol. III. Edited by Samuel Annesley. London: James Nichols, 1844.

——— "Christ is All in All – Col 3:11" (n.d.) In *The Select Works of Thomas Watson.* New York: Robert Carter & Brothers, 1855. https://archive.org/details/selectworksofrev00wats

Additional Primary Sources

Alleine, Richard. *Vindiciæ pietatis* (1665). Oxford: TCP, 2009. http://purl.ox.ac.uk/ota/A74976

Alsop, Vincent. *Decus & tutamen, or, Practical godliness the ornament and muniment of all religion.* (1696). Oxford: TCP, 2010. http://purl.ox.ac.uk/ota/A25204

Ames, William. *Marrow of Sacred Divinity.* (1642). Oxford: TCP, 2005. http://purl.ox.ac.uk/ota/A25291

Augustine. *De Civitate Dei.* Leipzig: BGT, 1877.

Baxter, Richard. *A Christian Directory* (1673). Oxford: TCP, 2004. http://ota.ox.ac.uk/id/A26892

———. *Gildas Salvianus, the reformed pastor* (1656). Oxford: TCP, 2012. http://purl.ox.ac.uk/ota/A26932

———. *The Practical Works of the Rev. Richard Baxter* Vol I-XXIII. Edited by John Orme. London: James Duncan, 1830.

——— *Reliquiæ Baxterianæ, or, Mr. Richard Baxters narrative of the most memorable passages of his life and times* (1696). Oxford: TCP, 2003. http://purl.ox.ac.uk/ota/A27006

———. *A Saint or a Brute the certain necessity and excellency of holiness* (1662). Oxford: TCP, 2006. http://purl.ox.ac.uk/ota/A27016

———. *The Saint's Everlasting Rest* (1650). Oxford: TCP, 2005. http://purl.ox.ac.uk/ota/N17286

Bayly, Lewis. *The Practice of Piety: Directing a Christian how to walk that he may please God.* London: Hamilton, Adams & Co. 1842.

Bernard of Clairvaux. "De Diligendo Deo," *Opera Omnia.* ed. Josse Clicthove. Lyons, 1538. Google Books edition. https://books.google.com.au/books?id=KbMqniK83w8C

———. "Sermon XXX: Mystical Vineyards and the Prudence of the Flesh," *Commentary on the Song of Songs*. ed. Darrell Wright. Internet Archive, 2008. https://archive.org/11/items/StBernards CommentaryOnTheSongOfSongs/StBernardOnTheSongOfSongsall.pdf

Beza, Theodore. *A brief declaration of the chiefe points of Christian religion set forth in a Table* (1613). Oxford: TCP, 2006. http://purl.ox.ac.uk/ota/A68592

Birkenhead, John. *Cabala, or, An impartial account of the non-conformists private designs, actings and ways* (1663). Oxford: TCP, 2009. http://purl.ox.ac.uk/ota/A28205

Blackburne Daniell, F. H. ed. *Calendar of State Papers Domestic: Charles II, 1678 With Addenda, 1674-9*. London: His Majesty's Stationery Office 1913. *British History Online*, http://www.british-history.ac.uk/cal-state-papers/domestic/chas2/addenda/1674-9

Blount, Henry. *Voyage into the Levant.* London, 1636. Google Books edition. https://books.google.com.au/books?id=f1ZzqBTjDVcC&q

Brakel, Wilhelmus à. *The Christian's Reasonable Service* (1700). Grand Rapids: Reformation Heritage, 1992.

Bunyan, John. *Seasonable counsel, or, Advice to sufferers* (1684). Oxford: TCP, 2012. http://purl.ox.ac.uk/ota/A30202

Burges, Cornelius. *A Vindication of the Ministers of the Gospel in and about London.* London: AM, 1648. https://catalog.hathitrust.org/Record/102258099

Calvin, John. *Institutio Christianae Religionis* (1536). Paris: Cherbuliez, c. 1834.

Christian Classics Ethereal Library edition. http://www.ccel.org/ccel/calvin/institutio1.i.html

———. *Institutes of the Christian Religion*. trans. Henry Beveridge. Edinburgh: Calvin Translation Society, 1845. https://www.ccel.org/ccel/calvin/institutes.iii.iii.html

Charnock, Stephen. *Complete Works of Stephen Charnock* Vols I-V. ed. James McCosh. Edinburgh: James Nichol, 1864.

———. *The Existence and Attributes of God.* Grand Rapids: Baker, 1996.

Church of England, The. *Constitutions and canons ecclesiasticall* (1640). Oxford: TCP, 2003. http://purl.ox.ac.uk/ota/A00089

Eaton, John. *The Honey-combe of Free Justification* (1642). London: Supralapsarian Press, 2016.

Fabricius, Johannes. *Al de Theologische en Practicale Werken van de Godvruchtige en zeer Geleerde Heer Thomas Watson.* Utrecht: Kemmer, 1665.

Faldo, Peter. *Quakerism no Christianity* (1673). Oxford: TCP, 2010. http://purl.ox.ac.uk/ota/A40785

Ferguson, Robert. *The Interest of Reason in Religion* (1675). Oxford: TCP, 2005. http://purl.ox.ac.uk/ota/A41173

Greenham, Richard. *The workes of the reuerend and faithfull seruant af Iesus Christ M. Richard Greenham* (1612). Oxford: TCP, 2004. http://purl.ox.ac.uk/ota/A02178

Hall, David D. *The Puritans: A Transatlantic History.* Princeton: Princeton University Press, 2019.

Hickman, Henry. *Speculum Sherlockianum: or, A looking-glass in which the admirers of mr. Sherlock may behold the man, as to his accuracy, judgement, orthodoxy.* London: Thomas Parkhurst, 1674. Google Books edition. https://books.google.com.au/books?id= 9NekFwfGjz4C

Historical Manuscripts Commission. *The Manuscripts of the Duke of Leeds.* London: HMSO, 1888.

Jenkin, William. "The Humble Petition of William Jenkin." (1652). Oxford: TCP, 2009. http://purl.ox.ac.uk/ota/A46808

L'Estrange, Roger. *Considerations and Proposals In Order to the Regulation of the Press: together with diverse instances of treasonous, and seditious pamphlets, proving the necessity thereof.* (1663). Oxford: TCP, 2005. http://purl.ox.ac.uk/ota/A47832

Leigh, Edward. *A Systeme or Body of Divinity* (1654). Oxford: TCP, 2004. http://ota.ox.ac.uk/id/A47625

Newcome, Henry. *Autobiography of Henry Newcome.* Manchester: Charles Simms, 1852.

Owen, John. *ΧΡΙΣΤΟΛΟΓΙΑ, or, A declaration of the glorious mystery of the person of Christ* (1679). Dublin: Richard Moore Tims, 1831.

———. *Of Communion with God the Father, Sonne and Holy Ghost* (1657). Oxford: TCP, 2012. http://purl.ox.ac.uk/ota/A53713

———. *Of the Mortification of Sin in Believers* (1668). Oxford: TCP, 2006. http://purl.ox.ac.uk/ota/A53715

———. *Phronēma tou pneumatou or, The Grace and Duty of Being Spiritually Minded* (1681). Oxford: TCP, 2012. http://purl.ox.ac.uk/ota/A53719

———. *ΠΝΕΥΜΑΤΟΛΟΓΙΑ, or, A discourse concerning the Holy Spirit wherein an account is given of his name, nature, personality, dispensation, operations, and effects* (1676). Oxford: TCP, 2012. http://purl.ox.ac.uk/ota/A53720

———. *Vindiciae Evangelicae: or the Mystery of the Gospel defended and Socinianism Examined* (1655). Google Books edition. https://books.google.com.au/books?id=zX4yAgAAQBAJ

———. *The Works of John Owen* ed. William H. Goold. New York: Robert Carter and Brothers, 1852. Google Books edition. https://books.google.com.au/books?id=Xx1KAAAAMAAJ

Parliamentary Archives, United Kingdom. *Emanuel College – The whole number therein as ... taking the Protestation* (1642). http://digitalarchive.parliament.uk/HL/PO/JO/10/1/78/61

Parliament of England. "An Act for Approbation and Admission of Ministers of the Gospel to Benefices and Publick Lectures" (March 1659/60). *Acts and Ordinances of the Interregnum, 1642-1660.* London: Royal Stationary Office, 1911. *British History Online* http://www.british-history.ac.uk/no-series/acts-ordinances-interregnum/pp1459-1462

Patrick, Simon. *A Friendly Debate between a Conformist and a Non-conformist* (1668). Fascimile of original, Internet Archive, 2013. https://archive.org/details/frienbe00patr

Penn, William. *A Just Rebuke to One and Twenty Learned and Reverend Divines Being an Answer to an Abusive Epistle Against the People Call'd Quakers* (1674). Oxford: TCP, 2007. http://purl.ox.ac.uk/ota/A54003

Perkins, William. *A Golden Chaine, or the description of theologie containing the order of the causes of saluation and damnation, according to Gods word.* (1600). Oxford: TCP, 2006. http://purl.ox.ac.uk/ota/A09339

———. *A godlie and learned exposition upon the whole epistle of Iude* (1606). Oxford: TCP, 2005. http://purl.ox.ac.uk/ota/A09434

———. *A treatise tending unto a declaration whether a man be in the estate of damnation or in the estate of grace* (1590). Oxford: TCP, 2005. http://purl.ox.ac.uk/ota/A09466

Polhill, Edward. *An Answer to the Discourse of William Sherlock.* London: Foster, 1675. Google Books edition. https://books.google.com.au/books?id=ETR9QYJcPtUC

Prideaux, John. *The Doctrine of the Sabbath* (1634). Oxford: TCP, 2003. http://ota.ox.ac.uk/id/A10094

Reynolds, Edward. *Seasonable Exhortation of Sundry Ministers in London.* London: E.M., 1660. https://www.westminsterassembly.org/primary-source/a-seasonable-exhortation-of-sundry-ministers-in-london-to-the-people-of-their-respective-congregations/ Accessed 08/05/18.

Rich, Mary. *Memoir of Lady Warwick.* London: Religious Tract Society, 1847. https://archive.org/details/autobiographyofm00warwiala Accessed 21/06/18.

Rolls, Samuel. *Prodromus or the Character of Mr Sherlock's book: called a Discourse of the Knowledg of Jesus Christ.* London, 1674. Google Books edition. https://books.google.com.au/books?id=cH5nAAAAcAAJ

Sherlock, William. *A Discourse Concerning the Knowledge of Jesus Christ* (1674). Oxford: TCP, 2005. http://purl.ox.ac.uk/ota/A59816

———. *A defence and continuation of the discourse concerning the knowledge of Jesus Christ* (1675). Oxford: TCP, 2005. http://purl.ox.ac.uk/ota/A59809

Sibbes, Richard. *The Bruised Reede and Smoaking Flax* (1630). Oxford: TCP, 2005. http://purl.ox.ac.uk/ota/A12171

Solemn League and Covenant (1643). https://en.wikisource.org/wiki/Solemn_League_and_Covenant Accessed 21/02/18.

Ussher, James. *A Body of Divinitie* (1645) Oxford: TCP, 2005. http://purl.ox.ac.uk/ota/A64622

———. *A copie of the proceedings of some worthy and learned divines* (1641) Oxford: TCP, 2012. http://purl.ox.ac.uk/ota/A32992

Vere, Mary. "The Will of Lady Mary Vere." Probate 11/338/214. London: National Archives, 1670.

Vincent, Thomas. *An Explicatory Catechism* (1675) Oxford: TCP, 2004. http://purl.ox.ac.uk/ota/A64986

Wesley, Charles. "Hymn for Christmas Day." *Hymns and Sacred Poems.* London: William Strahan, 1739.

SECONDARY SOURCES

Watson specific:

Barker, William S. "A Body of Divinity by Thomas Watson." In *The Devoted Life: The Invitation to the Puritan Classics.* Edited by Kelly M. Kapic and Randall C. Gleason, Downers Grove: IVP 2004.

Beeke, Joel R. and Randall J. Pederson. "Thomas Watson." In their *Meet the Puritans.* Grand Rapids: Reformation Heritage Books, 2006.

Haukenfrer, Norbert. "Bellows of Affection: The Meditative Spirituality of Thomas Watson." Master of Christian Studies Thesis. Vancouver: Regent College, 1998.

Hughes, Jack. *Expository Preaching with Word Pictures.* Fearn: Christian Focus, 2001.

Jenkins, Christopher. "Thomas Watson and how to live a Godly Life." In *The Power of God in the Life of Man.* London: Westminster Conference, 2005.

Lee, Chris. "Thomas Watson as Pastor and Scholar." *Founders Journal* 88 (Spring 2012): 3-22. http://founders.org/fj88/thomas-watson-as-pastor-and-scholar/ Accessed 21/09/15.

Neimeyer, Jennifer. "Thomas Watson: The Necessity of Meditation." *Puritan Reformed Journal* 2:1 (2010): 166-181.

Schwanda, Tom. "'Sweetnesse in Communion with God': The Contemplative Mystical Piety of Thomas Watson." *Journal for the History of Reformed Pietism* 1:1 (January 2015): 45-68.

———. "The Saints' Desire and Delight to be with Christ." In *Puritanism and Emotion in the Early Modern World.* Edited by Alec Ryrie and Tom Schwanda. Basingstoke: Palgrave Macmillan, 2016.

Till, Barry. "Watson, Thomas." *Oxford Dictionary of National Biography*. Oxford: Oxford University Press, 2004. https://doi.org/10.1093/ref:odnb/28867 Accessed 6/10/15.

Wallace, Dewey D. "Thomas Watson." In *Puritans and Puritanism in Europe and America.* Edited by Francis J. Bremer and Tom Webster. Santa Barbara: ABC Clio, 2006.

Wilsey, John D. "English Puritan views on Assurance: John Owen and Thomas Watson" https://www.academia.edu/11430265/ Accessed 30/09/15.

General

Alexander, H. G. *Religion in England 1558-1662.* London History Series. London: University of London Press, 1968.

Allison, Gregg. *Historical Theology.* Grand Rapids: Zondervan, 2011.

Appleby, David. *Black Bartholomew's Day: Preaching, Polemic and Restoration Nonconformity.* Manchester: Manchester University Press, 2007.

———. "From Ejectment to Toleration in England, 1662-89." In *The Great Ejectment of 1662: Its Antecedents, Aftermath and Ecumenical Significance.* Edited by Alan Sell. Eugene: Wipf & Stock, 2012.

Azmeh, Aziz al-. "Rhetoric for the Senses: A Consideration of Muslim Paradise Narratives." *Journal of Arabic Literature* 26:3 (1995): 215-231.

Bakratcheva, Albena. *Visibility of the Invisible: The Poetic Discourse of American Transcendentalism.* Amsterdam: Rodopi, 2013.

Barrett, Matthew and Michael Haykin. *Owen on the Christian Life: Living for the Glory of God in Christ.* Wheaton: Crossway, 2015.

Battles, Ford Lewis. *Piety of John Calvin.* Philipsburg: P&R, 2009.

Bebbington, David. *Evangelicalism in Modern Britain: A History from the 1730s to the 1980s.* London: Routledge, 2003.

Beeke, Joel and Mark Jones. *A Puritan Theology: Doctrine for Life.* Grand Rapids: Reformation Heritage Books, 2012.

Beeke, Joel and Randall J. Pederson. *Meet the Puritans.* Grand Rapids: Reformation Heritage Books, 2006.

Beeke, Joel. "Calvin on piety." In *The Cambridge Companion to John Calvin.* Edited by Donald McKim. Cambridge: Cambridge University Press, 2004.

———. *Puritan Reformed Spirituality.* Grand Rapids: Reformation Heritage Books, 2006.

Benge, Dustin W. *"Sweetly Set on God" The Piety of David Brainerd.* Profiles in Reformed Spirituality. Grand Rapids: Reformation Heritage Books, 2016.

Bennett, Martyn. *Historical Dictionary of the British and Irish Civil Wars 1637-1660.* London: Rowman & Littlefield, 2016.

Besant, Walter. *London in the Time of the Stuarts.* London: A&C Black, 1903.

Bidwell, Kevin. "A Puritan Theology (Review)." *Evangelical Times* (July 2013) https://www.evangelical-times.org/book/13010/a-puritan-theology/ Accessed 13/03/18.

Bolam, C. G. and Jeremy Goring. "The Cataclysm." In *The English Presbyterians: From Elizabethan Puritanism to Modern Unitarianism.* Edited by Bolam, C. G. and Jeremy Goring. London: Allen & Unwin, 1968.

Bozeman, Theodore. *The Precisianist Strain: Disciplinary Religion and Antinomian Backlash in Puritanism to 1638.* Chapel Hill: University of North Carolina Press, 2004.

Brady, Gary. *The Great Ejection.* Darlington: EP, 2012.

Branch, Lori. *Rituals of Spontaneity.* Waco: Baylor, 2006.

Bremer, Francis J. *Congregational Communion: Clerical Friendship in the Anglo-American Puritan Community 1610-1692.* Boston: Northeastern University Press, 1994.

Britton, Joseph H. *Abraham Heschel and the Phenomenon of Piety.* London: T&T Clark, 2015.

Brown, Raymond. *Spirituality in Adversity: English Nonconformity in a Period of Repression, 1660-1689.* Milton Keynes: Paternoster, 2012.

Carlyle, E. I. "Watson, Thomas." *DNB* 1885-1900 Vol. 60. London: Smith, Elder & Co., 1899. https://en.wikisource.org/wiki/Watson,_Thomas_(d.1686)_(DNB00) Accessed 02/05/18.

Carmichael, Casey B. *A Continental View: Johannes Cocceius's Federal Theology of the Sabbath.* Gottingen: Vandenhoeck & Ruprecht, 2019.

Champion, Justin. "Heaven Taken by Storm: Christopher Hill, Andrew Marvell and the Dissenting Tradition." Christopher Hill Memorial Lecture. London, 2019. https://www.versobooks.com/ blogs/4311-heaven-taken-by-storm-christopher-hill-andrew-marvell-and-the-dissenting-tradition Accessed 11/09/19.

Clarke, Elizabeth. "Elizabeth Jekyll." In *The Encyclopedia of English Renaissance Literature* Vol I. Edited by Garrett Sullivan and Alan Stewart. Chichester: Wiley & Blackwell, 2012.

———. *Politics, Religion and the Song of Songs in Seventeenth Century England.* Basingstoke: Palgrave Macmillan, 2011.

Coffey, John and Paul Lim. *The Cambridge Companion to Puritanism.* Cambridge: Cambridge University Press, 2008.

Cohen, Charles Lloyd. *God's Caress: The Psychology of Puritan Religious Experience.* Oxford: Oxford University Press, 1986.

Collinson, Patrick. *Godly People: Essays on English Protestantism and Puritanism.* London: Hambledon Press, 1983.

———. *The Elizabethan Puritan Movement.* Oxford: Clarendon, 1990.

———. "Antipuritanism." In *The Cambridge Companion to Puritanism.* Edited by John Coffey and Paul Lim. Cambridge: Cambridge University Press, 2008.

Como, David. *Blown by the Spirit: Puritanism and the Emergence of an Antinomian Underground in Pre-Civil War England.* Stanford: Stanford University Press, 2004.

———. "Radical Puritanism c. 1558–1660." In *The Cambridge Companion to Puritanism.* Edited by John Coffey and Paul Lim. Cambridge: Cambridge University Press, 2008.

Condie, Keith. "The Theory, Practice and Reception of Meditation in the Thought of Richard Baxter." PhD Thesis. Sydney: University of Sydney, 2010.

Cooper, Tim. *John Owen, Richard Baxter and the Formation of Nonconformity.* Surrey: Ashgate, 2011.

———. "John Owen, Richard Baxter and the Battle for Calvin in Later-Seventeenth Century England." *SBJT* 20.4 (2016): 63-78.

Craig, John. "Beadle, John." In *Puritans and Puritanism in Europe and America.* Edited by Francis Bremer and Tom Webster. Santa Barbara: ABC Clio, 2006.

Cosby, Brian H. "Towards a Definition of 'Puritan' and 'Puritanism': A Study in Puritan Historiography." *Churchman* 122:4 (2008): 297-314.

———. *Suffering and Sovereignty: John Flavel and the Puritans on Afflictive Providence*. Grand Rapids: Reformation Heritage, 2012. Kindle Edition.

Dahl, Gina. *Book Collections of Clerics in Norway, 1650-1750*. Leiden: Brill, 2010.

Davies, Julian. *The Caroline Captivity of the Church: Charles I and the Remoulding of Anglicanism 1625-1641*. Oxford: Clarendon, 1992.

De Krey, Gary S. *London and the Restoration, 1659–1683*. Cambridge: Cambridge University Press, 2005.

———. "The First Restoration Crisis: Conscience and Coercion in London, 1667-73." *Albion* 25:4 (1993): 565-580.

Dieleman, Kyle J. *The Battle for the Sabbath in the Dutch Reformation: Devotion or Desecration?* Gottingen: Vandenhoeck & Ruprecht, 2019.

Durston, Christopher and Jacqueline Eales. *The Culture of English Puritanism 1560-1700*. London: Palgrave MacMillan, 1996.

Eales, Jacqueline. "Anne and Thomas Fairfax and the Vere Connection." In *England's Fortress: New Perspectives on Thomas, 3rd Lord Fairfax*. Edited by Andrew Hopper and Philip Major. London: Routledge, 2014.

———. "Vere, Mary" in *Oxford Dictionary of National Biography*. https://doi.org/10.1093/ref:odnb/40534 Accessed 6/10/15.

Erdt, Terrence. "The Calvinist Psychology of the Heart and the 'Sense' of Jonathan Edwards." *Early American Literature* 13:2 (1978): 165-180.

Ferguson, James. *Robert Ferguson, "The Plotter."* Edinburgh: David Douglas, 1887.

Ferris, John P. "HARLEY, Sir Robert (1579-1656)." In *The History of Parliament: the House of Commons 1604-1629*. Edited by Andrew Thrush and John P. Ferris. Cambridge: Cambridge University Press, 2010. http://www.historyofparliamentonline.org/volume/1604-1629/member/harley-sir-robert-1579-1656 Accessed 06/12/17.

Fesko, J. V. "John Owen on Union with Christ and Justification." *Themelios* 37:1 (2012): 7-19.

Foster, Stephen. *The Long Argument: English Puritanism and the shaping of New England culture 1570-1700*. Chapel Hill: University of North Carolina Press, 1991.

Frost, Ronald. *Richard Sibbes: God's Spreading Goodness*. Vancouver: Cor Deo, 2012.

Fungaroli, Carole S. "Unitarianism." In *Britain in the Hanoverian Age, 1714-1837: An Encyclopedia*. Edited by Gerald Newman. New York, Garland, 1997.

Garrison, James D. *Pietas from Vergil to Dryden*. University Park: Pennsylvania University Press, 1992.

Gibson, William. *Religion and the Enlightenment 1600-1800: Conflict and the Rise of Civic Humanism in Taunton*. Oxford: Peter Lang, 2007.

Gordon, Alexander. "Gouge, Thomas." In *Dictionary of National Biography* 1885-1900 Vol. 22. https://en.wikisource.org/wiki/Gouge,_Thomas_(1609-1681)_(DNB00) Accessed 19/06/18.

Goss, Charles W. F. *Crosby Hall: A Chapter in the History of London*. London: Crowther & Goodman, 1908.

Granquist, Mark. "Sunday and Sabbatarianism." *Dictionary of Luther and the Lutheran Traditions*. Edited by Timothy Wengart. Grand Rapids: Baker, 2017.

Greaves, Richard L. *Enemies under His Feet: Radicals and Non-conformists in Britain 1664-1677*. Stanford: Stanford University Press, 1990.

———. *Glimpses of Glory: John Bunyan and English Dissent*. Stanford: Stanford University Press, 2002.

———. "Presbyterians, Religious." In *Historical Dictionary of Stuart England 1603-1689*. Edited by Ronald H. Fritze and William B. Robison. London: Greenwood, 1996.

Gribben, Crawford. *John Owen and English Puritanism Experiences of Defeat*. Oxford: Oxford University Press, 2016. Kindle Edition.

———. *Introduction to John Owen: A Christian Vision for Every Stage of Life*. Wheaton: Crossway, 2020.

Ha, Polly. *English Presbyterianism, 1590-1640.* Stanford: Stanford University Press, 2011.

Haigh, Christopher. *The Plain Man's Pathways to Heaven: Kinds of Christianity in Post-Reformation England, 1570-1640*. Oxford: Oxford University Press, 2007.

Hambrick-Stowe, Charles. *The Practice of Piety: Puritan Devotional Disciplines in Seventeenth-Century New England.* Chapel Hill: University of North Carolina Press, 1986.

———. "Practical Divinity and Spirituality." In *The Cambridge Companion to Puritanism*. Edited by John Coffey and Paul Lim. Cambridge: Cambridge University Press, 2008.

Haykin, Michael. "Word and Space, Time and Act: The Shaping of English Puritan Piety." *SBJT* 14.4 (2010): 38-46.

———. *Rediscovering the Church Fathers*. Wheaton: Crossway, 2011.

Heath, John Benjamin. *Some account of the Worshipful Company of Grocers of the City of London.* London: W. Marchant, 1829.

Helm, Paul. *Calvin and the Calvinists.* Edinburgh: Banner of Truth, 1982.

Henry, Matthew. *The Life of Mr. Philip Henry.* London: J. S. Hughes, 1825.

Hesselink, I. John. "Calvin, Theologian of Sweetness" *CTJ* 37 (2002): 318-332.

Heumann, Mark. "London, Great Fire of." In *Historical Dictionary of Stuart England 1603-1689*. Edited by Ronald H. Fritze and William B. Robison. London: Greenwood, 1996.

———. "London, Plague of." In *Historical Dictionary of Stuart England 1603-1689*. Edited by Ronald H. Fritze and William B. Robison London: Greenwood, 1996.

Hindson, Edward., ed. *Introduction to Puritan Theology: A Reader.* Grand Rapids: Baker, 1976.

Hope, Nicholas. *German and Scandinavian Protestantism 1700-1918.* Oxford: Clarendon, 1995.

Horton, Michael. *The Christian Faith: A Systematic Theology for Pilgrims on the Way.* Grand Rapids: Zondervan, 2011.

Hyde, Daniel. "Regulae de Observatione Sabbathi: The Synod of Dort's (1618–19) Deliverance on the Sabbath" *PRJ* 4:1 (2012): 161–183.

Hynes, Sandra. "Mapping Friendship and Dissent." In *Varieties of Seventeenth- and Early Eighteenth-Century English Radicalism in Context.* Edited by Ariel Hessayon and David Finnegan. London: Routledge, 2016.

Johnston, Warren. "The Patience of the Saints, the Apocalypse, and Moderate Nonconformity in Restoration England." *Canadian Journal of History* 38:3 (2003): 505-520.

Jones, Mark. *Antinomianism: Reformed Theology's Unwelcome Guest?* Phillipsburg: P&R, 2013. Kindle Edition.

Jung, Joanne. *Godly Conversation: Rediscovering the Puritan Practice of Conference*. Grand Rapids: Reformation Heritage Books, 2011. Kindle Edition.

Kapic, Kelly. *Communion with God: The Divine and the Human in the Theology of John Owen.* Grand Rapids: Baker, 2007.

———. "Evangelical Holiness: Assumptions in John Owen's Theology of Christian Spirituality." In *Life in the Spirit: Spiritual Formation in Theological Perspective*. Edited by Jeffrey P. Greenman and George Kalantzis. Downers Grove: IVP, 2010.

Kapic, Kelly and Mark Jones eds. *The Ashgate Companion to John Owen's Theology*. Farnham, Surrey: Ashgate, 2012.

Karfikova, Lenka. *Grace and the Will According to Augustine.* Leiden: Brill, 2012.

Keeble, N. H. and Geoffrey F. Nuttall. *Calendar of the Correspondence of Richard Baxter* Vol. II 1660-1696. Oxford: Clarendon, 1991.

Keeble, N. H. *The Restoration: England in the 1660s.* Oxford: Blackwell, 2002.

Kendall, R. T. *Calvin and English Calvinism.* Oxford: Oxford University Press, 1980.

Kim, Mark. "Michael Horton's Covenant Theology as a Defense of Reformation Theology in the Context of Current Discussions." ThD Thesis, Toronto: Wycliffe, 2013.

King, David. M. "Affective Spirituality of John Owen." *Evangelical Quarterly* 68:3 (1996): 223-233.

Lake, Peter. "The Laudian Style: Order, Uniformity and the Pursuit of the Beauty of Holiness in the 1630s." In *The Early Stuart Church, 1603-1642*. Edited by Kenneth Fincham. London: MacMillan, 1993.

———. "Post-Reformation Politics, or On not looking for the long-term causes of the English Civil War." In *The Oxford Handbook of the English Revolution.* Edited by Michael J. Braddick. Oxford: Oxford University Press, 2015.

Lane, Anthony. *John Calvin: Student of the Church Fathers.* Edinburgh: T&T Clark, 1999.

Lane, Calvin. *The Laudians and the Elizabethan Church: History, Conformity and Religious Identity in Post-Reformation England.* London: Routledge, 2013.

Lee, Hangsang. "Trinitarian Theology and Piety: The Attributes of God in the Thought of Stephen Charnock (1628-1680) and William Perkins (1558-1602)." DPhil Thesis, Edinburgh: New College, 2009.

Leith, John H. *Assembly at Westminster: Reformed Theology in the Making.* Richmond: John Knox, 1973.

Letham, Robert. *The Westminster Assembly: Reading its Theology in Historical Context.* Philipsburg: P&R, 2009.

Lim, Paul C. H. *Mystery Unveiled: The Crisis of the Trinity in Early Modern England.* Oxford: Oxford University Press, 2012.

Liu, Tai. *Puritan London: A Study of Religion and Society in the City Parishes.* Newark: University of Delaware Press, 1986.

Lorimer, William. "To the Reader." In Thomas Watson, *A Body of Practical Divinity.* London: Thomas Parkhurst, 1692.

Louth, Andrew. "Augustine." In *The Study of Spirituality.* Edited by Cheslyn Jones, Geoffrey Wainwright and Edward Yarnold. London: SPCK, 1986.

Lovelace, Richard. "The Anatomy of Puritan Piety: English Puritan Devotional Literature, 1600-1640." In *Christian Spirituality: Post-Reformation and Modern* Vol III. Edited by Louis Dupre and Don Saliers. New York: Crossroad, 1989.

Mallinson, Jeffrey. *Faith, Reason and Revelation in Theodore Beza, 1519-1605.* Oxford: Oxford University Press, 2003.

Mares, Henry. "Criminal Informations of the Attorneys-General in the King's Bench from Egerton to North." In *Law and Legal Process: Substantive Law and Procedure in English Law History.* Edited by Matthew Dyson and David Ibbetson. Cambridge: Cambridge University Press, 2013.

Matar, Nabil. *Islam in Britain 1558-1685.* Cambridge: Cambridge University Press, 1998.

Mattes, Mark. "Luther on Justification as Forensic and Effective." In *The Oxford Handbook of Martin Luther's Theology.* Edited by Robert Kolb et. al. Oxford: Oxford University Press, 2014.

Matthews, A. G. *Calamy Revised: being a revision of Edmund Calamy's Account of the ministers and others ejected and silenced, 1660-2.* London: Clarendon, 1988.

McGee, J. Sears. *The Godly Man in Stuart England: Anglicans, Puritans and the Two Tables, 1620-1670.* New Haven: Yale, 1976.

McGraw, Ryan. *Reformed Scholasticism: Recovering the Tools of Reformed Theology.* London: T&T Clark, 2019.

McKelvey, Robert J. "'That Error and Pillar of Antinomianism:' Eternal Justification." In *Drawn into Controversie: Reformed Theological Diversity and Debates within Seventeenth-Century British Puritanism.* Edited by Michael Haykin and Mark Jones. Gottingen: Vandenhoeck & Ruprecht, 2011.

Miller, Perry. *New England Mind: The Seventeenth Century.* Vol I. Cambridge: Harvard University Press, 1983.

———. *New England Mind: From Colony to Province.* Vol II. Cambridge: Harvard University, Press, 1953.

Miller, John. "Restoration." In *Historical Dictionary of Stuart England 1603-1689.* Edited by Ronald H. Fritze and William B. Robison. London: Greenwood, 1996.

Mohler, Albert J. "Confessional Evangelicalism." In *Four Views on the Spectrum of Evangelicalism.* Edited by A. D. Naselli and C. Hansen. Grand Rapids: Zondervan, 2011.

Morgan, Irvonwy. *Puritan Spirituality.* London: Epworth Press, 1973.

Morgan, John. *Godly Learning: Puritan attitudes towards reason, learning, and education.* Cambridge: Cambridge University Press, 1986.

Morrill, John. "The Puritan Revolution." In *The Cambridge Companion to Puritanism.* Edited by John Coffey and Paul Lim Cambridge: Cambridge University Press, 2008.

Muller, Richard. *Post-Reformation Reformed Dogmatics: The Rise and Development of Reformed Orthodoxy ca. 1520 to ca. 1725* Vols I-III. Grand Rapids: Baker, 2003.

Murray, Germaine Fry. *A Critical Edition of John Beadle's A Journall or Diary of a Thankfull Christian.* New York: Garland, 1996.

Murray, Iain H. *The Puritan Hope: A Study in Revival and the Interpretation of Prophecy.* Edinburgh: Banner of Truth Trust, 1971.

Mursell, Gordon. *English Spirituality: From Earliest Times to 1700.* Louisville: Westminster John Knox, 2001.

Neal, Daniel. *History of the Puritans or Protestant Non-Conformists.* New York: Harper & Bros., 1843.

Nuttall, Geoffrey. *The Holy Spirit in Puritan Faith and Experience.* Chicago: University of Chicago Press, 1992.

Packer, J. I. *A Quest for Godliness: The Puritan Vision of the Christian Life.* Wheaton: Crossway, 1990.

Parker, Kenneth L. *The English Sabbath: A Study of Doctrine and Discipline from the Reformation to the Civil War.* Cambridge: Cambridge University Press, 1988.

Parker, Thomas H. L. *Calvin: An Introduction to his Thought.* Louisville: Westminster John Knox, 1995.

Pastoor, Charles and Galen K. Johnson. *Historical Dictionary of the Puritans.* Lanham: Scarecrow Press, 2007.

Pederson, Randall J. *Unity in Diversity: English Puritans and the Puritan Reformation, 1603-1689.* Leiden: Brill, 2014.

Plant, David. "Army Remonstrance." British Civil Wars Project. 2008. http://bcw-project.org/church-and-state/second-civil-war/army-remonstrance Accessed 20/04/18.

———. "Pride's Purge, 1648." *British Civil Wars Project.* 2008. http://bcw-project.org/church-and-state/second-civil-war/prides-purge Accessed 20/04/18.

Porter, Stephen. *The Great Plague.* Stroud: Amberly, 2009.

Reuver, Arie. *Sweet Communion: Trajectories of Spirituality from the Middle Ages through the Further Reformation.* Grand Rapids: Reformation Heritage Books, 2007.

Roberts, S. Bryn. *Puritanism and the Pursuit of Happiness: The Ministry and Life of Ralph Venning, c. 1621-1674.* Suffolk: Boydell, 2015.

Rudy, Gordon. *The Mystical Language of Sensation in the Later Middle Ages.* London: Routledge, 2013.

Ryken, Leland. *Worldly Saints: The Puritans as they Really Were.* Grand Rapids: Zondervan, 1986.

Ryrie, Alec. *Being Protestant in Reformation Britain.* Oxford: Oxford University Press, 2013.

———. *Private and Domestic Devotion in Early Modern Britain.* Oxford: Routledge, 2016.

Schaefer, Paul R. *Spiritual Brotherhood: Cambridge Puritans and the Nature of Christian Piety.* Grand Rapids: Reformation Heritage Books, 2013.

Schneider, Hans. *A Catalogue of British Devotional and Religious Books in German Translation, from the Reformation to 1700*. Berlin: de Gruyter, 1996.

Schwanda, Tom. *Soul Recreation: The Contemplative-Mystical Piety of Puritanism*. Eugene, Oregon: Pickwick, 2012.

Seaver, Paul S. *Puritan Lectureships: The Politics of Dissent 1560-1662*. Stanford: Stanford University Press, 1970.

Seccombe, Thomas. "Vere, Horace." In *Dictionary of National Biography 1885-1900*. Vol. 58. London: Smith, Elder & Co., 1904. https://en.wikisource.org/wiki/Vere,_Horace_(DNB00) Accessed 22/03/17.

Sell, Alan. "The Doctrinal and Ecumenical Significance of the Great Ejectment." In *The Great Ejectment of 1662: Its Antecedents, Aftermath and Ecumenical Significance*. Edited by Alan Sell. Eugene: Wipf & Stock, 2012.

Shaw, William A. "Rolle, John." In *Dictionary of National Biography 1885-1900* Vol. 49. London: Smith, Elder & Co. 1897. https://en.wikisource.org/wiki/Rolle,_John_(1598-1648)_(DNB00) Accessed 02/05/18.

Siddiqui, Mona. "Death, Resurrection, and Human Destiny: Qura'nic and Islamic Perspectives." In *Death, Resurrection, and Human Destiny: Christian and Muslim Perspectives.* Edited by David Marshall and Lucinda Mosher. Washingston: Georgetown University Press, 2014.

Siekawitch, Larry Daniel. "Stephen Charnock's Doctrine of the Knowledge of God: A Case Study of the Balance of Head and Heart in Restoration Puritanism." PhD Thesis, Bangor: University of Wales, 2007.

Skea, Kinda. "The Ecclesiastical Identities of Puritan and Nonconformist Clergy, 1640-1672." PhD Thesis, Leicester: University of Leicester, 2015.

Smith, Charlotte F. *Mary Rich, Countess of Warwick*. London: Longmans, Green & Co., 1901.

Spurgeon, Charles. "Brief Memoir of Thomas Watson." In Thomas Watson, *A Body of Divinity*. London: Passmore & Alabaster, 1878.

Spurr, John. *English Puritanism 1603-1689.* Social History in Perspective. London: Palgrave Macmillan, 1998.

Strange, Alan D. "The Imputation of the Active Obedience of Christ at the Westminster Assembly." In *Drawn into Controversie: Reformed Theological Diversity and Debates within Seventeenth-Century British Puritanism*. Edited by Michael Haykin and Mark Jones. Gottingen: Vandenhoeck & Ruprecht, 2011.

Swanton, R. "The Theology of Westminster." *Reformed Theological Review* (May 1943): 28-41.

Sytsma, David. "The Logic of the Heart: Analyzing the Affections in Early Reformed Orthodoxy." In *Church and School in Early Modern Protestantism: Studies in Honor of Richard A. Muller on the Maturation of a Theological Tradition*. Edited by Jordan J. Ballor. Leiden: Brill, 2013.

Tipson, Baird. *Hartford Puritanism: Thomas Hooker, Samuel Stone, and Their Terrifying God*. Oxford: Oxford University Press, 2015.

Trevor-Roper, Hugh. *The Crisis of the Seventeenth Century: Religion, the Reformation and Social Change*. Indianapolis: Liberty Fund, 1999.

Trueman, Carl. *The Claims of Truth: John Owen's Trinitarian Theology*. Carlisle: Paternoster, 1998.

———. *John Owen: Reformed Catholic, Renaissance Man*. Aldershot: Ashgate, 2007.

———. "Reformed Orthodoxy in Britain," *SBJT* 14:4 (2010): 4-18.

Underdown, David. *Royalist Conspiracy in England, 1649-1660*. Hamden: Archon, 1971.

Vallance, Edward. *Revolutionary England and the National Covenant: State Oaths, Protestantism and the Political Nation 1553-1682*. Suffolk: Boydell Press, 2005.

Vernon, E. C. "ROBINSON, Ralph." In *The Oxford Dictionary of National Biography* https://doi.org/10.1093/ref:odnb/23864 Accessed 6/10/15.

Wakefield, Gordon. *Puritan Devotion: Its place in the development of Christian Piety*. Eugene, Oregon: Wipf & Stock, 2015.

Wallace, Dewey. *Spirituality of the Later English Puritans: An Anthology*. Macon: Mercer University Press, 1987.

———. "Puritan polemical divinity and doctrinal controversy." In *The Cambridge Companion to Puritanism*. Edited by John Coffey and Paul Lim. Cambridge: Cambridge University Press, 2008.

Walsham, Alexandra. *Charitable Hatred: Tolerance and Intolerance in England, 1500-1700*. Manchester: Manchester University Press, 2006.

Walton, Brad. *Jonathan Edwards: Religious Affections and the Puritan Analysis of True Piety, Spiritual Sensation and Heart Religion*. Lewiston: Edwin Mellen, 2002.

Ward, Joseph P. *Metropolitan Communities: Trade Guilds, Identity and Change in Early Modern London*. Stanford: Stanford University Press, 1997.

Ward, Rowland S. "Introduction." *The Westminster Assembly's Grand Debate*. Edited by Chris Coldwell. Dallas: Naphtali Press, 2014.

Webster, Tom. *Godly Clergy in Early Stuart England*. Cambridge: Cambridge University Press, 2003.

———. "Early Stuart Puritanism." In *The Cambridge Companion to Puritanism*. Edited by John Coffey and Paul Lim. Cambridge: Cambridge University Press, 2008.

White, James G. *A History of the Ward of Walbrook in the City of London.* London: Bowlbs and Sons, 1914.

Whitely, W. T. "The Great Raid of 1670 on certain London churches under the new Conventicle Act." *Baptist Quarterly* 9:4 (1938): 247-251.

Whiting, C. E. *Studies in English Puritanism from the Restoration to the Revolution, 1660-1668.* London: Frank Cass & Co. 1968.

Wilson, Harry Bristow. *A History of the Parish of St. Laurence Pountney*, London. London: Rivington, 1831.

Wilson, John F. Pulpit in Parliament: *Puritanism during the English Civil Wars 1640-1648.* Princeton: Princeton University Press, 1969.

Wilson, Walter. *The History and Antiquities of Dissenting Churches and Meeting Houses.* London W. Button & Son, 1808.

Wood, Laurence. *God and History.* Lexington: Emeth Press, 2005.

Wright, Shawn D. "Justification by Faith Alone: The Perspectives of William Kiffen and John Owen." *SBJT* 20.4 (2016): 25-42.

Yuille, Stephen. Puritan Spirituality: *The Fear of God in the Affective Theology of George Swinnock.* Milton Keynes: Paternoster, 2007.

General Index